T0257968

Encyclopedia of MATLAB: Science and Engineering

Volume III

Encyclopedia of MATLAB: Science and Engineering
Volume III

Edited by **Louis Young**

LANRYE
INTERNATIONAL

New Jersey

Published by Clanrye International,
55 Van Reypen Street,
Jersey City, NJ 07306, USA
www.clanryeinternational.com

Encyclopedia of MATLAB: Science and Engineering
Volume III
Edited by Louis Young

International Standard Book Number: 978-1-63240-191-5 (Hardback)

This book contains information obtained from authentic and highly regarded sources. Copyright for all individual chapters remain with the respective authors as indicated. A wide variety of references are listed. Permission and sources are indicated; for detailed attributions, please refer to the permissions page. Reasonable efforts have been made to publish reliable data and information, but the authors, editors and publisher cannot assume any responsibility for the validity of all materials or the consequences of their use.

The publisher's policy is to use permanent paper from mills that operate a sustainable forestry policy. Furthermore, the publisher ensures that the text paper and cover boards used have met acceptable environmental accreditation standards.

Trademark Notice: Registered trademark of products or corporate names are used only for explanation and identification without intent to infringe.

Printed in the United States of America.

Contents

Preface

The multi-paradigm numerical computing environment of MATLAB (Matrix Laboratory) has been elaborated in this book. It discusses MATLAB based applications in nearly every domain of science consisting of a compilation of comprehensive articles on this fourth-generation programming language. This book deals with the electronic engineering and computer science aspects of language, MATLAB/SIMULINK as a tool for engineering applications, applications in telecommunication and communication systems and MATLAB toolboxes as useful tools for allowing accessibility to symbolic computing capabilities.

The researches compiled throughout the book are authentic and of high quality, combining several disciplines and from very diverse regions from around the world. Drawing on the contributions of many researchers from diverse countries, the book's objective is to provide the readers with the latest achievements in the area of research. This book will surely be a source of knowledge to all interested and researching the field.

In the end, I would like to express my deep sense of gratitude to all the authors for meeting the set deadlines in completing and submitting their research chapters. I would also like to thank the publisher for the support offered to us throughout the course of the book. Finally, I extend my sincere thanks to my family for being a constant source of inspiration and encouragement.

Editor

Electronic Engineering and Computer Science

Two Novel Implementations of the Remez Multiple Exchange Algorithm for Optimum FIR Filter Design

Muhammad Ahsan and Tapio Saramäki

Additional information is available at the end of the chapter

1. Introduction

One of the main advantages of the linear-phase FIR filters over their IIR counterparts is the fact that there exist efficient algorithms for optimizing the arbitrary-magnitude FIR filters in the minimax sense. In case of IIR filters, the design of arbitrary-magnitude filters is usually time-consuming and the convergence to the optimum solution is not always guaranteed. The most efficient method for designing optimum magnitude linear-phase FIR filters with arbitrary-magnitude specifications is the Remez algorithm and the most frequent method to implement this algorithm is the one originally proposed by Parks and McClellan. Initially, they came up with the design of conventional low-pass linear phase FIR filters, whose impulse response is symmetric and the order is even [5]. Later on, along with Rabiner they extended the original design technique in [7] such that the generalized algorithm is applicable to the design of all the four linear-phase FIR filter types with arbitrary specifications. Due to the initial work of Parks and McClellan for the extended algorithm, this algorithm is famously known as the Parks-McClellan (PM) algorithm.

The PM algorithm was generated in the beginning of 1970 by using FORTRAN. During that era, the computer resources were quite limited. When people applied this algorithm in practice for high-order filters, they failed to achieve the optimum results. This gave rise to two main doubts about the PM algorithm. The first doubt was that the algorithm is not properly constructed and is valid for only low-order filters design. However, after noticing that the maximum number of iterations in the algorithm implementation is set to only 25 which is quite low to achieve the optimum solutions for high order filters, it became clear that the first doubt is superfluous.

The second doubt was concerned with the implementation of the PM algorithm's search strategy for the "real" extremal points of the weighted error function, which is formed based on the "trial" extremal points. While mimicking the search technique included in the PM algorithm in various Remez-type algorithms for designing recursive digital filters [15, 16, 18, 19], it was observed that some of the them are quite sensitive to the selection of the initial set of the "trial" extremal points. Moreover, they suffered from certain issues which prevented them to converge at the optimum solution in some cases. For algorithms described in [15], and [18], the convergence issue was solved by increasing the maximum number of iterations in the above-mentioned manner. However, the algorithms described in [16] and [19] have still remained sensitive to the selection of the initial set of the "trial" extremal points. This sensitivity motivated the authors of this contribution to figure out how the search for the "true" extremal points is really carried out in the core discrete Remez algorithm part in the FORTRAN implementation of the PM algorithm. After a thorough study of the FORTRAN code, it was observed that this code utilizes almost twenty interlaced "go to" statements which are quite redundant for locating the "real" extremal points. Meticulous investigation of the code revealed that it is possible to decompose the one large chunk of the search technique into two compact search techniques referred to as *Vicinity Search* and *Endpoint Search* in such a manner that the same optimum solution can be achieved in an efficient manner as follows.

In *Vicinity Search*, the candidate "real" extremal point is located in the vicinity of each "trial" extremal point, which is bounded by the preceding and the following "trial" extremal points with the exception of the first (last) point for which the lower (upper) bound is the first (last) grid point in use. *Endpoint Search*, in turn, checks whether before the first (after the last) local extremum found by *Vicinity Search* there is an additional first (last) local extremum of opposite sign. If one or both of such extrema exist, then their locations are considered as candidate "real" extremal points of the overall search consisting of *Vicinity Search* and *Endpoint Search*. In this case, there are one or two more candidate "real" extremal points as *Vicinity Search* already provides the desired number of "real" extremal points. In the PM algorithm, the desired final "real" extremal points are determined according to the following three options:

Option 1: The additional last extremum exists such that its absolute value is larger than or equal to those of the first extremum of *Vicinity Search* and the possible additional first extremum.

Option 2: The additional first extremum exists such that its absolute value is larger than or equal to that of the first extremum of the *Vicinity Search* and larger than that of the possible additional last extremum.

Option 3: The conditions in *Options 1* and *2* are not valid.

For *Option 3*, the final "real" extremal points are the ones obtained directly from the *Vicinity Search*, whereas for *Option 1* (*Option 2*), these points are obtained by omitting the first (last) point based on *Option 3* and by replacing the last (first) point with the one found by *Endpoint Search*. Based on the above-mentioned facts, an extremely compact translation of the original FORTRAN implementation into a corresponding MATLAB implementation has been reporeted in [2].

The above study on how the PM algorithm performs the search for the "real" extremal points indicates that mimicking this search principle in the Remez-type algorithms proposed in [16], [19] does not give the flexibility to transfer two extremal points between the two consecutive bands, for example, from a passband to a stopband or vice versa, which is a necessary prerequisite for convergence to the optimum solution in certain cases. Most significantly, the search technique included in the PM algorithm does not follow the fundamental idea of the Remez multiple exchange (RME) algorithm when the approximation interval is a union of three or more disjoint intervals [8, 11, 20]. That is, if there are more candidate "real" extremal points than required, then the desired points should be selected in such a way that the ones corresponding to the largest absolute values of the weighted error functions are retained subject to the condition that the sign of the weighted error function alternates at the consecutive points. An efficient MATLAB based implementation following the above mentioned fundamental notion of the RME algorithm has been reported in [3] and provides significant improvements in designing the multiband FIR filters.

In the beginning, the main purpose of the authors of this contribution was to modify the core discrete Remez part of the PM algorithm in FORTRAN such that it follows the fundamental principle of the RME algorithm and can ultimately be incorporated in the algorithms proposed in [16] and [19]. However, during the course of modifications, it was observed that a modified MATLAB implementation mimicking the original FORTRAN implementation is quite effective and superior to already available MATLAB implementation of the algorithm in the function **firpm** [21]. Based on the above discussion, this chapter describes two novel MATLAB based implementations of the Remez algorithm within the PM algorithm. Implementation I is an extremely fast and compact translation of the Remez algorithm part of the original FORTRAN code to the corresponding MATLAB code and is valid for general purpose linear-phase FIR filters design [2]. It is worth noting that Implementation I imitates the implementation idea of the Remez algorithm presented in PM algorithm. Implementation II is based on the fundamental notion of the Remez algorithm as described in [20] and provides significant improvements in designing the multiband FIR filters [3]. It is important to note that this chapter emphasizes on the practical MATLAB based implementation aspects of the Remez algorithm. In order to get an overview of the theoretical aspects of the Remez algorithm, please refer to [10, 17]. The organization of this chapter is as follows. Section (2) formally states the problem under consideration, Section (3) describes the Implementation I in detail, Section (4) discusses the Implementation II in detail, and finally, the concluding remarks are presented in Section (5).

2. Problem statement

After specifying the filter type, the filter order, and the filter specifications such that the problem is solvable using the RME algorithm, the essential problem in the PM algorithm is the following:

Core Discrete Approximation Problem: Given $nz - 1$ [1], the number of unknowns $a[n]$ for $n = 0, 1, \ldots, nz - 2$, and the grid points $grid(k)$ included in the vector **grid** of length $ngrid$, which contains values between 0 and 0.5 [2], along with the vectors **des** and **wt** of the same length $ngrid$, the entries of which carry the information of the desired and weight values, respectively, at the corresponding grid points of the vector **grid**, find the unknowns $a[n]$ to minimize the following quantity:

$$\varepsilon = \max_{1 \leq k \leq ngrid} |E(k)|, \tag{1a}$$

---

[1] In this contribution, $nz - 1$ is chosen to be the number of adjustable parameters in both the FORTRAN and the MATLAB implementations of the PM algorithm because in this case nz stands for the number of extrema at which *Alternation Theorem* should be satisfied in order to guarantee the optimality of the solution.

[2] In the original PM algorithm, this range is the baseband for the so-called normalized frequencies from which the corresponding angular frequencies are obtained by multiplying these frequencies by 2π [17].

where

$$E(k) = \mathbf{wt}(k) \left[G(k) - \mathbf{des}(k) \right] \tag{1b}$$

and

$$G(k) = \sum_{n=0}^{nz-2} a[n] \cos[2\pi n \cdot grid(k)]. \tag{1c}$$

According to *Alternation (characterization) Theorem* [4, 12, 13], $G(k)$ of the form of (1c) is the best unique solution minimizing ϵ as given by (1a) if and only if there exists a vector $\ell_{\mathbf{opt}}$ that contains (at least) nz entries $\ell_{\mathbf{opt}}(1), \ell_{\mathbf{opt}}(2), \ldots, \ell_{\mathbf{opt}}(nz)$ having the values of k within $1 \leq k \leq ngrid$ such that

$$\ell_{\mathbf{opt}}(1) < \ell_{\mathbf{opt}}(2) < \ldots < \ell_{\mathbf{opt}}(nz-1) < \ell_{\mathbf{opt}}(nz)$$

$$E[\ell_{\mathbf{opt}}(m+1)] = -E[\ell_{\mathbf{opt}}(m)] \text{ for } m = 1, 2, \ldots, nz-1$$

$$\left| E[\ell_{\mathbf{opt}}(m)] \right| = \varepsilon \text{ for } m = 1, 2, \ldots, nz.$$

It is worth mentioning that the core discrete approximation problem is the same for both the implementations I and II as defined in the Introduction.

3. Implementation I

This section discusses Implementation I in detail as follows. First, the theoretical formulation of the algorithm is described so that the reader can grasp the very essence of the MATLAB code snippet provided later on in this section. Second, during this inclusion, it is emphasized that instead of using approximately 15 nested loops and around 300 lines of code, only 3 looping structures and approximately 100 lines of code are required by Implementation I. Third, it is shown, by means of four examples, that the overall CPU execution time required by the proposed implementation to arrive practically in the same manner at the optimum FIR filter designs is only around one third in comparison with the original implementation. Fourth, in the last two examples, there are unwanted peaks in the transition bands. In order to suppress these peaks to acceptable levels, two methods of including the transition bands in the original problem are introduced.

3.1. Theoretical formulation

The theoretical formulation of the proposed algorithm is roughly classified into the initialization phase and the iteration phase. The initialization phase performs the necessary initializations for the algorithm, whereas the iteration phase carries out the actual Remez exchange loop. In order to explain why Implementation I is a compact and efficient MATLAB based routine, the iteration phase is further decomposed into four well-defined primary segments. Each segment is constructed in such a way that before the start of the basic steps, there is a thorough explanation on the benefits of carrying out the segment under consideration with the aid of the proposed basic steps.

3.1.1. Initialization phase

The overall implementation starts with the following initializations:

- Initialize the element values of "trial" vector ℓ_{trial} of length nz for ℓ_{opt} as $\ell_{\text{trial}}(m) = 1 + (m-1)\lfloor(ngrid-1)/nz\rfloor$ for $m = 1, 2, \ldots, nz - 1$ and $\ell_{\text{trial}}(nz) = ngrid$. Here, $\lfloor x \rfloor$ stands for the integer part of x.

- Initialize the iteration counter as $niter = 1$ and set the maximum number of iterations as $itrmax = 250$.

3.1.2. Iteration phase

The Remez exchange loop iteratively locates the desired optimum vector ℓ_{trial} having as its entries the nz values of k within $1 \leq k \leq ngrid$, at which *Alternation Theorem* is satisfied as follows. In the first loop, the vector ℓ_{trial} found in the initialization phase is the first "trial" vector for being the desired optimum vector ℓ_{opt}. As this is extremely unlikely to happen, **Segment 1**, based on the vector ℓ_{opt}, generates the weighted error vector **wei_err**(k) for $1 \leq k \leq ngrid$ corresponding to $E(k)$, as given by (1b), in such a way that the $nz - 1$ unknowns $a[0], a[1], \ldots, a[nz-2]$ as well as dev [3] are implicitly found so that the following nz equations

$$\mathbf{wei\_err}(\ell_{\text{trial}}(m)) = (-1)^{m+1}dev \text{ for } m = 1, 2, \ldots, nz \tag{2}$$

are satisfied. When concentrating only on the values of k being the enteries of the "trial" vector ℓ_{trial}, this solution is the best one according to *Alternation Theorem*. However, when considering all the values of k within $1 \leq k \leq ngrid$, this solution is not the best one.

The efficiency of Implementation I in comparison with the original MATLAB function `firpm`, in terms of significant reduction in the code compactness and a considerable reduction in the CPU execution time for obtaining practically in the same manner the best linear-phase FIR solutions are mostly based on the following two novel facts. First, the steps under **Segment 1** are accomplished by employing the efficient MATLAB vectorization operations whenever possible and, most importantly, by avoiding the call for one subroutine by replacing this call with highly efficient matrix operations available in MATLAB. Second, as already mentioned in the introduction, the lengthy search technique involved in the function `firpm` for locating the true extremal points based on the weighted error function can be compressed into *Vicinity Search* and *Endpoint Search*. In the sequel, **Segment 2** and **Segment 3** will take care of *Vicinity Search* and *Endpoint Search*, respectively. More detail can be found in the actual implementations of Segments 1, 2, and 3.

Finally, **Segment 4** checks whether $\ell_{\text{real}} \equiv \ell_{\text{trial}}$ or not. If this equivalence is established, then the best solution has been found as in this case $\ell_{\text{opt}} \equiv \ell_{\text{real}} \equiv \ell_{\text{trial}}$. Otherwise, the whole process is repeated by using the "real" vector ℓ_{real} of the present iteration as a "trial" vector for the next iteration. This exchange of the vectors is continued until ℓ_{real} and ℓ_{trial} coincide or the maximum allowable number of the iterations is exceeded, which is extremely unlikely to occur.

Segment 1: After knowing the "trial" vector ℓ_{trial} that contains the nz trial values of k in the ascending order for $1 \leq k \leq ngrid$ in the present iteration, this first segment guarantees that

---

[3] It should be noted that the value of dev is either positive or negative.

Alternation Theorem is satisfied when concentrating only on those nz values of k being involved in the vector ℓ_{trial}. For this purpose, it generates the weighted error vector $\mathbf{wei\_err}(k)$ for $1 \leq k \leq ngrid$ such that the following system of nz equations:

$$\mathbf{wt}(\ell_{\text{trial}}(m)) \left[\sum_{m=0}^{nz-2} a(n) \cos\left(2\pi n \cdot grid(\ell_{\text{trial}}(m))\right) - \mathbf{des}(\ell_{\text{trial}}(m)) \right]$$

$$= (-1)^{m+1} dev \text{ for } m = 1, 2, \ldots, nz \qquad (3)$$

is implicitly solved for the $nz - 1$ unknowns $a[0], a[1], \ldots, a[nz-2]$ as well as for dev.[4] For this purpose, similar to the function **firpm**, for a given "trial" vector ℓ_{trial}, the value of $\mathbf{wei\_err}(k)$ at $k = \ell_{\text{trial}}(1)$, denoted by dev, the corresponding abscissa vector $\mathbf{x}$, the ordinate vector $\mathbf{y}$, and the coefficient vector $\mathbf{ad}$, each of which are of length nz, are determined. These vectors are required to express the zero-phase frequency response when using the Lagrange interpolation formula in the barycentric form at each value of k for $1 \leq k \leq ngrid$, thereby making the implementation of the Remez loop very accurate and efficient.

In comparison with many scattered scalar operations in the original function **firpm**, the MATLAB code snippet, which is available in the following subsection, is computationally efficient and is highly compact due to the above-mentioned vectors. In addition to that, the time consuming subroutine of "**remezdd**" is replaced with simple and highly efficient matrix operations. Further improvements are obtained by using the vector **grid**, which contains the grid points under consideration, as well as **des** and **wt**, which carry information of the desired values and weights at these grid points, respectively. With the above-mentioned data, the weighted error function is generated only once during each iteration and is a single vector **wei_err**. This vector plays a pivotal role in the implementations of *Vicinity Search* in **Segment 2** and *Endpoint Search* in **Segment 3**.

This segment is performed by using the following ten steps:

Step 1: Determine the entries of the vectors $\mathbf{x}$ and $\mathbf{ad}$ as

$$\mathbf{x}(m) = \cos[2\pi \cdot \ell_{\text{trial}}(m)] \text{ for } m = 1, 2, \ldots, nz \qquad (4)$$

and

$$\mathbf{ad}(m) = 1 \left/ \prod_{\substack{k=1 \\ k \neq m}}^{nz} [\mathbf{x}(m) - \mathbf{x}(k)] \right. \text{ for } m = 1, 2, \ldots, nz, \qquad (5)$$

respectively, as well as the corresponding deviation value as

$$dev = -\frac{\sum_{m=1}^{nz} \mathbf{ad}(m) \mathbf{des}[\ell_{\text{trial}}(m)]}{\sum_{m=1}^{nz} (-1)^{m-1} \mathbf{ad}(m) \mathbf{wt}[\ell_{\text{trial}}(m)]}. \qquad (6)$$

---

[4] It is worth emphasizing that implicit solutions for the calculation of $a[n]$'s are not required for the intermediate iterations. The explicit solution for the calculation of $a[n]$'s is needed only after achieving the convergence to the best solution.

Step 2: Determine the entries of the vector **y** as

$$\mathbf{y}(m) = \mathbf{des}[\ell_{\text{trial}}(m)] + (-1)^{m-1}\mathbf{ad}[\ell_{\text{trial}}(m)]/\mathbf{wt}[\ell_{\text{trial}}(m)] \quad \text{for } m = 1, 2, \dots, nz. \quad (7)$$

Step 3: Generate the entries of the abscissa vector **x_all** covering all the entries in the vector **grid** as

$$\mathbf{x\_all}(k) = \cos[2\pi \cdot \mathbf{grid}(k)] \quad \text{for } k = 1, 2, \dots, ngrid. \quad (8)$$

Step 4: Select the entries of the vectors **err_num** and **err_den** of length $ngrid$ to be zero valued, set $m = 1$, and go to the next step.

Step 5: Generate the entries of the vector **aid** as

$$\mathbf{aid}(k) = \mathbf{ad}(m)/[\mathbf{x\_all}(k) - \mathbf{x}(m)] \quad \text{for } k = 1, 2, \dots, ngrid \quad (9)$$

and update **err_num**(k) and **err_den**(k) for $k = 1, 2, \dots, nz$ as **err_num**$(k) = $ **err_num**$(k) + $ **y**(m)**aid**(k) and **err_den**$(k) = $ **err_den**$(k) + $ **aid**(k), respectively.

Step 6: Set $m = m + 1$. If $m > nz$, then go to the next step. Otherwise, go to the previous step.

Step 7: Generate the entries of the weighted error function **wei_err** for $k = 1, 2, \dots, ngrid$ as

$$\mathbf{wei\_err}(k) = [\mathbf{err\_num}(k)/\mathbf{err\_den}(k) - \mathbf{des}(k)]\mathbf{wt}(k). \quad (10)$$

The resulting **wei_err** contains undefined values at the entries of ℓ_{trial} due to the use of the Lagrange interpolation formula in the barycentric form. The undefined values can be conveniently filled based on the fact that at $\ell_{\text{trial}}(m)$ with m odd (even), the desired value is dev ($-dev$), where dev is given by (6). Hence, the vector **wei_err** can be completed by using the following three steps:

Step 8: Set $m = 1$ and go to the next step.

Step 9: Update the vector **wei_err** as

$$\mathbf{wei\_err}(\ell_{\text{trial}}(m)) = \begin{cases} +dev & \text{for } m \text{ odd} \\ -dev & \text{for } m \text{ even.} \end{cases} \quad (11)$$

Step 10: Set $m = m + 1$. If $m < nz + 1$, then go to the previous step. Otherwise, go to *Step 1* under **Segment 2**.

Segment 2: This segment explains how to perform *Vicinity Search* based on the values of the weighted error function **wei_err**(k) for $1 \leq k \leq ngrid$, which has been generated at **Segment 1**, and the "trial" vector ℓ_{trial}, which is under consideration in the present iteration. The key idea in *Vicinity Search* is to determine the mth entry of the "real" vector ℓ_{real}, denoted by $\ell_{\text{real}}(m)$ for $m = 1, 2, \dots, nz$, to be the value of k in the close vicinity of $k = \ell_{\text{real}}(m)$, where a local extremum of **wei_err**(k) with the same sign occurs. The location of these nz entries are simplified as follows.

In the first phase, the search of both local minima and maxima is reduced to that of local maxima by multiplying the values of **wei_err**(k) for $1 \leq k \leq ngrid$ by sign[**wei_err**$(\ell_{\text{trial}}(m))$] as in this case the values of the resulting signed weighted function sign[**wei_err**$(\ell_{\text{trial}}(m))$] $\times$

wei_err(k) become positive at $k = \ell_{\text{trial}}(m)$ as well as in its proximity. In the second phase, the proper location of each $\ell_{\text{real}}(m)$ for $m = 1, 2, \ldots, nz$ can be obtained conveniently based on the following facts. First **Segment 1** guarantees that for $m > 1$ $[m < nz]$, the "signs" of **wei_err**(k) at both $k = \ell_{\text{trial}}(m-1)$ and $k = \ell_{\text{trial}}(m+1)$ is opposite to that of $k = \ell_{\text{trial}}(m)$, or correspondingly, at $k = \ell_{\text{real}}(m)$. Second, during the course of the present search, $\ell_{\text{real}}(m-1)$ is located before $\ell_{\text{real}}(m)$ in such a way that the sign of **wei_err**(k) at $k = \ell_{\text{real}}(m-1)$ is opposite to that of the sign of **wei_err**(k) at $k = \ell_{\text{real}}(m+1)$. The above mentioned facts together with the reasoning that the lowest value of k for locating $\ell_{\text{real}}(1)$ is 1 and the highest value of k for locating $\ell_{\text{real}}(nz)$ is $ngrid$ inherently lead to carrying out *Vicinity Search* by using the following three steps:

Step 1: Set $m = 1$ and go to the next step.

Step 2: Find the mth element, denoted by $\tilde{\ell}_{\text{real}}(m)$, at which the vector

$$\mathbf{err\_vicinity} = \text{sign}[\mathbf{wei\_err}(\ell_{\text{trial}}(m))]\,\mathbf{wei\_err}(low : upp), \tag{12a}$$

where

$$low = \begin{cases} 1 & \text{for } m = 1 \\ \max\{\ell_{\text{trial}}(m-1)+1, \ell_{\text{real}}(m-1)+1\} & \text{for } 2 \le m \le nz \end{cases} \tag{12b}$$

and

$$upp = \begin{cases} \ell_{\text{trial}}(m+1) - 1 & \text{for } 1 \le m \le nz - 1 \\ ngrid & \text{for } m = nz \end{cases} \tag{12c}$$

achieves the maximum value. Generate $\ell_{\text{real}}(m) = \tilde{\ell}_{\text{real}}(m) + low - 1$. If $m = 1$ $[m = nz]$, then store the corresponding maximum value as **err_vic**(1) [**err_vic**(nz)] to be used in *Endpoint Search* at **Segment 3**. Update $\ell_{\text{real}}(m)$ as $\ell_{\text{real}}(m) = \tilde{\ell}_{\text{real}}(m) + low - 1$.

Step 3: Set $m = m + 1$. If $m < nz + 1$, then go to the previous step. Otherwise, go to *Step 1* under **Segment 3**.

Segment 3: This segment explains how to perform *Endpoint Search*. After *Vicinity Search*, the role of *Endpoint Search* is to check whether the weighted error function **wei_err**(k) contains an additional local extremum before $k = \ell_{\text{real}}(1)$ [after $k = \ell_{\text{real}}(nz)$] such that its sign is opposite to that of occurring at $k = \ell_{\text{real}}(1)$ $[k = \ell_{\text{real}}(nz)]$. It is worth emphasizing that in order to take into account all the candidate extrema, *Endpoint Search* is necessary to be used after *Vicinity Search* as *Vicinity Search* totally omits the existence of these possible additional extrema.

The appearance of the additional first local extremum implies that [5]

$$upp_{\text{end}} = \min\{\ell_{\text{trial}}(1) - 1, \ell_{\text{real}}(1) - 1\} \tag{13}$$

---

[5] *Vicinity Search* automatically guarantees that the sign of the weighted error function **wei_err**(k) is same at both $k = \ell_{\text{trial}}(1)$ and $k = \ell_{\text{real}}(1)$. Hence, upp_{end} is the smallest value of k, where the sign of **wei_err**(k) can be opposite before these values. Similarly, the sign of **wei_err**(k) is same at both $k = \ell_{\text{trial}}(nz)$ and $k = \ell_{\text{real}}(nz)$ and low_{end} as given by (14) is the largest value of k, where the sign of **wei_err**(k) can be opposite after these values.

is larger than or equal to 1. If this fact holds true, then the largest entry in the sub-vector $-\text{sign}[\mathbf{wei\_err}(\ell_{\text{real}}(1))] \cdot \mathbf{wei\_err}(1 : upp_{\text{end}})$ should be positive. Similarly, the existence of the additional last local extremum implies that

$$low_{\text{end}} = \max\{\ell_{\text{trial}}(nz) + 1, \ell_{\text{real}}(nz) + 1\} \tag{14}$$

is smaller than or equal to $ngrid$. If this fact holds true, then the largest entry in the subvector $-\text{sign}[\mathbf{wei\_err}(\ell_{\text{real}}(nz))] \cdot \mathbf{wei\_err}(low_{\text{end}} : ngrid)$ should be positive.

If no additional extremum exists, then the "final" ℓ_{real} is the one found in *Vicinity Search*. Otherwise (that is, one or both the additional extrema exist), the final ℓ_{real} is constructed according to the following alternatives:

Alternative 1: The additional last extremum exists such that its absolute value is larger than or equal to those of the first extremum found by *Vicinity Search* and the possible additional first extremum.

Alternative 2: The additional first extremum exists such that its absolute value is larger than or equal to that of the first extremum found by *Vicinity Search* and larger than that of the possible additional last extremum.

If *Alternative 1* (*Alternative 2*) is valid, then the final ℓ_{real} is formed such that the first (last) entry of ℓ_{real} of *Vicinity Search* is disregarded and the last (first) entry is the value of k for $1 \leq k \leq ngrid$, where the additional last (first) maximum of the signed weighted error function $-\text{sign}[\mathbf{wei\_err}(\ell_{\text{real}}(nz))] \cdot \mathbf{wei\_err}(k)$ $[-\text{sign}[\mathbf{wei\_err}(\ell_{\text{real}}(1))] \cdot \mathbf{wei\_err}(k)]$ occurs.

The above explanation is the key idea to perform *Endpoint Search* in the function `firpm`. However, the function `firpm` performs *Endpoint Search* in a lengthier manner and in order to exactly follow this strategy, it is carried out by using the following eight steps:

Step 1: Set $endsearch = 0$.

Step 2: Determine upp_{end} according to (13). If $upp_{\text{end}} = 0$, then set $\mathbf{err\_end}(1) = 0$. Otherwise, find the index, denoted by $\ell_{\text{end\_real}}(1)$, where the vector

$$\mathbf{err\_endpoint} = -\text{sign}[\mathbf{wei\_err}(\ell_{\text{real}}(1))] \cdot \mathbf{wei\_err}(1 : \ell_{\text{end}}(1)) \tag{15}$$

achieves the corresponding maximum entry value. Store this maximum entry value as $\mathbf{err\_end}(1)$.

Step 3: If $\mathbf{err\_end}(1) < \mathbf{err\_vic}(nz)$, where $\mathbf{err\_vic}(nz)$ has been saved at *Step 2* under **Segment 2**, then go to the next step. Otherwise, set $endsearch = 1$.

Step 4: Determine low_{end} according to (14). If $low_{\text{end}} = ngrid + 1$, then go to *Step 6*. Otherwise, find the index, denoted by $\tilde{\ell}_{\text{end\_real}}(nz)$, where the vector

$$\mathbf{err\_endpoint} = -\text{sign}[\mathbf{wei\_err}(\ell_{\text{real}}(nz))] \cdot \mathbf{wei\_err}(low_{\text{end}} : ngrid) \tag{16}$$

achieves its maximum entry value. Set $\ell_{\text{end\_real}}(nz) = \tilde{\ell}_{\text{end\_real}}(nz) + low_{\text{end}} - 1$ and store the corresponding maximum entry value as $\mathbf{err\_end}(nz)$.

Step 5: If $\mathbf{err\_end}(nz) < \max\{\mathbf{err\_end}(1), \mathbf{err\_vic}(1)\}$, where $\mathbf{err\_vic}(1)$ has been saved at *Step 2* under **Segment 2**, then go to the next step. Otherwise, set $endsearch = 2$.

Step 6: If *endsearch* = 0, then go to *Step 1* under **Segment 4**. Otherwise, go to the next step.

Step 7: If *endsearch* = 1, then set $\ell_{\text{real}}(nz+1-m) = \ell_{\text{real}}(nz-m)$ for $m = 1, 2, \ldots, nz-1$ and $\ell_{\text{real}}(1) = \ell_{\text{end\_real}}(1)$ and got to *Step 1* under **Segment 4**. Otherwise, go to the next step.

Step 8: If *endsearch* = 2, set $\ell_{\text{real}}(m) = \ell_{\text{real}}(m+1)$ for $m = 1, 2, \ldots, nz-1$ and $\ell_{\text{real}}(nz) = \ell_{\text{end\_real}}(nz)$. Go to *Step 1* under **Segment 4**.

Segment 4: This concluding segment check the convergence of the Remez exchange loop as follows. If the entries of the vectors ℓ_{trial} and ℓ_{real} are the same, then stop as in this case the ultimate goal $\ell_{\text{opt}} \equiv \ell_{\text{real}} \equiv \ell_{\text{trial}}$ has been achieved. Otherwise, use the present "real" vector ℓ_{real} as the "trial" vector for the subsequent iteration by using the substitution $\ell_{\text{trial}} = \ell_{\text{real}}$ and go to *Step 1* under **Segment 1**. Continue the Remez loop until ℓ_{trial} and ℓ_{real} coincide or the value of the iteration counter *niter* exceeds *itrmax* = 250, which is extremely unlikely to occur.

This segment requires only the following two basic steps:

Step 1: If ℓ_{trial} and ℓ_{real} coincide, then stop. Otherwise, go to the next step.

Step 2: Set $\ell_{\text{trial}} = \ell_{\text{real}}$ and *niter* = *niter* + 1. If *niter* > *itrmax*, then stop. Otherwise, go to *Step 1* under **Segment 1**.

3.2. MATLAB code snippet

The code pasted below has been tested for realizing Implementation I by using MATLAB version 7.11.0.584($R2010b$). In order to embed this code snippet in the MATLAB function **firpm**, edit the function by taking away the code between lines 214 and 514, introduce the function call (the first line of the function of **remez_imp1**) and copy the function at the end of the file. Remember to take the backup copy of the original function. It is worth emphasizing that the implementation of Remez algorithm in the function **firpm** uses approximately 15 nested loops and 300 lines of code, whereas the code snippet provided below requires only 3 looping structures and approximately 100 lines of code to achieve the same optimum solution.

```
1   function [x,y,ad,dev] = remez_imp1(nz,iext,ngrid,grid,des,wt)
2   % remez_imp1 implements the Segments 1 - 4 described in the preceding
3   % section, the function needs to be inserted within the MATLAB function
4   % firpm. The input argument values come directly from the function firpm
5   % and the output arguments are required to perform the Inverse Fourier
6   % transform in order to calculate the filter coefficients. In case of
7   % any issues send an e-mail to muhammad"dot"ahsan"at"tut "dot" fi.
8   % Last updated 04.15.2012 4:15 AM (UTC/GMT+2)
9
10  % INITIALIZATIONS PHASE
11  niter = 1;         % Initialize the iteration counter.
12  itrmax = 250;      % Maximum number of iterations.
13  l_trial = iext(1:nz)';  % Startup value of l_trial.
14
15  % ITERATION PHASE
16  % REMEZ LOOP FOR LOCATING DESIRED nz INDICES AMONG THE GRID POINTS
17  while (niter < itrmax)
18
19  % SEGMENT 1: BASED ON THE PRESENT 'TRIAL' VECTOR l_trial, GENERATE THE
```

```
20   % WEIGHTED ERROR FUNCTION wei_err(k) AT ALL THE GRID POINTS
21       x = cos(2*pi*grid(l_trial));  % Step 1: Lagrange abscissa vector x.
22       A = x'*ones(1,nz)-ones(nz,1)*x;
23       A(eye(nz)==1) = 1;
24       ad = prod(A);
25       ad = ad * (-2)^(nz-1);  % Step 1: Lagrange coefficient vector ad...
26       ad = 1./ad;  % found efficiently without using the function remezdd.
27       add = ones(size(ad));
28       add(2:2:nz) = -add(2:2:nz);
29       dnum = ad*des(l_trial)';
30       dden = add*(ad./wt(l_trial))';
31       dev = -dnum/dden;  % Step 1: Current value of deviation.
32       % Step 2: Lagrange ordinate vector y
33       y = des(l_trial) + dev*add./wt(l_trial);
34       % Step 3: Overall abscissa vector x_all
35       x_all = cos(2*pi*grid(1:ngrid));
36       err_num = zeros(1,ngrid);  % Step 4: Initializations of err_num...
37       err_den = err_num;  % and err_den.
38       for jj = 1:nz  % Steps 5 and 6: Intermediate evaluations for...
39           aid = ad(jj)./(x_all - x(jj));  % obtaining the weighted error...
40           err_den = err_den + aid;  % wei_err(k) at all the grid points.
41           err_num = err_num + y(jj)*aid;
42       end
43       err_cy = err_num./err_den;
44       wei_err = (err_cy - des).*wt;  % Step 7: Generate the vector wei_err.
45       dev_vect = ones(size(l_trial));  % Steps 8-10: Fill in the undefined
46       dev_vect(2:2:length(l_trial)) = -dev_vect(2:2:length(l_trial));
47       dev_vect = dev_vect * dev;  % entries of wei_err at l_trial(1:nz)...
48       wei_err(l_trial)=dev_vect;  % by using the values of dev (-dev).
49
50   % SEGMENT 2: PERFORM VICINITY SEARCH
51       for k=1:nz                % Steps 1,2, and 3: Start of Vicinity search.
52           if k==1
53               low = 1;
54               err_vicinity = sign(wei_err(l_trial(k)))*...
55               wei_err(low:l_trial(2)-1);
56           elseif k==nz
57               low = max(l_trial(k-1)+1,l_real(k-1)+1);
58               err_vicinity = sign(wei_err(l_trial(k)))*wei_err(low:ngrid);
59           else
60           low = max(l_trial(k-1)+1,l_real(k-1)+1);
61           err_vicinity = sign(wei_err(l_trial(k)))* ...
62           wei_err(low:l_trial(k+1)-1);
63           end
64           [~,ind_vicinity]=max(err_vicinity);  % tilde operator does not...
65           % work with older MATLAB releases If you are running an older...
66           % MATLAB version, considering replacing it with a dummy value.
67           l_real(k) = ind_vicinity+low-1;
68           if k==1 || k==nz  % Step 3: Find err_vic(1)=wei_err(l_real(1))...
69               err_vic(k) = wei_err (l_real(k));
70           end  % and err_vic(nz)=wei_err(l_real(nz)) for use at STEP III.
71       end                        % Steps 1, 2, and 3: End of Vicinity search.
72
73   % SEGMENT 3: PERFORM ENDPOINT SEARCH
74       endsearch=0;  % Step 1: Start Endpoint search.
75       err_end(1) = 0;  % Step 2: Needed for the case, where upp_end = 0.
76       if l_real(1)>1 && l_trial(1)> 1  % Step 2: Find l_end_true(1)...
77           upp_end = min(l_real(1)-1,l_trial(1)-1);  % and err_end(1).
78           err_endpoint = -sign(wei_err(l_real(1)))*wei_err(1: upp_end);
79           [~,ind_endpoint]=max(err_endpoint);
```

```
80          l_end_real(1) = ind_endpoint;
81          err_end(1) = -sign(wei_err(l_real(1)))*wei_err(l_end_real(1));
82          if err_end(1) > abs(err_vic(nz))   % Step 3:Use 'endsearch=1'...
83              endsearch=1;  % or not?
84          end
85      end
86      if l_real(nz) < ngrid & l_trial(nz) < ngrid  % Step 4: Find...
87          low_end = max(l_real(nz)+1,l_trial(nz)+1);  % l_end_real(nz)...
88          err_endpoint = -sign(wei_err(l_real(nz)))*wei_err(low_end:ngrid);
89          [~,ind_endpoint]=max(err_endpoint);  % and err_end(nz).
90          l_end_real(nz) = ind_endpoint+low_end-1;
91          err_end(nz) = -sign(wei_err(l_real(nz)))*wei_err(l_end_real(nz));
92          if err_end(nz) > max(abs(err_vic(1)), err_end(1))  % Step 5:...
93              endsearch=2;  % Use 'endsearch=2' or not?
94          end
95      end
96      if endsearch == 1    % Step 7: 'endsearch=1' is valid. Form...
97          l_real=[l_end_real(1) l_real(1:nz-1)];  % l_real accordingly.
98      elseif endsearch == 2    % Step 8: 'endsearch=2' is true. Form...
99          l_real=[l_real(2:nz) l_end_real(nz)];  % l_real accordingly.
100     end                                      % End of Endpoint search.
101
102 % SEGMENT 4: TEST CONVERGENCE
103     if (l_real == l_trial)  % Step 1: The real and trial vectors...
104         break;  % coincide. Hence, stop. Remez loop ended successfully.
105     else
106         l_trial = l_real;  % Step 2: Otherwise, replace the values of...
107         niter = niter + 1;  % l_trial with the values of l_real and...
108     end % continue.
109 end % END OF THE OVERALL REMEZ LOOP
```

3.3. Performance comparison

This section presents a performance comparison between the Implementation I and the implementation available in the MATLAB function **firpm**. The performance measurement criteria is the time taken by both the implementations to design a particular filter and is measured with the help of MATLAB built-in function **profiler**. This function indicates the CPU execution time taken by a function and provides the following information:

- Calls — The number of times the function was called while profiling was on.
- Total Time — The total time spent in a function, including all child functions called, in seconds.
- Self Time — The total time taken by an individual function, not including the time for any child functions called, in seconds.

Time measurement was carried out on an IBM ThinkCentre machine equipped with Intel Core 2 Duo processor E6550 running at a speed of 2.33 GHz with a memory of 3 GB.

The following four filters were designed with both implementations. After the examples, the time taken by them will be tabulated in Table 1.

Example 1: It is desired to design a lowpass filter meeting the following criteria:

$$\omega_p = 0.05\pi, \omega_s = 0.1\pi, \delta_p = 0.01, \text{ and } \delta_s = 0.001.$$

The minimum order to meet these criteria is 108 and the relevant MATLAB commands are

```
1  >> [N,F,A,W] = firpmord([0.05 0.1],[1 0],[0.01 0.001]);
2  >> firr_coeff = firremez_impl(N+6,F,A,W);
3  >> fvtool(firr_coeff); % filter visualization tool
```

The magnitude response of the resulting filter is shown in Fig. 1.

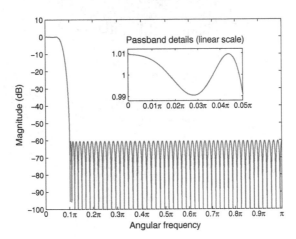

Figure 1. Magnitude response of the lowpass filter of Example 1.

Example 2: It is desired to design a highpass filter meeting the following criteria:

$$\omega_s = 0.02\pi, \omega_p = 0.05\pi, \delta_p = 0.01, \text{ and } \delta_s = 0.001.$$

The minimum order to meet these criteria is 172 and the relevant MATLAB commands are

```
1  >> [N,F,A,W] = firpmord([0.02 0.05],[0 1],[0.001 0.01]);
2  >> firr_coeff = firremez_impl(N-4,F,A,W);
```

The magnitude response of the resulting filter is shown in Fig. 2.

Example 3: It is desired to synthesize a bandpass filter meeting the following criteria:

$$\omega_{s1} = 0.2\pi, \omega_{p1} = 0.25\pi, \omega_{p2} = 0.6\pi, \omega_{s2} = 0.7\pi, \delta_p = \delta_{s2} = 0.01, \text{ and } \delta_{s1} = 0.001.$$

The minimum order required to meet the criteria is 102 and the relevant MATLAB commands are

```
1  >> [N,F,A,W] = firpmord([0.2 0.25 0.6 0.7],[0 1 0],[0.001 .01 .01]);
2  >> firr_coeff = firremez_impl(N,F,A,W);
```

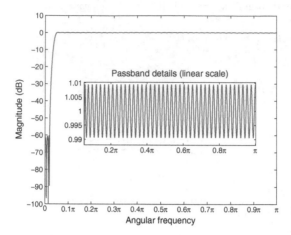

Figure 2. Magnitude response of the highpass filter of Example 2.

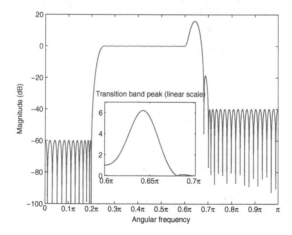

Figure 3. Magnitude response and the highest transition band peak of the bandpass filter of Example 3.

Figure 3 illustrates the magnitude response of the resulting filter. Although the amplitude response is optimal according to *Alternation Theorem*, it is worth noting that this particular filter has an extra peak in the second transition band region of approximately 16 dB. This is because of the fact that the approximation interval is a union of passband and stopband regions and transition bands are considered as "don't care" regions. This assumption works perfectly for filters having bands less than three. However, in case of three or more bands, there is no guarantee that the response is well-behaved in the transition bands, even though it is optimal according to the approximation theory. This fact is especially prominent if any one of the following holds true [9]:

- Transition bandwidths are very large compared to the passband and/or stopband widths.
- Width of transition bands is different; the larger the difference, the greater the problem.

In order to conveniently avoid the appearance of the unwanted transition peaks, consider an original problem stated for linear-phase Type I and Type II filters as follows.

First, there are R interlaced passband and stopband regions as given by

$$\Omega_\kappa = \left[\omega_\kappa^{(low)}, \omega_\kappa^{(upp)}\right] \text{ for } \kappa = 1, 2, \ldots, R. \tag{17a}$$

Such that these regions do not overlap. The lower and upper limits for the zero-phase frequency response in these bands are, respectively, specified as

$$L_\kappa^{(low)} = D_\kappa - \delta_\kappa \text{ and } L_\kappa^{(upp)} = D_\kappa + \delta_\kappa \tag{17b}$$

Here, the D_κ's alternatingly achieve the values of zero and unity such that the first value is zero (unity) if the first band is a stopband (passband). For this original problem, the overall approximation region is

$$\Omega = \Omega_1 \cup \Omega_2 \cup \ldots \cup \Omega_R. \tag{17c}$$

This region can be extended to cover the transition bands as follows:

$$\hat{\Omega} = \Omega_1 \cup \Omega_1^T \cup \Omega_2 \cup \Omega_2^T \cup \ldots \Omega_{R-1}^T \cup \Omega_R, \tag{17d}$$

where

$$\Omega_\kappa^T = [\omega_\kappa^{(upp)} + \alpha, \omega_\kappa^{(low)} - \alpha] \text{ for } \kappa = 1, 2, \ldots, R - 1. \tag{17e}$$

In order to guarantee that $\hat{\Omega}_\kappa$ is still a closed subset of $[0, \pi]$, α should be a small positive number. [6] There are two natural ways to state the transition band constraints, referred to as *Type A* and *Type B* transition band constraints. For both types, the upper and lower limits for the zero-phase frequency response in the κth transition band Ω_κ^T are specified as follows. For both *Type A* and *Type B*, the upper limit is[7]

$$\hat{L}_\kappa^{(upp)} = \max\{D_\kappa + \delta_\kappa, D_{\kappa+1} + \delta_{\kappa+1}\}, \tag{17f}$$

whereas the lower limits depend on the type as follows:

$$\hat{L}_\kappa^{(low)} = \begin{cases} \min\{D_\kappa - \delta_\kappa, D_{\kappa+1} - \delta_{\kappa+1}\}, & \text{for } Type\ A \\ -\hat{L}_\kappa^{(upp)} & \text{for } Type\ B \end{cases} \tag{17g}$$

The above limits for *Type A* are determined such that if the filter meets the overall criteria, then the maximum (minimum) value of the zero-phase frequency response in each transition band

---

[6] The only condition for α is that it should be small enough to avoid the extra peaks between the adjacent passbands and the newly formed intervals in the transition band regions.

[7] It is worth emphasizing that the use of $\max\{D_\kappa + \delta_\kappa, D_{\kappa+1} + \delta_{\kappa+1}\}$ implies that the maximum allowable value in the nearest passband is the upper limit. Similarly, in the following equation, $\min\{D_\kappa - \delta_\kappa, D_{\kappa+1} - \delta_{\kappa+1}\}$ means that the lower limit is the one in the nearest stopband.

is less than or equal to the stated upper limit in the nearest passband region (larger than or equal to the stated lower limit in the nearest stopband region). For *Type B*, in turn, the upper limit is the same, whereas the lower limit is obtained from the upper limit by changing its sign, thereby indicating that the magnitude response of the filter is less than or equal to the stated upper limit in the nearest passband region.

The desired value in the κth transition band Ω_κ^T for both types is the average of the corresponding lower and upper limits, whereas the admissible deviation is the difference between the upper limit and the above-mentioned desired value. Hence, in Ω_κ^T for $\kappa = 1, 2, \ldots, R - 1$ the desired values, denoted by $\widehat{D}_\kappa$, and the admissible deviations, denoted by $\widehat{\delta}_\kappa$, are as follows:

$$\widehat{D}_\kappa = \begin{cases} \left[\max\{D_\kappa + \delta_\kappa, D_{\kappa+1} + \delta_{\kappa+1}\} + \min\{D_\kappa - \delta_\kappa, D_{\kappa+1} - \delta_{\kappa+1}\} \right]/2 & \text{for } \textit{Type A} \\ 0 & \text{for } \textit{Type B}. \end{cases} \quad (17h)$$

and

$$\widehat{\delta}_\kappa = \begin{cases} \max\{D_\kappa + \delta_\kappa, D_{\kappa+1} + \delta_{\kappa+1}\} - \widehat{D}_\kappa & \text{for } \textit{Type A} \\ \max\{D_\kappa + \delta_\kappa, D_{\kappa+1} + \delta_{\kappa+1}\} & \text{for } \textit{Type B}. \end{cases} \quad (17i)$$

The following MATLAB function converts the original design specifications into those ones including either *Type A* or *Type B* transition band constraints as follows. The first three input parameters **F_ori**, **Des_ori**, and **Dev_ori** contain the $2R$ edges of the R bands as a fraction of π as well as the desired values and the admissible deviations from these values in the R bands in the original specifications. . "alpha" corresponds directly to α which is used in (17e), whereas *itype=1* (*itype=2*) means that *Type A* (*Type B*) transition band constraints are in use. The output of this function consists of vectors **F**, **Des**, and **Wt** that are in the desired form when calling the MATLAB function **firpm** in its original form or its modifications referred to as Implementation I or II in this contribution.

```
1   function [F,Des,Wt]=convert2constrt(F_ori, Des_ori,Dev_ori,alpha,itype)
2   % This function converts the original deisgn specifications into Type A
3   % or Type B  transition band constraints compatible specifications.
4   %
5   % Input parameters:
6   % - F_ori contains the edges of the R bands, where R = length(Des_s).
7   % - Des_ori contains the desired values in the R bands.
8   % - Dev_ori contains the admissiable deviations in the R bands.
9   % - alpha is a small positive constant.
10  % - type=1 (2) generates Type A (B) transition band constraints.
11  %
12  % Output parameters
13  % - F contains the edges of the 2R-1 bands.
14  % - Des contains the desired values on all the edges of 2R-1 bands.
15  % - Wt contains the weights in the 2R-1 bands.
16
17  % Check if the input data is correct
18  if (alpha < 0)
19      error('alpha should be a small positive number.');
20  end
21  R = numel(Des_ori);
22
```

```
23  % Generate the output parameters
24  for k=1:R
25      F(4*(k-1)+1)=F_ori(2*k-1); F(4*(k-1)+2)=F_ori(2*k);
26      Des(2*(k-1)+1)=Des_ori(k); Dev(2*(k-1)+1)=Dev_ori(k);
27  end
28  for k=1:R-1
29      F(4*(k-1)+3)=F_ori(2*k)+alpha;F(4*(k-1)+4)=F_ori(2*k+1)-alpha;
30      aid1=max(Des_ori(k)+Dev_ori(k),Des_ori(k+1)+Dev_ori(k+1));
31      aid2=min(Des_ori(k)-Dev_ori(k),Des_ori(k+1)-Dev_ori(k+1));
32      if itype==1
33          Des(2*k) = (aid1+aid2)/2;
34          Dev(2*k) = aid1-Des(2*k);
35      elseif itype==2
36          Des(2*k) = 0;
37          Dev(2*k) = aid1;
38      else
39          error('Type should be either 1 or 2.');
40      end
41  end
42  temp = Des(ones(2,1),:);
43  F = F';
44  Des = temp(:);
45  Wt = (1./Dev)';
```

When using the above MATLAB function with $\alpha = 0.0005$, the ten band-edges of the five bands as fractions of π for both *Type A* and *Type B* transition band constraints become

$$\widehat{\Omega}_\kappa = [0, 0.2, 0.2005, 0.2495, 0.25, 0.6, 0.6005, 0.6995, 0.7, 1].$$

The corresponding desired and weight values for *Type A* and *Type B* transition band constraints are, respectively,

$$D_A = [0, 0.5045, 1, 0.5, 0]$$
$$W_A = [1000, 1.9782, 100, 1.9608, 100],$$

and

$$D_B = [0, 0, 1, 0, 0]$$
$$W_B = [1000, 0.9901, 100, 0.9901, 100].$$

The relevant MATLAB commands are

```
1  >> % Data for Type A design
2  >> [F1,A1,W1] = convert2constrt([0 0.2 0.25 0.6 0.7 1],[0 1 0],...
3     [.001 .01 .01],0.0005,1);
4  >> N1 = 103; firr_coeff1 = firremez_imp1(N1,F1,A1,W1);
5  >> % Data for Type B design
6  >> [F2,A2,W2] = convert2constrt([0 0.2 0.25 0.6 0.7 1],[0 1 0],...
7     [.001 .01 .01],0.0005,2); firr_coeff2 = firremez_imp1(N1,F2,A2,W2);
```

As seen in Fig. 4, by increasing the original filter's order from 102 to 103, the transition bands constraints guarantee that the overall response of the filters stays within the desired limits.

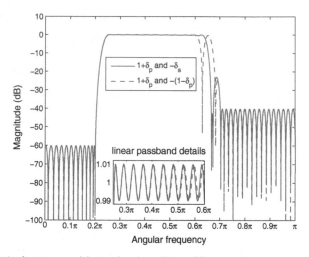

Figure 4. Magnitude response of the two bandpass filters of Example 3.

Example 4: It is required to synthesize a bandstop filter meeting the following criteria:

$$\omega_{p1} = 0.15\pi, \omega_{s1} = 0.3\pi, \omega_{s2} = 0.6\pi, \omega_{p2} = 0.65\pi, \delta_{p1} = \delta_{p2} = 0.01, \text{ and } \delta_s = 0.001.$$

The minimum order required to meet these criteria is 102 and the relevant MATLAB commands are

```
1  >> [N,F,A,W] = firpmord([0.15 0.3 0.6 0.65],[1 0 1],[0.01 0.001 0.01]);
2  >> firr_coeff = firremez_impl(N-4,F,A,W);
```

The magnitude response of the resulting bandstop filter is shown in Fig. 5. This response is the best one according to *Alternation Theorem*, but contains two extra peaks of approximately 33 and 15 dB in the first transition band. By using the technique described above, the transition band peaks can be attenuated to an acceptable level. The relevant MATLAB commands are

```
1  >> % Data for Type A design
2  >> [F1,A1,W1] = convert2constrt([0 0.15 0.3 0.6 0.65 1],[1 0 1],...
3  [0.01 0.001 0.01],0.0005,1);
4  >> N1 = 102; firr_coeff1 = firremez_impl(N1,F1,A1,W1);
5  >> % Data for Type B design
6  >> [F2,A2,W2] = convert2constrt([0 0.15 0.3 0.6 0.65 1],[1 0 1],...
7  [0.01 0.001 0.01],0.0005,2); firr_coeff2 = firremez_impl(N1,F2,A2,W2);
```

As seen in Fig. 6, the overall response of the filters of the same order as the original one, that is, 102, stay within the desired limits for both *Type A* and *Type B* transition band constraints. Among these two constrained designs, *Type A* constrained design is preferred as for it the undershoot of the zero-phase frequency response is limited to be larger than or equal to $-\delta_s = -0.001$. Furthermore, the response in the first passband remains equiripple.

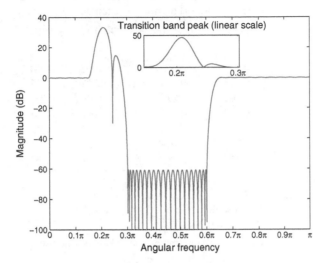

Figure 5. Magnitude response of the bandstop filter of Example 4.

Table 1 indicates the outcomes obtained from the original implementation and the Implementation I of the Remez algorithm, both of which work practically in the same manner. It is evident that the time required by the Implementation I is almost one third of the time taken by the original implementation and illustrates the superiority of the proposed MATLAB implementation of the algorithm.

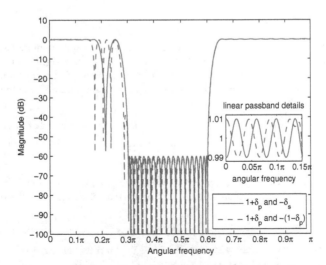

Figure 6. Magnitude response of the two bandstop filters of Example 4.

Example	Original Implementation		Implementation I	
	Total Time*	Self Time	Total Time	Self Time
1	0.152	0.125	0.032	0.032
2	0.235	0.136	0.064	0.064
$3^{\top}$	0.159	0.120	0.032	0.032
$3^{\perp A}$	0.262	0.191	0.056	0.056
$3^{\perp B}$	0.307	0.184	0.061	0.061
$4^{\top}$	0.198	0.138	0.047	0.047
$4^{\perp A}$	0.272	0.169	0.051	0.051
$4^{\perp B}$	0.318	0.186	0.055	0.055

*Time in seconds
$^{\top}$ Transition bands are excluded.
$^{\perp A}$ Type A transition band constraints are used.
$^{\perp B}$ Type B transition band constraints are used.

Table 1. Performance Comparison of Original Implementation and Implementation I

4. Implementation II

This section discusses the Implementation II in detail. First, a theoretical formulation of the algorithm is presented and, then, the corresponding MATLAB code is specified. After that, a detailed comparison shows how this implementation is superior to the original implementation of the Remez algorithm in the function **firpm**, in terms of significant reductions in the number of iterations and the CPU execution time required to generate the same optimum solution, especially in multiband cases.

4.1. Theoretical formulation

As mentioned in the introduction, the key difference between Implementations I and II is the search strategies employed for the "real" extremal points of the weighted error function, which is formed based on the "trial" extremal points. Consequently, **Segment 1** and **Segment 4** are same for both the implementations. The remaining **Segment 2** and **Segment 3** along with the accompanying steps are as follows.

Segment 2: Based on the values of **wei_err**(k) for $1 \leq k \leq ngrid$ generated at **Segment 1**, this main step generates the vector $\ell_{\text{real}}^{(\text{start})}$ to include as many entries as possible in the ascending order subject to the following three conditions:

Condition 1: At each entry of $\ell_{\text{real}}^{(\text{start})}$, **wei_err**$(k)$, when regarded as a function of k, achieves a local extremum whose absolute value is larger than or equal to $|dev|$, where $|dev|$ is determined according to (6).

Condition 2: In case of several consecutive local extrema of **wei_err**(k) with the same sign for $k^{(low)} \leq k \leq k^{(upp)}$, only one entry is included in $\ell_{\text{real}}^{(\text{start})}$ and its value is the value of k for $k^{(low)} \leq k \leq k^{(upp)}$, where $|\textbf{wei\_err}(k)|$ achieves its maximum value.

Condition 3: The sign of **wei_err** as a function of k alternates at the consecutive enteries of $\ell_{\text{real}}^{(\text{start})}$.

This vector $\ell_{\text{real}}^{(\text{start})}$ serves as a start-up vector for generating the "real" vector ℓ_{real} at **Segment 3**. This segment is carried out using the following four steps:

Step 1: Find all the values of k in the range $1 \leq k \leq ngrid$, where a local extremum of **wei_err**(k) occurs. Store these values of k in the ascending order into the vector ℓ_{aid1}.

Step 2: Extract those entries from ℓ_{aid1}, where the absolute value of **wei_err** is larger than or equal to $|dev|$, and store these entries into the vector ℓ_{aid2}.

Step 3: Split the range $1 \leq \kappa \leq n_{\text{aid2}}$, where n_{aid2} is the length of ℓ_{aid2}, into the sub-ranges $\kappa^{(low)}(m) \leq \kappa \leq \kappa^{(upp)}(m)$ for $m = 1, 2, \ldots, n_{\text{aid2}}$ in such a way that the signs of **wei_err**$(\ell_{\text{aid2}}(\kappa))$ in the mth sub-range as given by $\kappa^{(low)}(m) \leq \kappa \leq \kappa^{(upp)}(m)$ are the same.

Step 4: Generate the vector $\ell_{\text{real}}^{(\text{start})}$ of length nz_{start} such that its mth entry is the value among $\ell_{\text{aid2}}(\kappa)$ for $\kappa^{(low)}(m) \leq \kappa \leq \kappa^{(upp)}(m)$, at which $|$**wei_err**$(\ell_{\text{aid2}}(\kappa))|$ achieves its maximum value. Go to *Step 1* under **Segment 3**.

Segment 3: Based on the vector $\ell_{\text{real}}^{(\text{start})}$ generated at **Segment 2**, this main step extracts from its enteries the nz enteries to be included in the "real" vector ℓ_{real} such that the largest absolute values of **wei_err**(k), when regarded as a function of k, are retained subject to the condition that the maxima and minima alternate at the consecutive extracted enteries. If the length of $\ell_{\text{real}}^{(\text{start})}$ is nz, then $\ell_{\text{real}} \equiv \ell_{\text{real}}^{(\text{start})}$ and no extraction is required. Otherwise, the extraction is performed using the following steps:

STEP A: Denote the length of $\ell_{\text{real}}^{(\text{start})}$ by $n_{\text{real}}^{(\text{start})}$. If $n_{\text{real}}^{(\text{start})} - nz$ is an odd integer, then the first (last) entry is discarded from $\ell_{\text{real}}^{(\text{start})}$ if the absolute value of **wei_err**(k) at $k = \ell_{\text{real}}^{(\text{start})}(1)$ is less than or equal (larger) than the corresponding value at $k = \ell_{\text{real}}^{(\text{start})}$ $(k = n_{\text{real}}^{(\text{start})})$. Go to the next step.

STEP B: Denote the remaining vector and its length by $\tilde{\ell}_{\text{real}}^{(\text{start})}$ and $\tilde{n}_{\text{real}}^{(\text{start})}$, respectively. If $\tilde{n}_{\text{real}}^{(\text{start})} - nz = 0$, then stop. Otherwise go to the next step.

STEP C: Since $\tilde{n}_{\text{real}}^{(\text{start})} - nz$ is an even integer, two entries of $\tilde{\ell}_{\text{real}}^{(\text{start})}$ should be simultaneously discarded. There are altogether $\tilde{n}_{\text{real}}^{(\text{start})}$ optional pairs such that the first pair consists of the first and last entries of $\tilde{\ell}_{\text{real}}^{(\text{start})}$ and the remaining ones are $\tilde{n}_{\text{real}}^{(\text{start})} - 1$ consecutive entry pairs. The pair to be discarded is the pair, where the maximum of two absolute values of **wei_err**(k) is the smallest. Go to *STEP C*.

This segment is carried out using the following seven steps:

Step 1: Set $\ell_{\text{real}}^{(\text{init})} = \ell_{\text{real}}^{(\text{start})}$. If $nz_{\text{real}}^{(\text{init})} - nz$, where $nz_{\text{real}}^{(\text{init})}$ is the length of $\ell_{\text{real}}^{(\text{init})}$, is zero, then set $\ell_{\text{real}} = \ell_{\text{real}}^{(\text{init})}$ and go to *Step 1* under **Segment 4**. Otherwise, go to the next step.

Step 2: If $nz_{\text{real}}^{(\text{init})} - nz$ is an even integer, then go to *Step 4*. Otherwise, go to the next step.

Step 3: If $|\mathbf{wei\_err}(\ell_{\text{real}}^{(\text{init})}(1))| \leq |\mathbf{wei\_err}(\ell_{\text{real}}^{(\text{init})}(nz_{\text{real}}^{(\text{init})}))|$, then discard the first entry from $\ell_{\text{real}}^{(\text{init})}$. Otherwise, discard the last entry from $\ell_{\text{real}}^{(\text{init})}$. Go to the next step.

Step 4: If $nz_{\text{real}}^{(\text{init})} - nz$, where $nz_{\text{real}}^{(\text{init})}$ is the length of the remaining vector $\ell_{\text{real}}^{(\text{init})}$, is zero, then set $\ell_{\text{real}} = \ell_{\text{real}}^{(\text{init})}$ and go to *Step 1* under **Segment 4**. Otherwise, go to the next step.

Step 5: Determine the entries of the vector **wei_comp** as follows:

$$\mathbf{wei\_comp}(m) = \max\left(|\mathbf{wei\_err}(\ell_{\text{real}}^{(\text{init})}(m))|, |\mathbf{wei\_err}(\ell_{\text{real}}^{(\text{init})}(m+1))|\right)$$
$$\text{for } m = 1, 2, \ldots, nz_{\text{real}}^{(\text{init})} - 1. \tag{18}$$

Step 6: If $\max\left(|\mathbf{wei\_err}(\ell_{\text{real}}^{(\text{init})}(1))|, |\mathbf{wei\_err}(\ell_{\text{real}}^{(\text{init})}(nz_{\text{real}}^{(\text{init})}))|\right)$ is less than or equal to the largest entry of **wei_comp**, then remove the first and last entries from $\ell_{\text{real}}^{(\text{init})}$ and go to *Step 4*. Otherwise, go to the next step.

Step 7: Find the entry of **wei_comp** with the smallest value. If this is the mth entry, then remove the mth and the $(m+1)$th entries from $\ell_{\text{real}}^{(\text{init})}$. Go to *Step 4*.

4.2. MATLAB code snippet

The code pasted below has been tested and implemented with MATLAB version 7.11.0.584 (R2010b). It can be embedded into the MATLAB function **firpm** in a similar fashion to Implementation I.

```
1  function [x,y,ad,dev] = remez_imp2(nz,iext,ngrid,grid,des,wt)
2  % remez_imp1 implements the Segments 1 - 4 described in the preceding
3  % section, the function needs to be inserted within the MATLAB function
4  % firpm. The input argument values come directly from the function firpm
5  % and the output arguments are required to perform the Inverse Fourier
6  % transform in order to calculate the filter coefficients. In case of
7  % any issues send an e-mail to muhammad"dot"ahsan"at"tut "dot" fi.
8  % Last updated 04.15.2012 4:54 AM (UTC/GMT+2)
9
10 % INITIALIZATIONS PHASE
11 niter = 1;            % Initialize the iteration counter.
12 itrmax = 250;    % Maximum number of iterations.
13 l_trial = iext(1:nz)';  % Startup value of l_trial.
14
15 % ITERATION PHASE
16 % REMEZ LOOP FOR LOCATING DESIRED nz INDICES AMONG THE GRID POINTS
17 while (niter < itrmax)
18
19     % STEP I: BASED ON THE PRESENT 'TRIAL' VECTOR l_trial, GENERATE THE
20     % WEIGHTED ERROR FUNCTION wei_err(k) AT ALL THE GRID POINTS
21     x = cos(2*pi*grid(l_trial));  % Step 1: Lagrange abscissa vector x.
22     A = x'*ones(1,nz)-ones(nz,1)*x;
23     A(eye(nz)==1) = 1;
24     ad = prod(A);
25     ad = ad * (-2)^(nz-1);  % Step 1: Lagrange coefficient vector ad...
26     ad = 1./ad;  % found efficiently without using the function remezdd.
27     add = ones(size(ad));
```

```
28      add(2:2:nz) = -add(2:2:nz);
29      dnum = ad*des(l_trial)';
30      dden = add*(ad./wt(l_trial))';
31      dev = -dnum/dden;  % Step 1: Current value of deviation.
32      % Step 2: Lagrange ordinate vector y
33      y = des(l_trial) + dev*add./wt(l_trial);
34      % Step 3: Overall abscissa vector x_all
35      x_all = cos(2*pi*grid(1:ngrid));
36      err_num = zeros(1,ngrid);  % Step 4: Initializations of err_num...
37      err_den = err_num;  % and err_den.
38      for jj = 1:nz  % Steps 5 and 6: Intermediate evaluations for...
39          aid = ad(jj)./(x_all - x(jj));  % obtaining the weighted error...
40          err_den = err_den + aid;  % wei_err(k) at all the grid points.
41          err_num = err_num + y(jj)*aid;
42      end
43      err_cy = err_num./err_den;
44      wei_err = (err_cy - des).*wt;  % Step 7: Generate the vector wei_err.
45      dev_vect = ones(size(l_trial));  % Steps 8-10: Fill in the undefined
46      dev_vect(2:2:length(l_trial))= -dev_vect(2:2:length(l_trial));
47      dev_vect = dev_vect * dev;  % entries of wei_err at l_trial(1:nz)...
48      % by alternatingly using the values of dev and -dev.
49      wei_err(l_trial)=dev_vect;
50
51  % STEP II DETERMINE THE VECTOR l_real_start
52      % Step 1: Find l_aid1.
53      l_aid1  = find(diff(sign(diff([0  wei_err  0]))));
54      % Step 2: Determine l_aid2.
55      l_aid2  = l_aid1(abs(wei_err(l_aid1)) >= abs(dev));
56      [~,ind]  = max(sparse(1:length(l_aid2),...        % Step 3
57          cumsum([1,(wei_err(l_aid2(2:end))>=0)  ...
58          ~=(wei_err(l_aid2(1:end-1))>=0)]),...
59          abs(wei_err(l_aid2))));
60      l_real_start  = l_aid2(ind);  % Step 4: Determine l_real_start.
61
62  % STEP III DETERMINE THE VECTOR l_real
63      l_real_init  = l_real_start;  % Step 1
64      if rem(numel(l_real_init)  - nz,2)  == 1 % Step 2: odd difference.
65          if abs(wei_err(l_real_init(1)))  <=  abs(wei_err(l_real_init(end)))
66              l_real_init(1)  = [];  % Step 3: discard the first entry...
67          else  % of l_real_init.
68              l_real_init(end)  = [];  % otherwise discard the last entry.
69          end
70      end
71      while numel(l_real_init)  > nz  % Step 4
72          wei_real=abs(wei_err(l_real_init));  % Start of Step 5
73          wei_comp=max(wei_real(1:end-1),...
74          wei_real(2:end));                        % End of Step 5
75          if max(abs(wei_err(l_real_init(1))),...    % Start of Step 6
76              abs(wei_err(l_real_init(end))))<=  min(wei_comp)
77              l_real_init  = l_real_init(2:end-1);        % End of Step 6
78          else
79              [~,ind_omit]=min(wei_comp);              % Start: Step 7
80              l_real_init(ind_omit:ind_omit+1)  = [];      % End: Step 7
81          end
82      end
83      l_real = l_real_init;
84
85  % STEP IV: TEST CONVERGENCE
86      if (l_real == l_trial)  % Step 1: The real and trial vectors...
87          break;  % coincide. Hence, stop. Remez loop ended successfully.
```

```
88      else
89          l_trial = l_real;   % Step 2: Otherwise, replace the values of...
90          niter = niter + 1;  % l_trial with the values of l_real and...
91      end % continue.
92  end % END OF THE OVERALL REMEZ LOOP
```

4.3. Performance comparison

This subsection shows how the proposed Implementation II, following the fundamental principle of the RME algorithms, outperforms the original implementation in terms of significant reductions in both the number of iterations and the CPU execution time required to arrive at the same optimum solution. For this purpose, four practical filter design examples are discussed. In all these examples, the problem is to design a filter having five interlaced passbands and stopbands. In order to achieve the accepted behavior in the transition band regions, the last two examples require the use of the *Type A* or *Type B* transition band constraints described in Subsection 3.3.

Example 5: It is desired to design a five-band filter with two passbands and three stopbands meeting the following specifications:

$$\omega_{s1} = 0.17\pi, \omega_{p1} = 0.23\pi, \omega_{p2} = 0.47\pi, \omega_{s2} = 0.53\pi, \omega_{s3} = 0.67\pi, \omega_{p3} = 0.73\pi,$$

$$\omega_{p4} = 0.82\pi, \omega_{s4} = 0.88\pi, \delta_{s1} = \delta_{s2} = \delta_{s3} = 0.001, \text{ and } \delta_{p1} = \delta_{p2} = 0.01.$$

The minimum order to meet the criteria is 91 and the relevant MATLAB commands are

```
1  >> [n,f,a,w] = firpmord([.17 .23 .47 .53 .67 .73 .82 .88],...
2  [0 1 0 1 0], [.001 .01 .001 .01 .001]);
3  >> firr_coeff = firremez_imp2(n+4,f,a,w);
```

The magnitude response of the resulting filter is shown in Fig. 7.

Example 6: It is desired to design a five-band filter with three passbands and two stopbands with following specifications:

$$\omega_{p1} = 0.1\pi, \omega_{s1} = 0.15\pi, \omega_{s2} = 0.3\pi, \omega_{p2} = 0.35\pi, \omega_{p3} = 0.75\pi, \omega_{s3} = 0.8\pi, \omega_{s4} = 0.85\pi,$$

$$\omega_{p4} = 0.9\pi, \delta_{p1} = \delta_{p2} = \delta_{p3} = 0.01, \text{ and } \delta_{s1} = \delta_{s2} = 0.001.$$

The minimum order to meet the criteria is 106 and the relevant MATLAB commands are

```
1  >> [n,f,a,w] = firpmord([.1 .15 .3 .35 .75 .8 .85 .9],[1 0 1 0 1],...
2  [.01 .001 .01 .001 .01]); firr_coeff = firremez_imp2(n,f,a,w);
```

The magnitude response of the resulting filter is shown in Fig. 8.

Example 7: It is desired to design a five-band filter with two passbands and three stopbands with following specifications:

$$\omega_{s1} = 0.15\pi, \omega_{p1} = 0.2\pi, \omega_{p2} = 0.45\pi, \omega_{s2} = 0.55\pi, \omega_{s3} = 0.7\pi, \omega_{p3} = 0.8\pi, \omega_{p4} = 0.85\pi,$$

$$\omega_{s4} = 0.93\pi, \delta_{s1} = \delta_{s2} = \delta_{s3} = 0.001, \text{ and } \delta_{p1} = \delta_{p2} = 0.01.$$

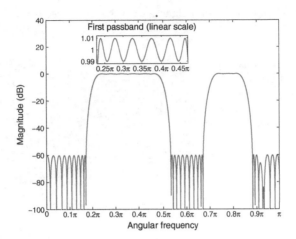

Figure 7. Magnitude response of the five-band filter of Example 5.

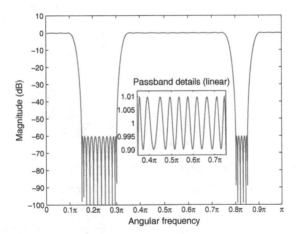

Figure 8. Magnitude response of the five-band filter of Example 6.

The minimum filter order required to meet these specifications is 100. The magnitude response of the resulting filter designed without any constraints in the transition bands is shown by the solid blue line in Fig. 9. It is observed that in the second and third transition bands there are unwanted peaks of approximately 9 dB and 16 dB, respectively. These undesired peaks can be avoided by using *Type A* and *Type B* transition band constraints in the approximation problem according to the discussion of Subsection 3.3. When using $\alpha = 0.0005$, the minimum order to meet the resulting criteria for both *Type A* and *Type B* constraints is 101. The responses of the resulting filters meeting these additional constraints are depicted in Fig. 9 by using a dashed red line and a dot-dashed black line, respectively.

The relevant MATLAB commands for designing the above-mentioned three filters are

```
1  >> % Filter design without transition band constraints
2  >> [n,f,a,w] = firpmord([.15 .2 .45 .55 .7 .8 .85 .93],...
3  [0 1 0 1 0],[.001 .01 .001 .01 .001]);
4  >> N1 = 101;h = firremez_imp2(n-2,f,a,w);
5  >> % Filter design with Type A transition band constraints
6  >> [F1,A1,W1] = convert2constrt([0 .15 .2 .45 .55 .7 .8 .85 .93 1],...
7  [0 1 0 1 0],[.001 .01 .001 .01 .001],0.0005,1);
8  >> htbi1 = firremez_imp2(N1,F1,A1,W1);
9  >> % Filter design with Type B transition band constraints
10 >> [F2,A2,W2] = convert2constrt([0 .15 .2 .45 .55 .7 .8 .85 .93 1],...
11 [0 1 0 1 0],[.001 .01 .001 .01 .001],0.0005,2);
12 >> htbi2 = firremez_imp2(N1,F2,A2,W2);
```

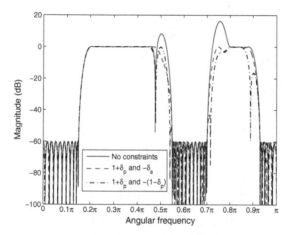

Figure 9. Magnitude responses of the three five-band filters of Example 7.

Example 8: It is desired to design a five bands filter with three passbands and two stopbands with following specifications:

$$\omega_{p1} = 0.17\pi, \omega_{s1} = 0.27\pi, \omega_{s2} = 0.47\pi, \omega_{p2} = 0.52\pi, \omega_{p3} = 0.69\pi, \omega_{s3} = 0.79\pi, \omega_{s4} = 0.87\pi,$$

$$\omega_{p4} = 0.92\pi, \delta_{p1} = \delta_{p2} = \delta_{p3} = 0.01, \text{ and } \delta_{s1} = \delta_{s2} = 0.001.$$

The minimum filter order to meet these specifications is 102. The magnitude response of the resulting filter designed without any constraints in the transition bands is shown by the solid blue line in Fig. 10. It is observed that in the first, second, and third transition bands, there are undesired peaks of approximately 1 dB, 2 dB, and 1.7 dB, respectively. These undesired peaks can be avoided in a manner similar to that used in the previous example. In this example, for *Type A* and *Type B* constraints, the minimum filter orders are 104 and 102, respectively, whereas the responses of the resulting filters are depicted in Fig. 10 using a dashed red line and a dot-dashed black line, respectively.

The relevant MATLAB commands for designing the above-mentioned three filters are

```
 1  >> % Filter design without transition band constraints
 2  >> [n,f,a,w] = firpmord([0.17 0.27 0.47 0.52 0.69 0.79 0.87 0.92],...
 3  [1,0,1,0,1],[0.01,0.001,0.01,0.001,0.01]);
 4  >> h = firremez_imp2(n-4,f,a,w);
 5  >> % Filter design with Type A transition band constraints
 6  >> [F1,A1,W1] = convert2constrt([0 0.17 0.27 0.47 0.52 0.69 0.79,...
 7  0.87 0.92 1], [1,0,1,0,1],[0.01,0.001,0.01,0.001,0.01],0.0005,1);
 8  >> N1 = 104; htbi1 = firremez_imp2(N1,F1,A1,W1);
 9  >> % Filter design with Type B transition band constraints
10  >> [F2,A2,W2] = convert2constrt([0 0.17 0.27 0.47 0.52 0.69 0.79,...
11  0.87 0.92 1], [1,0,1,0,1],[0.01,0.001,0.01,0.001,0.01],0.0005,2);
12  >> N2 = 102; htbi2 = firremez_imp2(N2,F2,A2,W2);
```

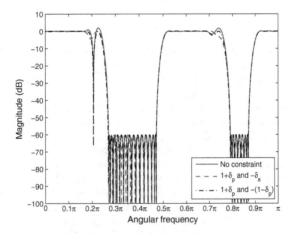

Figure 10. Magnitude response of three five-band filters of Example 8.

Example	Original Implementation		Implementation II		Reduction Percentage(%)	
	Iterations	Time*	Iterations	Time	Iterations	Time
1	34	0.223	7	0.024	79	89
2	35	0.269	16	0.040	54	85
$3^{\top}$	15	0.160	15	0.033	–	79
$3^{\perp A}$	93	0.617	23	0.055	75	91
$3^{\perp B}$	38	0.283	20	0.051	47	82
$4^{\top}$	11	0.146	11	0.029	–	80
$4^{\perp A}$	49	0.360	37	0.082	24	77
$4^{\perp B}$	66	0.398	23	0.057	65	86

*Time in seconds
$^{\top}$ Transition bands are excluded.
$^{\perp A}$*Type A* transition band constraints are used.
$^{\perp B}$*Type B* transition band constraints are used.

Table 2. Performance Comparison of Original Implementation and Implementation II.

The number of iterations as well as the CPU execution times required by the original implementation and the proposed second implementation are summarized in Table 2 for synthesizing all the eight filters considered in this section. The hardware and MATLAB versions are the same as used earlier during the comparison of the original and the proposed first implementations. It is seen that the reduction in the numbers of iterations is 79 and 54 percent, respectively, when synthesizing the filters in Example 5 and 6. In case of examples 7 and 8 with the transition band constraints in effect, the reduction in the numbers of iterations is 45 percent (*Type A*), 38 percent (*Type B*) and 18 percent (*Type A*), and 55 percent (*Type B*), respectively. The reduction percentage in the CPU execution time is between 71 and 86 percent for all the eight filter designs under consideration. Hence, the proposed second implementation is highly efficient in the design of multiband filters.

5. Conclusion

This chapter has introduced two novel MATLAB based Remez algorithms for the design of optimum arbitrary-magnitude linear-phase FIR filters. The first algorithm is a highly optimized and compact translation of the PM algorithm from its original FORTRAN code to its MATLAB counterpart in comparison with the existing MATLAB function **firpm**. These attractive properties have been achieved by first observing that the PM algorithm's very lengthy search strategy for the "real" extremal points of the weighted error function, which is formed based on the "trial" extremal points, can be compressed into two very compact basic search techniques. Second, the MATLAB vectorization techniques are employed whenever possible. As a result, the CPU execution time is roughly one third to synthesize linear-phase FIR filters practically in the same manner in comparison with the function **firpm** being more or less a direct translation from the FORTRAN code. Moreover, the code complexity is reduced to a considerable extent. The original implementation utilizes approximately 15 nested loops and around 300 lines of code whereas the first proposed implementation uses only 3 looping structures and approximately 100 lines of code. Thus, same efficient results are achieved with one fifth of the looping structures and one third of the code lines in the original implementation.

It is, however, important to note that the first technique does not follow the fundamental idea of Remez algorithm as suggested in [20] as it tries to find the new "trial" extremal points in the vicinity of previously found points as well as in the surroundings of the first and last grid points under consideration.

The second implementation obeys the fundamental principle of the Remez multiple exchange algorithm. This means that while searching for the "real" set of extrema, there is a possibility to obtain more than the required points in intermediate calculations. In this situation, the idea is to keep as many extremal points as possible subject to the condition that the corresponding error values are the maximum absolute ones and they obey the sign alternation property. Another prominent feature is that the weighted error function is calculated over the entire grid. This, not only makes sure that no potential extremal frequency point is skipped during a particular iteration, but also enables to transfer the two extremal points between the consecutive bands which, in some cases, is a necessary prerequisite for the algorithms in [16] and [19] to converge. Furthermore, the number of iterations as well as the CPU execution times required by the proposed second implementation to design the linear-phase FIR filters in comparison with the existing MATLAB function **firpm**, especially in multi-band cases, are significantly lower. Examples have shown that in most five-band cases with some constraints in the transition bands, the reduction in the number of iteration is more than 50 percent, whereas the reduction in the CPU execution time is around 80 percent.

The quality of the filters designed with the proposed implementations is analogous to that of the PM algorithm with the added advantages of less number of iterations and CPU execution time.

The proposed two implementations have concentrated only on the core discrete Remez part of the PM algorithm. Future work is devoted to explore the possibilities of further improvements in the overall function **firpm** and reimplementing the other portions of this function efficiently.

Author details

Muhammad Ahsan and Tapio Saramäki
Tampere University of Technology, Tampere, Finland

6. References

[1] Ahsan, M. (2008). Design of optimum linear phase FIR filters with a modified implementation of the Remez multiple exchange algorithm, In:*Department of Signal Processing, Tampere University of Technology*, Master's thesis, (Sep. 2008), Tampere, Finland, 107 pages.

[2] Ahsan, M. & Saramäki, T. (2009). Significant improvements in translating the Parks-McClellan algorithm from its FORTRAN code to its corresponding MATLAB code, In:*IEEE Symp. Circuits Syst.*, (May 2009), Taipei, Taiwan, pp. 289-292.

[3] Ahsan, M. & Saramäki, T. (2011). A MATLAB Based Optimum Multiband FIR Filters Design Program Following the Original Idea of the Remez Multiple Exchange Algorithm, In:*IEEE Symp. Circuits Syst.*, (May 2011), Rio de Janiero Brazil, pp 137-140.

[4] Cheney, W. E. (1966). *Introduction to Approximation Theory*, AMS Chalsea Publishing.

[5] McClellan, J. H. & Parks, T. W. (1972). A program for the design of linear phase finite impulse response digital filters, In: *IEEE Trans. Audio Electroacoust.*, Vol. AU-20, (Aug. 1972) pp. 195-199.

[6] McClellan, J. H. & Parks, T. W. (1973). A unified approach to the Design of Optimum FIR linear phase digital filters, In: *IEEE Trans. Circuit Theory*, Vol. 20, (Nov. 1973) pp. 697-701.

[7] McClellan, J. H. & Parks, T. W. & Rabiner, L. R. (1973). A computer program for designing optimum FIR linear phase digital filters, In: *IEEE Trans. Audio Electroacoust.*, Vol. 21, (Dec. 1973) pp. 506-526.

[8] Novodvorskii, E. P. & Pinsker, I. S. (1951). The process of equating maxima, In: *Uspekhi Mat. Nauk (USSR)*, Vol. 6, (1951) pp. 174-181 (Engl. transl. by A. Schenitzer).

[9] Rabiner, L. R., Kaiser, J. F. & Schafer, R. W. (1974). Some considerations in the design of multiband finite-impulse-response digital filters, In: *IEEE Trans. Acoust. Speech, Signal Processing*, Vol. 22, (Dec. 1974) pp. 462-472.

[10] Rabiner, R. L., Gold, G. (1975). *Theory and Application of DIGITAL SIGNAL PROCESSING*, Prentice Hall.

[11] Remez, E. (1934). Sur le calcul effectifdes polynomes d'approximation de Tchebychef, In: *Compt. Rend. Acad. Sci*, Vol. 199, (1934) pp. 337-340.

[12] Rice, R. J. (1964). *The Approximation of Functions. Volume 1: Linear Theory*, Addison-Wesley Pub (Sd).

[13] Rivlin, J. T. (2010). *An Introduction to the Approximation of Functions*, Dover Publications.

[14] Saramäki, T. (1981). Design of digital filters requiring a small number of arithmetic operations, In:*Dept. of Electrical Engineering, Tampere University of Technology*, Dr. Tech. Dissertation, Publ. 12, Tampere, Finland, 1981,226 pages.

[15] Saramäki, T. (1987). Efficient iterative algorithms for the design of optimum IIR filters with arbitrary specifications, In:*Proc. Int. Conf. Digital Signal Process.*, Florence,Italy, (Sep. 1987) pp. 32-36.

[16] Saramäki, T. (1992). An efficient Remez-type algorithm for the design of optimum IIR filters with arbitrary partially constrained specifications, In:*IEEE Symp. Circuits Syst.*, Vol. 5, (May 1992) San Diego CA, pp. 2577-2580.

[17] Saramäki, T. (1993). Finite impulse response filter design, In:*Handbook for Digital Signal Processing*, Mitra, S. K. & Kaiser, J. F. , (Eds.), Ch. 4, (1993) New York, NY:John Wiley and Sons, pp. 155-277.

[18] Saramäki, T. (1994). Generalizations of classical recursive digital filters and their design with the aid of a Remez-type Algorithm, In:*IEEE Symp. Circuits Syst.*, Vol. 2, (May 1994), London UK, pp. 549-552.

[19] Saramäki, T. & Renfors, M. (1995). A Remez-type algorithm for designing digital filters composed of all-pass sections based on phase approximations, In:*Proc. 38th Midwest Symp. Circuits Syst.*, Vol. 1, (Aug. 1995), Rio de Janiero Brazil, pp. 571-575.

[20] Temes, G. C. & Calahan, D. A. (1967). Computer-aided network optimization the state-of-the-art, In:*Proc. IEEE*, Vol. 55, (Nov. 1967), pp. 1832-1863. Nov. 1967.

[21] The MathWorks Inc. (2009). Filter design toolbox user's guide, In:*MATLAB Product Help*, Version 4.6, (Sep. 2009), The MathWorks Inc., Natick, MA.

Chapter 2

MATLAB COM
Integration for Engineering Applications

Mariano Raboso, María I. Jiménez, Lara del Val,
Alberto Izquierdo, Juan J. Villacorta and Myriam Codes

Additional information is available at the end of the chapter

1. Introduction

COM (Component Object Model) is a Microsoft framework designed for Windows platforms for developing and integrating software components. Software components and reusability techniques have interesting advantages, as component base software engineering has shown through the last years.

The most powerful idea around component-based software, is that components can be implemented by a programmer and reused by others without having knowledge of the source code. Components are binary packages that can be deployed and further integrated with others written on different programming languages. As component selection and integration is usually an easy and well-known process, components are also called COTS (Commercial Off-The-Shelf).

Software components are also very useful for evaluating several implementations for different vendors. Engineers can analyse and compare them in terms of cost, performance and security. Furthermore, component software integration is a key tool for rapid-prototyping software developments.

A component may be implemented with a high specialized language suitable for specific tasks and used by clients written on more general languages. For example, we could be interested on implementing a specialized component in Matlab, and integrating it into a GUI written on Visual Basic or Tcl/Tk. This situation may be comparable to software written on assembly language (specific and low-level) and linked into C programs using libraries or object code.

On the other hand, using software components also involves some risks. Software development must follow its own methodologies, standards and rules that must be taken into account when integrating external objects made from third parties. Fortunately this can be accomplished by following the rules that the component-based software methodologies suggest.

Microsoft has developed some technologies around COM. OLE (Object Linking and Embedding) and DDE (Dynamic Data Exchange) were the first tools capable of transferring objects between applications and creating links among them. They were available on the earliest Windows versions. In 1996 OLE technology was fused with Internet capabilities and was renamed as ActiveX, providing ActiveX controls, Active Documents and Active Scripting.

COM+ are COM based services first developed for Windows 2000. They extend COM technology with advanced services to manage resource pools, disconnected applications and event publication.

DCOM (Distributed Component Object Model) is a Microsoft technology that enables communication links among distributed components running on network interconnected machines. DCOM extends COM and COM+ using new services based on DCE (Distributed Computing Environment) and RPC (Remote Procedure Call).

Nowadays, Microsoft recommends using .Net technology instead, as it has already integrated COM services. Many powerful programming languages can use COM components; Visual Basic, Matlab, Visual C++, C# and Tcl/Tk are good examples.

The next sections will describe COM technology and related Matlab resources. Section 2 explains COM basis and history, as well as some terminology that will be useful to the reader for better understanding the following concepts. Section 3 describes Matlab COM interface, specifically the COM automation server and interface methods. Some real examples given will be useful to the novel engineer that wants to work with COM technology. In Section 4, a real application called XBDK that makes use of COM services is described. Finally, some conclusions are made to summarize this technology and to give the reader the opportunity to explore deeper inside COM and .Net technology.

2. Microsoft COM technology

A COM component is an instance of the component object class that runs on the COM server and is accessible from a variety of clients. There are several platforms that can serve COM objects and many clients that can use them.

Matlab COM components are very useful to integrate tasks implemented on this language and exported to others applications. These components can be used later in Microsoft Office Applications (for example Microsoft Excel), Microsoft Visual C++, C#, VB, Tcl/Tk, or even other Matlab clients, in local or distributed applications.

2.1. COM interfaces

COM component implementation is hidden to clients through convenient encapsulation, as the only way to access the component is through a public interface. An interface is a set of public methods, events and properties declarations defining the way an encapsulated object can be accessed. The component manufacturer is responsible for providing the corresponding interface information, with the necessary method details. As this information is all the knowledge of the component, it is necessary to give as much information as possible in order to ensure the component is suitable to be integrated into a third party system. Interface details are usually transparent to users. Applications as Microsoft Visual Studio provide tools for using COM objects and other resources for .Net platforms (Gunderloy, 2001).

There are four basic COM interfaces:

- IUnknown. It is a basic standard interface that is compulsory to every COM object.
- IDispatch. It is a standard interface for obtaining general information about the object and specifically about methods and properties than can be accessible.
- Custom. It is a custom interface. It can be user defined.
- Dual. It is a combination from IDispatch and Custom.

These interfaces are provided by corresponding server types.

2.2. COM clients

A COM client is a program that uses COM Objects that are provided by COM servers. An example can be a spreadsheet built with Microsoft Excel integrated into a Matlab client. Matlab can be used as a COM client or server.

In this chapter, we are concerned with developing COM server objects using Matlab. Therefore, Matlab client details will be omitted.

2.3. COM server types

COM model defines three types of servers, depending on the interfaces implemented (The Mathworks, 2012):

- **Automation.** This type of server can be accessed by all clients. It supports the OLE Automation standard, and servers are based on IDispatch interfaces.
- **Custom.** These servers are used when a special client requires specific and faster access.
- **Dual.** It is a combination of the above types.

Depending on the locations of the component and client the server can be one of these two types:

- **In-Process server.** In this configuration, the client accesses the components using a DLL (dynamic link library) or an ActiveX. Both client and server run in the same process so they share a unique context.
- **Out-Process server.** The component is implemented as an independent executable (.exe) file. The client can access this program with either local or remote configuration. It depends on the location of the client and server. For local access, performance can be reduced compared to an In-Process configuration. For remote access configuration, it can be only accomplished on systems supporting DCOM (Distributed COM).

2.4. Programmatic identifiers

A programmatic identifier is a unique string that identifies an instance of a COM object. It is usually defined by the vendor.

Users can access different services using different identifiers. For example, Matlab provides three identifiers with several versions to provide such services. If there were more than one version of the software installed, each one would have its own identifier.

Figure 1 shows how a programmatic identifier can be found. It corresponds to an object available in the Windows registry. Besides finding out the existing programmatic identifiers, explore the registry (regedit32.exe) is a good way to verify if the COM servers are properly installed. Another option is to use the Microsoft Visual Studio object explorer or reference explorer.

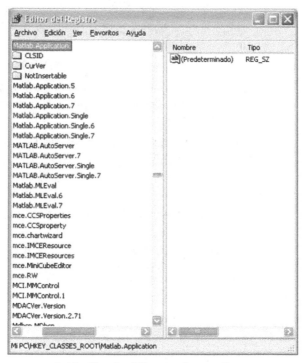

Figure 1. Matlab programmatic identifiers for different package versions.

This is very useful if the client must start an instance of a specific version of the software, because each version has its own programmatic identifier. The identifier has also a suffix with a major, followed by a minor, version to identify it (for example 7.3). If no identifier is used, the most recently version will be selected. This situation is not very common, but it can be used to compare the different behaviour of the different versions.

3. Matlab COM server

Matlab COM server is included in the default software installation. With COM enabled, developers can implement COM components and use other COM objects. Developers may insert Matlab applications on web (html code) pages or use Microsoft Excel spreadsheets to present numerical results.

Integration of COM Matlab objects can also be distributed, so components may be run from remote machines. This is mainly used for developing parallel solutions, which are typical on many engineering applications, specifically in digital signal processing.

The next sections will explain how Matlab COM server works. Furthermore, COM objects are illustrated with some real examples.

3.1. Matlab programmatic identifiers

As shown above in figure 1, Matlab provides three programmatic identifiers to access COM servers:

- **Matlab.Application.** This identifier is used to start a Matlab Automation server on an independent window. A command window will appear to enter commands. Note that if several versions exist, the most recently Automation Server version run will be selected.
- **Matlab.Autoserver.** A Matlab Automation server is started on an independent command window. The most recent install version is selected if no version is specified.
- **Matlab.Desktop.Application.** With this configuration, a Matlab full desktop is started. The most recently installed version will run, if no version is specified.

By running the registry tool in Windows, we will be able to find out the identifiers for accessing the COM servers (see figure 1):

- **Matlab.Application**
- **Matlab.Application.Single**
- **Matlab.AutoServer**
- **Matlab.AutoServer.Single**

The *single* attribute will make the server to run on an exclusive mode. Otherwise the server will starts on a shared configuration.

3.2. Matlab Client/Server architecture

Matlab client-server architecture defines how client and server relationships can be established. Four different models are available:

- Matlab client (In-Process Server). Using this architecture, Matlab clients access services by ActiveX controls or DLL libraries. Both client and server run on the same process. Communication is extremely efficient as both share the same context. If a DLL is used, it runs on a separate window.

- Matlab client (Out-Process Server). Client accesses server resources using an executable (.exe) file. The component instantiates on a separate process. Communication is not as effective as in the In-Process configuration.
- Matlab application and Matlab server (Automation Server). Using this configuration, a client application (called controller) accesses the services provided by the Automation server. The services make possible to run commands and transfer variables into Matlab workspace. The server may run locally or on a remote machine using DCOM services (see section 2.3). This configuration is affected from networks issues, specifically by bandwidth bottlenecks and latency problems.
- Client application and Matlab server (engine server). Matlab offers a faster interface called IEngine to be used with C, C++ and Fortran clients.

3.3. Linking references to COM servers

When using developing tools as Microsoft Visual Studio, some previous configuration must be made before writing the code. Specifically, COM references must be included into the project configuration. Figures 2 and 3 show how these references can be added:

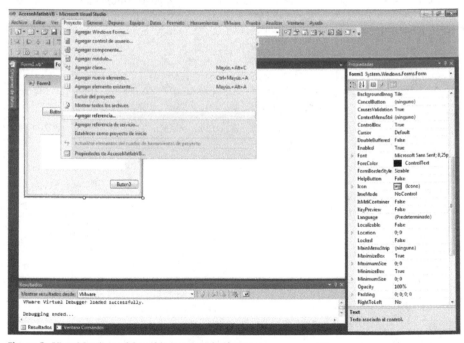

Figure 2. Visual Studio tool for adding external references.

By clicking on project tab and selecting "add reference", the references window appears, and shows the applications that provides COM servers (figure 3).

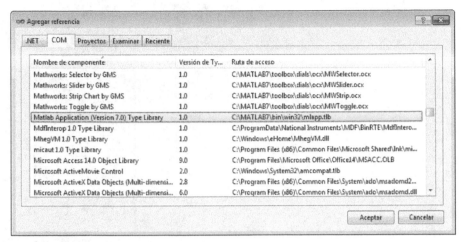

Figure 3. Adding Matlab COM references.

The reference selected is identified by a version number, and a path for the library location. If the server is located on a remote machine, then, the identifier will contain the path to the server having Matlab installed. The next figure shows a remote server accessible by the path "\\hiseuibd01\home$\matlab2\bin":

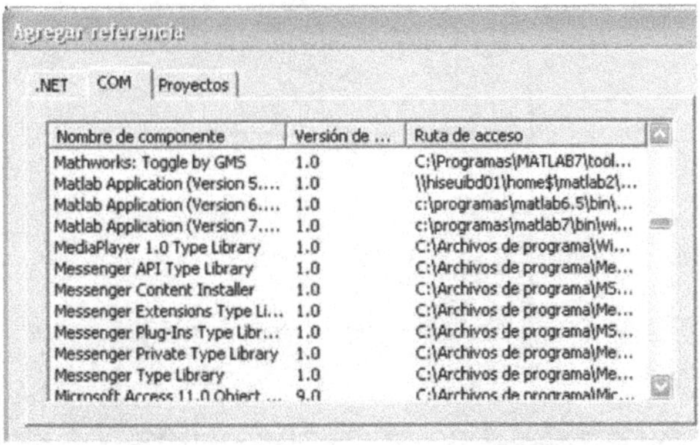

Figure 4. Matlab COM references for different package versions and locations.

References to other different hosts make it possible to access Matlab remote servers using DCOM. With this configuration Matlab software must be also installed on the local host, because some Matlab components must be accessible locally.

Once the references are added, Matlab objects links can be used in the source code. This is usually made by the "new" construct or "CreateObject" function. If the interface IMLApp is used, the methods available can be shown by the source code interactive help system. Otherwise methods can be viewed using the object explorer menu option (figure 5 and 6):

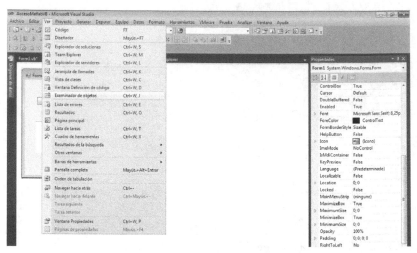

Figure 5. Visual Studio object explorer window.

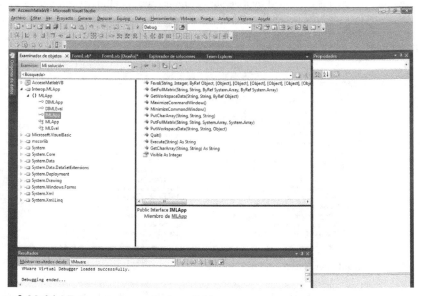

Figure 6. Matlab MLApp interface methods available.

Figure 6 shows the available interface methods. The most useful are:

- MLApp.Execute(). This method executes a Matlab command on the COM server.
- MLApp.Feval(). This method evaluates a Matlab function.
- MLApp.GetFullMatrix(). This method is useful to copy a matrix from Matlab workspace.
- MLApp.PutFullMatrix().This method is useful to copy a matrix into Matlab workspace.

- MLApp.PutWorkspaceData(). This method is used to put variables into Matlab workspace.
- MLApp.GetWorkspaceData(). This method is used to read variables from Matlab workspace.
- MLApp.Quit(). It must be used to force exit when the host application finalizes.

3.4. Accessing Matlab resources from the source code

The next sections will describe how to create and reference COM objects using different languages.

3.4.1. Creating COM objects

Microsoft .Net technologies provide resources to access COM objects from different languages. For convenience, the following examples are written in Visual Basic. Users that prefer other languages may use COM objects and references on the same way.

The following example makes use of the easy graphical user interface that provides Visual Basic. Matlab specific routines are accessed by adding references into the Visual Basic code. The next code is an example of running a Matlab server that exchanges data from the workspace. The application simply runs an interactive tool to access some Matlab resources using COM services.

```
Public Class Form1
    'Dim Matlab as Object and use CreateObject method
    'use MLApp library and New MLApp method to see the methods available
    Dim MatlabCommand As String
    'Dim Matlab As MLApp.MLApp
    Dim Matlab As Object
    Dim ArrayA() As Double = {1, 2, 3, 4}
    Dim ArrayB() As Double = {5, 6, 7, 8}
    Dim ArrayC() As Double = {0, 0, 0, 0}
    Dim ArrayImg() As Double = {0, 0, 0, 0}
Private Sub Button1_Click(ByVal sender As System.Object, ByVal e As
System.EventArgs) Handles Button1.Click
        Matlab = CreateObject("Matlab.Application")
End Sub
Private Sub Button3_Click(ByVal sender As System.Object, ByVal e As
System.EventArgs) Handles Button3.Click
        Matlab.Quit()
        Me.Close()
End Sub
```

Table 1. GetFullMatrix() and PutFullMatrix() methods example.

Note that before using COM objects, some declarations must be made in order to instantiate the objects.

Figure 7 shows how the "execute()" method can be used for running commands inside the Matlab environment. Methods "GetFullMatrix()" and "PutFullMatrix()" are used in the example to exchange data between the application and the Matlab workspace.

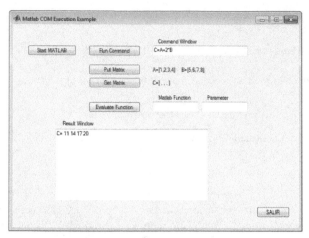

Figure 7. Matlab Execute(), PutFullMatrix() and GetFullMatrix() interface methods example.

Matlab Execute() method provides a powerful tool to use Matlab server. It is probably the most frequent method used. The source code associated with the task shown in figure 7 is the following:

```
Private Sub Button2_Click(ByVal sender As System.Object, ByVal e As
System.EventArgs) Handles Button2.Click
        Dim StringResult As String
        MatlabCommand = CommandBox.Text
        StringResult = Matlab.Execute(MatlabCommand)
        ResultBox.Text = StringResult
End Sub

Private Sub Button4_Click(ByVal sender As System.Object, ByVal e As
System.EventArgs) Handles Button4.Click
        Dim ArrayA() As Double = {1, 2, 3, 4}
        Dim ArrayB() As Double = {5, 6, 7, 8}
        Dim ArrayC() As Double = {0, 0, 0, 0}
        Dim ArrayImg() As Double = {0, 0, 0, 0}

        Matlab.PutFullMatrix("A", "base", ArrayA, ArrayImg)
        Matlab.PutFullMatrix("B", "base", ArrayB, ArrayImg)
End Sub

Private    Sub    Button5_Click(sender    As    System.Object,    e    As
System.EventArgs) Handles Button5.Click
        Dim ArrayC() As Double = {0, 0, 0, 0}
        Dim ArrayImg() As Double = {0, 0, 0, 0}

        Matlab.GetFullMatrix("C", "base", ArrayC, ArrayImg)
        ResultBox.Text   =   "C=   "   +   ArrayC(0).ToString()   +   "  "   +
ArrayC(1).ToString()   +   "  "   +   ArrayC(2).ToString()   +   "  "   +
ArrayC(3).ToString()
End Sub
```

Table 2. Matlab Execute(), GetFullMatrix() and PutFullMatrix() methods example.

Figure 8 shows how the Feval() method can be used to evaluate a trigonometric function inside Matlab environment. This method allows parameter exchange, so you can pass or receive the necessary arguments (sin(π) in the example).

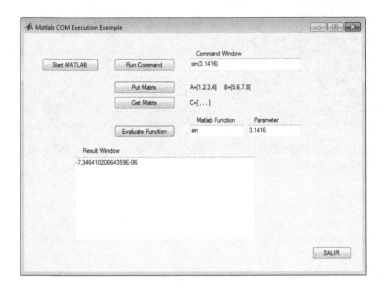

Figure 8. Feval() interface method.

The source code fragment for the application that it is shown in figure 8 is the following:

```
Private     Sub     Button6_Click(sender     As     System.Object,     e     As
System.EventArgs) Handles Button6.Click
        Dim MatlabFunction As String
        Dim out As Object
        Dim x As Double

        x = Parameter.Text
        MatlabFunction = FunctionBox.Text
        Matlab.Feval(MatlabFunction, 1, out, x)
        ResultBox.Text = out(0).ToString
End Sub
```

Table 3. Feval() method example.

Finally, the next code fragment shows an example for transferring data between the application and Matlab workspace, using "PutWorkspaceData()" and "GetWorkspaceData()" interface methods:

```
Private    Sub    Button7_Click(ByVal    sender    As    Object,    ByVal    e    As
System.EventArgs) Handles Button7.Click
        Dim nombre As String
        Dim matriz(,) As Integer = New Integer(,) {{0, 1}, {2, 3}}
        Dim S2X2(,) As Short = New Short(,) {{5, 6}, {7, 8}}

        nombre = TextBox5.Text
        Matlab.PutWorkspaceData(nombre, "base", matriz)
End Sub

Private    Sub    Button6_Click(ByVal    sender    As    Object,    ByVal    e    As
System.EventArgs) Handles Button6.Click
        Dim resultado As Object
        Dim nombre As String

        nombre = TextBox5.Text
        Matlab.GetWorkspaceData(nombre, "base", resultado)
        TextBox7.Text = resultado
End Sub
```

Table 4. Example using PutWorkspaceData() and GetWorkspaceData() interface methods.

Both examples transfer variables using the default "base" workspace and custom variable names read from a text box.

3.4.2. Creating COM objects using Tcl/Tk

Tcl (Tool Command Language) is a very powerful and easy language to learn. It is useful for automation, test, programming embedded systems, web applications and database access (Tcl community, 2009).

It was developed in 1988 by John K. Ousterhout at the University of California, and later maintained by Sun Microsystems Laboratories by the group SunScript. One of its great advantages is that it is multiplatform. There are versions for Windows, Mac OS X and most versions of Unix: Linux, Solaris, IRIX, AIX, BSD...

The language is constantly evolving, so new versions of interpreters are frequently released, along with extensions that extend the functionality of the language.

Tcl is flexible and open source, so any developer can investigate the language details, include new features, modify existing ones, and even develop new commercial versions. Extensions are usually of the same type of license, although it depends on each developer.

Associated with Tcl, there is a toolkit for developing graphical user interface called Tk (Tool Kit), which is the most popular Tcl extension. Tk was also developed by John Ousterhout and provides an interpreter that adds Tcl commands and others capable of creating graphical user interface components such as buttons, panels, combo boxes and dialog boxes. It is usually distributed into a package called Tcl/Tk.

Recent versions of Tcl/Tk include a package to access COM objects through a very extensive API, replacing the traditional interpreter by a compiler that translates source code to bytecodes, which then runs another interpreter (Huang, 2006). Although this improvement allows substantial increase of the execution speed, it cannot be still compared with other compiled languages.

The following code shows how Matlab COM server can be created using a Tcl/Tk script:

```
package require tcom
set application [::tcom::ref createobject  "Matlab.Application.7"]
```

Table 5. Example creating a COM reference from Tcl.

Once the reference is created, all methods will be accessible. The next lines show how to run a Matlab .m program and get the result (Matlab diagram variable) from the "base" workspace, into the local variable "diagrama".

```
$application Execute "run('C:/smi.m')"
$application GetWorkspaceData "diagram" "base" "diagrama"
```

Table 6. Example using Execute and GetWorkspaceData interface methods for Tcl.

4. XBDK, a TCL/TK platform using Matlab and other COM objects

XBDK stands for XML-Based Beamforming Development Kit. It is a software platform designed for aiding the engineer through the beamforming development process (Raboso et al., 2003, 2007, 2009). It is a CASE (Computer Aided Software Environment) tool that integrates several interesting applications related to software modelling, simulation and XML parsing and manipulation. The applications are written in Java and Matlab, and are integrated using a script language (Tcl/Tk).

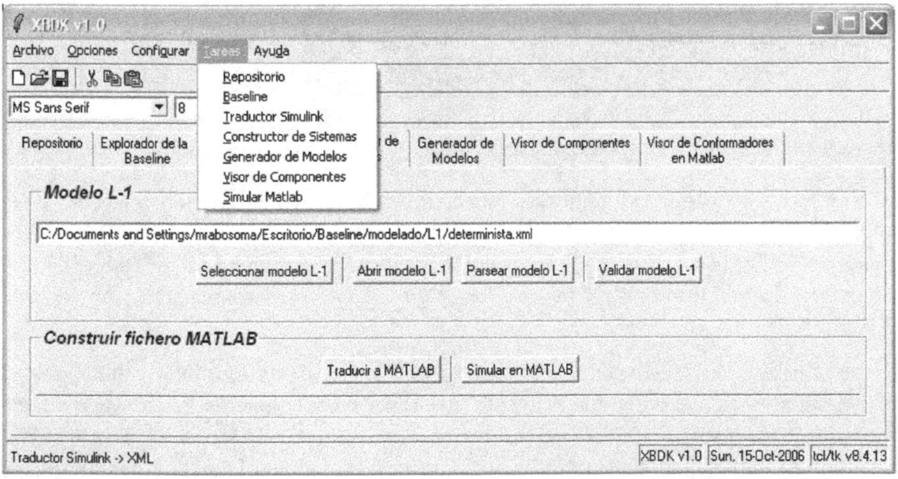

Figure 9. XBDK main menu.

Three COM servers are used for implementing different tasks:

- Matlab COM server is used for running Matlab programs for simulation tasks.
- Altova XML COM server is used for XML parsing and validation.
- Microsoft Excel COM server is used for data management.

XBDK uses a data model that gives a high-level abstraction management of a variety of signal processing systems, specifically for Beamformers (Raboso et al. 2003). Beamformers are array signal processing systems that process the receiving or transmitting signals of an array of sensors (antennas) for obtaining interesting radiation properties as high directivity, low sidelobe levels or nulls for some directions of arrivals. Beamformers developed with XBDK are described using XML language, providing a natural human description of such systems. The abstraction model architecture is shown in figure 10. The specific tools to manage the information of each level are located at the right side of each layer.

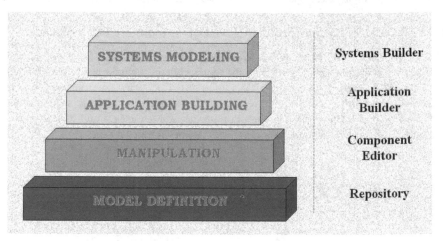

Figure 10. Beamforming XML data representation.

Beamformers are designed and later written in XML using two abstraction levels corresponding to the upper two levels of the pyramid. For XML data manipulation, files must be well-formed and validated. As XBDK is also responsible of these tasks, this tool integrates several routines that use another COM server designed by Altova (AltovaXML).

The next figure and source code below shows a .Net example performing validation and well-forming tasks. Note that the Altova COM server must be started before the methods are called. As a result, a window with the server is automatically launched. This window can be push into background until the application is closed. As the quit() method is not implemented in the interface, close operation must be done manually with CTRL+C key combination or using the task manager.

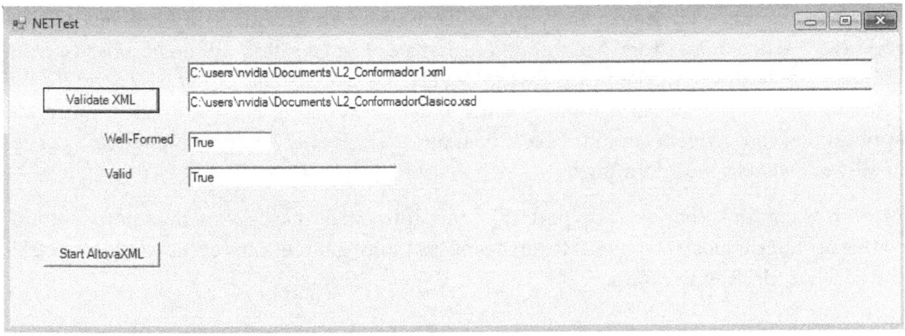

Figure 11. Beamforming XML data representation.

The following code corresponds to the example below:

```
Private  Sub  Button1_Click(ByVal  sender  As  Object,  ByVal  e  As
System.EventArgs) Handles Button1.Click
        Dim resultado As String

        AltovaXMLNET.XMLValidator.InputXMLFileName = TextBox1.Text
        AltovaXMLNET.XMLValidator.SchemaFileName = TextBox4.Text
        resultado = AltovaXMLNET.XMLValidator.IsWellFormed()
        TextBox2.Text = resultado
        If (resultado) Then
            'resultado = AltovaXMLNET.XMLValidator.IsValid()
            resultado                                                =
AltovaXMLNET.XMLValidator.IsValidWithExternalSchemaOrDTD()
            TextBox3.Text = resultado
        Else
            TextBox3.Text = "The document is not well-formed"
        End If
End Sub

Private  Sub  Button2_Click(sender  As  System.Object,  e  As
System.EventArgs) Handles Button2.Click
        AltovaXMLNET = New Altova.AltovaXML.Application
End Sub
```

Table 7. Example using AltovaXML COM server.

5. Conclusions

COM technology is a useful tool for integrating software from different vendors. This is specifically interesting for engineering applications, which have to integrate a great variety of software functionality, from specialized and low-level task, to intuitive GUIs.

Fortunately, software component industry has provided solutions to properly combine software components to get a complete solution without implementing the software from scratch. This can be made using reusability techniques following the standards defined by the Component Base Software Engineering (CBSE).

Engineers working with Matlab and other software can take advantage of CBSE using COM and .Net technologies from Microsoft. Furthermore, integrating different objects from different applications accelerates software development and reduces costs. Today, COTS (Commercial Off-The-Shelf) components are ready to be integrated into the engineering applications and vendors exploit these advantages developing components while assuring quality and standard conforming.

After reading this chapter, I expect that the interested reader can take into account component technology on their future projects, and gain effectiveness on the overall software development process.

Author details

Mariano Raboso and Myriam Codes
Universidad Pontificia de Salamanca (Facultad de Informática), Spain

María I. Jiménez, Lara del Val, Alberto Izquierdo and Juan J. Villacorta
Universidad de Valladolid, Spain

Acknowledgement

This research has been supported by projects: 10MLA-IN-S08EI-1 (Pontifical University of Salamanca), and PON323B11-2 (Junta de Castilla y León). I also want to thank the work made by professors Maribel and Domingo, who carefully made the technical review of the chapter.

6. References

Gunderloy, M. (2001). Calling COM Components from .NET clients, In: *MSDN Library*, 23.03.2012, Available from: http://msdn2.microsoft.com/en-us/library/ms973800.aspx

Huang, C. (2006). Tcom, In: *Access and implement Windows COM objects with Tcl*, 23.03.2012, Available from: http://www.vex.net/~cthuang/tcom/

Raboso, M.; Izquierdo, A. & Villacorta J.J. (2003). Beamforming Systems Modeling using Component Reusability with XML Language, Proceedings of the International Signal Processing Conference, ISPC 2003, Dallas, Texas, USA, March 31-April 3, 2003.

Raboso, M. (2007). *Beamforming Systems Modeling Using XML Language, based on Software Component Reuse*, ProQuest Information and Learning, ISBN 978-0-549-26134-6, USA

Raboso M.; Izquierdo A.; Villacorta J.; del Val L. & Jiménez, M. (2009). Integración de componentes COM de MATLAB/SIMULINK en el entorno CASE XBDK para el modelado de sistemas de conformación de haz. *Ingeniare, Revista chilena de ingeniería*, Vol.17, No.1, (January 2009), pp. 122-135, ISSN 0718-3305

Tcl community (2009). Tcl and Tk manual pages, In: *Tcl/Tk Documentation*, 23.03.2012, Available from: http://www.tcl.tk/doc/

The Mathworks (2012). MATLAB COM Automation Server Support, In: *Matlab R2012a Documentation*, 23.03.2012, Available from:
http://www.mathworks.es/help/techdoc/matlab_external/brd0v3w.html

Chapter 3

Mobile Radio Propagation Prediction for Two Different Districts in Mosul-City

Farhad E. Mahmood

Additional information is available at the end of the chapter

1. Introduction

Since the nineties, a great progress observed in wireless and mobile communications field. Mobiles make many tasks simple and easily to be accomplished. This requires imperatively good and accurate knowing and describing radio propagation for the intended area. Propagation of mobile radio signals is complex, and depend on the applied environment (Theodore S Rappaport, 2002).

In this chapter, two theoretical models considered for the prediction of path loss in two different districts at Mosul city, using MATLAB 7.4 program. The propagation of radio wave of built-up area strongly influenced by the nature of environment, Parameters like antennas height, frequency band, interference, polarization etc, have an influence upon channel behavior. Reflection, diffraction and scattering from building add multipath, fast fading and slow fading effects to the signal.

The Walfisch-Ikegami (W-I) model used for uniform heights and similar buildings in the Karama district to calculate the path loss. The other model used is Okumura-Hata (OH) model applied for irregular and dissimilar buildings (M.O. Kabaou 2007) in the Almajmoa'a district. The information buildings heights for two areas obtained from the Civil Engineering Department, in the University of Mosul.

2. Cellular concept

The key idea of mobile communication system is to offer possibility for a communication link in the serving area of the mobile network regardless of the location of the user. These demand two requirements for service providers (operators) of mobile communication system. Firstly, the service area has to be geometrically large area in order to provide services for a large number of costumers. Secondly, the network has to be able to guarantee mobility, i.e., customers have to be able to move even considerably long distances without breaking already establish connections. Achieving this requirement is technically challenging, and more over there is limited amount of air interface frequency band available (T. Rappaport 2002).

One solution to satisfy these requirements is utilization of *cellular concept* (Lioh. Wacker. 2006). in cellular concept, the basic approach is to divide a large service area into smaller sub areas called cells. The main advantage of cellular solution is increasing capacity. Since the limited radio frequency, range used only in small areas. The same radio frequency can utilized again after a certain physical distance. Once other advantage is that, the base station antenna heights can be much lower due to smaller serving areas. This enables the usage of lower transmit powers, which also saves the battery of the mobile. Furthermore, change capacity and coverage demands for different area can be easily adopted using smaller cells where the traffic density is higher.

In Fig.1, cells depicted with a shape of hexagon. In practice, the concept of hexagonal cells is conceptual due to non-homogenous environment. The morphology of the terrain introduces different propagation environments (e.g., open areas, forests, and waters) and topography fluctuations of the terrain. If the radio wave attenuation is enough, or the distances between the sites are long enough, it is possible to reuse frequencies after a certain distance. The frequencies used in all the grey areas of the figure could be the same, as well as those in the white and the lined areas, respectively, this increase the capacity of cellular communication system. The cellular concept introduces also some disadvantages. Due to the large service area covered by multiple cells, the system has to know the location of the users in order to, e.g., route an incoming call. Thus, some signaling capacity needed in order to control the communications. Another problem arises when continuous service provided for the mobiles on move. To solve these problems, the network management system becomes more complicated, expensive, and more difficult to handle.

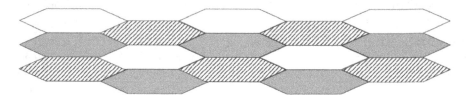

Figure 1. Cellular Concept

3. An environment classification for a mobile radio channel

The propagation of radio wave of built-up district strongly influenced by the nature of environment, in particular the density and size of buildings. In propagation studies for mobile radio, a qualitative description of the environment area is often employed using term such as dense urban, urban, sub urban and rural. 'Dense urban' area generally defined as being dominated by tall buildings, office blocks and other commercial buildings. Whereas suburban areas comprise residential houses, parks and gardens. The term 'rural' defines open farmland with sparse buildings, forest and woodland. When the effects of environment have been conceder, six factors are useful in classifying land usage (J.D.Parson 2000):

- Building density (percentage of area covered by building).
- Building height.
- Building size (area covered by building)
- Building location.
- Vegetation location.
- Terrain density.

Mobile radio channels needs a rigorous vision of channel characterization; the study of channel will be useful for mobile wireless communication to make the best decision between source and destination, and even advising recommendations and directives for dimensioning exploited network (antenna heights, carrier, network architecture, etc...).

4. Radio mobile channel characterization

Propagation channel is a linear system defining a transformation between an input and an output signal, for best understanding the channel and overcome its eventual imperfections. In fact, signal affronts many distortions like delays, spreading. These distortions induced by various reflections that signal faces up during the Emission- Reception path. Consequently, other additive signals will be perceived by the receiver besides the main transmitted signal which must be captured in ideal situations. These additional signals have followed various and different paths. That is what usually named: Multipath. With higher rates used in digital communications e.g., symbols have small duration in comparison with the delay spreading scale and a really superposition between them will be observed.

4.1. Multipath propagation

Multipath is a phenomenon that happens in the channel of mobile systems when the transmitted signal arrives at the receiver via different paths due to reflection, diffraction and scattering resulting in fading. There is only one transmitted signal, due to obstacles like buildings, hills, trees, and so on, in the signal paths that cause different signals to arrive at the receiver from various directions with different delays (M. Rahnema 2008). In such situations, receiver will collect light of seen's (LOS) rays but also other rays having arrived over indirect ways. They know as Non-light of Sight (NLOS) rays. More further, are Emission and the Reception one side from the other, more lower will be chosen the used frequency. Possible paths will consequently be higher. Propagation channel causes then Inter Symbol Interferences (ISI). For that, the parameter conditioning propagation delay spread values must imperatively specify. Fig. 2. illustrates three propagation components.

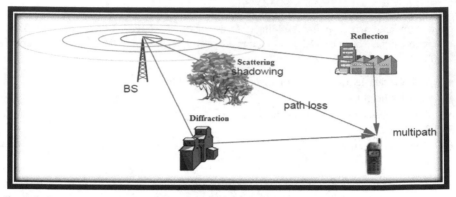

Figure 2. Propagation Component between Base Station and Mobile Station

Where (L. Poole 2006):

- Path loss: decay of the signal strength with distance.
- Slow fading (Shadowing): is due to obstruction of the signal by natural obstacles.
- Fast fading: due to the multipath reflection of the transmitted signal.

Signals coming from the same source will arrive to at the receiver side affected by different delays. Delay spread evaluated as (S. Tabbane 2000):

$$\text{Multi path spread} = \frac{\text{longest path} - \text{shortest path}}{c} \tag{1}$$

Where c commonly known light celerity. Table below shows and gives better and more accurate idea.

Environment type	Delay spread (s)
Free space	< 0.2
Rural area	1
Mountainous area	30 to 50
Suburban area	0.5
Urban area	3
Indoor area	0.1

Table 1. Comparison of delay spread in different environments.

We can particularly note that delays caused indoor are fewer than other referred to abroad situations (some tens of s) (M. J. Nawrocki 2006). For that, a suitable modeling must accomplished for each situation often named Indoor/Outdoor. Therefore, the channel has many dimensions, giving a particular description as indicated in the fig. 3. (V. Erceg 2005)

Parameters like antennas heights, frequency band, interference, polarization etc, and have an influence upon channel behavior indicated above in the fig. 3.

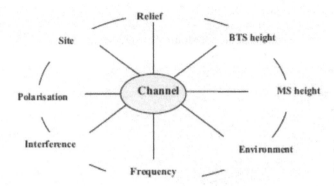

Figure 3. Channel characterization versus different vision

Direction and distance between reflectors (buildings, mountains, walls, cars) influence channel awkward and followed channel. The IR of a dispersive delay channel depends then on number of physical factors. The delay spread value varies from ten nanoseconds for indoor propagation up to some microseconds in outdoor propagation case as indicated in Table 1 for different areas and situations (J.D.Parson 2000).

4.2. Slow and fast fading

In addition to distance dependent path loss, the received signal level experiences also fluctuations that called slow and fast fading. When the receiver placed in, a coverage area that either omits the LOS component or other dominant component, the receiver is considered shadowed. Usually these shadowing obstacles are big trees, buildings, or in rural environment the hills. Slow fading is shown to follow log-normal distribution, and thus it is also called log-normal fading.

Fast fading is a consequence of the multipath propagation phenomena. As described earlier, the multipath propagated signal components can received either constructively or de-constructively depending on the relative phase difference between the components. This causes very rapid fluctuations in the received signal level. Slow and fast fading components of received signal illustrated in Fig.4. in respect to receiver-transmitter distance.

4.3. Rayleigh fading

After reflection, the phases and magnitude of the radio wave might be attaint attenuation or fading phenomena cause essentially temporal variations in phases. These come from additive multiple signals In this case; the resulting received signal in the receiver could be null or a very weak signal. Multiple received signals could also add in a constructive manner and the resulting received signal will have a magnitude greater than signal issued along directly path. Taking account of propagation conditions's variation between kinds of domains, we must note fading depends on the following (J. S. Seybold 2005):

- Transmitted Signal's bandwidth,
- Delay spread of the received signal,
- Random phase and magnitude of Multipath components,
- Transmitter, receiver and around existing objects position cause CIR's temporal fluctuations.

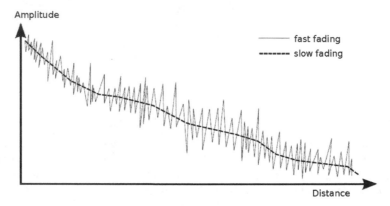

Figure 4. Slow and fast fading of propagated signal in respect to receiver-transmitter distance

4.4. Doppler shift

This phenomena result from Displacement and mobility of the MS in relation to BS. This introduces frequency shift of the received signal. Frequency shift depends essentially on:

- Mobile position,
- The speed of the receiver according to the emitter.

If we note:

- λ is the wavelength,
- f the carrier used frequency.

The frequency received by a receiver moving at elative speed v relatively to the emitter is given by the following (F.I . Mahmoud 2008).

$$f' = f - \frac{v}{\lambda} \qquad (2)$$

Doppler shift causes a random frequency modulation for the signal, and could introduce Multipath Signals. Positive and negative shifts both introduced.

5. Path loss models

Free space:

The free space path loss used in many areas for predicting radio signal strengths that may expected in a radio system. Although it does not hold for most terrestrial situations as there are several situations in which it can be used and it also useful as the basis for understanding many real life radio propagation situations.

Calculation of free-space path loss:

The free space path loss formula or free space path loss equation is quite simple to use. Not only is the path loss proportional to the square of the distance between the transmitter and receiver, but the signal level is also proportional to the square of the frequency (T. Rappaport, 2002).

$$FSPL = (4\pi d/\lambda)^\wedge 2 \tag{3}$$

Where:

FSPL is the Free space path loss

d is the distance of the receiver from the transmitter (metres)
λ is the signal wavelength (metres)
f is the signal frequency (Hertz)
c is the speed of light in a vacuum (metres per second)

due to multipath effect and fading it cannot depend on free space formula to find path loss there are empirical model used to find path loss.

Methods to model the mobile radio propagation channel are (M.O. Kabaou 2007):

- Statistical models ,like (Okumura-Hata) ,
- Physical Models ,like (Walfisch-Ikegami),
- Mixed Models,
- In addition, References Models.

We study only the first two cases.

5.1. Okumura-Hata Model (OH), statistical models

Okumura-Hata Model is an Empirical model; which based on a Statistical Analysis of a great number of experimental measures that takes in account many parameters such as buildings, Base stations (BS) and Mobile stations heights (S.A.Mawjoud 2008). The model based on the field measurements made by Okumura in Tokyo in 1968. Okumura's measurements were later fitted in a mathematical formula by Hata . The Okumura-Hata model is valid for frequency range of 150–1500 MHz, the BS height is 30-200m, the MS height is 1-10m and the distance is 1-20km. Because of the frequency band limitation of the Okumura-Hata model, the original model was later extended by the European CO-operation in the field of Scientific and Technical research (COST 231) to the frequency band of 1500–2000 MHz , which covers the bands allocated to the 3G networks (E. Damasso 1999), is given in equation (4)

$$L\ (urban)(dB) =$$
$$46.3 + 33.9\ log(f_{MHz}) - 13.82 \log(h_b) - a(h_m) + (44.9 - 6.55 \log(h_b)) \log(d_{km}) \tag{4}$$

Where:

f_{MHz} is the operating frequency in MHz   (1500 MHz -2000 MHz).

h_b the base station(BS) antenna height in meter (30m- 200m).
h_m the mobile(MS) antenna height in meter   (1m – 10m) .
d_{km} the distance between BS and MS in km.
$a(h_m)$ the correction factor for mobile antenna height which is given by:

$$a(h_m)_{dB} = (1.1 \log(f_{MHz}) - 0.7)h_m - 1.56 \log(f_{MHz}) - 0.8 \qquad (5)$$

Where: $1 \text{ m} \leq h_m \leq 10 \text{ m}$

Equation (3) is an extension version of original Hata model to work up to 2GHz by The European comparative for scientific and technical research (EURO-COST) (M. J. Nawrocki 2006).

The BS antenna height must be above the rooftop level of the buildings adjacent to the BS. Thus, the model is proposed to be used in propagation studies of macro-cells. There are several weaknesses in the empirical or semi-empirical models for propagation studies in micro-cellular environments. If the BS antenna height is below the level of the rooftop of surrounding buildings, the nature of the propagation phenomena will changes. This situation cannot be analyzed with statistical methods because the individual buildings are too large compared with the cell size and the exact geometrical properties of the buildings can no longer be ignored as they can in macro cellular models.

5.2. Walfisch-Ikegami Model (W-I) physical models

This model based on the assumption that the transmitted wave propagates over the rooftops by a process of multiple diffraction in regular area, regular area has rows of buildings, which are nearly of equal and uniform height and are located on flat terrain. The building are organized along the street grid with little or no side-to-side spacing and nearly equal front-to-front and back-to-back spacing. The propagation takes place primarily over building (T. Rappaport. 2002). The model considers the impact on rooftops and building heights using diffraction to predict average signal strength at street level. The models consider the path loss (L) to be the product of three factors (J.D.Parson 2000):

- Free space loss.
- Losses added by diffraction.
- Losses introduced by rooftops near the studied area.

The geometry used in the Walfisch model shown in fig.5.

From fig. 5, it can be noted that the diffracted signals arrive at the receiver from the 1st, 2nd and 3rd as if the model show that the signals travels from rooftops.

This model depends on:

1.   The height of the buildings.
2.   The width of the streets and the width of the buildings.

3. The distance between buildings.
4. The orientation of the streets relative to the line of sight (LOS) and non line of sight (NLOS).
5. The distance between the Tx. and receiver Rx, the heights of Tx. and Rx. antennas and the frequency of operation.

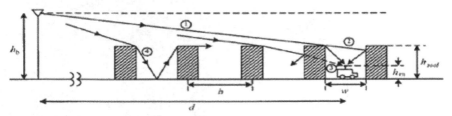

Figure 5. Propagation geometry for Walfisch– Ikegami model

COST 231 Walfisch–Ikegami (WI) model is the most widely used empirical model today, being an extension of the models from J. Walfisch and F. Ikegami. To work up to 2GHz by The European comparative for scientific and technical, research (EURO-COST). It has been adopted as a standard model for 3G IMT 2000/UMTS systems. It is valid within the following constraints:

- BS height: 4–50m.
- MS height: 1–3m.
- BS to MS separation : 0.02–5 km.

The Walfisch – Ikegami equation is given by:

$$L = L_O + L_{rts} + L_{msd} \tag{6}$$

Where:
L_O : free space loss.
L_{rts} : rooftop to street diffraction and scatter loss.
L_{msd} : multi screen diffraction loss due to the rows of building .

$$L_o = 32.4 + 20 \log d_{km} + 20 \log f_{MHz} \tag{7}$$

$$L_{rts} = -16.9 - 10 \log w + 10 \log f_{MHz} + 20 \log(h_{roof} - h_m) - L_{ori} \tag{8}$$

Where:
h_{roof}: The height of the buildings.

$$L_{ori} = \begin{cases} -10 + 0.354 \dfrac{\varphi}{\deg} & \text{for } 0^\circ \leq \varphi < 35^\circ \\[2mm] 2.5 + 0.075\left(\dfrac{\varphi}{\deg} - 35\right) & \text{for } 35^\circ \leq \varphi < 55^\circ \\[2mm] 4.0 - 0.114\left(\dfrac{\varphi}{\deg} - 55\right) & \text{for } ^\circ 55 \leq \varphi < 90^\circ \end{cases} \tag{9}$$

φ is the angle between incident wave and street oriented.

$$L_{msd} = L_{bsh} + k_a + k_d \log(d_{Km}) + k_f \log(f_{MHz}) - 9\log(b) \tag{10}$$

Where   b: The distance between buildings.

$$L_{bsh} = \begin{cases} -18 Log\left[1 + \left(h_b - h_{Roof}\right)\right] & \text{for } h_b > h_{Roof} \\ 0 & \text{for } h_b \le h_{Roof} \end{cases} \tag{11}$$

$$k_a = \begin{cases} 54 & \text{for } h_b > h_{Roof} \\ 54 - 0.8\left(h_b - h_{Roof}\right) & \text{for d>0.5km and } h_b \le h_{Roof} \\ 54 - 0.8\left(h_b - h_{Roof}\dfrac{d_{km}}{0.5}\right) & \text{for d<0.5km and } h_b \le h_{Roof} \end{cases} \tag{12}$$

$$k_d = \begin{cases} 18 & \text{for } h_b > h_{Roof} \\ 18 - 15\dfrac{\left(h_b - h_{Roof}\right)}{h_{Roof}} & \text{for } h_b \le h_{Roof} \end{cases} \tag{13}$$

$$k_f = -4 + 1.5 \left(\frac{f_{MHz}}{925} - 1\right) \tag{14}$$

The term k_a represents the increase in path loss when the base station antenna is below rooftop height. k_d and k_f allow for the dependence of the diffraction loss on range and frequency, respectively .

6. Radio network planning

Mosul city have large variation in topography there are terrain and water, shown in fig.6, two regions have been investigated, for terrain there is nonhomogenous area like Almajmoa'a region, also there is the Karama region that have regular area with equal height for all building. Usually the OH model used by mobile companies in all Mosul city because it is assumed irregular region, but regular region can be seen in Karama district (building structure is nearly equal), W-I propagation model is applicable to district of uniform area buildings, which is appropriate for Karama region.

6.1. Path loss study for Almajmoa'a region using Okumura-Hata Model

In Almajmoa'a region, shown in fig.7. , all buildings are irregular and not of uniform shape, for these reasons W-I model cannot be applied but OH is more suitable.

- Simulations for *OH Model* in Almajmoa'a:

i.   Study of coverage range in OH model:

Fig.9. Shows the variation of path loss with distance, which shows that as the coverage of cell increases the path loss increases, using equation 4 & 5 for operation frequency of 2000MHz, 1.5m mobile antenna height and 25m base station antenna height. That is mean when mobile move far from base station the received signal decreases gradually.

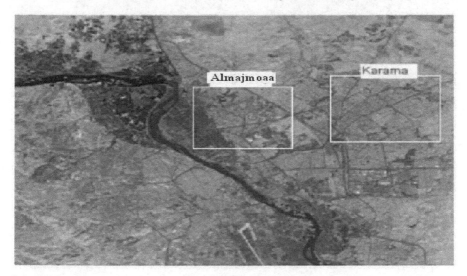

Figure 6. Mosul city map by Google Earth

Figure 7. Almajmoa'a region in Mosul city.

Figure 8. Karama region in Mosul city.

ii.   Study of BS height in OH model:

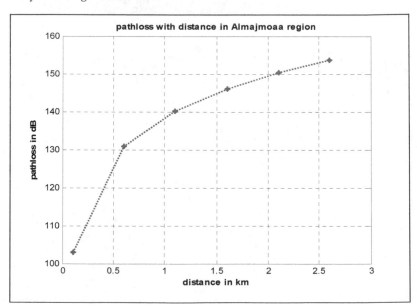

Figure 9. Path loss versus distance for O-H in Almajmoa'a region.

The result in Fig.10., shows the variation of path loss with distance for four antennas height of base station (30m,50m,70m and 100m), which shows that as the antenna height of base station increases, path loss decreases. Therefore, the coverage of cell will increases, which mean for BS height 30m the coverage of cell, could be 5km, where for 100m the coverage may arrive 35km. Therefore, inside the city where there are large number of building and MS, this demand large number of BS, if the coverage of these BSs is large, that mean the interference among these cells will increase, then the blocking probability will increase. Therefore, it must decrease BSs height inside cities to reduce this interference. However, for outside cities, where there are large area, small building and small number of MSs, it recommended to increase BSs height to increase coverage to cover as large area as can.

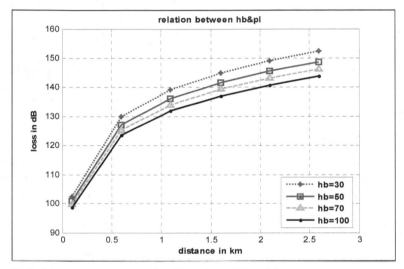

Figure 10. Path loss versus distance for four BS heights in OH model

6.2. Path loss study for karama region using Walfisch-Ikegami (W-I) model

In karama region shown in fig. 8, buildings are regular and of uniform shape, for these reasons W-I model can be applied. (karama's information which is used in simulation, are given from Civil Engineering Department in Mosul university).

• Simulations for W-I in karama:
a. Study of coverage range in W-I model:

Buildings in this region have three floors with 3m height for each floor, i.e. the whole building's height (h_{roof}) is 9m. Base station's height (h_b) is 25m. buildings distance (b) are 6m , street width (w) is 4m, operating frequency 2000MHz, mobile antenna's height (h_m) is 1.5 m . Fig.11. shows the relation between path loss and distance in Karama district with W-I model, this figure show that as the coverage of cell increases the path loss increases in mobile unit at cell boarder.

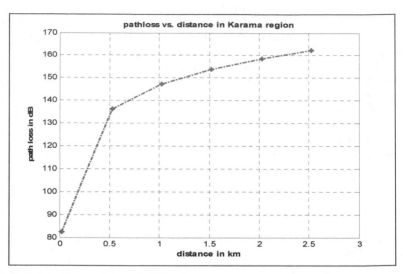

Figure 11. Path loss versus distance for W-I in Karama

b.   Study of BS height in W-I model :

Fig.12. shows the variation of path loss with distance for three BSs height (hb=25m>hroof , hb=9m= hroof & hb=5m<hroof) this figure shows that to reduce the path loss they must increase BS height to become higher than buildings height, to avoid reflection from buildings .

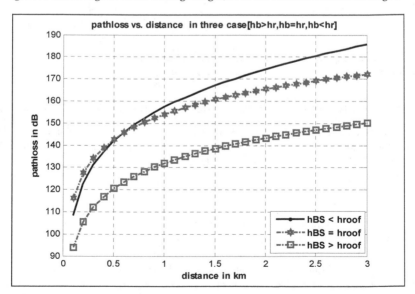

Figure 12. Path loss versus distance for different BS heights.

The BS height larger than rooftop case, it can be seen that there are difference by about 20 dB from rooftop BS height, regardless of distance between BS and MS.

However, for BS height less than rooftop the difference in bath loss increase gradually to be 10 dB at 3km, where in 600 meter the difference could be zero.

7. Comparison between O-H and W-I

The simulation results of the two different districts considered are shown in fig.13. (for same BS and MS antenna height and same operating frequency),which shows that Karama region using W-I model have larger path loss than Almajmoa'a region using OH model about 7 - 10dB, because of rooftop and multi-screen effects in karama region which makes more diffraction for signal.

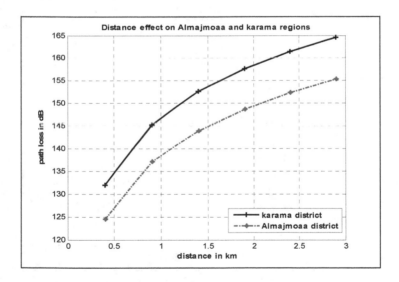

Figure 13. Path loss versus distance in karama and Almajmoa'a regions

The path loss verses base stations height for O-H model and W-I model is shown in fig. 14., this result show that the path loss verses BS antenna height in karama district is higher than that for Almajmoa'a district, which can be attributed to high signal diffraction on roof top in karama region, and this figure shows that the decrease path loss in karama region greater than that in Almajmoa'a region by 7dB, due to the signals in karama region are release from rooftop and multi-screen effects for increasing BS height over the rooftop of karama regular buildings.

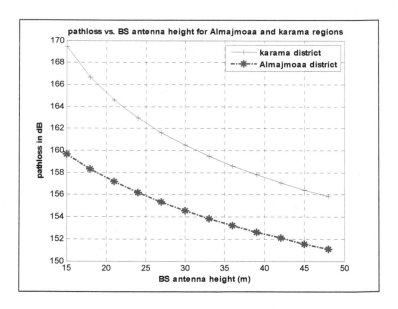

Figure 14. Path loss versus BS antenna height.

8. Conclusions

In this study, two districts in Mosul city were investigated, one (Karama district) which has large number of similar and uniform building, Walfisch-Ikegami model is used which is suitable for radio network planning. The other is the Almajmoa'a district, which has dissimilar and irregular building, and less buildings density than Karama, Okumura-Hata model is applicable. Statistical Models are easier to be used than the physical ones. They do not need e.g. geographic databases. However, validity domain is often limited: Okumura-Hata model cannot be used for distances less than 1 km.

Author details

Farhad E. Mahmood
Electrical Department, College of Engineering, University of Mosul, Iraq

9. References

Theodore S Rappaport, "Wireless communications principles and practice". John Wiely&Sons, 2002.

J.D.Parson " The mobile radio propagation channel " second edition . John Wiely&Sons, 2000.

M.O. Kabaou."Multipath propagation models for radio mobile channel " Fourth international multi-conference on systems ,signals & devices .vol .3 2007 . Tunisia .

S.A.Mawjoud "Estimation of design parameters for cellular WCDMA network" .AL-Rafidain engineering journal .vol 16. No .4 . Oct. 2008.

M. J. Nawrocki M. Dohler "Understanding UMTS Radio Network Modelling, Planning and Automated Optimisation" John Wiley & Sons Ltd . 2006.

F.I . Mahmoud & S.A.Mawjoud " planning and design of a WCDMA network compatible with existing GSM system in Mosul city " 5th international multi-conference on systems ,signals & devices. IEEE . 2008. Jordan .

M. Rahnema, "UMTS Network Planning Optimization, and Inter-Operation with GSM", First Edition, John Wiley and Sons (Asia) Ltd, India, 2008.

L. Poole, "Cellular Communications Explained from Basics to 3G", First Edition, Elsevier Ltd, England, 2006.

S. Tabbane. *Handbook of Mobile Radio Networks*. Artech House Boston London, 2000.

V. Erceg. *Channels Modeling suitable for MBWA*. Activity report, Junary 2003.

J. S. Seybold, Introduction to RF Propagation. Wiley-IEEE, 2005.

E. Damasso and L. M. Correia, Eds., Digital Mobile Radio towards Future Generation Systems, COST 231 Final Report, 1999.

H. Holma and A. Toskala, WCDMA for UMTS: HSPA Evolution and LTE, 4th ed. John Wiley & Sons, 2007.

J. Laiho, A. Wacker, and T. Novosad, Radio Network Planning and Optimisation for UMTS, 2nd ed. John Wiley & Sons, 2006.

MATLAB/SIMULINK and Its Engineering Applications

A Virtual Laboratory: Teaching and Research Tool in Control Engineering Education

Prashant M. Menghal and A. Jaya Laxmi

Additional information is available at the end of the chapter

1. Introduction

A virtual laboratory for Automatic Control Engineering can provide easy access to university students with regard to engineering applications at anytime and from any computing environment. This interactive learning environment, consist of simulations, demonstrations and exercises, which can fulfill the role of a bridge from passive learning to active engagement and accordingly stimulate deeper thinking; grounding a problem based-learning environment. The applications are also very important for relating theory to practice, so that the students develop engineering judgment and understand how process behavior can be captured using mathematical models. The undergraduate control engineering at engineering colleges is based on a strong "hands-on" laboratory experience. Regardless of how many fine lectures are given or how many homework problems assigned, the students do not see how control systems work in the real world until they get into the laboratory. They do not understand that they can modify the performance of a physical system to meet design specifications. Only after they complete the laboratory course do they understand the power that they have to become "control gods." After completing the lab experiments on virtual laboratory, the students first characterize the performance of a second order system (a dc servomechanism ES-130).Virtual Laboratory (VLab) has been developed to control Engineering by using MATLAB/SIMULINK. This chapter will also emphasize on the use of Mathematical Modeling and simulation of Feed back Servo trainer (33-100) and study their behavior by using the MATLAB/SIMULINK models and Graphical User Interface (GUI). A graphical user interface is developed which is user friendly and does not require the knowledge of MATLAB. This user can change the parameters of the systems as per his choice or required condition, this computational tool as a part of laboratory experiments will enhance laboratory experience by providing students with the opportunity to compare the practical results with those obtained by computer simulation. Such an opportunity helps the students of all courses to realise the limitations of hardware.

With the growing popularity and possibilities of the Internet, web-based teaching is becoming more and more popular in education. The new trend focuses on developing more effective and efficient teaching methods for large groups of students by using interactive web based material. Control systems curricula are often viewed by students as theoretical and highly mathematical. Students are often unable to relate theory to applications in the real world. The obvious solution to this problem, is to include the virtual lab experiment in the control curriculum. Simulation tools are frequently used as an educational aid in automatic control courses. Initially, analog computers with electronic circuits were used for simulating different types of physical processes. When digital computers were present several simulation packages based on numerical techniques were obatinable. Personal computers with low price are universally acknowledged. MATLAB/SIMULINK is a Windows based engineering and science toolbox, which offers valuable interactive demonstrations or the possibility to easily create different simulations related to the theory. It is an integrated technical computing environment that combines numeric computation, advanced graphics and visualization, through powerful Graphical User Interface (GUI). The undergraduate(UG) level engineering lecture class are co- requisites with the lab experiments selected to support and complement the lectures. Most of the universities cover the following lab experiments at UG level:

i.   Modeling mechanical, electrical and electromechanical systems.
ii.   Transfer function, Block diagram and Manson's rules.
iii. DC Servo Mechanism: Open loop and Closed loop systems.
iv.   Steady state and transient time response analysis.
v.   Root locus and introduction to root locus design.
vi.   Frequency response analysis: Bode and Nyquist plots etc.

The above listed experiments are performed with the help of feedback mechanical unit 33-100 and feedback analog unit 33-002 which are as shown in fig.1 and Fig.2.

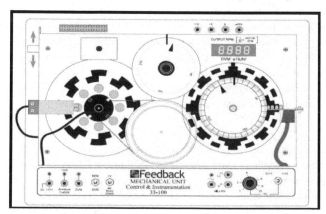

Figure 1. Feed back Mechanical Unit 33-100

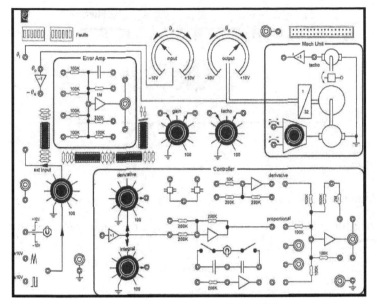

Figure 2. Feedback Analog Unit 33-002

It is usually recognized that, by studying and experimenting the simulation model a student can experiment with systems that are impossible. He can also work in a laboratory which are being potentially dangerous or huge dimension or very a expensive processes. By using a virtual laboratory, it is possible to obtain some knowledge about its model, operation or stability of the system without using a actual hardware.

2. Mathematical modelling and simulation

Modeling a system and writing the simulation program contributes to better understanding of its physical principles and properties. By defining the equations of the different parts of the system and how they interact with each other, a student can obtain the clear understanding about the system structure and the way it operates. The feedback mechanical unit 33-100 is a electromechanical unit which comprises of a dc motor, analog tachogenerator, analog input and output potentiometers, absolute and incremental digital encoders and magnetic break as shown in fig.1. The main component of feedback mechanical unit is a DC motor. The mathematical model of DC motor in armature control mode has been carried out by writing differential equations which are as follows:

The air gap flux is proportional to field current,

$$\Phi = K_f i_f$$

Where K_f is a constant.

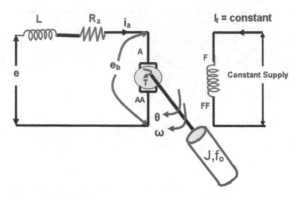

Figure 3. Armature controlled DC Motor

The torque T_m developed by the motor is proportional to the product of the armature current and air gap flux,

$$T_m = K_1 K_f i_f i_a$$

Where K_1 is constant. In the armature controlled DC motor field current is kept constant, so the above equation can be written as

$$T_M = K_T i_a$$

Where K_T is known as motor torque constant. The motor back emf being proportional to speed is given as

$$e_b = K_b \, d\theta/dt$$

where K_b equals to back emf constant.

The differential equation of the armature circuit is

$$L_a \, d/dt \, (i_a) + R_a i_a + e_b = e_a$$

The torque equation is

$$J d^2/dt^2 \, (\theta) + f_o \, d\theta/dt = T_M = K_T i_a$$

Thus, from above equations, the transfer function of DC motor is as follows:

$$T(s) = K_T / \, [s\{(R_a + s L_a)(Js + f_o) + K_T K_b\}] \qquad (1)$$

The simulink model of DC motor is derived from the equation 1 is shown in fig. 4. It is the universal model for performing the control system engineering practical in virtual laboratory.

The front end user interface is created to perform the control system practicals with the help of GUI platform of the MATLAB as shown in fig. 5.

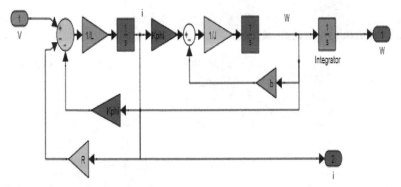

Figure 4. Simulink Model of DC Motor Model

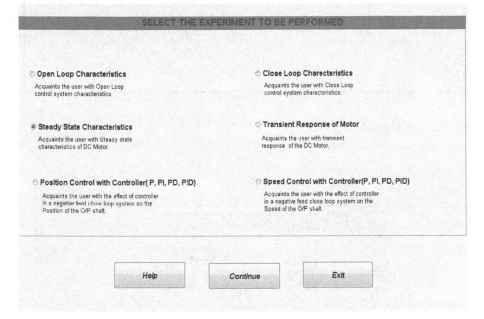

Figure 5. Front End User Interface of Virtual Laboratory

2.1. Open loop characteristics

The aim of this experiment is to acquaint the user with Open Loop control system characteristics. The circuit diagram for performing this experiment on Analog Servo trainer – Analog unit 33-110 is as shown in fig. 6.

The simulation model created with the help of SIMULINK is shown in fig. 7. The response of the open loop system is shown in fig. 8.

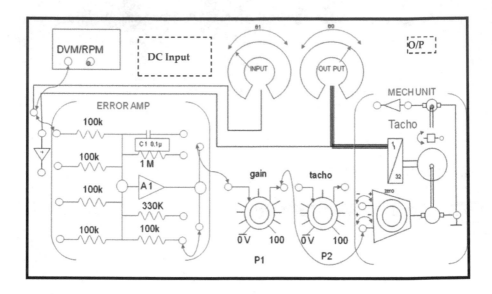

Figure 6. Open Loop system

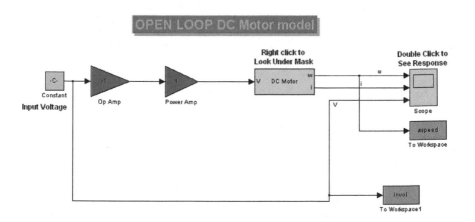

Figure 7. Simulink Model of Open Loop Control System

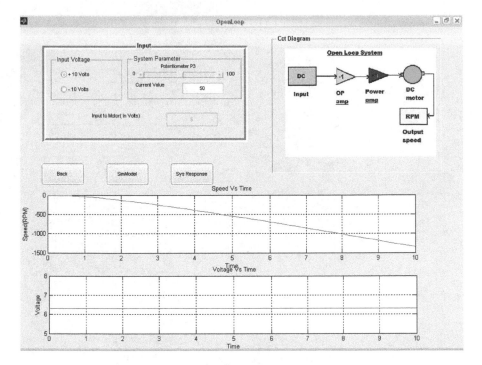

Figure 8. Output Response of Open Loop Control System

by modeling and simulating of each experiment with the help of MATLAB/SIMULINK. A complete Virtual Laboratory has been developed and successfully implemented. The Virtual Laboratory performs the following experiments:

a. Open Loop Control System.
b. Closed Loop Control System
c. Steady State Characteristics of DC Motor.
d. Transient Response of DC Motor.
e. Position Control with Controller (P, PI, PD, PID).
f. Speed Control of DC Motor with Controller (P, PI, PD and PID).

An interactive user interface has been developed using GUI feature of MATLAB to ease and help the user in better understanding and performing of above mentioned practicals. The following are the graphs generated to show the system response in the above mentioned practicals.

a. Speed Vs Input voltage. (b) Step Response. (c) Root locus. (d) Bode plots.
b. Nyquist plots. (f) Pole Zero Map.

2.2. Simulation results

The simulation results which are obtained by Virtual Laboratory are as follows:

a.   Closed Loop Control System

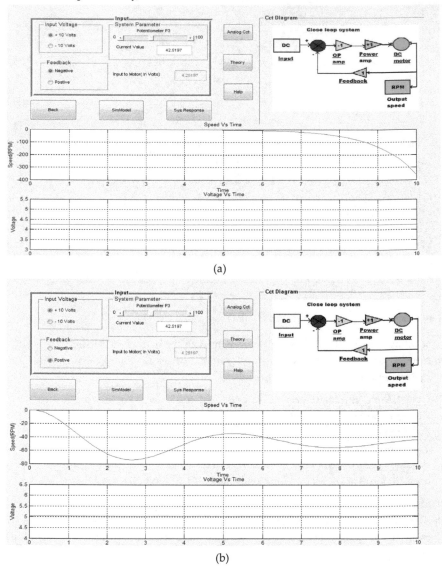

Figure 9. (a) Closed loop with Negative Feedback; (b) Closed loop with Positive Feedback

3. Need of controller (P, PD, PI & PID)

Every practical system takes finite time to reach its steady state and during this period , it oscillates or increases exponentially.The behaviour of the system gets decided by the type and location of closed loop poles in s–plane. The closed loop poles are dependent on selection of the parmeters of the system. Every system has a tendency to oppose the oscillatory behaviour of the system which is called as **damping.** Now this tendency controls the type of closed loop poles and hence the nature of the response. This damping is measured by a factor called damping ratio of the system. Damping ratio indicates how much dominant the opposition from the system is to the oscillations in the output. In some systems it will be low where system will oscillate but slowly i.e. with damped frequency. If damping ratio is high, system output will not oscillate at all and not only it will be exponential, but also so slow that it will take a very long time to reach a steady state. That is why all practical systems are designed for the damping ratio less than 1 i.e. underdamped.

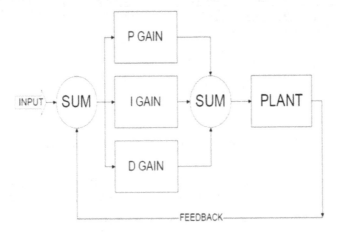

Figure 10. PID Controller

A Proportional, Integral, Derivative controller (PID controller) is a controller which attempts to correct the error between a measured process variable and a desired set point by calculating and then outputing a corrective action that can adjust the process accordingly. The PID controller calculation (algorithm) involves three separate parameters; the Proportional, the Integral and the Derivative values. The Proportional value determines the reaction to the current error, the Integral determines the reaction based on the sum of recent errors and the Derivative determines the reaction to the rate at which the error has been changing. The weighted sum of these three actions is used to adjust the process via a control element. By "tuning" the three constants in the PID controller algorithm, the PID can provide control action designed for specific process requirements. The response of the controller can be described in terms of the responsiveness of the controller to an error, the degree to which the controller overshoots the set point and the degree of system oscillation. The use of the PID algorithm for control does not guarantee optimal control of the system or system stability. Some applications may necessitate using only one or two modes to provide the appropriate system control. This is achieved by setting the gain of undesired control outputs to zero. A PID controller will be called a PI, PD, P or I controller in the absence of the respective control actions.

A proportional controller (K_p) will have the effect of reducing the rise time and will reduce, but never eliminate, the steady-state error. An integral control (K_i) will have the effect of eliminating the steady-state error, but it may make the transient response worse. A derivative control (K_d) will have the effect of increasing the stability of the system, reducing the overshoot, and improving the transient response. Effects of each of controllers K_p, K_d, and K_i on a closed-loop system are summarized in the table shown below:

CONTROLLER	RISE TIME	OVERSHOOT	SETTLING TIME	STEADY STATE ERROR
K_p	Decrease	Increase	Small Change	Decrease
K_i	Decrease	Increase	Increase	Eliminate
K_d	Small Change	Decrease	Decrease	Small Change

Table 1. Effects of Controller of Time Response.

The transfer function for PID controller is

$$\text{Transfer Function} = K_p + K_d S + K_i / \qquad (2)$$

3.1. Simulation results & analysis

The simulation results which are obtained by virtual laboratory for DC motors with controller are as follows.

The simulation results of transient behavior of DC motor are shown from Fig. 12 to Fig. 33. The following inferences are drawn from the simulation results of DC Servomechanism:

i.   From the output response of the DC motor, it is observed that for every increase in input voltage the output response (i.e. Current and Speed) also increases and reaches its steady state value faster as shown in Fig. 12

ii. When proportional controller is used the response is oscillatory and underdamped. It takes more settling time to reach the steady state value as shown in Fig. 13. By using PD controller, the peak overshoot is reduced and thus transient response is improved as shown in Fig.14. System without controller is type I system. The integral controller of the system increases from I to II. As type of system is increased, steady state errors are reduced as shown in Fig. 15. Transient response as well as steady state response can be improved by adjusting value of derivative gain and integral gain as shown in Fig. 16.

iii. By using PID controller the transient as well as steady state response improves as shown in Fig. 14, Fig. 15 and Fig. 16.

iv. The comparison of the transient response of DC motor is shown in Fig. 33 with P, PI, PD and PID controller. As the Integral gain is increased the system response becomes more sluggish, however the tuning of the controller can be judged by deciding on the proper gain of Derivative and Integral Controller.

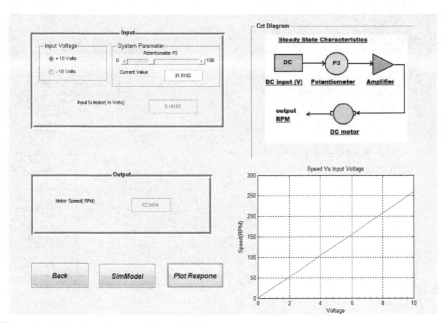

Figure 11. Steady State Characteristics of DC Motor

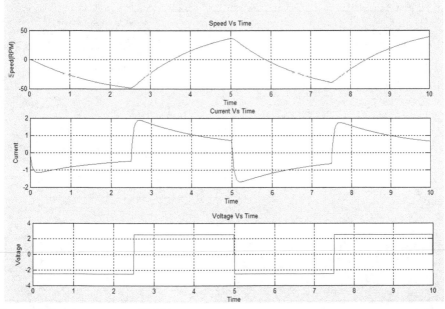

Figure 12. Transient response of DC Motor

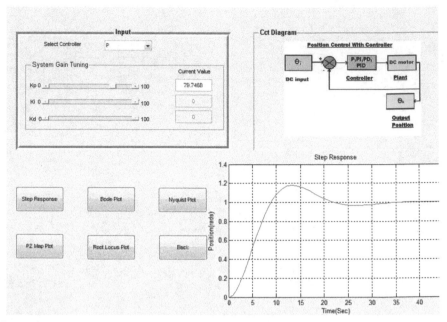

Figure 13. Transient Response of the DC motor without Controller.

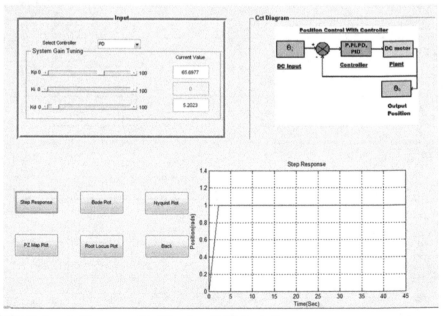

Figure 14. Transient Response of the DC motor with PD Controller

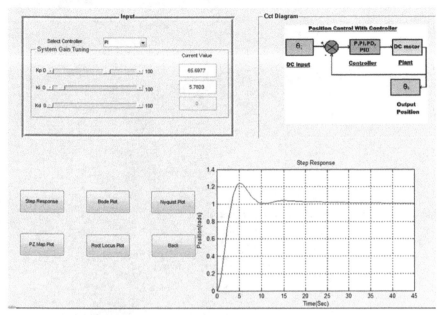

Figure 15. Transient Response of the DC motor with PI Controller

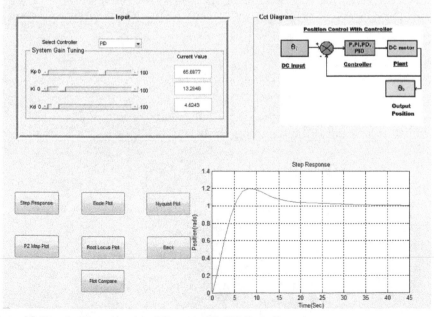

Figure 16. Transient Response of the DC motor with PID Controller

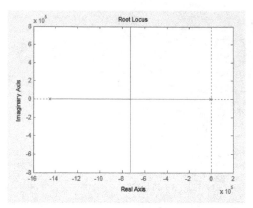

Figure 17. Root Locus of the DC motor without Controller

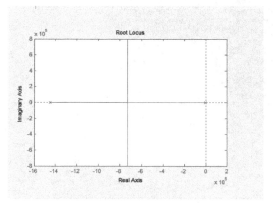

Figure 18. Root Locus of the DC motor with PD Controller

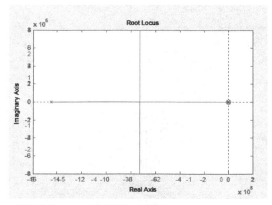

Figure 19. Root Locus of the DC motor with PI Controller

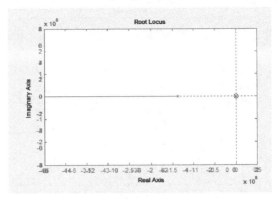

Figure 20. Root Locus of the DC motor with PID Controller

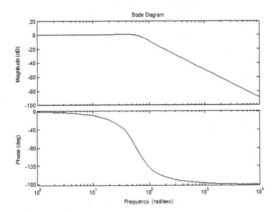

Figure 21. Bode plot of the DC motor without Controller

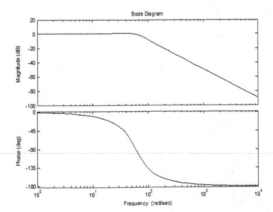

Figure 22. Bode plot of the DC motor with PD Controller

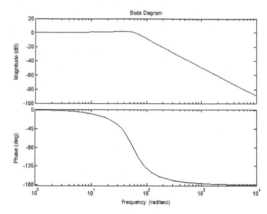

Figure 23. Bode plot of the DC motor with PI Controller

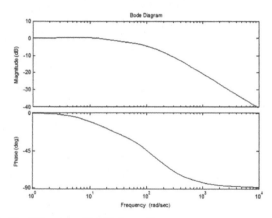

Figure 24. Bode plot of the DC motor with PID Controller

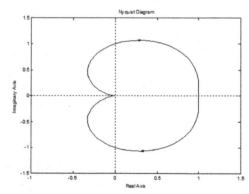

Figure 25. Nyquist plot of the DC motor without Controller

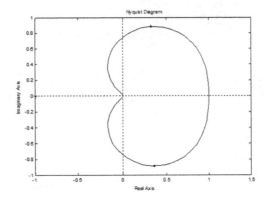

Figure 26. Nyquist plot of the DC motor with PD Controller

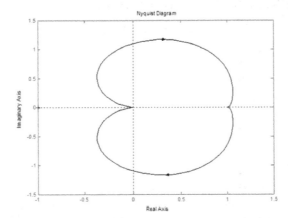

Figure 27. Nyquist plot of the DC motor with PI Controller

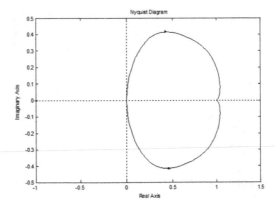

Figure 28. Nyquist plot of the DC motor with PID Controller

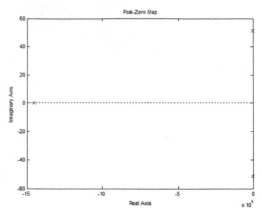

Figure 29. Pole Zero Map of the DC motor without Controller

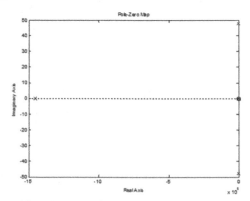

Figure 30. Pole Zero Map of the DC motor with PD Controller

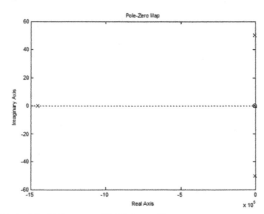

Figure 31. Pole Zero Map of the DC motor with PI Controller

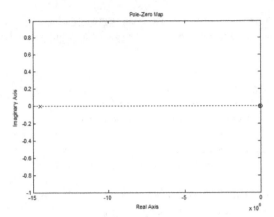

Figure 32. Pole Zero Map of the DC motor with PID Controller

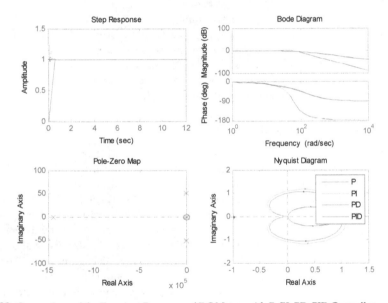

Figure 33. Comparison of the Transient Response of DC Motor with P, PI, PD, PID Controller

4. Integration of Virtual laboratory into Control Engineering courses

The Virtual laboratory for control system has been developed using MATLAB/SIMULINK and integrated into the Control Engineering Curriculum of UG courses. It consists of the complete details of mathematical modeling using the modules available in SIMULINK for open loop, closed loop, PID control, Transient, frequency response of DC Motor, Position and speed control of DC motor using controller experiments. Then the programming of each selected module is carried out. For the ease of an user, a graphical user interface is modeled for all the above said experiments on a single platform as shown in Fig. 5. The platform includes

a. Buttons to perform all the experiments.
b. Controls to change the system parameters.
c. View the results of the experiments in the graphical form.
d. Compare system response such time and frequency domain .
e. A menu bar on activation of which brief description along with the transfer function of the experiments performed can be viewed.
f. A menu bar to simulate directly the SIMULINK circuits diagrams and see the results in separate window.
g. SIMULINK diagram of the current experiment.
h. An EXIT button to come out of the GUI page of project.
i. A refresh button to clear all the graphs and diagram displayed earlier.
j. A button to see the SIMULINK diagram of each experiments.
k. Menu bar to see different values in the graph, to zoom in/out and other controls.
l. A course ware for each experiment is prepared and successfully integrated into the control engineering laboratory. Vlab is very useful for performing experiments and understanding the basic concepts of feedback systems in the control system laboratory. It is a fundamental system which is useful to any course of instruction including basic subjects in electronics and mechanical at undergraduate level.

4.1. The educational use of the model

The mathematical model of DC Motor is very useful for carrying out transient and steady state analysis and understanding the basic concepts of control systems with and without the controller. It is a fundamental system useful to any course of instruction including basic subjects in Engineering at undergraduate courses. The MATLAB/SIMULINK model and GUI representation of DC motor using controller will definitely work as a teaching tool and support the classroom teaching by enabling the faculty, with   the computer-generated graphics, to illustrate transient and steady-state performance and stability analysis of DC motor under various parameter controls. The user can change the parameters of the system as per his/her choice or required condition. Thus this computational tool as a part of laboratory experiments will enhance laboratory experience by providing students with the opportunity to compare the results of laboratory experiments with those obtained by computer simulation. Such an opportunity helps students of all courses realise the limitations of hardware.

5. Conclusion

The MATLAB/SIMULINK models and GUI representation of closed loop, open loop, PID Control, etc. of Feedback Control System 33-001 will definitely work as a teaching tool and support the classroom teaching by enabling the faculty, through the computer-generated graphics, to illustrate transient and steady-state performance and stability analysis of control system under various parameter controls. The user can change the parameters of the systems as per his choice or required condition. Such an opportunity helps students of all courses realise the limitations of hardware. A Virtual laboratory for Automatic Control (AC) allows students an easy access to different applications, simulations related to the theory they studied. These interactive demos present in a tutorial manner the influence of the different parameters of the mathematical model to the system behavior. These simulations provide a more intuitive and more practical approach for the abstract theory of Automatic Control. The advantage of the approach presented here is the use of the available simulation tools. The user can focus on the learning and understanding of problems and concepts, as he/she doesn't have to master the MATLAB programming environment. The scope of this Vlab is extending to the remote control laboratory using MATLAB /SIMULINK applications to control system engineering. The MATLAB/SIMULINK models and GUI representation of DC Motor using controller will definitely work as a teaching tool and support the classroom teaching by enabling the faculty, with the computer-generated graphics, to illustrate transient and steady-state performance and stability analysis of DC motor under various parameter controls. The user can change the parameters of the system as per his/her choice or required condition. Thus, this computational tool, as a part of laboratory experiments will enhance practical experience by providing students with the opportunity to compare the results of laboratory experiments with those obtained by computer simulation. Such an opportunity helps students of all courses realize the limitations of hardware.

Author details

Prashant M. Menghal
Radar & Control System Dept, Faculty of Electronics, Military College of Electronics and Mechanical Engineering, Secunderabad, Andhra Pradesh, India

A Jaya Laxmi
Electrical & Electronics Engg. Dept. Jawaharlal Nehru Technological University, Hyderabad College of Engineering, Kukatpally, Hyderabad, Andhra Pradesh, India

Acknowledgement

Eric Hoffer, in **"Reflections On the Human Condition"** quotes "the hardest arithmetic to master is to enable us to count our blessings." In pursuit of accomplishing a goal, there is incessant need for constant stimulation and inspiration to persevere and attain. There are also times when obscurity threatens to conceal the desire to succeed with the drape of uncertainnities and hindrances and it is in those hours of trepidation that the Guru rekindles the spark within us with flames of guidance and mentoring. This is a humble effort on the part of me to undertake the enormous responsibility of expressing in words the emotions and gratitude felt towards all our gurus, without whose ardor and continuous assurances, this voyage of intense erudition would not have been possible. I would like to thank Head of Department (Radar & Control System), V. K. Pokhriyal, Dean Faculty of Electronics V S

Randhwa,Head of Institution SM Mehta SM,VSM**,who unlocked for me the opportunities and the resources to explore potentials beyond my envision through his inexorable confidence in my capabilities. I am obliged to the unrelenting espousal and conviction of my Ph.D. supervisor, Dr A. Jaya Laxmi, who was a catalyst in leading towards the completion of this chapter.

Once again we would like to express our heartfelt gratitude to each and every person who was pivotal in the successful architecting and completion of this chapter and without whom this chapter would not have been a reality.

6. References

Saffet Ayasun, Chika O. Nwankpa (2005). Induction motor tests using MATLAB/SIMULINK and their integration into undergraduate electric machinery courses, IEEE Transactions on education, vol. 48 No.1 Feb 2005, pp 37-46.

O. I. Okoro C.U. Ogbuka M.U.Agu (2008). Simulation of D.C. machines transient behaviours: Teaching and Research, Pacific journal of science and technology vol.9 No.-1 May-June 2008 pp.142-148.

Erin Harley, G.R.Loftus (2000). MATLAB and graphical user interfaces: Tools for experimental management, Behavior Research Methods, Instruments and Computers 2000 vol 32(2) pp 290-296.

M. Javed, H. Aftab, M.Qasim, M.Sittar (2008). RLC Circuit response and Analysis (using State Space Method, International journal of computer science and network security vol.8. No.4 April 2008 pp-48-54.

Richard C. Dorf, Robert H.Bishop (2009). Modern Control Systems, Second Edition, Pearson Education India.

Stephen J. Chapman (2007). MATLAB Programming for Engineers, Second Edition Thomson Publication India.

Hanselman and Littlefield (2007). Mastering MATLAB 7, Second Edition Thomson Publication India.

www.mathworks.com

Chapter 5

Matlab/SystemC for the New Co-Simulation Environment by JPEG Algorithm

Walid Hassairi, Moncef Bousselmi, Mohamed Abid and Carlos Valderrama

Additional information is available at the end of the chapter

1. Introduction

The functionality of embedded systems as well as the time-to-market pressure has been continuously increasing in the past decades. Simulation of an entire system including both hardware and software from early design stages is one of the effective approaches to improve the design productivity. A large number of research efforts on hardware/software (HW/SW) co-simulation have been made so far. Real-time operating systems have become one of the important components in the embedded systems. However, in order to validate function of the entire system, this system has to be simulated together with application software and hardware. Indeed, traditional methods of verification have proven to be insufficient for complex digital systems. Register transfer level test-benches have become too complex to manage and too slow to execute. New methods and verification techniques began to emerge over the past few years. High-level test-benches, assertion-based verification, formal methods, hardware verification languages are just a few examples of the intense research activities driving the verification domain.

Our work articulates on three contributions which are the proposal for solutions to the implementation of the different parts of the architecture using SystemC and Matlab/Simulink simulators. Secondly, the definition of a co-simulation environment based on the automatic generation of the interfaces required to the integration of these simulators. Finally, the proposal of a new verification framework based on SystemC Verification standard that uses MATLAB/Simulink to accelerate the test-bench development. This chapter attempts to give a guide for the implementation of real-time control systems, using the **S-function** of matlab/Simulink, as a practical tool for students in control engineering. The MATLAB/Simulink to SystemC interface and the advanced version of transactors are combined in a scalable multi-abstraction level verification platform. The proposed refined co-simulation platform enables co-simulation with hardware models written in SystemC.

On that platform, application software and hardware modules are directly executed on a host computer, which leads to a high co-simulation speed. The MATLAB/SystemC interface is mainly used for the verification of the lower abstraction levels with a high level model of their execution environment.

The integration of SystemC within MATLAB/Simulink and the resulting verification flow is tested on the JPEG compression algorithm. The required synchronization of both simulation environments, including data type conversion, is solved by using the proposed co-simulation flow. The application is divided into two JPEG encoder parts: the DCT (Direct Cosine Transform), the HW part implemented in SystemC, and the QEE (Quantization and Entropy Encoding), the SW part implemented in Matlab. With this research premise, this study introduces a new HW implementation of the DCT algorithm in SystemC. For the communication and synchronization between these two parts we use the S-Function and the MATLAB/Simulink engine. In addition, we compare the co-simulation results to a pure software simulation.

In this chapter, the related work is discussed in Section 2 and the proposed co-simulation methodology is presented in Section 3. Then, in Section 4, we propose the implementation of the JPEG image compression as a case study. We present the steps in matlab for the implementation of the JPEG algorithm. In Section 5, we summarize the proposed approach and co-simulation results. Finally, we sum up the proposal including suggestions and recommendations to future works.

2. Related work

First of all, we present the chosen two simulators: Matlab and SystemC.

The MATLAB environment is a high-level technical computing language for algorithm development, data visualization, data analysis and numerical computing. One of the key features of this tool is the integration ability with other languages and third-party applications. MATLAB also included the Simulink graphical environment used for multi-domain simulation and model-based design. Signal processing designers take advantage of Simulink as it offers a good platform for preliminary algorithmic exploration and optimization. A hardware designer doesn't like C/C++ environment because of:

- Concurrency support is missing (HW is inherently parallel)
- No notion of time (clock, delays)
- Communication model (function calls & parameters) is very different from actual HW model (pins & signals)
- Weak/complex reactivity to events
- Some data types missing (logic values, bit vectors, fixed point).

The resulting modelling language is System C.

Connecting Simulink and SystemC together have already been tried in the literature. Authors in [6] propose a solution to integrate SystemC models in Simulink. A wrapper is created using S-Functions to combine SystemC modules with Simulink.

This wrapper initializes the SystemC kernel and converts Simulink data type to SystemC signals and vice versa. Simulation control is entirely handled by Simulink. Some extensions of the SystemC kernel are required for initialization and simulation tasks. In [7], SystemC calls MATLAB using the engine library. MATLAB provides interfaces to external routines written in other programming languages. Using the C engine library, it is possible to share data between SystemC models and MATLAB. This simple working demo shows how to use the library to send, to retrieve data from the MATLAB workspace and to plot some results. The main difference with [6] is with the simulation control: SystemC is now the master of the simulation and MATLAB operates as a slave process. Also, Simulink is not supported in this example.

In a similar way, MathWorks provides a commercial solution to close the gap between the algorithmic domain and the hardware design. The link for ModelSim [8] is a co-simulation interface that integrates MATLAB and Simulink into the hardware design flow. It provides a link between MATLAB/Simulink and Model Technology's HDL simulator, ModelSim. This interface makes the verification and co-simulation of RTL-level models possible from within MATLAB and Simulink. As opposed to the two previous techniques, there is no support for system level languages like SystemC.

These approaches [6, 7, 8] all try to reduce the barrier that exist between higher level modeling and existing hardware design flow. While [8] is a fully functional commercial tool for RTL verification, [6, 7] suffer from their embryonic stage (i.e. incomplete solutions for hardware design and verification).

The authors in [9] look at the problem of cosimulating continuous systems with discrete systems. The increasing complexity of continuous/discrete systems makes their simulation and validation a demanding task for the design of heterogeneous systems. They propose a co-simulation interface based on Simulink and SystemC. The main objective of the proposed solution is to provide a framework to evaluate continuous/discrete systems modeling and simulation.

In work [10], the authors have created a tool called: co-simulation COLIF that defines a subset of Matlab / simulink and combines a set of descriptive rules allows for the specification and functional validation efficient algorithms for the application. To reduce the "gap" between the functional model and architecture model in SystemC, they proposed a new intermediate transactional model in Simulink executable that combines both the algorithm and architecture in a single model representation. To validate their work, they applied to decoder MPEG Layer III. They found that the simulation model in Simulink is 50 times faster than the macro-level architecture. The difference is mainly due to the complexity of the description and details of the communication are present at the macro architecture.

In our former work [11], we adopted the methodology of communication and synchronization. To exchange data between a Simulink model and SystemC module, the co-simulation interface must integrate a bridge between the two simulators. This bridge is built with two Simulink S-Functions. An S-Function is a computer language description of a Simulink block. It uses syntax of call allowing us to interact with Simulink solvers. For our bridge, we create two C++ S-Functions.

The representation of simulation time differs significantly from SystemC and Matlab. SystemC is cycle-based simulator and simulation occurs at multiples of the SystemC resolution limit. The default time resolution is one picosecond. This limit can be changed with the function sc_set_time_resolution. However, Simulink maintains simulation time as a double precision value scaled to seconds. Thus, our co-simulation interface uses a one-to-one correspondence between simulation time in Simulink and SystemC.

3. Methodologies

The implementation of applications on embedded systems is a very time expensive task using the standard development tools. The proposed heterogeneous model is also executable to simulate the co-design implementation. Such simulation of the heterogeneous model is realized using SystemC. In fact, a description of a hardware module is transformed into a structural description with SystemC components (RT-level). Then, the interface between hardware and software parts is implemented using special SystemC constructs. This interface can be compared with the interface of the implementation in the real system. SystemC provides several levels of abstraction to describe hardware. For the simulation of hardware modules in the shown design flow given by figure Fig1, the cycle accurate level (CA) of SystemC is used. The interface to the software kernel is untimed functional level (UTF). A wrapper was designed to connect the modules to the software kernel. This wrapper is based on two shell-blocks which connect the CA-model to the software kernel by realizing an interface between the CA- and the UTF-model (Untimed Functional) of SystemC.

Simulink is a commonly used tool for designing DSP applications. It supports with a lot of libraries distinguished suppositions to develop single machine vision operators, e.g. the possibility to generate intelligent test environments for image. To use the tool for generation of hardware operators, an interface between SystemC and Simulink was developed. Thus, the visualized tool in more common design flows is integrated using Simulink S-Functions. Those Functions provide a powerful mechanism for extending Simulink with custom blocks and can be implemented as C++ Code. Within the S-Function the output is calculated from input and from states at each time step using a cycle by cycle SystemC-simulation as a fixed-step discrete time solver. The initialization of the SystemC kernel should be separated from simulation.

To meet these requirements a wrapper has been inserted between the S-Function and the SystemC model (Fig. 1). The wrapper functionalities are:

- connecting Simulink ports to a SystemC-TM-Block,
- converting Simulink data types to SystemC-TM signals and vice versa,
- initializing of the SystemC-Kernel,
- converting events; function call from Simulink to sc_cycle(),
- providing a DLL interface to the Simulink S-Function.

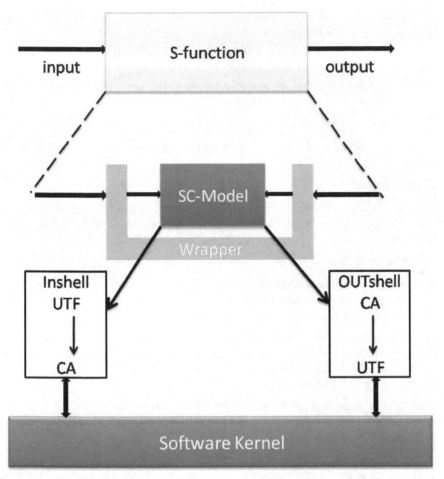

Figure 1. Integrated SystemC in Simulink S-Function.

So, our methodology tries to push the idea a step further than just a co-simulation interface. It is a complete verification solution. It uses MATLAB external interfaces, similar to the example described in [6], to exchange data between SystemC and Simulink. Once this link is established, it opens up a wide range of additional capability to SystemC, like stimulus generation and data visualization [10]. We also based our methodology on a portion of the methodology in the work [11]. In this work, they are based on the transformation of a task in SystemC. The first advantage of our technique is to use the right tool for the right task. Complex stimulus generation and signal processing visualization are carried out with MATLAB and Simulink while hardware verification is performed with SystemC verification standard. The second advantage is to have a SystemC centric approach allowing greater flexibility and configurability.

With this approach the overall system simulation can be controlled by Simulink through settings of duration time and step size.

There are three new call-backs provided via virtual methods for classes derived from sc_module, sc_port, sc_export, and sc_prim_channel. These call-backs will be invoked by the SystemC simulation kernel when certain phases of the simulation process occur. The new methods are:

void before_end_of_elaboration();

This method is called just before the end of elaboration processing is to be done by the simulator.

void start_of_simulation();

This method is called just before the start of simulation. It is intended to allow users to set up variable traces and other verification functions that should be done at the start of simulation.

void end_of_simulation();

If a call to sc_stop() had been made this method will be called as part of the clean up process as the simulation ends. It is intended to allow users to perform final outputs, close files, storage, etc.

It is also possible to test whether the callbacks to the start_of_simulation methods or end_of_simulation methods have occurred. The Boolean functions sc_start_of_simulation_invoked() and sc_end_of_simulation_invoked() will return true if their respective callbacks have occurred.

The tasks at the transactional level under Simulink are included in a software knot represented by a sub-system having the prefix ' SW_ ' in its name. These tasks are modelled under Simulink in several ways.

They can be trained by a merger of several blocks in one under system having the name preceded by the prefix ' TASK _ ' either they are trained by individual blocks. These last ones, in turn can be predefined blocks of the library either Functions modelled in language C.

In what follows, the modelling of the tasks in SystemC will be explained before describing the various manners admitted to transform the tasks of transactional Simulink into tasks described in SystemC.

For the modelling and description of the tasks in SystemC, we used the notion of "SC_MODULE". A module can be hierarchical containing the other modules, or elementary containing an active or passive behaviour using the elementary modules "SC_CTHREAD". On the other hand, the communication is determined through an interface of communication. This last one is described through a set of ports which can be inputs, output or inputs / output ones. SystemC also supplies a specific port for the modelling of a physical clock. The figure 2 shows the header file of a task described in SystemC. The interface of this module is formed by an input   port and an output   port of   type 'long int'. The task has a service port 'SAP', which allows synchronization of tasks in the co-simulation.

```
SC_MODULE (SF_SYNCRO)
{
va_in_mac_pipe<long int> DATA_IN1;
va_in_mac_pipe<long int> DATA_OUT1;

va_synchro  TSAP2;
void SF_SYNCRO_beh();
SC_CTOR(SF_SYNCRO)
{
SC_CTHREAD( SF_SYNCRO_beh,TSAP2.pos())
};
};
```

Figure 2. Example of a file header. "h" has a corresponding TASK SystemC.

However, the figure 3 shows the main file. "cpp'. The main calculation is done to the body of this task. The communication of this module with the system is through the interfaces represented by the ports of entry and exit 'DATA_IN1'and 'DATA_OUT1' by means of APIs defined in the library.

```
#include <stdio.h>
#include <stdlib.h>
#include"SF_SYNCRO.H"
void SF_SYNCRO::SF_SYNCRO_BEH()
{
        long int entreel;
        long int sortiel;
            for(;;)
            {
                entreel= DATA_IN1.Get();
                //calcul
                DATA_OUT1.Put(sortiel);
            };
}
```

Figure 3. Example of a file header. "cpp" has a corresponding task SystemC.

3.1. Transformation the S-functions of Simulink in task SystemC

SystemC is used by the synthesis tools and co-simulation in the stream of conception flow of the proposed heterogeneous Systems. The conception process always begins with the specification of the application in the Simulink environment using S-Functions blocks. The S-Functions are developed in language C according to precise rules and through methods decided by the Simulink simulator. An S-Function is formed by four essential methods. In our work, a block S-Function will be converted in a module in SystemC trained by a ' thread ' sensitive to a signal ' SAP '. The file S-function C will be processed in a direct manner in a header file and the implementation file in C++. To understand better the transformation of one S-Function into a task, we divided into four parts.

In the first part, we define global variables and we include the header files. 'H'. **S-function**: header files of the library of Simulink (Simstruct.h ...) macros, header files of the code, and global variables are defined. **SystemC**: The header files of the SystemC library, macros, code header files and global variables are defined.

In the second part, the initialization of variables and definition of input ports and output are included in this section. **S-function**: This part is formed by the method mdlInitializeSizes (SimStruct * S) where variables are initialized, and the number and size of ports of entry and exit are defined. **SystemC**: This part is divided on the header file and implementation file for SystemC. In the first type of port is defined. In the second module ports are declared and initialized. The type of the port depends on the type of communication used by the port (Shared memory, FIFO, signal synchronization).

In the third part, the APIs and the communication are the main calculation developed in this part along a loop that is repeated several times. **S-function**: Method mdloutput (SimStruct *S) is used in this part. The main calculation of the block is made. The data to be transmitted are affected ports by using the operator "=". This is a communication primitive. **SystemC**: The loop for (;;) in the implementation file contains the main calculation module. The calculation code in C is similar to that of the S-function.

The difference in this part occurs at the level of communication primitives. In S-function, a reading and writing data port is through the assignment operator "=". In SystemC there are two types of communication primitives:

- The Get () and Put () to communicate through a FIFO.
- The operator "=" to read and write to shared memory.

In the final part, there is the last part that runs at the end of the simulation. **S-function**: This part is formed by the method mdlterminate (SimStruct * S). **SystemC**: This part is after the end of the loop for (;;) of Part III and the end of the module.

3.2. Creating a task from a SystemC predefined block in the Simulink library

In the case of an elementary block a different type of S-function included in a software node (a subsystem with the prefix 'SW_'), the generation of the tasks SystemC is made from a bookshop of functions describing the behaviour of all the blocks Simulink used in the application.

Each function has the same name as the Simulink block and the corresponding module in our methodology. However, reading and writing data are specific through the APIs to each communication protocol. These APIs exist in the communication library. The type of communication protocol is identified in the 'Port' of each module in our methodology. Figure 4 shows the generation of a task in SystemC from an individual block in Simulink transaction, this block is transformed into a parameterized module under our methodology.

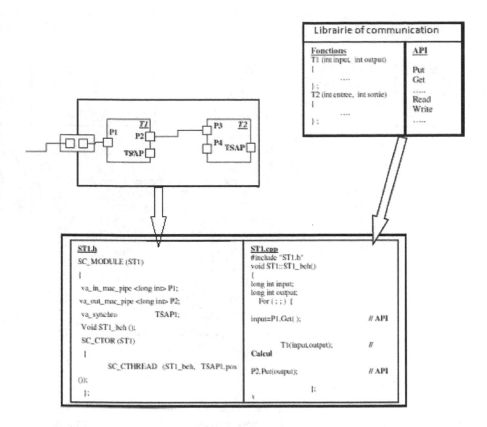

Figure 4. Generating a task from a basic block.

3.3. Fusion of several blocks Simulink in one task SystemC

In the case where several units are grouped in a subsystem representing a task whose name is prefixed with 'TASK_' the generation of the task SystemC is by assembling several library functions into a single task SystemC. Functions have the same names of the blocks. These functions exchange data via common variables. Communication with the system 'inter_Thread' is via the APIs generated following the protocol communication defined in our methodology.

Figure 5 illustrates the merger of several blocks in Simulink transactional to generate a task in SystemC. The functions of the library F0 (), F1 () have the same names as the blocks F0, F1. The generation of APIs is done by identifying the type of protocol in each port of the module in the virtual architecture of our methodology.

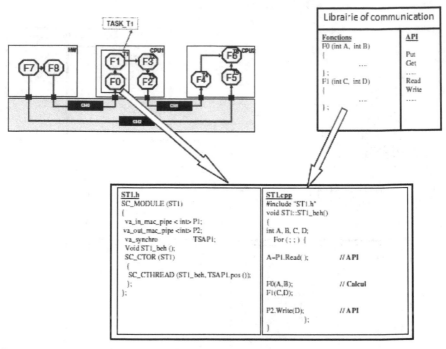

Figure 5. Generating a task from a set of blocks in Simulink.

4. JPEG compression algorithm

The baseline JPEG compression algorithm is the most basic form of sequential DCT based compression [12]. The process of JPEG-based encoding and decoding of images vary according to color depth (8, 24 or 32 bits). However, the basic ideology for all color depths is same. The bitmap image stores raw pixel-by-pixel color values. In addition, 54 bytes are stored at the start of file as header information that includes image width and height, image file size, image color depth, etc. These 54 bytes must be taken into account whenever working with the bitmap images. Following the 54-byte header, the bitmap image holds the color values of each pixel that varies for different color depths. For an 8-bit image, this is simply one byte (8-bits) per pixel and for a 32-bit image; they are 4 bytes per pixel. For 8-bit pixels, the pre-processing stage divides image data into 8x8 blocks that are shifted from unsigned integers with range $[0, 2^8 - 1]$ to signed integers with a range of $[-2^7, 2^7 - 1]$ and then individually compressed at the 8x8 block level. The compression process for each block goes through the following processes in addition to preprocessing.

- Discrete Cosine Transform (DCT)
- Quantization
- Zigzag
- Entropy Encoding (commonly Huffman)

Decompression is an inverse process that performs the individual inverse of all the above processes.

4.1. 8x8 FDCT and IDCT

At the input to the encoder, source image samples are grouped into 8x8 blocks, shifted from unsigned integers with range $[0, 2^7 - 1]$ to signed integers with range $[-2^7{-}1, 2^{7-1}{-}1]$, and input to the Forward DCT (FDCT). At the output from the decoder, the Inverse DCT (IDCT) outputs 8x8 sample blocks to form the reconstructed image. The following equations are the idealized mathematical definitions of the 8x8 FDCT and 8x8 IDCT:

$$F(u,v) = 1/4C(u)C(v)[\textstyle\sum_{x=0}^{7}\sum_{Y=0}^{7} f(x,y) * \cos((2x+1)u\pi)/16 * \cos((2y+1)v\pi/16] \quad (1)$$

$$x,y = 0,1...7$$

$$c(u,v) = \begin{cases} \dfrac{1}{2}\,where, u=v=0 \\[2mm] \dfrac{1}{\sqrt{2}}\,where, u=0, v\neq0 \\[2mm] \dfrac{1}{\sqrt{2}}\,where, u\neq0, v=0 \\[2mm] 1, atherwise \end{cases}$$

$$f(x,y) = 1/4[\textstyle\sum_{u=0}^{7}\sum_{v=0}^{7} C(u)C(v)F(u,v) * \cos((2x+1)u\pi)/16 * \cos((2y+1)v\pi)/16] \quad (2)$$

The DCT is related to the Discrete Fourier Transform (DFT). Some simple intuition for DCT-based compression can be obtained by viewing the FDCT as a harmonic analyzer and the IDCT as a harmonic synthesizer. Each 8x8 block of source image samples is effectively a 64-point discrete signal which is a function of the two spatial dimensions x and y. The

FDCT takes such a signal as its input and decomposes it into 64 orthogonal basis signals. Each contains one of the 64 unique two-dimensional (2D) "spatial frequencies" which comprise the input signal's "spectrum." The ouput of the FDCT is the set of 64 basis-signal amplitudes or "DCT coefficients" whose values are uniquely determined by the particular 64-point input signal.

The DCT coefficient values can thus be regarded as the relative amount of the 2D spatial frequencies contained in the 64-point input signal. The coefficient with zero frequency in both dimensions is called the "DC coefficient" and the remaining 63 coefficients are called the "AC coefficients." Because sample values typically vary slowly from point to point across an image, the FDCT processing step lays the foundation for achieving data compression by concentrating most of the signal in the lower spatial frequencies. For a typical 8x8 sample block from a typical source image, most of the spatial frequencies have zero or near-zero amplitude and need not be encoded.

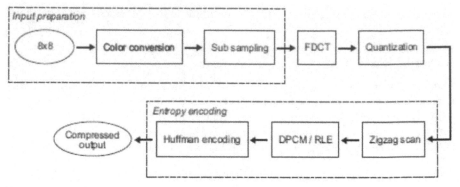

Figure 6. The JPEG decoder.

At the decoder the IDCT reverses this processing step. It takes the 64 DCT coefficients (which at that point have been quantized) and reconstructs a 64-point ouput image signal by summing the basis signals. Mathematically, the DCT is one-to-one mapping for 64-point vectors between the image and the frequency domains. If the FDCT and IDCT could be computed with perfect accuracy and if the DCT coefficients were not quantized as in the following description, the original 64-point signal could be exactly recovered. In principle, the DCT introduces no loss to the source image samples; it merely transforms them to a domain in which they can be more efficiently encoded. Some properties of practical FDCT and IDCT implementations raise the issue of what precisely should be required by the JPEG standard. A fundamental property is that the FDCT and IDCT equations contain transcendental functions.

4.2. Quantization

After output from the FDCT, each of the 64 DCT coefficients is uniformly quantized in conjunction with a 64-element Quantization Table, which must be specified by the application (or user) as an input to the encoder. Each element can be any integer value from 1 to 255, which specifies the step size of the quantizer for its corresponding DCT coefficient. The purpose of quantization is to achieve further compression by representing DCT coefficients with no greater precision than is necessary to achieve the desired image quality. Stated another way, the goal of this processing step is to discard information which is not visually significant. Quantization is a many-to-one mapping, and therefore is fundamentally lossy. It is the principal source of lossiness in DCT-based encoders.

Quantization is defined as division of each DCT coefficient by its corresponding quantizer step size, followed by rounding to the nearest integer:

$$F^Q(u,v) = IntegerRound\left(\frac{F(u,v)}{Q(u,v)}\right) \qquad (3)$$

This output value is normalized by the quantizer step size. Dequantization is the inverse function, simply means in this case that the normalization is removed by multiplying by the step size, which returns the result to a representation appropriate for input to the IDCT:

$$F^Q(u,v) = F^Q(u,v) * Q(u,v) \qquad (4)$$

When the aim is to compress the image as much as possible without visible artifacts, each step size ideally should be chosen as the perceptual threshold or "just noticeable difference" for the visual contribution of its corresponding cosine basis function. These thresholds are also functions of the source image characteristics, display characteristics and viewing distance. For applications in which these variables can be reasonably well defined, psycho visual experiments can be performed to determine the best thresholds.

4.3. DC Coding and Zig-Zag sequence

After quantization, the DC coefficient is treated separately from the 63 AC coefficients. The DC coefficient is a measure of the average value of the 64 image samples. Because there is usually strong correlation between the DC coefficients of adjacent 8x8 blocks, the quantized DC coefficient is encoded as the difference from the DC term of the previous block in the encoding order (defined in the following), as shown in Figure 7. This special treatment is worthwhile, as DC coefficients frequently contain a significant fraction of the total image energy.

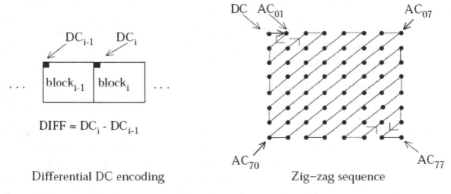

Differential DC encoding   Zig–zag sequence

Figure 7. Preparation of Quantized Coefficients for Entropy Coding

Finally, all of the quantized coefficients are ordered into the "zig-zag" sequence, also shown in Figure 7. This ordering helps to facilitate entropy coding by placing low-frequency coefficients (which are more likely to be nonzero) before high-frequency coefficients.

4.4. Entropy coding\Huffman

Huffman coding is a technique which will assign a variable length codeword to an input data item. Huffman coding assigns a smaller codeword to an input that occurs more frequently. It is very similar to Morse code, which assigned smaller pulse combinations to letters that occurred more frequently. Huffman coding is variable length coding, where characters are not coded to a fixed number of bits.

This is the last step in the encoding process. It organizes the data stream into a smaller number of output data packets by assigning unique codewords that later during decompression can be reconstructed without loss. For the JPEG process, each combination of run length and size category, from the run length coder, are assigned a Huffman codeword.

4.5. Decomposition and implementation of the JPEG algorithm

It is possible to increase speed and to reduce power consumption by running portions of the algorithm implemented in the custom hardware. To do this, parts of the algorithm remains the SW and the other part goes to HW area and must be well chosen. This is called hardware partitioning software (HW / SW partitioning). Many factors must be considered when the HW / SW partitioning is done. The problem is to use the right amount of material. Using too much material implies a rise in costs and probably increase the time of placing on the market.

The first step in a HW / SW partitioning is to identify the parts of the algorithm that consumes a lot of time if left in the software or by the implementation of the algorithm entirely in software or perform estimates on the number of cycles. The next step is to evaluate and decide which parts need to be moved to the HW area. It is important to take into account more things than just a party that consumes more cycles of the software. Perhaps it is better to leave this part of computation in software intensive and move some other parts in HW, the parts that are better suited for hardware implementation. This is of course possible only if time constraints may even now be suffering the most intense in the software calculation.

To make a good HW / SW partitioning a simulation tool is needed where much can be moved from HW field to SW field and vice versa. In addition, it should be possible to specify the execution time for different parts. This part of the design process is important and time spent here is well spent and often reduces the work in phases. If the processor architecture also must be chosen in the design process, the problem becomes even more complicated. With a more powerful processor, it is probably possible to do more in software and thus reduce the cost of designing and manufacturing the hardware. The question then is of course how this affects the total cost. The entire HW / SW partitioning problem is an optimization problem where constraints are typical on the surface of silicon, energy, monetary cost and execution time. So the time aspect of the market must be considered. In this section, we illustrate the approach we have followed for the implementation of JPEG through our methodology. As we have previously presented the most important part of the chain compression and DCT part, it has a lot of calculating. In this case we will implement this part with SystemC and the rest of the chain compression is implemented on MATLAB.

The following attempts to give a guide for the implementation of the JPEG compression algorithm in Figure 8.

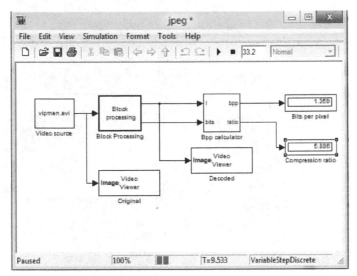

Figure 8. Implementing the JPEG algorithm.

Matlab let us to choose the video when we click on the video source. A window is opened where we specify the video place and its parameter as it is presented in figure 9.

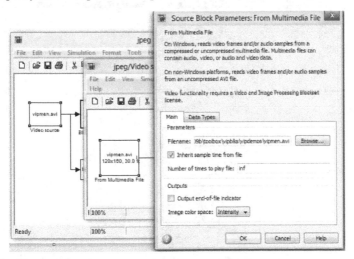

Figure 9. Choosing the video.

A click on the Block Profession opens window. In this window, there are the parameters of this block as a number of input, in our case , we put 1, number of output, in our case, we put 2 and two parameters are block size and overlap. A click the open Subsystem opens another window opens in which we find the block that we have just parameterize as indicated in figure 10.

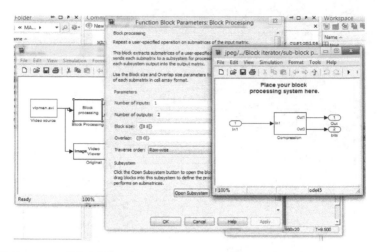

Figure 10. Parameter of Block Processing.

Figure 11 below, shows the different parts of the implementation of the JPEG encoder.

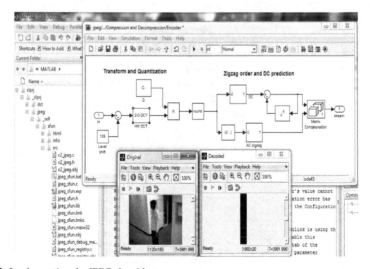

Figure 11. Implementing the JPEG algorithm.

As motion in the chair, the DCT is the most important and contains much of calculation. This part of the chain will be developed in SystemC, and represents the Hardware part. We explain it using an example process named 'DCT' (in JPEG encoder) in SystemC as shown in Figure 12.

```
struct fdct : sc_module {
sc_out<double> out64[8][8]; // the dc transformed 8x8 block
sc_in<double> fcosine[8][8]; // cosine table input
sc_in<FILE *> sc_input; // input file pointer port
sc_in<bool> clk; // clock signal
char input_data[8][8]; // the data read from the input file
void read_data( void ); // read the 8x8 block
void calculate_dct( void ); // perform dc transform
// define fdct as a constructor
SC_CTOR( fdct ) {
// read_data method sensitive to +ve & calculate_dct sensitive to
// -ve clock edge, entire read and dct will take one clock cycle
SC_METHOD( read_data ); // define read_data as a method
dont_initialize();
sensitive_pos << clk;
SC_METHOD( calculate_dct );
dont_initialize();
sensitive_neg << clk;
}
};
```

Figure 12. The DCT in SystemC.

It has two FIFO channels, one for receiving data and the other for sending data. From the SystemC code, we remove all SystemC dependent statements and exchange the FIFO read/write.

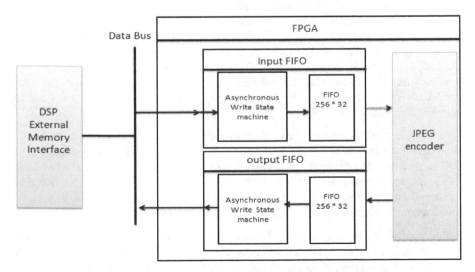

Figure 13. Two FIFO channels.

To proceed to an FPGA implementation, the resulting netlist from the previous stage has to be mapped to the FGPA's logic block structure and interconnect. The main outcome of this technology mapping, placing, and routing is a bit stream which can be programmed into a FPGA figure 13.

4.6. Results

The virtual architecture model is described using SystemC language and is generated according to the parameters specified in the initial Simulink model. SystemC allows modeling a system at different abstraction levels from functional to pin accurate register transfer level.

The virtual architecture is modeled using transaction level modeling (TLM) techniques that allow analyzing FPGA architecture in an earlier phase of design, software development and timing estimation. At the virtual architecture level, the Simulink functions of the application are transformed into systemC program code for each task. This step is very similar to the code generation performed by Real Time Workshop (RTW).

Contrary to the RTW which generates only single task code, the software at the virtual architecture level represents a multitasking systemC code description of the initial Simulink application model. The generation has to support also user defined systemC codes integrated in the Simulink model as S-functions. For the S-functions, the task code represents a function call of the user written systemC function. The semantics of the argument passing are identical to those of the definition in the configuration panel of the S-Function Builder tool in Simulink. The hardware is refined to a set of abstract SystemC modules (SC_MODULE) for each subsystem. The SC_MODULE of the processor includes the tasks modules that are mapped on the processor and the communication channels for the intra-subsystem communication between the tasks inside the same processor. The communication channels between the tasks mapped on the FPGA is implemented using standard SystemC channels. The tasks modules are implemented as SystemC modules (SC_MODULE). The development of the JPEG Decoder application in Simulink requires 7 S-Functions in order to integrate the systemC code of the main parts of the decoding algorithm. Which are: jpeg_sfun_h, dct_sfun_h, sfc_sf.h, sfc_mex.h, sfcdebug.h, jpeg_sfun.mexw32, dct_sfun.mexw32.

Once this link is established, it opens up a wide range of additional capability to SystemC, like stimulus generation and data visualization. The first advantage of our technique is to use the right tool for the right task. Complex stimulus generation and signal processing visualization are carried out with MATLAB and Simulink while hardware verification is performed with SystemC verification standard. The second advantage is to have a SystemC centric approach allowing greater flexibility and configurability.

In this part, we make a comparison between the previous methodology based on the communication and the synchronization between both simulators and the new approach which is based on the integration of systemC in matlab / Simulink in other applications.

CODIS (COntinuous DIscrete Simulation) is a tool which can automatically produces co-simulation instances for continuous/discrete systems simulation using SystemC and Simulink simulators. This is done by generating and providing co-simulation interfaces and the co-simulation bus. To evaluate the performances of simulation models generated in CODIS, they measured the overhead given by the simulation interfaces. The experiments have shown synchronization overhead of less than 30 % in simulation time [9]. In the [5] A Software-Defined Radio (SDR) is a combination of digital filters, analog components and processors, each requiring different design approaches with a different tool or language. Using a traditional design flow, where the verification effort represents 70% of the total design time, will yield in more time spent on test-bench development and simulation runs. The result is 192 days as the total development time for this project, compared to 131 days using the improved design flow. This represents a productivity gain of around 32% over a traditional design flow that has limited test-bench components reuse and software interoperability. But the implementation HW/SW reduced the number of clock cycle: 1334722 to 158044 times of execution. The reduction on the total execution time of the JPEG algorithm was 88. 15%.

5. Conclusion

In this chapter, we presented a new approach based on the integration systemC in matlab / simulink. The capital advantage of this approach is the possibility of modeling and verifying the overall system within the same design environment. The result is shorter design cycles for applications using heterogeneous architectures. The co-simulation interface we presented a method for reducing the time spent on validation and verification while improving overall test-bench quality. MATLAB/Simulink assists the SystemC verification environment in a unified approach. It has been shown that the methodology allows complex stimulus generation and exhaustive data analysis for the design under verification. As FPGA designs encompass larger and larger systems, the need to efficiently model the complex external environment during the architecture and verification phases becomes greater. The whole verification flow has been evaluated, using an example. It has been shown, that the usage of the extended verification flow saves a significant amount of time during the development process. The proposed platform is tested on the JPEG compression algorithm. The execution time of such algorithm is improved by 88.15% due to the hardware implementation of the Matlab mult16 Function using SystemC. As future works, we aim to test our platform with the whole video compression chain using MPEG4 modules and Software-Defined Radio (SDR). It includes hardware and software components that require rigorous verification all along the design flow.

Author details

Walid Hassairi, Moncef Bousselmi, Mohamed Abid and Carlos Valderrama
UMons University of Mons, Electronics & Microelectronics Dpt., Mons, Belgium
Laboratory CES, National School of Engineers of Sfax, Tunisia

6. References

[1] A. Avila, *"Hardware/Software Implementation of a Discrete Cosine Transform Algorithm Using SystemC"* Proceedings of the 2005 International Conference on Reconfigurable Computing and FPGAs (ReConFig 2005)

[2]   M.Abid, A. Changuel, A. Jerraya," *Exploration of Hardware/Software Design Space through a Codesign of Robot Arm Controller*" EURO-DAC '96 with EURO-VHDL '96 pp 17-24

[3]   L. Benini, D. Bertozzi, D. Bruni, N. Drago, F. Fummi, M. Poncino, "*SystemC Cosimulation and Emulation of Multiprocessor SoC designs,*" Computer Magazine, April 2003 pp: 53 – 59

[4]   The Open SystemC Initiative (OSCI) http://www.systemc.org

[5]   J.F. Boland "*Using MATLAB and Simulink in a SystemC Verification Environment*", Proc. of Design and Verification Conference & Exhibition, San Jose, Californie, Février 2005

[6]   F. Czerner and J. Zellmann. "*Modeling cycle-accurate hardware with matlab/ simulink using systemc*". 6th European SystemC Users Group Meeting (ESCUG), October 2002.

[7]   C. Warwick. Systemc calls matlab. MATLAB Central, March 2003.

[8]   The MathWorks. Link for ModelSim 2.0, 2006.

[9]   F. Bouchhima, M. Briere, G. Nicolescu, M. Abid, and E.M. Aboulhamid. *A SystemC/Simulink co-simulation framework for continuous/discrete-events simulation.* In Behavioral Modeling and Simulation Workshop, Proceedings of the 2006 IEEE International, pages 1–6, 2006

[10] Youssef ATAT "*Conception de haut niveau des MPSoCs à partir d'une spécification Simulink : Passerelle entre la conception au niveau Système et la génération d'architecture*"21 Mai 2007

[11] W.hassairi, M.Bousselmi, M.Abid,C.valderama "*Using Matlab And Simulink In SystemC Verification Environment By JPEG Algorithm*"ICECS 2009 ,page 912-915

[12] Draft Standard SystemC Language Reference Manual April 25 2005

[13] Independent JPEG Group, http://www.ijg.org

[14] Hiroyasu Mitsui "*A Student Experiment Method for Learning the Basics of Embedded Software Development Including HW/SW Co-design*" 22nd International Conference on Advanced Information Networking and Applications – Workshops 2008 pp.1367-1376

[15] James Rosenthal " *JPEG Image Compression using an FPGA*" A Thesis submitted in partial satisfaction of the requirements for the degree Master of Science in Electrical and Computer Engineering *December 2006*

Chapter 6

Matlab Simulink as Simulation Tool for Wind Generation Systems Based on Doubly Fed Induction Machines

Moulay Tahar Lamchich and Nora Lachguer

Additional information is available at the end of the chapter

1. Introduction

In the last years, Matlab-Simulink has become the most used software for modeling and simulation of dynamic systems. It provides a powerful graphical interface for building and verifying new mathematical models as well as new control strategies particularly for non linear systems. Then, using a dSPACE prototype, these new control strategies can be easily implemented and tested.

The study of wind turbine systems generators are an example of such dynamic systems, containing subsystems with different ranges of the time constants: wind, turbine, generator, power electronics, transformer and grid.

There are two principle-connections of wind energy conversion. The first one is connecting the wind-generator to grid at grid frequency. While connected to grid, grid supplies the reactive VAR required for the induction machines. Often, a DC-link is required to interface the wind-generator system with a certain control technique to the utility grid. The second is connecting the wind-generator system to isolated load in remote areas.

A wound rotor induction machine, used as a Doubly Fed Induction Generator (DFIG) wind turbines are nowadays becoming more widely used in wind power generation. The DFIG connected with back to back converter at the rotor terminals provide a very economic solution for variable speed application. Three-phase alternative supply is fed directly to the stator in order to reduce the cost instead of feeding through converter and inverter. For the control of these converters different techniques will be adopted.

The network side converter control has been achieved using Field Oriented Control (FOC). This method involves the transformation of the currents into a synchronously rotating dq reference frame that is aligned with one of the fluxes.

The Direct Torque Control (DTC) is used for the rotor side converter. The DTC is mostly used in the objective to improve the reduction of the undulations or the flux's distortion, and to have good dynamic performances. It's essentially based on a localization table which allows selecting the vector tension to apply to the inverter according to the position of the stator flux vector and of the direct control of the stator flux and the electromagnetic torque.

Also, we have chosen to develop the case where a conventional neural controller associated with a reference model, represented by a Fuzzy logic corrector, for the learning phase is used to control the generator speed.

The main structure of this control scheme, as used in the Matlab/Simulink environment, is shown by the following figure.

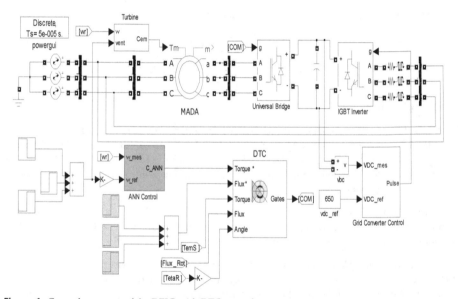

Figure 1. General structure of the DFIG with DTC control

An overview of Matlab Simulink, particularly the blocks concerned by the study of wind turbine generators based on DFIG will be presented.

In order to analyze the dynamic and/or steady state behaviour of the control of DFIG for wind generation, the basic components of a wind turbine structured in these libraries: Mechanical Components, Electrical Machinery, Power Converters, Common Models, Transformations, Measurements and Control, will be developed

SimPowerSystems DEMOS present good support and examples for the study of power systems and particularly the components of the wind generation energy systems. These tools can help for modeling and simulating basic electrical circuits and detailed electrical power systems. These tools let you model the generation, transmission, distribution, and consumption of electrical power, as well as its conversion into mechanical power. SimPower Systems is well suited to the development of complex, self-contained power systems, such as those in automobiles, aircraft, manufacturing plants, and power utility applications.

In this chapter, we will be focalized on the following sections to show how we can use these libraries to develop a model of electrical generation based wind systems in step by step.

The different sections on the analysis and the development of such a system will concern:

- Dynamic model of DFIG in terms of dq windings
- Wind turbine simulator
- Control of rotor side converter based DTC:
  - Switching table elaboration
  - Rotor flux and torque control
  - Reference value of the torque given by a PI controller which parameters are adapted by a fuzzy logic inference system

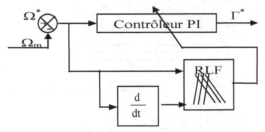

Figure 2. Speed control bused a PI adapted by a Fuzzy logic inference system

- Control of grid side converter based voltage oriented control
- Control of DFIG speed based on a fuzzy neural corrector

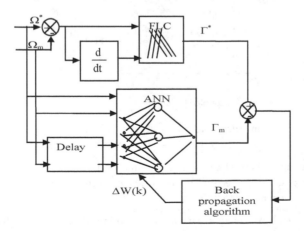

Figure 3. Control of DFIG speed based on a fuzzy neural corrector

2. An overview of wind turbine control blocksets in Matlab Simulink

In order to analyze the dynamic behaviour of a wind turbine generation systems, different blocksets exist in the Matlab Simulink environment. The power scheme of the wind generation system can be divided into many blocs:

*   The wind turbine or a simulator based on electrical machines for the comportment of this turbine. The principal object is to convert the aerodynamic variables (particularly wind power under variable wind speeds) to the mechanical power;
*   The electrical generator witch permits to convert this energy to electrical power;
*   The power converters used to connect this system and permits its control;
*   The connection to the grid with filter structure constitutes the last bloc.

Different control blocs of this structure complete the general scheme.

In this chapter, we have chosen to show the simulation of wind turbine associated with a doubly fed induction generator.

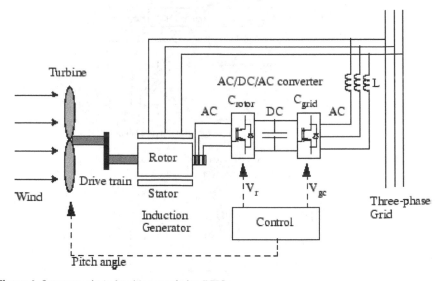

Figure 4. Structure of wind turbine coupled to DFIG

In this structure, two converters; the rotor-side converter and the grid-side converter, are Voltage-Sourced Converters that use forced-commutated power electronic devices (IGBTs).

A coupling inductor L is used to connect the inverter to the grid. The three-phase rotor winding is connected to the rectifier by slip rings and brushes and the three-phase stator winding is directly connected to the grid.

The power captured by the wind turbine is converted into electrical power by the induction generator and it is transmitted to the grid by the stator and the rotor windings.

The control system generates the pitch angle command and the voltage command signals for the rectifier and the inverter respectively in order to control the power of the wind turbine, the DC bus voltage and the reactive power or the voltage at the grid terminals.

2.1. Wind turbine model

This model is based on the steady-state power characteristics of the turbine. In fact, to simulate the behavior of the wind turbine, the torque that it exerts on the mechanical shaft must verify the relation:

$$T_{turbine} = T_{em_{mec}} = \frac{P_m}{\Omega_t} \tag{1}$$

where Pm is the output power of the turbine (mechanical power extracted from the wind) given by the following:

$$P_m = \frac{1}{2} \rho \, S \, C_p(\lambda \, , \, \beta) \, v^3_{wind} \tag{2}$$

where:

ϱ Air density (kg/m)
S   Turbine swept area (m)
Cp   Performance coefficient of the turbine

Vwind   Wind speed (m/s)

λ Tip speed ratio of the rotor blade tip speed to wind speed
β Blade pitch angle (deg)

Ω_t (rad/s) is the mechanical speed of the turbine

$$\Omega_t = \frac{\lambda \, v_{wind}}{R_t} \tag{3}$$

By introducing another parameter, coefficient of torque, $C_m = \frac{C_p}{\lambda}$, the mechanical shaft is defined as

$$T_{em_{mec}} = \frac{1}{2} . \rho . \pi . R_t^3 . C_m . v^2_{wind} \tag{4}$$

The Cp(λ) characteristics, for different values of the pitch angle β, are illustrated below.

We can note that the maximum value of the performance coefficient Cp (Cpmax = 0.48) is achieved for β = 0 degree and for λ = 8.1. This particular value of λ is defined as the nominal value (λ_nom).

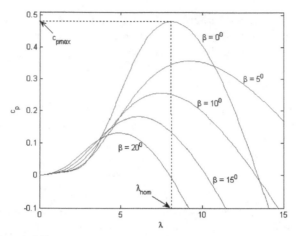

Figure 5. Cp(λ) characteristics

A generic equation can be used to model cp(λ,β). This equation, based on the modeling turbine characteristics, is represented as:

$$c_p(\lambda,\beta) = c_1(\frac{c_2}{\lambda_i} - c_3\beta - c_4)e^{\frac{-c_5}{\lambda_i}} + c_6\lambda \tag{5}$$

where:

$$\frac{1}{\lambda_i} = \frac{1}{\lambda + 0.08\,\beta} - \frac{0.035}{\beta^3 + 1} \tag{6}$$

The coefficients c1 to c6 are respectively: c1 = 0.5176, c2 = 116, c3 = 0.4, c4 = 5, c5 = 21 and c6 = 0.0068.

In our simulation case, we have adopted the following relation for the evaluation of coefficient C_m as a parameter of λ.

$$C_p = (0.44 - 0.0167.\beta).\sin\left[\frac{\pi.(\lambda - 3)}{(15 - 0.3.\beta)}\right] - 0.00184.(\lambda - 3.\beta) \tag{7}$$

The torque reference corresponding to a level of wind turbine speed and generator speed is evaluated as represented by the following scheme.

A second model of wind turbine behavior could be the use of a DC machine to generate the reference mechanical torque corresponding to the wind speed plan.

A separately excited DC machine is used, in this case, with the control of the field terminals and the armature circuit connected to converters. The inputs are respectively the rotor speed and electromagnetic torque of the generator.

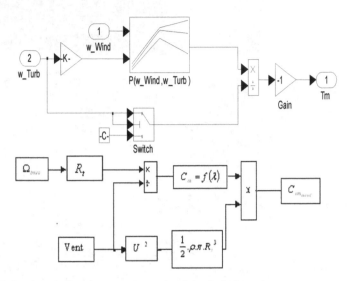

Figure 6. Estimation of reference torque (general and detailed schemes)

The mechanical power / speed characteristic, obtained at different wind speeds, is represented by the following figure.

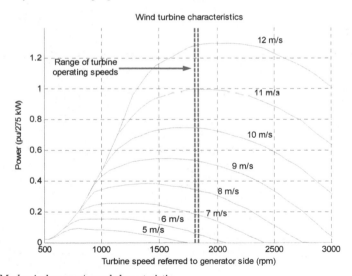

Figure 7. Mechanical power / speed characteristic

The reference field current is deduced from a lockup table with rotor speed as entry. The mechanical torque deduced form a wind and rotor speeds permits to impose the armature current.

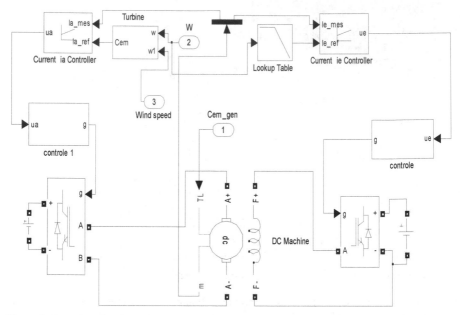

Figure 8. Second model of turbine based DC machine

2.2. Wind turbine control

For example, the wind turbine doubly fed induction generator is studied. The operating principle of the power flow is described as follows:

The mechanical power and the stator electric power output are defined by:

$$P_m = T_m \, \omega_r \quad ; \quad P_s = T_{em} \, \omega_s \tag{8}$$

For a loss less generator, the mechanical equation is:

$$J \frac{d\omega_r}{dt} = T_m - T_{em} \tag{9}$$

For a loss less generator and in steady-state at fixed speed, we have: $T_m = T_{em}$; $P_m = P_s + P_r$

It follows that: $P_r = -s\, P_s$, where $s = \dfrac{\omega_s - \omega_r}{\omega_s}$ is defined as the slip of the generator

Generally, Pr is only a fraction of Ps (the absolute value of slip is much lower than 1) and the sign of Pr is opposite to the slip sign. Pr is transmitted to or is taken out of DC bus capacitor. The control of grid converter permits to generate or absorb the power Pgc in order to keep the DC voltage constant. In steady-state for a loss less converters, Pgc is equal to Pr.

The converters have the capability of generating or absorbing reactive power and could be
used to control the reactive power or the voltage at the grid terminals.

The rotor-side converter is used to control the wind turbine output power and the voltage
(or reactive power) measured at the grid terminals.

The grid-side converter is used to regulate the voltage of the DC bus capacitor. It's also used
to generate or absorb reactive power.

2.2.1. Power control

The power is controlled in order to follow a pre-defined power-speed characteristic. An
example of such a characteristic showing also tracking characteristic represented by the
ABCD curve, is illustrated in the following figure.

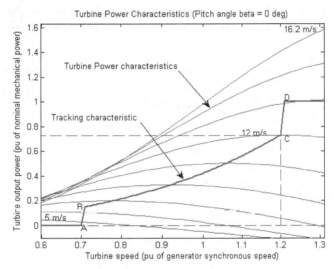

Figure 9. Power / speed characteristic and tracking characteristic

The actual speed of the turbine ωr is measured and the corresponding mechanical power of
the tracking characteristic is used as the reference power for the power control loop. We can
note that between points B and C, the tracking characteristic is the locus of the maximum
power of the turbine (maxima of the turbine power versus turbine speed curves).

For the power control loop, the actual electrical output power, measured at the grid
terminals of the wind turbine, is added to the total power losses (mechanical and electrical)
and is compared with the reference power obtained from the tracking characteristic. A
Proportional-Integral regulator is used and its output is the reference rotor current that must
be injected in the rotor by the rotor converter. This is the current component that produces
the electromagnetic torque Tem.

2.2.2. Reactive power control

The reactive power at grid terminals or the voltage is controlled by the reactive current flowing in the rotor converter. When the wind turbine is operated in var regulation mode the reactive power at grid terminals is kept constant by a var regulator.

The output of the voltage regulator or the var regulator is the reference d-axis current that must be injected in the rotor by the rotor converter. The same current regulator as for the power control is used to regulate the actual direct rotor current of positive-sequence current to its reference value.

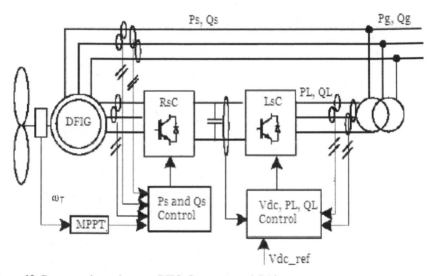

Figure 10. Powers exchange between DFIG, Converters and Grid

The rotor side converter ensures a decoupled active and reactive stator power control, Ps and Qs, according to the reference torque delivered by the Maximum Power Point Tracking control (MPPT). The grid side converter control the power flow exchange with the grid via the rotor, by maintaining the dc bus at a constant voltage level and by imposing the reactive power QL at zero.

2.2.3. Pitch angle control

The pitch angle is kept constant at zero degree until the speed reaches point D speed of the tracking characteristic.

Beyond point D, the pitch angle is proportional to the speed deviation from point D speed. The control system is illustrated in the following figure.

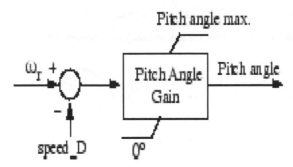

Figure 11. Pitch angle control

3. Doubly fed induction generator

3.1. Advantages of DFIG in wind turbine systems

The doubly-fed induction generator phasor model is the same as the wound rotor asynchronous machine (see the Machines library) with the following two points of difference:

- Only the positive-sequence is taken into account, the negative-sequence has been eliminated.
- A trip input has been added. When this input is high, the induction generator is disconnected from the grid and from the rotor converter.

The DFIG, in the wind turbine system, presents the following attractive advantages:

- The active and reactive power can be controlled independently via the current of the rotor;
- The magnetization of the generator can be achieved via the rotor circuit and not necessarily via the grid.
- The DFIG is capable of producing reactive power that it is delivered through the grid-side converter. Usually, this converter operates under constant unity power factor and it is not involved in reactive power trading with the grid. Also, the DFIG can be regulated in order to produce or consume a certain amount of reactive power. This way, the voltage control is achieved in cases of weak distribution grids.
- The converter size is not determined according to the total power of the generator but according to the decided speed range of the machine and therefore the slip range. For example, if the speed range is controlled between ±30% of the nominal speed, the nominal power of the converter is equal to the 30% of the nominal power of the generator. The selected speed range is decided according to the economical optimization and the increased performance of the system.

In this part, the dynamic model of DFIG in the dq frame is succinctly presented.

3.2. Dynamic model of DFIG in terms of dq windings

The general model for wound rotor induction machine is resumed as follows.

- Stator and rotor voltage equations :

$$\underline{V}_s = R_s \, \underline{i}_s + \frac{d\underline{\varphi}_s}{dt} + j \, \omega_s \underline{\varphi}_s \qquad (10)$$

$$\underline{V}_r = R_r \, \underline{i}_r + \frac{d\underline{\varphi}_r}{dt} - j \, \omega \underline{\varphi}_r \qquad (11)$$

where Rs, Rr, φs and φr are the stator and rotor resistances and flux
ωs is the synchronously frequency and ω = ωs - ωr is the slip frequency.
- Stator and rotor flux equations :

$$\underline{\varphi}_s = L_s \, \underline{i}_s + L_m \, \underline{i}_r \qquad (12)$$

$$\underline{\varphi}_r = L_r \, \underline{i}_r + L_m \, \underline{i}_i \qquad (13)$$

where Ls = Lsλ + Lm and Lr = Lrλ + Lm
Lsλ and Lrλ are stator and rotor leakage inductances
Lm is the mutual inductance
- Power and torque equations :

The electromechanical torque and the electrical power will be:

$$T_e = \text{Im}\left[\varphi_s \, i_s^*\right] \qquad P_e = \text{Im}\left[\varphi_r \, i_r^*\right] \qquad (14)$$

Referring to the model developed in Matlab Simulink and defining the different parameters of the induction machines (DFIG in particularly), the DFIG equations can be resumed as follows:

$$v_{sd} = R_s \, i_{sd} + \frac{d\varphi_{sd}}{dt} - \omega_s \, \varphi_{sq} \quad v_{sq} = R_s \, i_{sq} + \frac{d\varphi_{sq}}{dt} + \omega_s \, \varphi_{sd} \qquad (15)$$

$$v_{rd} = R_r \, i_{rd} + \frac{d\varphi_{rd}}{dt} - \omega_r \, \varphi_{rq} \quad v_{rq} = R_r \, i_{rq} + \frac{d\varphi_{rq}}{dt} + \omega_r \, \varphi_{rd} \qquad (16)$$

$$\varphi_{sd} = (L_{is} + L_m) \, i_{sd} + L_m \, i_{rd} \quad \varphi_{sq} = (L_{is} + L_m) \, i_{sq} + L_m \, i_{rq} \qquad (17)$$

$$\varphi_{rd} = (L_{ir} + L_m) \, i_{rd} + L_m \, i_{sd} \quad \varphi_{rq} = (L_{ir} + L_m) \, i_{rq} + L_m \, i_{sq} \qquad (18)$$

In most practical work, the DFIG will have a non-unity turns ratio, n witch must be included in the flux linkage equations. Also, it will be useful to define the d- and q-axis magnetizing current.

Including magnetizing currents and turns ratio, the flux linkage equations must be rewritten and finally the electrical model of the machine is schematised as follow (case of d-axis seen from stator):

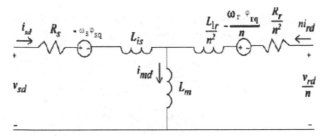

Figure 12. Electrical model in d-axis seen from stator

4. Control of rotor side converter based DTC

To control the torque and power factor of a doubly fed machine used in wind power generation system, a Direct Torque Control (DTC) method is adopted. As well known, a DTC technique is based on switching table which permits to choose an adequate inverter voltage vector to be applied to the converter according to flux and torque errors. These ones are deduced by a comparison between the references and estimated or measured values of flux and torque.

The DTC technique has the following steps:

- calculating the estimated torque and rotor flux of the DFIG;
- determining the reference torque from the wind and a rotor speed;
- evaluating the desired rotor flux ;
- selecting an inverter voltage vector from the torque error, the flux error and the rotor angle.

The control bloc of this strategy is shown by the following figure:

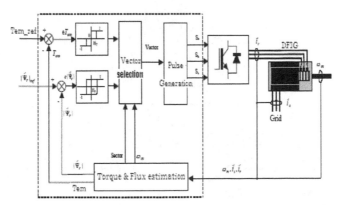

Figure 13. DTC principle of DFIG

4.1. Rotor flux and torque control

For the control of the electromagnetic torque, we can use a three level hysteresis comparator which permits to have the two senses of motor rotation. The output of this corrector is represented by a Boolean variable $Ccpl$ indicating directly if the amplitude of the torque must be increased, decreased or maintained constant $(ccpl = 1, -1, 0)$.

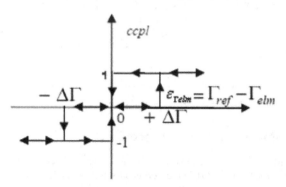

Figure 14. Three level hysteresis comparator

The control of the flux is carried out by selecting a suitable voltage vector with the inverter.

A two level hysteresis comparator could be used for the control of the flux. So, we can easily control and maintain the flux vector Φ_r in hysteresis bound as shown in the following Figure.

The output of this corrector is represented by a Boolean variable $cflx$ which indicates directly if the amplitude of flux must be increased $(cflx = 1)$ or decreased $(cflx = 0)$ so as to maintain: $\left| (\Phi_r)_{ref} - \Phi_r \right| \le \Delta\Phi_r$, with $(\Phi_r)_{ref}$ the flux reference value and $\Delta\Phi_r$ the width of the hysteresis corrector.

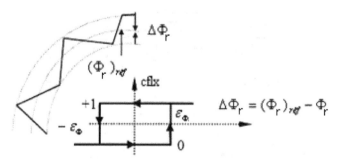

Figure 15. Flux hysteresis corrector

The reference value of the torque is given by a PI controller which is able to reach the reference speed. The PI parameters are adapted by a fuzzy logic inference system.

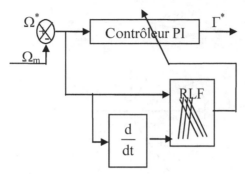

Figure 16. Torque reference estimation

The rotor flux amplitude is controlled in order to keep the unity power factor of the rotor current and rotor voltage. This is obtained if the rotor flux amplitude has to be the orthogonal projection of the stator vector. So, the reference value of the rotor flux is defined by:

$$\left|\varphi_r\right| = \frac{L_m}{L_s}\left|\varphi_s\right|\cos(\theta) \tag{19}$$

θ is the angle between the rotor and the stator flux.

Another issue for calculating the rotor flux reference, tested in our case, is defined as:

$$\varphi_r^* = \sqrt{\left(\frac{\sigma L_s L_r}{L_m}\frac{T_e^*}{\left|\hat{\psi}_s\right|}\right)^2 + \left(\frac{L_r}{L_m}\left|\hat{\psi}_s\right| + \frac{\sigma L_s L_r Q^*}{\omega_e L_m\left|\hat{\psi}_s\right|}\right)^2} \tag{20}$$

4.2. Switching table

As mentioned below, the Direct Torque Control of DFIG is directly established through the selection of the appropriate stator vector to be applied by the inverter. To do that, in first state, the estimated values of stator flux and torque are compared to the respective references, and the errors are used through hysteresis controller.

The phase plane is divided, when the DFIG is fed by two-level voltage inverter with eight sequences of the output voltage vector, into six sectors.

When the flux is in a sector (i), the control of flux and torque can be ensured by the appropriate vector tension, which depends on the flux position in the reference frame, the variation desired for the module of flux and torque and the direction of flux rotation:

	Φs increase, Γelm increase	Φs increase, Γelm decrease	Φs decrease, Γelm increase	Φs decrease, Γelm decrease
Vector tension selected	V$_{i+1}$	V$_{i-1}$	V$_{i+2}$	V$_{i-2}$

Table 1. Selection of vector tension

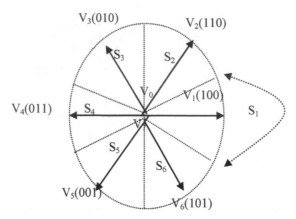

Figure 17. Stator vectors of tensions delivered by a two level voltage inverter

This selection is schematized by the following figure:

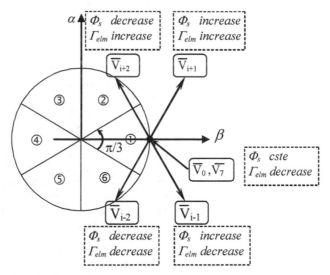

Figure 18. Selection of vector tension

The implemented switching table consents to give the right pulses to the rotor side converter having as inputs the sector in which the rotor flux lies and the values of the hysteretic controllers.

The null vectors (V0, V7) could be selected to maintain unchanged the rotor flux.

According to the table 2, the appropriate control voltage vector (imposed by the choice of the switching state) is generated:

Cflx	ccpl	S_1	S_2	S_3	S_4	S_5	S_6
1	1	V_2	V_3	V_4	V_5	V_6	V_1
	0	V_7	V_0	V_7	V_0	V_7	V_0
	-1	V_6	V_1	V_2	V_3	V_4	V_5
0	1	V_3	V_4	V_5	V_6	V_1	V_2
	0	V_0	V_7	V_0	V_7	V_0	V_7
	-1	V_5	V_6	V_1	V_2	V_3	V_4

Table 2. Voltage vector selected (for each sector S_i)

The following figure shows the selected voltage vector for each sector to maintain the stator
flux in the hysteresis bound.

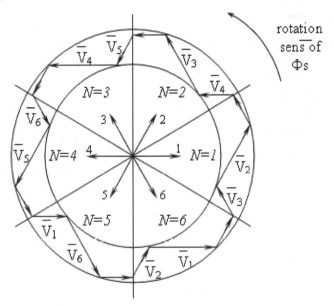

Figure 19. Selection of vector tension

5. Control of grid side converter based voltage oriented control

The applied vector control is based on a synchronously rotating, stator flux oriented d-q
reference frame, which means that the d-axis is aligned with the vector of the grid voltage
and the q component is zero.

For this technique of control of the inverter connected to the network, we proceed as
follows:

- We establish a regulation of the DC bus voltage to its reference by a PI corrector. The
  output of this corrector is the direct current reference.

- The current measured at the output of the inverter connecting the MADA to the network is transformed into its dq components.
- By imposing the quadrature component of reference voltage to zero, and then, performing the regulation of the direct and quadrature components of the output voltage of the network side converter, we obtain the two components voltage to be imposed.
- After decoupling and compensation procedures, followed by transformation into Cartesian coordinates, we define the control signals of the converter with a simple modulation based on level comparators.

A simplified diagram in Matlab Simulink environment of this control is then presented.

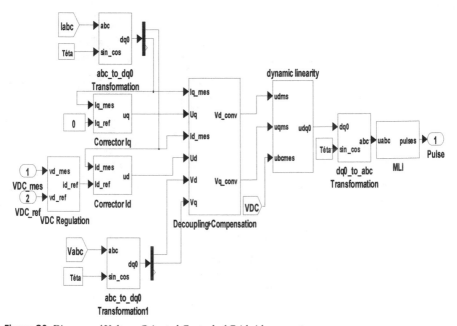

Figure 20. Diagram of Voltage Oriented Control of Grid side converter

6. Simulation results

Simulations were performed to show the behavior of the Doubly Fed Induction generator connected to the grid by a bi-directional converter.

The torque reference value is deduced from the regulation of the wind generator speed according to the wind speed and using a PI corrector. In this example, we have used three levels of wind speed. We have chosen to present the results corresponding to the rotation speed evolution, the electromagnetic torque, the flux evolution in the αβ subspace and the stator currents.

The obtained simulation results show that:

- trajectory of the stator flux, represented by its two components in the αβ phase plane, is in a circular reference (Figure 21)
- phase current obtained by this strategy is quasi-sinusoidal (Figure 22)
- speed track its reference with good performance (Figure 8)
- overshoot on torque is limited by saturation on the reference value (Figure 8)

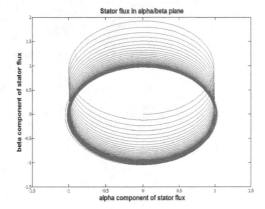

Figure 21. Stator flux in the αβ phase plane

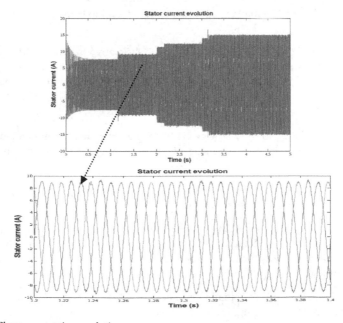

Figure 22. Phase current time evolution

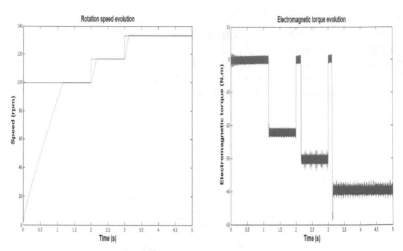

Figure 23. Time evolution of mechanical speed and electromagnetic torque

7. Conclusion

Through a concrete example of implementation of a prototype simulation of a system of wind power generation based on a doubly fed induction machine, we have highlighted some of the tools offered by Matlab / Simulink to design and to help for the complete study for such system.

The Direct Torque Control (DTC) is an important alternative method for the doubly fed induction machine drive based wind turbine, with its high performance and simplicity. The control of the DFIG connected to the grid with back to back converter, using two control techniques: DTC for the rotor side converter and Voltage Oriented Control for the grid converter present good performance and undulations reduction.

The effectiveness of the proposed scheme control is demonstrated by simulation using the blocks PSB of Matlab / Simulink and the results corresponding to the test of three levels of wind speed.

Finally, we can conclude that the control methods applied to DFIG present most interest and contribute to improvement of system response performances.

The first investigations, presented here, of the DFIG control prove its effectiveness and its high dynamics. It will be completed in a future work by considering others control techniques and particularly limiting torque undulations and resolving the problem of variable switching frequency.

Also, we conclude that Matlab / Simulink is a powerful tool in the comprehensive study of dynamical systems and particularly in what concerns us the power generation based on renewable and new energy.

Author details

Moulay Tahar Lamchich and Nora Lachguer
Cadi Ayyad University, Faculty of Sciences Semlalia, Department of Physic, Work group EERI,
Marrakech, Morocco

8. References

H. Akagi, Y. Kanazawa and A. Nabae Instantaneous reactive power compensators comprising switching devices without energy storage components, In: IEEE Transactions on Industry Applications. Vol. IA-20, No. 3, May/June 1984, p. 625-630.

Y. Komatsu and T. Kawabata, "Characteristics of Three Phase Active Power Filter using Extension pq Theory," Proceedings of the IEEE International Symposium on Industrial Electronics (ISIE), Guimaraes, Portugal, 1997, pp. 302-307.

A. Jami, S.H. Hosseini, Implementation of a novel control strategy for shunt active filter, ECTI, Trans. On Electrical Eng., Electronics and communications, Vol. 4, N° 1, February 2006, p. 40-46.

Dell'Aquila, A. Lecci, A current control for three-phase four-wire shunt active filters, Automatika 44, 3-4, 2003, 129-135.

Z. Y. Zhao, M. Tomizuka, S. Isaka, Fuzzy gain scheduling of PID controllers, IEEE Trans. On Systems, Man and Cybernetics, Vol. 23, Issue 5, Sep/Oct 1993, p. 1392-1398.

M. Chakphed, P. Suttichai, Active power filter for three-phase four-wire electric systems using neural networks, Electric Power Systems Research, Elsevier Science, 60, p. 179-192, 2002.

S. Seman, J. Niiranen, A. Arkkio, Ride-Through Analysis of Doubly Fed Induction Wind-Power Generator under Unsymmetrical Network Disturbance, IEEE Transaction on Power Systems, 2006.

Takahachi, I. & Noguchi, T. (1986). A new quick response and high efficiency control strategy of an induction motor. IEEE *Trans on Industry Application*, Vol.IA-22.N°5, pp 820-827, September/October 1986.

Baader, U. & Depenbroch, M. (1992). Direct Self Control (DSC) of inverter fed induction machine −A basis for speed control without speed measurement. IEEE. *Trans on Industry Application*. Vol.IA-288.N°3, pp 581-588, May/June 1992.

PUJOL, A.A. (2000). Improvement in direct torque control of induction motors. *Thesis of doctorate of the university polytechnic of Catalonia*, Spain, 2000.

Ozkop, E. & Okumus, H.I. (2008). Direct Torque Control of Induction Motor using Space Vector Modulation (SVM-DTC). MEPCON *12th International Middle-East, Power System Conference*, pp 368-372, March 2008.

Cirrinciane, M., Pucci, M. & Vitale, G. (2003). A Novel Direct Torque Control of Induction Motor Drive with a Three-Level Inverter. IEEE *Power Tech Conference Proceeding*, Vol.3, 7pp, Bologna, June 2003.

Xiying Ding, Qiang Liu, Xiaona Ma, Xiaona. He & Qing Hu (2007). The Fuzzy Direct Torque Control of Induction Motor based on Space Vector Modulation. *Third International Conference on, Natural Computation* ICNC 2007, Vol.4, pp 260-264, Aug.2007.

Guohan Lin & Zhiwei Xu (2009). Direct Torque Control of an Induction Motor using Neural Network. *1st International Conference on, Information Science and Engineering* (ICISE), pp 4827-4830, 28 December.2009.

Martins, A.C., Roboam, X., Meynard, T.A. & Carvaiho, A.C. (2002). Switching Frequency Imposition and Ripple Reduction in DTC Drives by using Multilevel Converter. IEEE *Trans, on Power Electronics*, Vol.17 N°2, March 2002.

Yang Xia & Oghanna, W. (1997). Study on Fuzzy control of induction machine with direct torque control approach. Industrial Electronics. ISIE 97, *Proceeding of the International Symposium*, Vol.2, pp 625-630, Jul.1997.

Yang, J., Ryan, M. & Power, J. (1994). Using Fuzzy Logic," Prentice Hall, 1994.

Kumar, R., Gupta, R.A., Bhangale, S.V. & Gothwal, H. (2008). Artificial Neural Network based Direct Torque Control of Induction Motor Drives. IETECH *Journal of Electrical Analysis*, Vol.2, N°3, pp 159-165, 2008.

Toufouti, R., Mezian, S. & Benalla, H. (2007). Direct Torque Control for Induction Motor using Intelligent Technique. *Journal of Theoretical and Applied Information Technology*, Vol.3, N°3, pp 35-44, 2007.

Dreyfus, G., Martinez, J., Samuelides, M., Gordon, M.B., Badran, F., Thiria, S. & Hérault, L. (2002). Réseaux de neurons : Méthodologie et applications. Editions Eyrolles, 2002.

Grabowski, P.Z., Kazmierkowski, M.P., Bose, B.K. & Blaabjerg, F. (2000). A simple Direct torque Neuro Fuzzy control of PWM Inverter fed Induction motor drive. IEEE *Trans. Electron.* 47 N° 4, pp 863-870, Aug 2000.

Viljamaa, P. (2000). Fuzzy gain scheduling and tuning of multivariable fuzzy control methods of fuzzy computing in control systems. *Thesis for the degree of doctor of technology, Temper University of technology*, Finland, 2000.

Barbara H. K. (2001). Stator and Rotor Flux Based Deadbeat Direct Torque Control of Induction Machines. IEEE *Industry Applications Society, Annual Meeting*, Chicago, September 30-October 4, 2001.

Casadei, D., Profumo, Serra, G. & Tani, A. (2002). FOC And DTC:Tox Viable Schemes For Induction Motors Torque Control. IEEE *trans.Power Electronics. On PE*, Vol.17, N°.5, Sept 2002.

Schibili, N., Nguyen, T. & Rufer, A. (1998). Three-Phase Multilevel Converter for High-Power Induction Motors. IEEE *trans. On Power Elect.* Vol. 13 N°.5, 1998.

Roboan, X. (1991). Variateur de vitesse pour machine asynchrone, Contrôle de la vitesse sans capteur mécanique. Thèse Doctorat De L'INPT, Toulouse, 1991.

Ould Abdeslam, D., Wira, P., Mercklé, J., Chapuis, Y.A. & Flieller, D. (2006). Stratégie neuromimétique d'identification et de commande d'un filtre actif parallèle. *Revue des Systèmes, Série Revue Internationale de Génie Electrique* (RS-RIGE), vol. 9, no. 1, pp 35-64, 2006.

Ould abdeslam, D. (2005). Techniques neuromimétiques pour la commande dans les systèmes électriques: application au filtrage actif parallèle. *Thèse de doctorat d'état en Electronique, Electrotechnique et Automatique*, Université de Batna, 2005.

Chapter 7

On Finite-Dimensional Transformations of Anisochronic Controllers Designed by Algebraic Means: A User Interface

Libor Pekař, Eva Kurečková and Roman Prokop

Additional information is available at the end of the chapter

1. Introduction

Linear time-invariant time delay systems (LTI TDS) have usually been assumed to contain delay elements in input-output relations only. All the system dynamics has been hence modeled by point accumulations in the form of a set of ordinary differential equations. The Laplace transform then results in a transfer function expressed by a serial combination of a delayless term and a delay element. However, this conception is somewhat restrictive in effort to fit the real plant dynamics because inner feedbacks are often of the time-distributed or delayed nature.

Anisochronic (or *hereditary*) TDS models, on the other hand, offer a more universal dynamics description applying both integrators and delay elements either in lumped or distributed form so that delays appear on the left side of a differential equation which is no longer *ordinary* (ODE) but rather *functional* (FDE) - this brings the concept of *internal* (or *state*) delays. In contrast to undelayed systems, the main difference in dynamics is that their spectra are infinite in general. In the further text, an abbreviation TDS means LTI TDS containing state delays with or without input-output delays.

Already in (Volterra, 1928) differential equations incorporating the past states when studying predator-pray models were formulated. The theory of these models has been then developed by many outstanding authors, see e.g. (Bellman & Cooke, 1963), (Krasovskii, 1963), (Kolmanovskii & Nosov, 1986), (Zítek, 1983), (Górecki et al., 1989), and especially (Hale & Verduyn Lunel, 1993) and (Nicolescu, 2001), to name a few. Aftereffect phenomenon is included in many processes, e.g. in chemical processes (Zítek & Hlava, 2001), heat exchange networks (Zítek, 1997), in models of mass flow in sugar factory (Findeisen et al., 1970), in metallurgic processes (Morávka & Michálek, 2008), etc. Plenty of references to examples of processes with internal delays, covering a wide range of human activities (e.g. biology, chemistry, economics, communication and information technologies, etc.) are introduced in (Kolmanovskii & Myshkis, 1999; Niculescu 2001; Richard, 2003). Capabilities and advantages of this class of models and controllers for modeling and process control were broadly discussed in (Manitius & Olbrot, 1979). TDS models can be used not only for description of those systems embodying internal delays but they are successfully capable to fit the dynamics of high-order systems and processes even without apparent delays (Zítek & Vítecek, 1999; Vyhlídal & Zítek, 2001; Simuenovic, 2011), which simplifies the processes description.

Using the Laplace transform applied to FDEs of TDS, input-output models in the single-input single-output (SISO) case can be expressed by the transfer function in the form of a fraction of so-called quasipolynomials (El'sgol'ts & Norkin, 1973) which can be viewed as polynomials in complex variable s over the ring of exponentials polynomials (or over a ring of linear combinations of real numbers and exponential functions in s). The concept of pseudopolynomials (Brethé & Loiseau, 1998), meromorphic functions (Zítek & Kucera, 2003) or a special ring (Gluesing-Lueerssen, 1997; Conte & Perdon, 2000), instead of quasipolynomials, can be used as alternatives; however, from the description point of view all these models are equivalent – their significance emerges while controller design.

Delay in the feedback control significantly deteriorates control performance, namely stability and periodicity, and makes controller design more complex – mainly if delays are not approximated or ignored. Therefore, design a suitable control law for such systems is a challenging task solved by various techniques and approaches; a plentiful enumeration of them can be found e.g. in (Richard, 2003). Due to the complexity of many direct methods, one can approximate an infinite-dimensional model by a finite-dimensional one to obtain a rational transfer function which can be handled by any standard control approach for undelayed plants. Similarly, in case of delayed (anisochronic) controllers obtained by controller design without delay approximation, one way how to implement these control laws on discrete-time-working machines such as PLC or PC is to find a delayless (i.e. finite-dimensional) approximating model followed by a discretization (e.g. by the z-transform with a holder).

This chapter aims two problems. First, output controller design for TDS models in a special ring is introduced. Second, resulting anisochronic controllers are approximated using various techniques for rational approximation of transfer function of TDS, which is the crucial part of the chapter. Hence, let us to make a brief insight into the two tasks.

Some authors, e.g. in (Brethé & Loiseau, 1998), pointed out that the use quasipolynomials does not permit to effectively handle some stabilization and control tasks, such as internal stability, controller properness etc. Hence, the quasipolynomial (meromorphic) description of TDS can be extended to a fractional one where a transfer function can be viewed as a field of fractions over a ring. The ring of stable and proper quasipolynomial (RQ) meromorphic functions ($\mathbf{R}_{MS}$) (Zítek & Kucera, 2003; Pekar & Prokop, 2010; Pekar & Prokop, 2011a, 2011b; Pekar et al., 2011) is a suitable candidate. Although the ring can be used for a description of even neutral systems (Hale & Verduyn Lunel, 1993) after some definition adjustment, only systems with so-called retarded structure are considered as the admissible class of systems in this paper. Contrary to some other algebraic approaches, the ring enables to handle systems with non-commensurate delays, i.e. it is not necessary that all system delays can be expressed as integer multiples of the smallest one. Control philosophy in this ring then utilizes the Bézout identity, to obtain stable and proper controllers, along with the Youla-Kučera parameterization for reference tracking and load disturbance rejection.

Final controllers, in most cases, evince internal delays. Hence, a special effort to apply the control law in discrete time when controllers' realization on computers must be made. To name just a few TDS discretization methods, state space approaches can be found e.g. in (Engelborghs & Roose, 2002) based on the so-called solution operator, or in (Breda et al., 2005) via the so-called infinitesimal generator, or using Taylor series expansion of the state vector in a neighborhood of the working point (Hofreiter, 2003). Input-output approaches include e.g. utilization of delta transform operators (Middleton & Goodwin, 1990; Zítek & Petrová, 2002). Nevertheless, all these methods consider a "very small" sampling period. An equivalent discrete-time model via the z-transform with a holder ought to be found when the sampling period is "higher". To utilize the z-transform, one has to find a finite-dimensional continuous model. This task is the primary aim of this chapter, i.e. to approximate an infinitesimal model of an anisochronic controller such that the final finite-dimensional model can be subjected to the z-transform.

In recent decades a huge number of papers and works have been focused on model reduction or rational approximation of TDS, see e.g. (Makilla & Partington, 1999a, 1999b; Battle & Miralles, 2000). A fair overview of some methods and approaches has been published in (Partington, 2004). An overwhelming majority of these methods, however, deals with input-output delays only ignoring internal or state delays on the left-hand side of differential equations, i.e. those transfer functions with exponential terms in the denominator. In the contrary, this chapter focuses transfer function rational approximations for TDS with internal (state) delays since there are no theoretical analytic results about approximations convergence and accuracy for such models up today (distinct from single input-output delay which has been deeply analysed by rigorous analytic means many times) and one can thus expect interesting numerical comparative results. The basic question is whether the higher order approximation yields the better (i.e. more accurate) finite dimensional approximating model. The appropriate methods are chosen so that they are easy to deal with and anyone can use them effortlessly. Namely, Padé approximation, shift operator approximations – Laguerre and Kautz shift - and Fourier analysis based method are introduced and benchmarked. The common principle of all approaches consists in substitution of exponential terms in the transfer function of TDS with a rational fraction in the Laplace complex variable s.

We made no attempts to deal with analytic mathematical proofs in this chapter. From the practical point of view, the efficiency and accuracy of the selected approaches is measured and compared via norms in the Hardy space, namely, H_∞ and H_2 norms, the definitions of which and some calculation tricks are presented here as well (Štecha & Havlena, 2000).

A Matlab-Simulink user-interface application has been programmed to make a benchmark of approximations easier which enables to enter an approximated (nominal) plant transfer function, to select methods to be compared and the choice of norms by which the accuracy of approximation is calculated. It is also possible to specify an order of the approximation for each selected approximation approach. As the outputs, a table of calculated norms and the gain Bode plot (that is relevant to the norms) are displayed. Some study cases on approximations of anisochronic controllers' derived by this algebraic method are introduced and compared in this contribution. For instance, control of an unstable system describing roller skater on a swaying bow (Zítek et al., 2008), or a laboratory heating system (Pekař et al., 2009), are taken as quasi-practical examples.

The chapter is organized as follows. In Section 2 a brief general input-output description of TDS is introduced together with the coprime factorization for the R_{MS} ring representation. Fundamentals of algebraic controller design in R_{MS} using a simple control feedback scheme are presented in Section 3. Section 4 introduces selected rational approximation methods for anisochronic controllers' transfer functions. Definitions and calculation issues regarding to norms for approximations' performance comparison are focused in Section 5. The application part of the chapter, i.e. Matlab-Simulink user interface, is described in Section 6. Finally, illustrative benchmark examples are presented in Section 7.

2. TDS models

Since the chapter applies finite-dimensional approximations of (controllers') transfer functions, there is no point to introduce TDS systems description in the state space, regardless of the fact that state-space models appear as a result of system modelling and it would be natural to mention them first. For further details about state-space TDS models the reader is referred to (Richard, 2003). The second aim of this section is to present the concept of fields of fractions as an extension of meromorphic description in the form of quasipolynomial fractions, namely the ring of quasipolynomial meromorphic functions, R_{MS}, which is suitable to meet some elementary. So-called retarded TDS are primarily focused; nevertheless, neutral ones have to be mentioned as well, since it is necessary to make the ring definition complete.

2.1. Input-output quasipolynomial model

Since the authors' interest lies in single-input single-output (SISO) TDS and their input-output models, they are concerned here. Namely, transfer functions in the form of quasipolynomial fractions giving rise to the meromorphic representation are taken as initial models to be approximated.

For both lumped (point-wise) and distributed input-output and internal delays in the system or model, the Laplace transform of a state space model (considering zero initial conditions) can be formulated as follows

$$G(s) = \frac{b(s)}{a(s)} \tag{1}$$

where $b(s)$, $a(s)$ are quasipolynomials of the general form

$$q(s) = s^n + \sum_{i=0}^{n} \sum_{j=1}^{h_i} m_{ij} s^i \exp(-s\vartheta_{ij}), \vartheta_{ij} \geq 0 \tag{2}$$

where n is the order of a quasipolynomial which usually agrees with the system degree (of a

state-space model), m_{ij} are real numbers and $\vartheta_{ij} \geq 0$ represent delays. If $\sum_{j=1}^{h_n} m_{nj} \exp(-\vartheta_{nj} s)$

does not equal a real constant, the system is called *neutral*; otherwise, the system is *retarded*.

2.2. TDS stability

A retarded system (1) is said to be *asymptotically* (exponentially) *stable* if all poles are located
in the open left half plane, $\mathbb{C}_0^-$, i.e. there is no s satisfying

$$a(s) = 0, \operatorname{Re} s \geq 0, b(s) \neq 0 \tag{3}$$

Condition $b(s) \neq 0$ in (3) is taken into accont if the system contains distributed delays since
there hence exist common roots of the transfer function numerator and denominator which
are *not* system poles.

A rather more complicated TDS stability conditions are given regarding to neutral systems,
since there may exist vertical strips of system poles tending to the imaginary axis of infinite
amplitude. Moreover, these strips can be sensitive to even infinitesimally small deviations in
delays, i.e. the position of system poles in the real axis is not continuous with respect to
delays. A neutral system (1) is exponentially stable if there is no s such that

$$a(s) = 0, \operatorname{Re} s \geq -\varepsilon, b(s) \neq 0 \tag{4}$$

for arbitrarily $\varepsilon > 0$.

A system is *strongly stable* if so-called associated difference equation (in state-space
formulation) remains asymptotically stable when subjected to small variations in delays
(Hale & Verduyn Lunel, 1993), i.e. a TDS remains *formally stable*, see details in (Byrnes et al.,
1984; Loiseau et al., 2002). Formal stability, roughly speaking, means that the rightmost
vertical strip of poles does not cross the imaginary axis. If this holds also under small delay
changes, the system is strongly stable. A necessary and sufficient strong stability (and thus
also formal stability) condition in the Laplace transform can be formulated as

$$\sum_{j=1}^{h_n} |m_{nj}| < 1 \tag{5}$$

according to e.g. (Zítek & Vyhlídal, 2008), where m_{nj} are real coefficients for the highest s-power in the denominator $a(s)$ of (1).

2.3. TDS model over RMS ring

Algebraic approaches for analysis and control of TDS can be performed either in the state space or in the realm of input-output models where fields, modules and rings as principal algebraic notions and tools are utilized. Usually, commensurate delays, i.e. those which can be expressed as integer multiples of the smallest one, are assumed; however, delays are naturally real-valued and thus this assumption is rather restrictive for real applications. Non-commensurate or rationally unapproximated delays results in a fraction of quasipolynomials as presented above. However, these transfer function representations are not suitable in order to satisfy some basic control requirements, e.g. controller feasibility, closed-loop (Hurwitz) and formal (strong) stability.

Rather more general approaches (Vidyasagar, 1985; Kučera, 1993) utilize a field of fractions where a transfer function is expressed as a ratio of two coprime elements of a suitable ring. A ring is a set closed for addition and multiplication, with a unit element for addition and multiplication and an inverse element for addition, i.e. division is not generally allowed. A powerful algebraic tool ensuring some basic control requirements, such as internal closed-loop stability and controller properness, is a ring of stable and proper RQ-meromorphic functions ($\mathbf{R}_{MS}$). Since the original definition of $\mathbf{R}_{MS}$ in (Zítek & Kučera, 2003) does not constitute a ring, some minor changes in the definition were made e.g. in (Pekař & Prokop, 2009). Namely, although the retarded structure of TDS is considered only, the minimal ring conditions require the use of neutral quasipolynomials at least in the numerator as well. In this chapter, the ring definition is reformulated once more to comprise models of neutral type, distributed delays and formal stability.

A term $T(s)$ from $\mathbf{R}_{MS}$ ring is represented by a proper ratio of two quasipolynomials $y(s) / x(s)$ where a denominator is a quasipolynomial of degree n and a numerator can be factorized as

$$y(s) = \tilde{y}(s)\exp(-\tau s) \qquad (6)$$

where $\tilde{y}(s)$ is a quasipolynomial of degree l and $\tau \geq 0$. Note that the degree of a quasipolynomial means its highest s-power. The element is analytic and bounded in $\mathbb{C}^{+}$, particularly, there is no pole s_0 such that $\operatorname{Re} s_0 \geq 0$ (or $\operatorname{Re} s_0 \geq -\varepsilon, \varepsilon > 0$, for neutral terms, more precisely, which can be taken as a generalization) - in other words, all possible roots of $x(s)$ in $\mathbb{C}^{+}$ are those of $y(s)$. Thus, it lies in the space $H_{\infty}(\mathbb{C}^{+})$ providing the finite norm defined as

$$\|T\|_{\infty} := \sup\{|T(s)| : \operatorname{Re} s \geq 0\} \qquad (7)$$

It is said that $T(s)$ is H_{∞} stable (Partington & Bonnet, 2004). That is, the system has finite $L_2(0,\infty)$ to $L_2(0,\infty)$ gain where $L_2(0,\infty)$ norm of an input or output signal $h(t)$ is defined as

$$\left\| h(t) \right\|_2 := \sqrt{\int_0^\infty \left| h(t) \right|^2 dt} \tag{8}$$

Notice, for instance, that $T(s)$ having no pole in the right-half complex plane but with a sequence of poles with real part converging to zero can be H_∞ unstable due to an unbounded gain at the imaginary axis.

Moreover, $T(s)$ is also formally stable which is guaranteed by condition (5) for $x(s)$. Unfortunately, strong stability can not be included in the ring definition since the product of two strongly stable terms can be strongly unstable. Although neutral TDS that are strongly stable can be H_∞ stable, see (Partington & Bonnet, 2004), yet they are not H_∞ (nor BIBO) stabilizable, (Loiseau et al., 2002). It can be shown that neglecting formal stability can bring the problem with ring axioms in controller design , i.e. H_∞ stability is not sufficient.

In addition, the ratio is proper, i.e. $l \leq n$. More precisely, there exists a real number $R > 0$ for which holds that

$$\sup_{\mathrm{Re}\,s > 0, |s| \geq R} \left| T(s) \right| < \infty \tag{9}$$

2.4. Coprime factorization in RMS

Let the plant be initially described by the transfer function

$$G(s) = \frac{b(s)}{a(s)} \tag{10}$$

where $a(s)$, $b(s)$ are quasipolynomials. Hence, using a coprime factorization, a plant model has the form

$$G(s) = \frac{B(s)}{A(s)} \tag{11}$$

where $A(s), B(s) \in \mathbf{R}_{MS}$ are coprime, i.e. there does not exist a non-trivial (non-unit) common factor of both elements. Details about divisibility can be analogously deduced from notes presented in (Pekař & Prokop, 2009). Note that a system of neutral type can induce problem since there can exist a coprime pair $A(s), B(s)$ which is not, however, Bézout coprime – which implies that the system can not be stabilized by any feedback controller admitting the Laplace transform (Loiseau et al., 2002); for instance when the system is not formally stable. More precisely, two coprime elements $A(s), B(s) \in \mathbf{R}_{MS}$ form a Bézout factorization if and only if

$$\inf_{\mathrm{Re}\,s \geq 0} \left(\left| A(s) \right|, \left| B(s) \right| \right) > 0 \tag{12}$$

3. Controller design in R$_{MS}$

The aim of this section is to outline controller design based on the algebraic approach in the R$_{MS}$ ring satisfying the closed loop stability in that sense that all transfer functions in the feedback are from the ring (i.e. they lies in H$_\infty$ and are proper and formally stable) controller feasibility, reference tracking and load disturbance rejection. As a control system, the simple feedback loop is chosen for the simplicity, see Fig. 1.

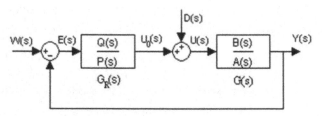

Figure 1. Control feedback scheme

For algebraic controller design in R$_{MS}$ it is initially supposed that not only the plant is expressed by the transfer function over R$_{MS}$ but a controller and all system signals are over the ring. Let $W(s)$ be the Laplace transform of the reference signal, $D(s)$ stands for that of the load disturbance, $E(s)$ is transformed control error, $U_0(s)$ expresses the controller output (control action), $U(s)$ represents the plant input affected by a load disturbance, and $Y(s)$ is the plant output controlled signal in the Laplace transform. The plant transfer function is depicted as $G(s)$, and $G_R(s)$ stands for a controller in the scheme.

External inputs, reference and load disturbance signals, respectively, have forms

$$W(s) = \frac{H_W(s)}{F_W(s)}, \ D(s) = \frac{H_D(s)}{F_D(s)} \tag{13}$$

where $H_W(s)$, $H_D(s)$, $F_W(s)$, $F_D(s) \in$ R$_{MS}$.

The following important feedback transfer functions can be derived

$$G_{WY}(s) = \frac{Y(s)}{W(s)} = \frac{B(s)Q(s)}{M(s)}, \ G_{DY}(s) = \frac{Y(s)}{D(s)} = \frac{B(s)P(s)}{M(s)}$$

$$G_{WE}(s) = \frac{E(s)}{W(s)} = \frac{A(s)P(s)}{M(s)}, \ G_{DE}(s) = \frac{E(s)}{D(s)} = -\frac{B(s)P(s)}{M(s)} \tag{14}$$

where the controller transfer function is factorized as follows

$$G_R(s) = \frac{Q(s)}{P(s)} \tag{15}$$

and the common denominator meromorphic function reads

$$M(s) = A(s)P(s) + B(s)Q(s) \tag{16}$$

Meromorphic functions $Q(s), P(s)$ are from $\mathbf{R}_{MS}$ and the fraction (16) is (Bézout) coprime. The numerator of $M(s) \in \mathbf{R}_{MS}$ agrees to the characteristic quasipolynomial of the closed loop generally defined in (2).

A brief description of basic control design steps follows.

3.1. Closed loop stabilization

Given a Bézout coprime pair $A(s), B(s) \in \mathbf{R}_{MS}$ the closed-loop system is stable if and only if there exists a pair $P(s), Q(s) \in \mathbf{R}_{MS}$ satisfying the Bézout identity

$$A(s)P(s) + B(s)Q(s) = 1 \tag{17}$$

A particular stabilizing solution of (17), say $P_0(s), Q_0(s)$, can be then parameterized as

$$
\begin{aligned}
P(s) &= P_0(s) \pm B(s)Z(s) \\
Q(s) &= Q_0(s) \mp A(s)Z(s)
\end{aligned}
\tag{18}
$$

where $Z(s) \in \mathbf{R}_{MS}$. Parameterization (18) is used to satisfy remaining control and performance requirements, such as reference tracking, disturbance rejection etc.

The proof of the statement above can be done analogously as in (Zítek & Kučera, 2003) where a three-step proof for a similar ring was presented. Condition (12) ensures i.a. that there can exist the ring inversion of $M(s)$ since it proves that there is no common zero of $A(s), B(s)$ in $\mathbb{C}^+$ (including infinity).

3.2. Reference tracking

The task of this subsection is to find $Z(s) \in \mathbf{R}_{MS}$ in (18) so that the reference signal is being tracked. The solution idea results from the form of $G_{WE}(s)$ defined in (14). Consider the limit

$$\lim_{t \to \infty} e_W(t) = \lim_{s \to 0} sE_W(s) = \lim_{s \to 0} sG_{WE}(s)W(s) = \lim_{s \to 0} sA(s)P(s)\frac{H_W(s)}{F_W(s)} \tag{19}$$

where $\cdot_W$ expresses that the signal is a response to the reference not influenced by other external inputs. Limit (19) reaches zero if $\lim_{s \to 0} E_W(s) < \infty$ and $E_W(s)$ is analytic and bounded in the right half-plane, i.e. $E_W(s) \in H_\infty(\mathbb{C}^+)$ – this requirement also satisfies that $\lim_{t \to \infty} \int_0^t e_W(\tau)d\tau < \infty$. Moreover, it must hold that $G_{WE}(s)$ is proper (or, equivalently, $E_W(s)$ is strictly proper) because of the feasibility (impulse free modes) of $e_W(t)$. If one wants to prevent the closed loop stability from the sensitivity to small delays, or to preserve formal stability at least, the denominator of $E_W(s)$ must be a (quasi)polynomial satisfying (5). This implies, in other words, that the reference tracking is fulfilled if $E_W(s) \in \mathbf{R}_{MS}$.

Alternatively, $F_W(s)$ must divide the product $A(s)P(s)$ in $\mathbf{R}_{MS}$. Hence, all unstable zeros (including infinity) of $F_W(s)$ must be those of $A(s)P(s)$ and, moreover, the quasipolynomial numerator of $F_W(s)$ is formally (strongly) stable. It means that one has to set all unstable zeros of $F_W(s)$ (with corresponding multiplicities) as zeros of $P(s)$ - if there is no one already contained in $B(s)$. Recall that zeros mean zero points of a whole term in $\mathbf{R}_{MS}$, not only those of a quasipolynomial numerator.

Note that the controller approach fails for formally unstable controlled processes since then the feedback loop remains formally unstable (neutral term can not be affected by a controller).

3.3. Load disturbance rejection

The attenuation of the load disturbance signal entering a plant model can be done analogously as for reference tracking. Thus, $Z(s)$ is chosen so that $Y_D(s) \in \mathbf{R}_{MS}$ which is clear from

$$\lim_{t \to \infty} y_D(t) = \lim_{s \to 0} sY_D(s) = \lim_{s \to 0} sG_{DY}(s)D(s) = \lim_{s \to 0} sB(s)P(s)\frac{H_D(s)}{F_D(s)} \qquad (20)$$

where $\cdot_D$ means that the output is influenced only by the disturbance. Or, $F_D(s)$ must divide the product $B(s)P(s)$ in $\mathbf{R}_{MS}$.

One has to be careful when deciding about the form of $Z(s)$ since both divisibility conditions must be fulfilled simultaneously. A detailed procedure of reference tracking and disturbance rejection briefly described above was presented e.g. in (Pekař & Prokop, 2011).

4. Selected transfer function rational approximations

Selected easy-handling transfer function rational approximation methods based on the substitution of exponential elements by a rational function are described in this section. The emphasis is put on the engineering usability of the methods.

4.1. Padé approximation

In the second half of the 19th century, a French mathematician Henry Padé devised a simple and, nowadays, one of the most used and favorite rational approximations which is based on the comparison of derivatives of the approximating and approximated functions in zero. More precisely, let $F(s)$ with $F(0) \neq 0$ be analytic in the neighborhood of zero. Then, the n-

n Padé approximation is the function $\Phi(s) = N_n(s)/D_n(s)$ where $N_n(s)$, $D_n(s)$ are polynomials of the nth order with $D_n(0) = 1$ and it holds that $F^{(i)}(0) = \Phi^{(i)}(0), i = 1,...,2n$.

Padé approximation of $F(s) = \exp(-sT)$, $T \geq 0$ is given by the following relation (Partington, 2004)

$$\exp(-sT) \approx \frac{P(-s)}{P(s)}$$

$$P(s) = \sum_{k=0}^{n} \binom{n}{k} \frac{(2n-k)!}{(2n)!}(sT)^k$$

(21)

where n is the order of the approximation. Obviously, one can approximate another function, e.g. the whole transfer function.

A method called *diagonal* Padé approximation, which is distinguished by some authors, see (Battle & Miralles, 2000; Richard, 2003) can be expressed as

$$\exp(-sT) \approx \frac{P(s)}{P(-s)}$$

$$P(s) = \sum_{k=0}^{n} \frac{(2n-k)!}{k!(n-k)!}(-sT)^k$$

(22)

However, it is easy to verify, that (21) and (22) represent the same approximations. In fact,

$$\binom{n}{k}\frac{(2n-k)!}{(2n)!} = \frac{n!}{(2n)!}\frac{(2n-k)!}{k!(n-k)!}$$

(23)

and $n!/(2n)!$ is the common factor of both, the approximating numerator and denominator, hence, the fractions are the same.

4.2. Shift operator approximations

Approaches based on operator shifting yields from the fact that a delay term $\exp(-sT)$ can be perceived as a shift operator and can be subjected to Maclaurin series expansion. Moreover, the variable s can be vied as a derivative operator.

Hence

$$sf(t) := f'(t)$$

$$\exp(-sT)f(t) := f(t-T) = f(t) - Tf'(t) + \frac{T^2}{2}f''(t) - \frac{T^3}{6}f'''(t) + ...$$

$$\exp(-sT)f(t) := \exp\left(-T\frac{d}{dt}\right)f(t) = \left(1 - T\frac{d}{dt} + \frac{T^2}{2}\frac{d^2}{dt^2} - \frac{T^3}{6}\frac{d^3}{dt^3} + ...\right)f(t)$$

(24)

A concise overview of some important shift operator approaches follows.

4.2.1. Laguerre shift

The eventual relation for this shift operator approximant is given by the formula

$$\exp(-sT) \approx \left(\frac{1 - \dfrac{sT}{2n}}{1 + \dfrac{sT}{2n}} \right)^{n} \tag{25}$$

where n is the order of the approximation again, see (Makilla & Partington, 1999a) for more details. The Laguerre shift is successfully used in robust control.

4.2.2. Kautz shift

As presented in (Makilla & Partington, 1999a), the nth order Kautz shift reads

$$\exp(-sT) \approx \left(\frac{1 - \dfrac{sT}{2n} + \dfrac{1}{2}\left(\dfrac{sT}{2n}\right)^{2}}{1 + \dfrac{sT}{2n} + \dfrac{1}{2}\left(\dfrac{sT}{2n}\right)^{2}} \right)^{n} \tag{26}$$

In the source referenced above, there has been analytically proved for input-output delays that the Kautz shift approximation is asymptotically twice more accurate than the Laguerre one.

4.2.3. Padé shift

This type of shift approximation is based on the second order Padé approximation (Makilla & Partington, 1999b; Battle & Miralles, 2000) and it is also called Padé-2. It can be formulated e.g. as follows

$$\exp(-sT) \approx \left(\frac{1 - \dfrac{sT}{2n} + \dfrac{1}{3}\left(\dfrac{sT}{2n}\right)^{2}}{1 + \dfrac{sT}{2n} + \dfrac{1}{3}\left(\dfrac{sT}{2n}\right)^{2}} \right)^{n} \tag{27}$$

4.2.4. Fourier analysis based method

This approximation methodology results from the analysis of the delay-in-feedback step response or, generally, the response to the input of the form $u(t) = t^{k}, t, k \geq 0$. It has been found that the feedback system response is a superposition of a periodic and an aperiodic signal. The Fourier series expansion of the periodic part of the response gives the resulting approximation.

To demonstrate the initial idea more precisely, consider a single delay term $\exp(-sT)$ in the simple negative feedback loop. Then the whole feedback transfer function $W(s)$ reads

$$W(s) = \frac{Y(s)}{U(s)} = \frac{\exp(-sT)}{1 + \exp(-sT)} \tag{28}$$

Hence

$$y(t) = -y(t - T) + u(t - T) \tag{29}$$

and the output $y(t)$ is assumed to be a superposition of a polynomial $q(t)$ and a periodic part $p(t)$

$$y(t) = q(t) + p(t) \tag{30}$$

Inserting (30) into (29) yields

$$y(t - T) - y(t) = \text{constant} \tag{31}$$

From the Fourier series expansion of $p(t)$ and some further nontrivial calculations, the following final relation can be obtained

$$W(s) = \frac{1}{2} - \frac{1}{4}Ts + \frac{2}{\pi^2}T^3s^3\sum_{k=0}^{n}\frac{1}{(2n+1)^2}\frac{1}{T^2s^2 + (2n+1)\pi} \tag{32}$$

The exponential term can be then approximated by the inverse of (28) as

$$\exp(-sT) = \frac{W(s)}{1 - W(s)} \tag{33}$$

The reader is referred to (Battle & Miralles, 2000) for more details about the derivation and methodology.

5. Approximation performance evaluation using norms

The accuracy of rational approximation methods and approaches has been usually measured and evaluated via conscientious and rigorous mathematic analytic proofs. The derivation of such results has been facilitated by the fact that delays in input-output relation only, ignoring the effect of internal delays, have been considered. This is the main gap which ought to be healed up; however, no analytic methods are used in this chapter anyway.

Transfer function norms in the Hardy space known from robust control for unstructured uncertainty measurement instead of any complex analytic method for the comparison of approximation accuracy are used in this contribution since this conception is sufficient for particular cases and for engineering practice. Moreover, analytic derivations of accuracies for internal delays would be much more difficult than those for input-output ones.

First of all, define the objective to be minimized in various meanings. The difference between the nominal G and approximated $\hat{G}$ transfer functions is taken as a measured expression G_M, i.e.

$$G_M = G - \hat{G} \tag{34}$$

We chose two the most used norms in the Hardy space, namely, H_2 and H_∞ norms, which are effective to express the proximity of transfer functions in the frequency domain. The definitions and some basic properties are then followed by some calculation tricks when dealing with the norms.

5.1. H2 norm

The H_2, sometimes called quadratic, norm of a stable strictly proper transfer function is defined as

$$\|G\|_2 = \frac{1}{\sqrt{2\pi}} \sqrt{\int_{-\infty}^{\infty} |G(j\omega)|^2 \, d\omega} \tag{35}$$

The norm is finite for strictly proper stable systems having no pole on the imaginary axis, and the meaning of H_2 is energy of G. A generalized strict properness can be expresses as follows

$$\lim_{R \to \infty} \sup_{\mathrm{Re}\,s > 0, |s| \geq R} |G(s)| = 0 \tag{36}$$

Note that for TDS with distributed delays, there can exist a denominator root (or roots) of G which is not the system pole.

In computer practice, i.e. working with discrete samples, the integral in (36) is calculated as a sum within a finite range of nonnegative frequencies, $\omega \in [0, \omega_{max}]$. Due to the symmetry, the resulting value is doubled finally. The value of ω_{max} can be chosen so that the frequency gain is "small enough".

Residual expansion can be used when analytic (and continuous) calculation of $\|G\|_2$, (Štecha & Havlena, 2000). It holds that

$$\|G\|_2 = \sqrt{\sum_{\mathrm{Re}\,s_i < 0} \operatorname*{res}_{s_i} G(s)G(-s)} \tag{37}$$

where s_i are (stable) system poles and resuduum of a complex function $F(s)$ reads

$$\operatorname*{res}_{s_i} F(s) = \frac{1}{(m-1)!}\lim_{s \to s_i}\left\{\frac{d^{(m-1)}}{ds^{(m-1)}}\left[F(s)(s-s_i)^m\right]\right\} \qquad (38)$$

where m is the multiplicity of a pole.

5.2. H∞ norm

The H-infinity (H_∞) norm is defined as

$$\|G\|_\infty = \sup_\omega |G(j\omega)| \qquad (39)$$

i.e. it expresses the supreme of the amplitude (gain) frequency characteristics of G, see Fig. 2. If the system is asymptotically (exponentially) stable and provides a finite H∞ norm, it is said that it is H∞ stable and lies in the space $H_\infty(\mathbb{C}^+)$ of functions analytic and bounded in the right-half complex plane.

The norm is also called L_2 gain, That is, the H∞ stable system has finite $L_2(0,\infty)$ to $L_2(0,\infty)$ gain where $L_2(0,\infty)$ norm of an input or output signal $h(t)$ is defined as

$$\|h(t)\|_2 := \sqrt{\int_0^\infty |h(t)|^2\, dt} \qquad (40)$$

The frequency characteristics supreme can be easily found by standard analytic means, or by mapping the values of $G(j\omega)$ when using digital computers.

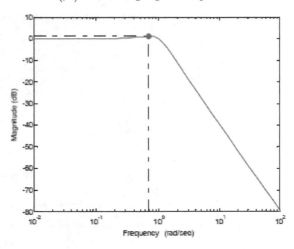

Figure 2. The meaning of H_∞ norm as the frequency characteristics supreme

Note, for instance, that a transfer function having no pole on the imaginary axis but a sequence of poles with real part converging to zero can have an infinite H_∞ norm due to an unbounded gain, see (Partington & Bonnet, 2004).

6. Matlab-Simulink user interface

The main application part of this chapter consists in development of a simulation program that can evaluate the quality of approximations. A user-friendly interface in Matlab-Simulink environment has been hence developed by the authors in order to provide testing and comparison of approximation approaches introduced above. The source code can be found in (Pekař & Kurečková, 2011).

Fig. 3 displays the working environment of the application. In the upper part of the user interface, one is allowed to enter a nominal plant transfer function as a numerator and denominator quasipolynomials. The user must be careful since the syntax scheme which is indicated by grey font (or by the help hint) in the edit box must be kept.

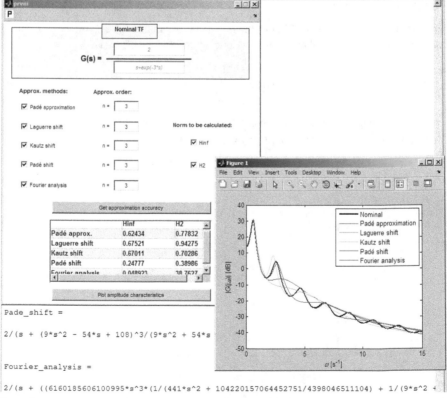

Figure 3. Matlab-Simulink user interface and working environment

Then, a user can select one or more approximation methods to be compared and check the choice of norms by which the accuracy of approximation is calculated. It is also possible to specify an order of the approximation for each selected method.

By clicking the button *Get approximation accuracy*, the programme returns a table of calculated norms in the text form. A graphical comparison of amplitude frequency responses for all chosen approximations is obtained by clicking the button *Plot amplitude characteristics*.

Final approximation controller transfer functions are returned to the Matlab workspace to the command line.

7. Benchmark examples

The aim of this section is to verify introduced approximation methods using the user interface. The approximation accuracy with respect to the order of an approximation is a very attractive question as well. As will be seen from the following examples, some rather surprising results can be obtained.

As mentioned above, results of the benchmark ought to be primarily used by the authors for the rational approximation of controllers with internal delays (also called anisochronic) as a first step of controllers' discretization via the z-transform, for the computer implementation.

Three examples of algebraic controller design with rational approximations using the user interface follow. The first one gives results for anisochronic controllers design in control of a hypothetic simple stable LTI with stepwise reference, to demonstrate mainly the design procedure. The second one presents the approximation of an anisochronic controller for an attractive unstable system of a skater on a swaying bow. The third example deals with control of a laboratory circuit heating system, as a typical real-life representative of retarded TDS.

7.1. Stable system with stepwise reference

Let the plant be described by the transfer function of a stable first order TDS model with both internal and input-output delays as

$$G(s) = \frac{b\exp(-\tau s)}{s + a\exp(-\vartheta s)}, \tau, \vartheta \geq 0, a\vartheta \in (0, 2\pi) \tag{41}$$

Condition $a\vartheta \in (0, 2\pi)$ ensures the asymptotic stability of the model.

Coprime (Bézout) factorization is the first step of controller design in $\mathbf{R}_{MS}$ ring as follows

$$G(s)\frac{\dfrac{b\exp(-\tau s)}{m(s)}}{\dfrac{s + a\exp(-\vartheta s)}{m(s)}} = \frac{B(s)}{A(s)}, A(s), B(s) \in \mathbf{R}_{MS} \tag{42}$$

where $m(s)$ is an appropriate stable (quasi)polynomial of the first order (due to the coprimeness). A suitable form of $m(s)$ is contentious and depends on user's requirements, let $m(s) = s + m_0, m_0 > 0$.

Consider the simplest practical case that both external inputs are from the class of step functions, hence

$$W(s) = \frac{H_W(s)}{F_W(s)} = \frac{\frac{w_0}{m_w(s)}}{\frac{s}{m_w(s)}}, \quad D(s) = \frac{H_D(s)}{F_D(s)} = \frac{\frac{d_0}{m_d(s)}}{\frac{s}{m_d(s)}} \tag{43}$$

where $m_w(s)$ and $m_d(s)$ are arbitrary stable (quasi)polynomials of degree one, say, for the simplicity, $s + m_0$ again, $H_W(s), F_W(s), H_D(s), F_D(s) \in \mathbf{R}_{MS}$ and w_0 and d_0 are real constants.

Find a stabilizing particular solution by (17). Set e.g. $Q_0 = 1$ which yields

$$P_0(s) = \frac{s + m_0 - b\exp(-\tau s)}{s + a\exp(-\vartheta s)} \tag{44}$$

Now parameterize the solution according to (18) to obtain controllers asymptotically rejecting the load disturbance and tracking the stepwise reference

$$P(s) = \frac{s + m_0 - b\exp(-\tau s)}{s + a\exp(-\vartheta s)} - \frac{b\exp(-\tau s)}{s + m_0} Z(s) \tag{45}$$

The numerator of $P(s)$ has to have at least one zero root. Moreover, it is appropriate to have $P(s)$ in a simple form, which is fulfilled e.g. when

$$Z(s) = \left(\frac{m_0}{b} - 1\right) \frac{s + m_0}{s + a\exp(-\vartheta s)} \tag{46}$$

providing

$$P(s) = \frac{s + m_0(1 - \exp(-\tau s))}{s + a\exp(-\vartheta s)}, \quad Q = \frac{m_0}{b} \tag{47}$$

Thus, final controller's structure is the following

$$G_R(s) = \frac{m_0[s + a\exp(-\vartheta s)]}{b[s + m_0(1 - \exp(-\tau s))]} \tag{48}$$

The obtained control structure can be easily compared with the well-known Smith predictor structure and note that the controller is of the anisochronic type because of delay in the transfer function denominator. It is naturally possible to take $m(s)$ as a quasipolynomial instead of polynomial; however, this option would make a controller more complicated. The importance of $m(s)$ reveals from the closed loop transfer function

$$G_{WY}(s) = \frac{Y(s)}{W(s)} = \frac{m_0 \exp(-\tau s)}{s + m_0}$$ (49)

i.e. $m(s)$ appears as a characteristic (quasi)polynomial of the closed loop.

Model (41) can to fit the dynamics of a high order undelayed system; for instance, a tenth order system governed by the transfer function

$$G_s(s) = \frac{1}{(2s+1)^{10}}$$ (50)

can be estimated by model (41) with $a = b = 6.5 \cdot 10^{-2}, \tau = 15.3, \vartheta = 6.7$, see (Zítek & Vyhlídal, 2003; Pekař & Prokop, 2008) for details. Hence, let the system has these parameters and $m_0 = 0.5$.

Let $n = \{1,2,3,4,5\}$, where n is the order of the approximation method, and test the accuracies for all methods introduced above. The best results for each of them measured by H_∞ and H_2 norms with the corresponding order are displayed in Table 1.

Obviously, the best result for H_∞ is given alongside by the Padé approximation and Laguerre shift of the first order, whereas, amazingly, higher orders make results worse. The Fourier analysis based methods yields almost the same score for all studied orders. The benchmark results for the H_2 norm with $\omega_{max} = 15$ introduced in Table 1 are almost identical with those for H_∞, i.e. the Padé approximation and Laguerre shift of the first order are the best and the Fourier analysis based methods gives almost the same results for all orders. The corresponding gain frequency responses for the approximations of orders as in the last column in Table 1 are displayed in Fig. 4.

Method	H_∞	n	H_2	n
Padé approx.	0.243	1	0.237	1
Laguerre shift	0.243	1	0.237	1
Kautz shift	0.408	5	0.299	3
Padé shift	0.277	1	0.29	1
Fourier analysis	0.38	1	0.354	5

Table 1. Comparison of rational approximations of (49) measured by H_∞ and H_2 norms

The approximating transfer function by Padé approximation and Laguerre shift with $n = 1$ is given by (51), which agrees with a conventional PID controller

$$\hat{G}_R(s) = \frac{0.7692s^2 + 0.506s + 0.0065}{s^2 + 0.2307s} \tag{51}$$

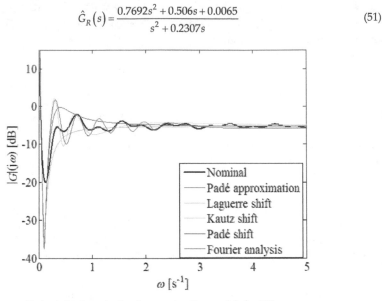

Figure 4. Bode magnitude plots of nominal and approximating models for (48)

7.2. Control of the roller skater on a swaying bow

Consider an unstable system describing roller skater on a swaying bow, (Zítek et al., 2008), governed by the transfer function

$$G(s) = \frac{Y(s)}{U(s)} = \frac{b\exp(-(\tau + \vartheta)s)}{s^2(s^2 - a\exp(-\vartheta s))} \tag{52}$$

see Fig. 5, where $y(t)$ is the skater's deviation from the desired position, $u(t)$ expresses the slope angle of a bow caused by force P, delays τ, ϑ means the skater's and servo latencies, respectively, and b, a are real parameters. Skater controls the servo driving by remote signals into servo electronics.

Let the model parameters be $b = 0.2$, $a = 1$, $\tau = 0.3$ s, $\vartheta = 0.1$ s, as in the literature, and design the controller structure analogously as in the previous subsection 7.1. Consider that the reference and load disturbance are in the form of step-wise functions. Then the final controller has the structure given by the following transfer function

$$G_R(s) = \frac{b(q_3 s^3 + q_2 s^2 + q_1 s + q_0)(s + m_0)^4 + p_0 m_0^4 s^2 (s^2 - a\exp(-\vartheta s))}{b\left[(s^3 + p_2 s^2 + p_1 s + p_0)(s + m_0)^4 - p_0 m_0^4 \exp(-(\tau + \vartheta)s)\right]} \tag{53}$$

where p_2, p_1, p_0, q_3, q_2, q_1, $q_0 \in \circ$ are free parameters, see details in (Pekař & Prokop, 2011b).
Using a quasi-optimal tuning algorithm, the parameters were set as

$$q_3 = 4.7587, q_2 = 2.1164, q_1 = 2.6252, q_0 = 0.4482, p_2 = 0.4636, p_1 = 0.529, p_0 = 4.6164 \quad (54)$$

and e.g. $m_0 = 5$.

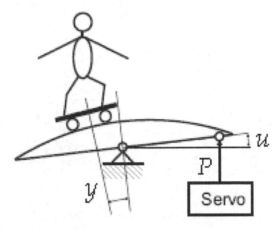

Figure 5. The roller skater on a swaying bow

The comparison of the best controller rational approximations can be found in Table 2.
Again, the method based on the Fourier series expansion very slowly approaches the limit
value of the H_2 norm (≈ 7.811) with the increasing n. The only method evincing the better
asymptotical results with the higher order approximation is the Kautz shift. Again, the Padé
and Laguerre approximations of the first order give very good results with the
approximating controller transfer function

$$\hat{G}_R(s) = \frac{\begin{matrix} 4.7587s^8 + 121.084s^7 + 1245.21s^6 + 20969.8s^5 + 90315.2s^4 + 39304.5s^3 \\ +56753.5s^2 + 9604.38s + 1400.63 \end{matrix}}{\begin{matrix} s^8 + 25.4636s^7 + 262.119s^6 + 1383.74s^5 + 3952.16s^4 + 6389.1s^3 + 8872.37s^2 \\ +18964.6s \end{matrix}} \quad (55)$$

Method	H_∞	n	H_2	n
Padé approx.	5.6674	1	8.577	1
Laguerre shift	5.6674	1	8.577	1
Kautz shift	6.0847	5	9.7446	5
Padé shift	6.0668	1	9.674	1
Fourier analysis	5.6674	1	7.8114	5

Table 2. Comparison of rational approximations of (53) measured by H_∞ and H_2 norms

Fig. 6 displays Bode magnitude plots for the best orders for H_2 (the last column in Table 2), which verifies a very good performance of all the approaches.

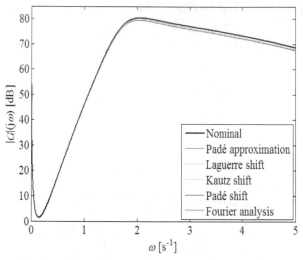

Figure 6. Bode magnitude plots of nominal and approximating models for (53)

7.3. Control of a circuit heating plant

The laboratory heating plant, a photo and a sketch of which, respectively, are displayed in Fig. 7, was assembled at the Faculty of Applied Informatics of Tomas Bata University in Zlín in order to test control algorithms for systems with dead time. The original description of the apparatus and its electronic circuits can be found in (Dostálek et al., 2008).

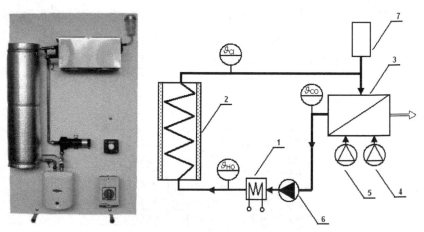

Figure 7. Bode magnitude plots of nominal and approximating models for (53)

The heat transferring fluid (namely distilled water) is transported using a continuously controllable DC pump {6} into a flow heater {1} with maximum power $P(t)$ of 750 W. The temperature of a fluid at the heater output is measured by a platinum thermometer giving value of $\vartheta_{HO}(t)$. Warmed liquid then goes through a 15 meters long insulated coiled pipeline {2} which causes the significant delay in the system. The air-water heat exchanger (cooler) {3} with two cooling fans {4, 5} represents a heat-consuming appliance. The speed of the first fan can be continuously adjusted, whereas the second one is of on/off type. Input and output temperatures of the cooler are measured again by platinum thermometers giving $\vartheta_{CI}(t)$, resp. $\vartheta_{CO}(t)$. The expansion tank {7} compensates for the expansion effect of the water.

Originally, it was intended to control input delays only; however, it was shown that the plant contains internal delays as well. A detailed mathematical model was presented in (Pekař et al., 2009). A linearized model of the relation between the power to the heater $P(t)$ and $\vartheta_{CO}(t)$ can be expressed by the transfer function

$$G(s) = \frac{\vartheta_{CO}(s)}{P(s)} = \frac{\left[b_{0D}\exp(-\tau_0 s)+b_0\right]\exp(-\tau s)}{s^3 + a_2 s^2 + a_1 s + a_0 + a_{0D}\exp(-\vartheta s)} \tag{56}$$

where all real parameters in the model are complex algebraic functions of physical quantities in the circuit and input and output steady states, see details in the literature. It was determined that for a certain working point, the parameters are

$$b_{0D} = 2.334 \cdot 10^{-6}, b_0 = -2.146 \cdot 10^{-7}, a_2 = 0.1767, a_1 = 0.009, a_0 = 1.413 \cdot 10^{-4},$$
$$a_{0D} = -7.624 \cdot 10^{-5}, \tau_0 = 1.5, \tau = 131, \vartheta = 143 \tag{57}$$

The controller structure obtained by controller design in $\mathbf{R}_{MS}$ yields

$$G_R(s) = \frac{P(s)}{\vartheta_{CO}(s)} = \frac{m_0^3\left(s^3 + a_2 s^2 + a_1 s + a_0 + a_{0D}\exp(-\vartheta s)\right)}{b_0(s+m_0)^3 - m_0^3\left[b_{0D}\exp(-\tau_0 s)+b_0\right]\exp(-\tau s)} \tag{58}$$

Table 3 displays the best values for approximations at their orders $n = \{1,2,3,4,5\}$. H_2 norm is measured within the frequency range $\omega \in [0.001;0.5]$ with the discretization step $\Delta\omega = 0.001$.

Method	H_∞	n	H_2	n
Padé approx.	27994.7	4	1197.3	5
Laguerre shift	28528.6	3	1194.3	2
Kautz shift	28365.9	2	1196.4	2
Padé shift	28650.2	3	1198.7	1
Fourier analysis	28760.9	1	1205.1	1

Table 3. Comparison of rational approximations of (56) measured by H_∞ and H_2 norms

Immense values of H_∞ norm are caused by a pair controller poles which is very close to the imaginary axis ($s_i = 0.0002 \pm 0.094\text{j}$) and the controller is obviously unstable. Padé approximation of the 4th order provides the best value for H_∞, whereas Laguerre shift of the 2nd order gives the best approximation measured by H_2 norm. Again, this example indicates that the higher order of the approximation does not mean the more accurate result automatically.

The comparison of Bode magnitude plots for the best orders (which are placed in the last column in Table 3) for H_2 can be seen in Fig. 8.

To conclude study cases above, it is startling that the best approximations measured by H_2 and H_∞ norms are mostly given by the well known and widely used Padé approximation of the first (or a low) order. By simulations, the higher order of an approximation does not generally yields the more accuracy finite dimensional model, which is in the contradiction with a general expectation and analytic results for rational approximations for TDS with input-outputs delays. Comparative Bode plots above indicate the usability and a very good efficiency of selected methods.

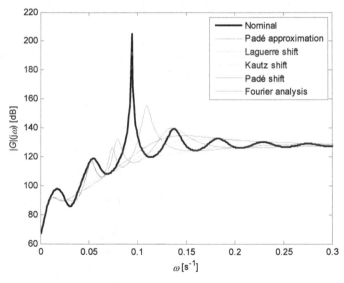

Figure 8. Bode magnitude plots of nominal and approximating models for (58).

8. Conclusion

This chapter intended to propound the reader a methodology for algebraic controller design for systems with internal delays, followed by a comparison of several easy-handling techniques for rational (i.e. finite-dimensional) approximation of anisochronic (i.e. infinite-dimensional) controllers – or their transfer functions, more precisely.

The first, controller design, part was based on the solution of the Bézout identity, to obtain stable and proper controllers, along with the Youla-Kučera parameterization for reference tracking and load disturbance rejection, in $\mathbf{R}_{MS}$ ring.

The second, controller approximation, part of this chapter intended to use five quite simple methods, namely Padé approximation, Laguerre, Kautz shift and Fourier analysis based method, how to approximate a delay exponential term in the transfer function. Two norms in the Hardy space, namely, H_2 and H_∞ norms were used as a measure for the accuracy and efficiency of the approaches since there are no rigorous analytic results about the approximation efficiency and accuracy in the literature and these norms are usually sufficient in technical practice. Approximation methods were selected so that they are serviceable also for people with basic mathematical background knowledge. The authors plan to use approximated controllers in their digital implementation on PC or PLC.

Matlab with Simulink was a very useful assistant here. The authors programmed a simple user interface which enables the user to enter a nominal transfer function and select approximation methods to be used and their orders. As a result, the program returns the accuracies in both text and graphical forms.

Simulation experiments with the program were made. Control of a simple stable TDS, control of unstable TDS of a skater on the swaying bow and control of a laboratory circuits heating plant were benchmark examples. The results were very interesting and startling because the habitual Padé approximation proved to be very good and, moreover, the higher order approximation did not automatically mean the better result for systems with internal delays.

Author details

Libor Pekař, Eva Kurečková and Roman Prokop
Tomas Bata University in Zlín, Czech Republic

Acknowledgement

The authors kindly appreciate the financial support which was provided by the Ministry of Education, Youth and Sports of the Czech Republic, under the project CEBIA-Tech No. CZ.1.05/2.1.00/03.0089.

9. References

Battle, C. & Miralles, A. (2000). On the Approximation of Delay Elements by Feedback. *Automatica*, Vol.36, No.5, pp. 659-664, ISSN 0005-1098
Bellman, R. & Cooke, K.L. (1963). *Differential-Difference Equations*, Academic Press, New York
Brethé, D. & Loiseau, J.J. (1998). An Effective Algorithm for Finite Spectrum Assignment of Single-Input Systems with Delays. *Mathematics and Computers in Simulation*, Vol.45, No.3-4, pp. 339-348, ISSN 0378-4754

Byrnes, C.I., Spong, M.W. & Tarn, T.J. (1984). A Several Complex Variables Approach to Feedback Stabilization of Neutral Delay-Differential Systems. *Mathematical Systems Theory*, Vol.17, No.1, pp. 97-133, ISSN 0025-5661

Conte, G. & Perdon, A.M. (2000). Systems over Rings: Geometric Theory and Applications. *Annual Reviews in Control*, Vol.24, pp. 113-124, 1367-5788

Dostálek, P., Dolinay, J. & Vašek, V. (2008). Design and Implementation of Portable Data Acquisition Unit in Process Control and Supervision Applications. *WSEAS Transactions on Systems and Control*, Vol.3, No.9, pp. 779-788, ISSN 1991-8763

El'sgol'ts, L.E. & Norkin, S.B. (1973). *Introduction to the Theory and Application of Differential Equations with Deviated Arguments*. Academic Press, New York

Findensen, W., Pulaczewski, J. & Manitius, A. (1970). Multilevel Optimization and Dynamic Coordination of Mass Flows in a Beet Sugar Plant. *Automatica*, Vol.6, No.4, 1970, pp. 581-589, ISSN 0005-1098

Gluesing-Lueerssen, H. (1997). A Behavioral Approach to Delay-Differential Systems. *SIAM Journal of Control and Optimization*, Vol.35, pp. 480-499, ISSN 0363-0129

Górecki, H.; Fuksa, S.; Grabowski, P. & Korytowski, A. (1989). *Analysis and Synthesis of Time Delay Systems*, John Wiley & Sons, ISBN 978-047-1276-22-7, New York

Hale, J.K., & Verduyn Lunel, S.M. (1993). *Introduction to Functional Differential Equations*. In: *Applied Mathematical Sciences*, Vol.99, Springer-Verlag, ISBN 978-038-7940-76-2, New York

Štecha, J., Havlena, V. (2000). *Modern Control Theory* (in Czech). ČVUT Publishing, ISBN 80-01-01971-3, Prague

Kolmanovskii, V.B. & Nosov, V.R. (1986). *Stability of Functional Differential Equations*, Academic Press, ISBN 0124179401, London

Kolmanovskii, V.B. & Myshkis, A. (1999). *Introduction to the Theory and Applications of Functional Differential Equations*, Cluwer Academy, ISBN 978-0792355045, Dordrecht, Netherlands

Krasovskii, N.N. (1963). *Stability of Motion*, Standford University Press, Chicago

Kučera V. (1993). Diophantine Equations in Control - A Survey. *Automatica*, Vol.29, No.6, pp. 1361-1375, ISSN 0005-1098

Loiseau, J.J., Cardelli, M. & Dusser, X. (2002). Neutral-Type Time-Delay Systems that are not Formally Stable are not BIBO Stabilizable. *IMA Journal of Mathematical Control and Information*, Vol.19, No.1-2, pp. 217-227, ISSN 0265-0754

Makilla, P.M. & Partington, J.R. (1999a). Laguerre and Kautz Shift Approximations of Delay Systems. *International Journal of Control*, Vol.72, No.10, pp. 932-946, ISSN 0020-7179

Makilla, P.M. & Partington, J.R. (1999b). Shift Operator Induced Approximations of Delay Systems. *SIAM Journal of Control and Optimization*, Vol. 37, No.6, pp. 1897-1912, ISSN 0363-0129

Manitius, A.Z. & Olbrot, A.W. (1979). Finite Spectrum Assignment Problem for Systems with Delays. *IEEE Transactions on Automatic Control*, Vol.24, No.4, pp. 541-553, ISSN 0018-9286

Morávka, J. & Michálek, K. (2008). Anisochronous Model of the Metallurgical RH Process. *Transactions of the VŠB – Technical University of Ostrava, Mechanical Series*, Vol.14, No.2, 2008, pp. 91–96, ISSN 1210-0471

Niculescu, S.-I. (2001). *Delay Effects on Stability*. In: *Lecture Notes in Control and Information Sciences*, Vol.269, Springer, ISBN 9781852332914, Berlin

Partington, J.R. (2004). Some Frequency-Domain Approaches to the Model Reduction of Delay Systems. *Annual Reviews in Control*, Vol.28, No.1, pp. 65-73, ISSN 1367-5788

Partington, J.R. & Bonnet, C. (2004). H_∞ and BIBO Stabilization of Delay Systems of Neutral Type. *Systems & Control Letters*, Vol.52, No.3-4, 2004, pp. 283-288, ISSN 0167-6911

Pekař, L. & Kurečková, E. (20/03/2011). Application for Transfer Function Rational Approximations for Time Delay Systems, In: *Faculty of Applied Informatics, Tomas Bata University in Zlín*, 22/03/2011, Available from: http://web.fai.utb.cz/?id=0_2_2_5&iid=0&lang=cs&type=0

Pekař, L. & Prokop R (2008). An approach for relay based identification of anisochronic models, *Proceedings of the 27th IASTED International Conference on Modelling, Identification and Control*, paper No. 596-061 [CD-ROM], ISBN 978-0-88986-712-3, Innsbruck, Austria, February 11-13, 2008

Pekař, L. & Prokop R (2009). Some Observations about the RMS Ring for Delayed Systems, *Proceedings of the 17th International Conference on Process Control '09*, pp. 28-36, ISBN 978-80-227-3081-5, Štrbské Pleso, Slovakia, June 9-12, 2009

Pekař, L. & Prokop, R. (2010). Control Design for Stable Systems with Both Input-Output and Internal Delays by Algebraic Means, *Proceedings of the 29th International Conference on Modelling, Identification and Control*, pp. 400-407, ISBN 978-0-88986-833-5, Innsbruck, Austria, February 15-17, 2010

Pekař, L. & Prokop, R. (2011a). On Reference Tracking and Disturbance Rejection for Time Delay Systems, *Proceedings of the 31st International Conference on Modelling, Identification and Control*, pp. 327-333, ISBN 978-088986863-2, Innsbruck, Austria, February 14-16, 2011

Pekař, L. & Prokop, R. (2011b). Implementation of a New Quasi-Optimal Controller Tuning Algorithm for Time-Delay Systems, In: *MATLAB for Engineers – Applications in Control, Electrical Engineering, IT and Robotics*, K. Perůtka, (Ed.), pp. 3-26. InTech, ISBN 978-953-307-914-1, Rijeka, Croatia

Pekař, L., Prokop, R. & Dostálek, P. (2009). Circuit Heating Plant Model with Internal Delays. *WSEAS Transactions on Systems*, Vol.8, No.9, pp. 1093-1104, ISSN 1109-2777

Pekař, L., Prokop, R. & Dostálek, P. (2011). Non-Stepwise Reference Tracking for Time Delay Systems, *Proceedings of the 12th International Carpathian Control Conference*, pp. 292-297, ISBN 978-1-61284-360-5, Velké Karlovice, Czech Republic, May 25-28, 2011

Richard, J.P. (2003). Time-delay Systems: an Overview of Some Recent Advances and Open Problems. *Automatica*, Vol.39, No.10, pp. 1667-1694, ISSN 0005-1098

Simuenovic, G. (2011). *Separate Identification of Coefficients and Delays in Time-Delay Systems*, Ph.D. Thesis, Faculty of Mechanical Engineering, Czech Technical University in Prague

Vidyasagar, M. (1985). *Control System Synthesis: A Factorization Approach*, MIT Press, ISBN 978-0262220279, Cambridge, M. A.

Volterra, V. (1928). Sur le Théorie Mathématique des Phénomenès Héreditaires. *Journal des Mathématiques Pures et Appliquées*, Vol.7, 1928, pp. 249-298

Vyhlídal, T. & Zítek, P. (2001). Control System Design Based on a Universal First Order Model with Time Delays. *Acta Polytechnica*, Vol.44, No.4-5, 2001, pp. 49-53, ISSN 1210-2709

Zítek, P. (1983). Anisochronic State Theory of Dynamic Systems. *Acta Technica ČSAV*, Vol.4, 1983, ISSN 0001-7043

Zítek, P. (1997). Frequency Domain Synthesis of Hereditary Control Systems via Anisochronic State Space. *International Journal of Control*, Vol.66, No.4, pp. 539-556, ISSN 0020-7179

Zítek, P. & Hlava, J. (2001). Anisochronic Internal Model Control of Time-Delay Systems. *Control Engineering Practice*, Vol.9, No.5, pp. 501-516, ISSN 0967-0661

Zítek, P. & Kučera, V. (2003). Algebraic Design of Anisochronic Controllers for Time Delay Systems. *International Journal of Control*, Vol.76, No.16, pp. 1654-1665, ISSN 0020-7179

Zítek, P.; Kučera, V. & Vyhlídal, T. (2008). Meromorphic Observer-based Pole Assignment in Time Delay Systems. *Kybernetika*, Vol.44, No.5, pp. 633-648, ISSN 0023-5954

Zítek, P. & Vítecek, A. (1999). *Control of Systems with Delays and Nonlinearities* (in Czech), ČVUT Publishing, ISBN 80-01-01939-X, Prague

Zítek, P. & Vyhlídal, T. (2003). Low Order Time Delay Approximation of Conventional Linear Model, *Proceedings of 4th IMACS Symposium on Mathematical Modelling*, 2003, pp. 28, ISBN 3-901608-24-9, Vienna, Austria, February 5-7, 2003

Zítek, P. & Vyhlídal, T. (2008). Argument-Increment Based Stability Criterion for Neutral Time Delay Systems, *Proceedings of the 16th Mediterranean Conference on Control and Automation*, pp. 824-829, ISBN 978-1-4244-2505-1, Ajaccio, Corsica, France, June 25-27, 2008

Matlab-Simulink® Coupling to Finite Element Software for Design and Analysis of Electrical Machines

Gaizka Almandoz, Gaizka Ugalde, Javier Poza and Ana Julia Escalada

Additional information is available at the end of the chapter

1. Introduction

Classical electric machine design processes normally do not take into account some specific aspects (PWM voltage supply, mechanical resonances, etc) of the application where the motor is integrated. Actually the electromagnetic properties of the machine can influence the overall performances of the system, or the performances of the motor can get worse due to the influence of other components that are connected to the motor. For example, at low speeds, the torque ripple produced by the machine could cause undesirable speed pulsations and inaccuracies in motion control. At the same time, machine performance could be negatively affected by the Power Converter. For instance, the large amount of harmonic components contained in a PWM wave can increase the iron losses. Furthermore, when long connection cables are used between motor and power converter, high dv/dt voltages, which are characteristic in PWM signals, might cause over voltages at motor terminals which could damage seriously the winding insulation.

A possible solution to identify these problems is to add a new step into the design process previously to the prototyping stage, where the behavior of the machine into the final application is analyzed, evaluating the interaction between different elements of the system.

In order to achieve this purpose, this chapter deals with the integration of the numerical magnetic field computation software FLUX® and the system simulator MATLAB-SIMULINK® into only one simulation tool. The electric machine is modeled with FLUX® software, whereas the control, the electric components and the mechanical systems are implemented in MATLAB-SIMULINK®. In addition, the Finite Element Method (FEM) for electrical motor design and analysis is described. On the other hand, MATLAB-SIMULINK® coupling to FEM software is explained and some clues related to this issue are given. And finally two case studies are presented in order to illustrate the benefits of this multi-domain simulation method. In both cases a surface mounted permanent magnet synchronous motor is analyzed.

2. Co-simulation tools for electrical machine design

Typically conventional electric machine design process is divided into two stages: an initial analytic design is complemented by a more accurate analysis based on FEM Software. A disadvantage of this methodology is that some specific aspects of the application for which the machine is designed are not entirely taken into account during the design process. Consequently, after integrating the machine into the final application, some performance problems may appear due to the interaction between the motor and different elements of the system. A new design step where these phenomena are identified by multi-domain analysis may help in the task of achieving an optimal design.

An electric drive is a non-linear multi-domain system which involves electric, electromagnetic, thermal and mechanical domains. The analysis of the whole system requires a specific simulation tool for each domain. But this way it is not possible to evaluate the interaction between different subsystems. A possible solution could be a simulation tool capable to integrate all domains. However, it is well known that the more are the domains of the simulation tool, the less is the accuracy. Therefore, a solution may be the integration of different simulation tools in a multi-domain analysis. Few years ago, that solution was impossible due to limitations in computation capacity of the computers and incompatibilities between different simulation software. Nevertheless, nowadays the development of new powerful work stations and updated simulation tools oriented to co-simulations make possible to analyze relatively complex multi-domain systems by means of co-simulations.

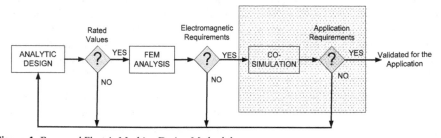

Figure 1. Proposed Electric Machine Design Methodology

In this section some useful co-simulation examples for electric machine design will be presented.

2.1. Coupling between control unit – Electric machine – Mechanical system

Normally the electromagnetic torque produced by an electric machine is not entirely smooth but it presents a certain ripple component. This oscillatory component is due to a non-sinusoidal spatial distribution of flux density in the air-gap, and due to the effect of slots known as cogging torque.

Regarding to the mechanical system, many times it may present resonances which can be excited by the drive. In that case important level of vibrations and noise can be produced.

Carrying out co-simulations concerning the control unit, the electric motor FEM model and the mechanical system model it is possible to evaluate the effect of torque ripple over the mechanical system (see Fig 2-A). Furthermore, this multi-domain simulation makes possible a pre-evaluation of control algorithms, analyzing the influence of different control strategies as well as the influence of regulator parameters upon system performances.

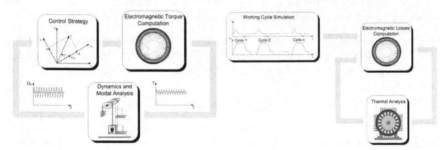

A) Control-Electromagnetic-Mechanical System Coupling

B) Electromagnetic-Thermal Coupling

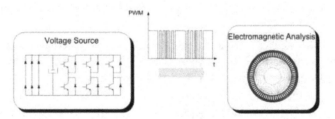

C) Power Electronics Converter–Electric Machine Coupling

Figure 2. Examples of different multi-domain simulations

2.2. Coupling between power electronics converter – Electric machine

Few decades ago, technological advances in power converters made possible the development of new variable speed drives, leading to important performance improvements in many applications. In this kind of drives, the speed of the motor is controlled varying the frequency of the supply voltage by means of an power converter, which generates a well known Pulse Width Modulated (PWM) voltage.

The high harmonics content of this non-sinusoidal supplying voltage causes significant increase in electromagnetic losses, leading to a less efficient motor. These losses could be taken into account in the electromagnetic – thermal coupling in order to compute the overall heating of the machine.

Another phenomenon caused by the mutual influence between the power converter and the machine is the overvoltage at machine terminals. This overvoltage is caused by the characteristic high dv/dt of PWM waveforms and it may appear when connection wires between power converter and machine are too long. In the worst case, this effect could irreversibly destroy the insulation of stator winding or even could damage some semiconductor of the converter.

Besides these two phenomena, a pulse width modulated voltage has another effect on machine performance. That kind of supplying voltage causes a non-sinusoidal current, which contributes to increase the ripple of the torque.

All these phenomena could be analyzed by multi-domain simulations concerning the electric and electromagnetic domains (see Fig 2-C). After identifying all these problems, several design modifications can be made in order to improve the performance of the electric drive.

2.3. Coupling between electromagnetic and thermal domains

It is widely known that the temperature is very critical parameter in the performance of electric machines. The overheating of the machine depends on various factors such as core losses, current amplitude and working cycles. Typically conservative thermal designs are applied which may lead to bigger and more expensive machines. In order to get more compact motors, it is necessary to optimize the thermal design according to the requirements of the application.

This electromagnetic-thermal coupling simulation (see Fig 2-B) permits the evaluation of the overheating of the machine depending on the working cycles of the application. Thus, the design can be adjusted to the application performance achieving a thermally optimized machine.

As a particular case, machines excited by means of Neodymium permanent magnets are very sensitive to the temperature. The main drawback of this kind of rare earth magnets is the low Curie temperature, about 300ºC, and the high temperature sensitivity. If the operation point of the magnet remains above the typical knee in its characteristic curve, the change due to temperature is fully reversible. However, if temperature causes a change in the operation point below the knee, the magnet gets partially de-magnetized. So, it is very important to evaluate the rotor temperature in order to prevent any problem related to partial de-magnetization of magnets.

3. FEM analysis of electrical machines

Software based on the Finite Element Method is known as very powerful tool for the design and analysis of electrical motors. FEM analysis makes possible an accurate evaluation of electromagnetic characteristics such as magnetic saturation level, torque or induced electromotive force, and it is also very useful for the computation of the lumped parameters of the equivalent electric circuit, i.e. inductances and iron losses resistance. In this section the basis of this numerical method are explained and some important details related to the FEM analysis of electrical machines are pointed out.

Simulations based on the FEM can be divided in three stages: Definition of the problem, resolution of the problem and results analysis. Next, these three stages are described briefly.

3.1. Definition of the electromagnetic problem

The definition of the problem is faced in three steps. First the geometry must be defined. After that the mesh may be created. And finally physical properties have to be defined. Undoubtedly meshing the problem is the most critical issue in the definition stage. It is widely known that the results accuracy depends strongly on the quality of the mesh. Therefore, normally the higher the amount of nodes is the more accurate the results are. On the other hand, the computational load also depends on the amount of nodes, so that the bigger the amount of nodes is the longer the required simulation time is. Thus, the meshing process is a trade of between accuracy and computational time.

3.2. Resolution of electromagnetic problems

Electric machines are non-linear problems so that they must be solved applying numerical iterative methods. In case of FLUX® electromagnetic non-linear problems are solved by the Newton-Raphson method. Regarding to the equations, in the solving process of electromagnetic problems the Maxwell's equations are considered.

$$\forall X \vec{E} = -\frac{d\vec{B}}{dt} \quad \forall \cdot \vec{B} = 0 \quad \forall X \vec{H} = \vec{J} + \frac{d\vec{D}}{dt} \quad \forall \cdot \vec{D} = \rho_v \tag{1}$$

E is the electric field, B is the magnetic flux density, H is the magnetic field, J is the current density, ρ_v is the volume charge density and D is the electric flux density. It is important to notice that in electromagnetic problems the fourth Maxwell's law, that concerning to the electrostatic Gauss's law, is not considered. In addition to the considered three Maxwell's laws, the following constitutive laws are taken into account as well.

$$\vec{B} = \mu \vec{H} \quad [T] \qquad \vec{J} = \sigma \vec{E} \quad [A/m^2] \tag{2}$$

μ is the permeability of the medium, and σ is the conductivity of the medium. To solve these equations a vector model is used, in which the magnetic vector potential $\vec{A}$ is considered as state variable. Applying this vector model the objective function (4) is solved at each node of the mesh, and the value of this state variable is obtained as result at each node.

The relationship between magnetic flux density and magnetic vector potential can be described as,

$$\vec{B} = \forall \times \vec{A} \quad [T] \tag{3}$$

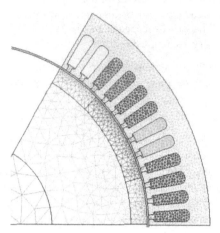

Figure 3. Meshing of the electric machine

Figure 4. Description of different stages in the FEM simulations

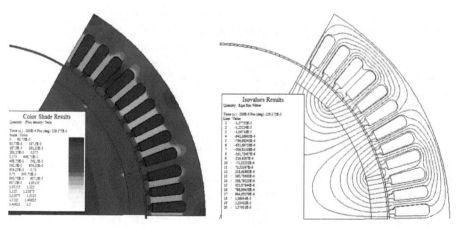

A) Spatial Distribution of the Flux Density   B) Representation of the EquiFlux Lines

Figure 5. Representation of the magnetic flux density and the EquiFlux lines

In transient magnetic model the problem can be considered as quasi-steady-state so that the variation in time of the electric flux density can be neglected ($\frac{d\vec{D}}{dt} = 0$) [1]. According to this assumption, the computed function at each node is simplified.

$$\forall \times \left(v_o[v_r](\forall \times \vec{A}) - \vec{H}_c\right) + [\sigma]\left(\frac{\partial \vec{A}}{\partial t} + \overrightarrow{grad}\,V\right) = 0 \tag{4}$$

v_o is the reluctivity of the vacuum ($v_o = \frac{1}{\mu_o}$), $[v_r]$ is the tensor of the relative reluctivity of the medium, H_c is the coercive magnetic field which is considered only in case of permanent magnets and V is the electric scalar potential.

3.3. Results analysis

During the resolution of the problem the magnetic vector potential is computed at every node of the mesh. After that, in the third stage different local and global results are analyzed which are derived from the magnetic vector potential. For example, the flux density is computed applying expression (3). Meanwhile, the magnetic flux crossing certain S surface can be computed by the following expression.

$$\phi = \int_S \vec{B} \cdot d\vec{s} = \int_S (\forall \times \vec{A}) \cdot d\vec{s} = \int_l \vec{A} \cdot d\vec{l} \quad [Webber] \tag{5}$$

The torque produced by the motor is computed applying the well known virtual work method [2].

$$T = \left.\frac{\partial W'(i,\theta)}{\partial \theta}\right|_{i=cte} = \frac{1}{2}\frac{\partial L}{\partial \theta}i^2 + \frac{1}{2}\frac{\partial \Re_g}{\partial \theta}\phi_{pm} + N\frac{\partial \phi_{pm}}{\partial \theta}i \quad [Nm] \tag{6}$$

W' is the co-energy stored in the air-gap, L is the self-inductance of stator winding, i is the supplying current, $\Re_g$ is the air-gap reluctance, ϕ_{pm} is the magnet flux, N is the number of turns per phase and θ is the mechanical angle of the rotor. As it is shown in expression (6) the torque produced by permanent magnet machines is the sum of three components. The first component is known as reluctance torque, the second term is known as cogging torque and the third term is known as electromagnetic torque. In the particular case of surface mounted motors, the first torque component is null. On the other hand the cogging torque is oscillatory so that it contributes to the torque ripple. Regarding to the electromagnetic torque it has a main average component but it has also certain torque ripple component. So the total torque ripple in permanent magnet motors is due to cogging torque and electromagnetic torque ripple. In the Fig 6 the cogging torque and the overall torque produced by the motor are shown during an electric period. In this particular case the order of the main cogging torque component is $n = 6$ meanwhile the order of the main total torque ripple component is $n = 12$. In the case study of section 6 de influence of this torque ripple upon the ride comfort in a lift is evaluated.

3.4. Iron losses computation by the FEM

The total iron losses in permanent magnet synchronous machines (PMSM) can be separated in two components: The Eddy current losses in permanent magnets and the iron losses in

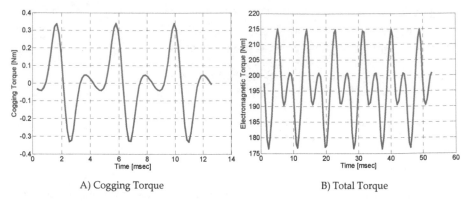

| A) Cogging Torque | B) Total Torque |

Figure 6. Different torque components in permanent magnet motors

electrical sheets. Hence, the computation of these losses components in FEM is carried out in two different ways. The Eddy current losses in permanent magnets are calculated as the active power dissipated in these regions considering the magnets as solid conductors. Meanwhile the losses in electrical sheets are computed by the tool so called Loss Surface Model (LSM) which is integrated in the FEM software FLUX® for that purpose.

Loss Surface Model (LSM) for Iron Losses Computation in Electrical Sheets

Normally FEM software do not consider the magnetic hysteresis cycle of electrical sheets in the solving process, but an approximated so called normal magnetization curve is taken into account. As the iron losses depend on the area enclosed by the hysteresis loop, these losses are not computed in the solving process and their calculation is addressed typically as a post processing task.

One calculation option consists in the local computation of the iron losses using the loss separation method and considering local induction waveforms calculated in the solving process. As main disadvantages, the accuracy of this computation method depends on some coefficients, and additional phenomenon as skin effect and minor loops are not normally considered.

FLUX®presents an alternative tool so called Loss Surface Model for iron losses computation. This tool is supposed to be more accurate than the method based on the losses separation theory, because it does not depend on empirical coefficients and it considers additional phenomena such as the skin effect or the minor loops [3]. Due to this fact, in this case the LSM has been used as post processing tool for the calculation of the losses in electrical sheets.

In Fig 7-B the iron losses computation process using the LSM is explained. First of all the electromagnetic problem is solved in the FEM calculating the temporal waveform of induction at each node of the mesh. In the post processing analysis the temporal waveforms of the magnetic field strength are reconstructed from the induction waveforms obtaining in this way local hysteresis loops. This reconstruction of the magnetic field strength is performed using a model based on one $H(B, dB/dt)$ surface curve which is characteristic to each material. This curve must be obtained by experimental characterization of the material. In Fig 7-A the surface curve of a given material is shown. The model that reconstructs the magnetic field strength can be described by the following expression.

$$H(B, dB/dt) = H_{static}(B) + H_{dynamic}(B, dB/dt)$$ (7)

In Fig 8 two different hysteresis loops reconstructed by the LSM tool at the same local point are shown. Resulting hysteresis loops with sinusoidal and PWM voltages are plotted. In this way the minor loops caused by the PWM voltages can be appreciated.

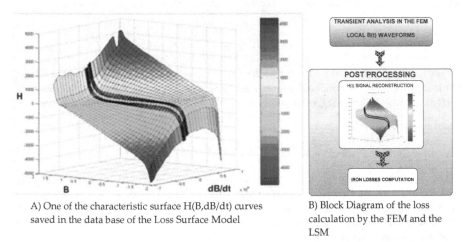

A) One of the characteristic surface H(B,dB/dt) curves saved in the data base of the Loss Surface Model

B) Block Diagram of the loss calculation by the FEM and the LSM

Figure 7. Electric sheet losses computation methodology based on the LSM tool

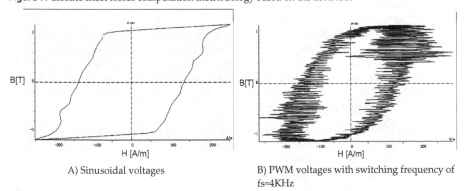

A) Sinusoidal voltages

B) PWM voltages with switching frequency of fs=4KHz

Figure 8. Local hysteresis loops reconstructed by the Loss Surface Model with sinusoidal and PWM voltages

Once the local hysteresis loops are obtained, the specific iron losses are computed integrating the area enclosed by each hysteresis loop.

$$P = \frac{1}{T}\int_T \int_B H \cdot dB \quad [W/m^3] \tag{8}$$

Eddy Current Losses in Permanent Magnets

In case of non-fractional machines normally the Eddy current losses in permanent magnets can be neglected. While in fractional machines these losses are more significant due to the high harmonic content of the armature field, so they cannot be neglected [4]. In order to make the proposed method usable to both non-fractional and fractional machines, the calculation of the permanent magnet losses is also addressed. Eddy current losses are due to the asynchronous harmonics of the magnetic field induced by the armature winding in the air-gap. The induced Eddy current density in the magnets can be expressed as in the following equation.

$$J_{eddy} = -\frac{1}{\rho}\int \frac{\partial B}{\partial t} \cdot r \cdot dt + C \quad [A/m^2] \tag{9}$$

Where J_{eddy} is the induced Eddy current density in the magnets, ρ is the electrical resistivity of the magnets, B is the armature magnetic field and r is the radius of the point in which the current density is represented. The Eddy current losses are computed using the following formula.

$$P_{eddy} = \frac{2p}{T}\int_0^\pi \int_{-\frac{\alpha}{2}}^{\frac{\alpha}{2}} \int_{R_1}^{R_2} J_{eddy}^2 \cdot \rho \cdot r \cdot dr \cdot d\theta \cdot dt \quad [W] \tag{10}$$

Where R_1 and R_2 are the inner and the outer radius of the magnets respectively, T is the period of the fundamental component of the armature field and α is the magnets span in mechanical degrees [5]. It is necessary to consider in the formula the constant C in order to assure that the induced Eddy currents are limited to one pole piece. That means that the different magnet poles are supposed to be electrically isolated.

Regarding to the computation of the magnetic field induced by the armature winding in the air-gap, there are two options for that purpose depending on if the Eddy current reaction field is neglected or not. In case this reaction field is neglected, the Eddy currents are considered resistance limited and this way they can be calculated performing magneto static simulations. However, in case the Eddy current reaction field has to be considered, it is necessary to perform time step simulations. In the proposed method, as the machine is co-simulated with MATLAB-SIMULINK®, the simulations are time stepped so the Eddy current reaction field is taken into account.

As far as the FEM simulation is concerned, magnets have to be defined as solid conductors. As the permanent magnets are electrically isolated, each one has to be associated to one solid conductor. In Fig 9 the electrical circuit associated to the permanent magnets is represented. It can be seen how each solid conductor has connected in parallel one resistor. It is because in the FEM software all the electrical components have to be connected in close circuit. These parallel resistances are set to very high values in order not to have influence on the losses computation.

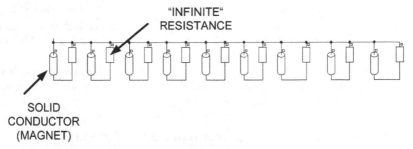

Figure 9. Associated electrical circuit to the permanent magnets

4. Matlab-simulink coupling to FEM software

Being MATLAB® numerical calculus software, FEM calculus can be carried out in MATLAB® without any external software. However the tendency is to use specialized FEM software for each physical domain like Electromagnetic, Fluid dynamics and so on. For example Cedrat's FLUX® software is well known electromagnetic FEM analysis software. Using FLUX® enables to design and study a wide range of electromagnetic devices such as different electrical machines, actuators or sensors.

However this software is usually generalist respect to the domain and an application approach of the software is usually desired for a more friendly use of the software by beginner users. That's why companies like Cedrat are providing programmatic tools for external piloting of their calculus Kernel.

Using some libraries, user can pilot a FLUX® file that has been prepared previously from MATLAB® for instance. Although several parameters are required to prepare the flux file, using external piloting, it is possible to limit the parametric study to a short number of parameters that are required to be visible by application user. The use of FLUX® calculus Kernel is now more application oriented and any user without FEM knowledge can use the calculus Kernel.

Another MATLAB® FEM collaboration example is the co-simulation. Usually the electromagnetic device that is being designed is connected to other external devices. Complex mechanical models, electrical circuits or hydraulic systems are some examples of models that can be easily modeled by MATLAB-SIMULINK® but cannot be included in the FEM software.

The simplest approximation to solve this multi-domain problem is the simplification of the electromagnetic device to an equivalent electric circuit based on lumped parameters such as resistance and inductances. This can be done with different levels of accuracy. For example, the inductance of a machine can be considered constant respect to the current of the machine. In a more precise approximation the saturation effect can be considered introducing a Look-up table to take into account the change of the inductance respect to the magnetic flux of the machine. In both cases, first FEM simulations are carried out and the values for the inductance are post processed to include them later in the MATLAB-SIMULINK® simulation. However this approximation cannot take into account torque ripples, instantaneous saturations and so on. If more accuracy is required, it is possible to couple the FEM problem to the MATLAB-SIMULINK® simulations. Cedrat provides a block to use in MATLAB-SIMULINK®. In this interface block inputs and outputs should be defined". Then, the FEM problem is solved at each time step of MATLAB-SIMULINK simulation. The convergence of this type of simulations is difficult but the accuracy is rather high.

5. Case study 1: Iron losses computation in electrical machines

It is widely known that the performances of electric machines depend strongly on the losses. The efficiency, the thermal behavior or the compactness are some of the design constrains which are strongly influenced by the losses. So it is very important to predict these losses accurately if an optimum design of the electric machine is required. The losses in electric machines can be divided in three main components: Joule losses, iron losses and additional or stray losses (mechanical losses, induced Eddy current losses in frames, etc). The Joule losses are relatively easy to compute from the armature resistance and current values. However, the other two components are rather more complicated to estimate. This work is focused on the calculation of iron losses which can be relevant in some cases depending on the machine topology, speed, saturation levels, etc.

Nowadays the majority of the electric machines are integrated in variable speed drives. That means that the motors are supplied by modulated voltages such as Pulse Width Modulated (PWM) voltages. It is well known that the additional current harmonics introduced by PWM voltages increase the iron losses. So it is necessary to consider the voltage characteristic in the computation process in order to achieve accurate results in loss computation.

The most extended way to define the iron losses is by the widely known loss separation method in which they are divided in three main components: hysteresis losses, classical Eddy losses and excess losses [6,7]. In case of non sinusoidal voltages, the high order harmonics of currents can accentuate the presence of some phenomena such as the skin effect or the minor loops which are not directly taken into account by theses classical methods. Many efforts have been dedicated to the adaptation of the initial definition of the iron losses given by *Bertotti* in [6] to consider all these phenomena. For instance, in [8] *Boglietti et al.* completes the expression of the classical Eddy losses component with the aim of taking into account also the skin effect. In [9] *Toda et al.* proposes a modification of the hysteresis losses formula in order to consider the minor loops. It is also possible to find in the literature some papers that deals with the iron losses computation under arbitrary supply voltages, mainly focused on pulse width modulated (PWM) voltages [8,10,11].

In this section a novel method for iron losses computation under non-sinusoidal supply voltages is proposed. The method consists in coupling the FEM software FLUX® from CEDRAT Company with the system simulator software MATLAB-SIMULINK®. The iron losses are computed by a post-processing analysis separating the computation of the Eddy current losses in the permanent magnets (PM) and the iron losses in electrical sheets. The simulation results have been compared with experimental results in order to validate the proposed method.

5.1. Iron losses computation by co-simulations

In the proposed methodology the steady state iron losses are computed by a co-simulation between the FEM software and the system simulator software. The power system comprising a two-level converter is simulated in MATLAB-SIMULINK®, whereas the electrical machine is modeled in the FEM software. This way it is possible to evaluate the performance of the electrical machine under the functioning conditions imposed by the converter, in a relatively short and rather accurate way.

The FEM software permits the coupling of electric circuits for transient analysis. Generally these circuits comprise passive elements such as resistances and inductances along with sinusoidal voltage and current sources. Nevertheless, if more sophisticated circuits are required to consider, for example a power converter, it is necessary to couple the FEM software with the circuit simulator software.

When the machine is supplied by a converter, it is driven by voltage. In these cases there is an inevitable transient period which takes several electrical cycles before the motor reaches the steady state. It is considered that at least a resolution of 10 samples per switching period is necessary to achieve accurate results. The simulation of several electric periods with so small step size would lead to such an amount of samples and such long time consumption that current driven simulations are chosen instead of voltage driven simulations. In current driven simulations it is enough considering only one electric period to compute the iron losses, which enables to decrease significantly the time consumption of the simulation. For example, taking 10 samples per switching period, one co-simulation characterized by a switching frequency of $fs=4KHz$ and a period of $T=25.82\ sec$, is carried out with a time step of $\Delta T=25\mu sec$ and it takes approximately 30 minutes.

The proposed method for iron losses computation is structured in three stages as it is shown in Fig 10. First of all the lumped parameters of the equivalent electrical circuit of the machine are calculated by the FEM. From this previous simulation the machine can be modeled with lumped parameters such as d-q axis inductances Ld and Lq, and the permanent magnet flux Ψpm. In the second stage the transient model of the machine in d-q axes is implemented in MATLAB-SIMULINK® using the lumped parameters previously estimated and a two level inverter is implemented as power supply. In this simulation the current waveforms in steady state are obtained for PWM voltages. Finally the co-simulation between the FEM software and MATLAB-SIMULINK® is carried out driving the FEM model of the electrical machine by current waveforms obtained in the previous stage. In this third stage the total iron losses are computed as the sum of the Eddy current losses in permanent magnets and the iron losses in electrical sheets.

In Fig 11 the total iron losses estimated by co-simulations for sinusoidal and PWM voltages are compared. It can be observed that the iron losses with PWM voltages are higher. Meanwhile in Fig 12 the resulting currents and electromagnetic torque are plotted for sinusoidal and PWM voltages. It can be noticed a significant difference in the ripples because of the PWM voltages.

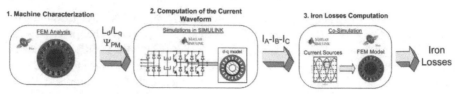

Figure 10. Proposed methodology for iron losses computation under non-sinusoidal voltages

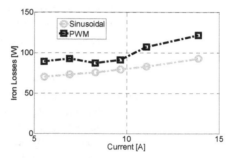

Figure 11. Iron losses computed with sinusoidal and PWM voltages with $f_s = 4KHz$

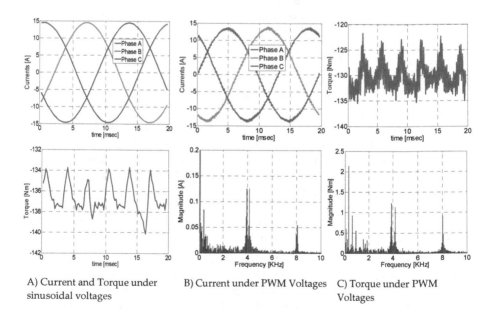

A) Current and Torque under
sinusoidal voltages

B) Current under PWM Voltages

C) Torque under PWM
Voltages

Figure 12. Co-simulation results obtained under sinusoidal and PWM voltages with $f_s = 4KHz$

5.2. Experimental results

In this section some experimental results are shown in order to prove the accuracy of the proposed method. For that purpose 7.4KW brushless motor has been analyzed in a test bench and the iron losses have been measured.

Description of the experimental test

In Fig 14 the test bench layout is shown. It consists of two machines, the one under test and the load motor, one torque sensor, one commercial controller for each machine and one power analyzer. During the test the controlled variables are the speed in case of the load machine and the torque in case of the machine under test. The test has been carried out controlling the d-axis current to zero avoiding in this way the functioning of the machine in the flux weakening operation mode. To calculate the losses, the loss segregation method has been implemented.

$$P_{in} - P_{cu} - P_{loss} - P_{mec} = 0 \tag{11}$$

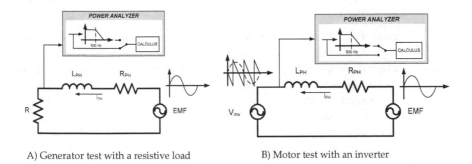

A) Generator test with a resistive load   B) Motor test with an inverter

Figure 13. Description of the performed tests in order to validate the sinusoidal losses computation method

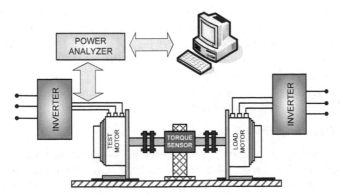

Figure 14. Test bench configuration

Where P_{in} is the active power consumed by the machine, P_{cu} are the Joule losses, P_{mec} is the mechanic power in the motor axis and P_{loss} is the sum of the iron losses and the mechanical losses. The value of P_{in} is calculated by the power analyzer which is connected to the input of the machine. To calculate the Joule losses, a high accuracy ohmmeter has been used due to the fact that the power balance is very sensitive to the errors in the resistance measurement. The mechanical power is calculated from the torque and speed measurements. As the test is carried out at constant speed, the mechanical power can be calculated as the following.

$$P_{mec} = T \cdot \Omega_m \quad [W] \tag{12}$$

Where T is measurement provided by the torque sensor and Ω_m is the mechanical speed measured by the encoder. In the power balance the only unknown variable is P_{loss} which involves two loss components, the iron losses and the mechanical losses. As the tests are performed at relatively low speeds (290 rpm) and the machine has been heated previously, the mechanical losses can be considered negligible in comparison with the iron losses. In addition all the tests have been carried out at constant speed in order to maintain the mechanical losses constant.

The configuration of the test bench does not allow supplying the machine with sinusoidal voltages. The possible solution would be to add RLC filters between the inverter and the machine or to use sinusoidal voltage supplies instead of the inverters. However in this case it has not been possible to implement neither of these solutions so finally it has been necessary to implement an alternative solution. The power analyzer comprises low pass band filters for the measured currents and voltage, which has been set to 500Hz. This way only the fundamental components of voltages and currents are considered for the computation of the power. The calculated power in this way is considered to be the power for sinusoidal voltages. However, before implementing this method, it has been validated performing two different tests which are described in Fig 13.

First of all the so called generator test is carried out. In this test a resistive load is connected to the terminals of the machine under test, which operates as a generator, and it is driven by the load motor at constant speed. This way the currents are sinusoidal and so the computed iron losses correspond to the sinusoidal voltages. After that the second test is performed using the inverter and with the machine working exactly at the same operation conditions that in the previous test. In this case the input filters of the power analyzer are configured to 500Hz. In both cases the resulting P_{loss} are very similar, with a difference less than 5%. Hence it is considered that the losses calculated with the filter are equivalent to the sinusoidal losses.

Validation of the simulation results

The proposed method to calculate the iron losses has been validated with experimental results. As the machine iron losses are closely related to the stator current density, the simulations and the tests have been done at same phase current magnitude. The switching frequency of the PWM voltage is fixed to $f_s = 4KHz$ during all the tests.

In Fig 15 the simulated torque and the experimental torque at different current values are shown for both cases, sinusoidal and PWM voltages. It can be noticed how the simulated and the experimentally measured torques are very similar.

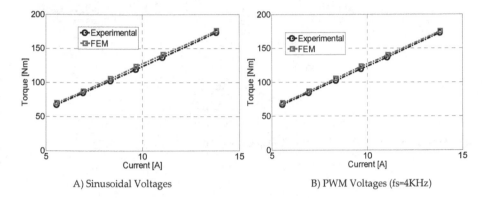

A) Sinusoidal Voltages   B) PWM Voltages (fs=4KHz)

Figure 15. Torque with Sinusoidal and PWM voltages

In Fig 16 the computed iron losses with sinusoidal and PWM voltages are shown. It is remarkable that certain differences arises between the co-simulation and the experimental results either with sinusoidal or PWM voltages. These differences are considered to be because of the mechanical losses which are not taken into account by the co-simulations. This difference is rather constant respect to the current and very similar in both cases with sinusoidal and PWM voltages. This behavior of the difference between simulations and test fits perfectly with the supposition that the difference is due to the mechanical losses.

Although there is a slight error in the prediction of the iron losses, an important point of this work is that the proposed methodology enables to calculate rather accurately the increase of the iron losses due to PWM voltages. In Fig 17-A the comparison between sinusoidal and PWM iron losses is shown. A coefficient can be defined to represent the increase of the losses due to the PWM modulation. This coefficient is defined as PWM losses factor K_{pwm} and it is calculated as following.

$$K_{pwm} = \frac{P_{PWM}}{P_{sin}} \tag{13}$$

P_{sin} are iron losses with sinusoidal voltages and P_{PWM} are iron losses under PWM voltages. As it is shown in Fig 17-B the PWM loss factor is approximately constant for every load conditions. So it can be concluded that the losses increase due to PWM voltages hardly depends on the current value. In the procedure presented in this work, the loss terms which are not taken into account are independent from the modulation which enables us to calculate very accurately the loss increase in spite of making a slight error in the loss estimation.

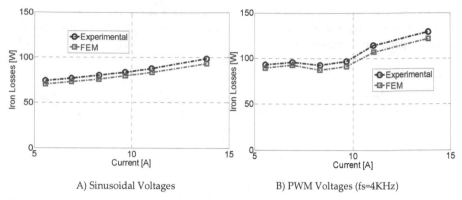

A) Sinusoidal Voltages   B) PWM Voltages (fs=4KHz)

Figure 16. Iron Losses with Sinusoidal and PWM voltages

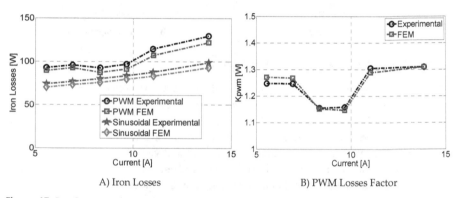

A) Iron Losses   B) PWM Losses Factor

Figure 17. Iron Losses and PWM losses factor K_{pwm}

6. Case study 2: Comfort analysis in elevators

The performance of the electric motor in an elevator is going to be studied by co-simulation. As the elevator is a very sensitive direct drive application, it is very important the smoothness of the torque. So in this case the influence of the torque ripple on the elevator performance is going to be evaluated.

In this study the overall elevator system is considered taken into account the control unit, the traction motor and the mechanical system. Thus, the control unit and the mechanical system are simulated in MATLAB-SIMULINK®, while the electric motor is simulated in the FEM software FLUX®.

6.1. Application description

An elevator is a complex system in sense that it may present resonances due to the elastic properties of ropes and the elasticity and damping effect between the frame and the cage of the lift [12]. Moreover, the resonant frequency of the system is variable, and depends upon the passenger load.

The elevator taken into analysis is a so-called 1:1 roping configuration which is shown in Fig 18-A. As main feature, it has a maximum speed of 1 m/s and a maximum acceleration of 0.5 m/s², with a capacity of 6 passengers. Considering a pulley diameter of 50 mm, rated value of 20 rad/sec and 200 Nm are required for the drive.

In Fig 18-B the frequency response of the acceleration of the cage to pulley torque variations for different load states is shown.

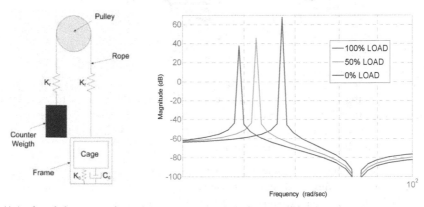

A) Analyzed elevator configuration   B) Bode diagram of the elevator system at
                                            different load conditions

Figure 18. Description of the analyzed elevator system

6.2. Co-simulation scheme

In Fig 19 the co-simulation block diagram is shown. The control strategy, the speed reference generator and the elevator model are implemented in MATLAB-SIMULINK®, while a precise machine model is simulated in FLUX®.

"Coupling with flux2d" function of MATLAB-SIMULINK® library allows data transfer between both simulation tools. In this function the following parameters have to be specified: the name of the FLUX® file, the input and output parameters, the sample time and the memory size to allocate. The inputs are the currents of phase A and B, and the mechanical speed. With these inputs, FLUX® model returns as outputs the electromagnetic torque and the position of the rotor. The torque is the input for the elevator model which computes the linear acceleration of the cage and the angular speed of the pulley. The speed is fed back along with the position which is aligned with the flux vector.

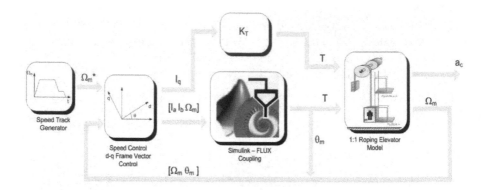

Figure 19. Co-simulation block diagram

Regarding to the speed of the elevator, it has to follow a specific track in order to get a good ride quality. In this case, this track is obtained by means of a speed track generator. The speed control is a vector control implemented in a d-q frame oriented to the magnet flux vector. The block diagram of that control is shown in Fig 20.

As it is shown in Fig 20, the electromagnetic torque is controlled acting upon Iq component. In this application flux weakening is not necessary, so Id component is null. Notice that current control is not implemented. The dynamic of current loops is so quick in comparison with the dynamic of the mechanical system that they can be omitted. So, control consists in a PI for speed regulation, a frame transformation from d-q to α-β and an inverse CLARKE transformation from α-β to abc.

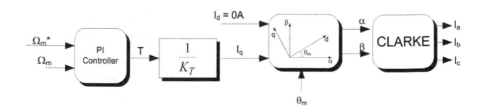

Figure 20. Speed Control Diagram

On the other hand, a proper choice of sample time is very important. It must not be too small in order to avoid too long simulation times. Otherwise, it has to have enough precision if accurate results are wanted. In this case, the aim of co-simulation is to evaluate the effect of torque ripple on vertical acceleration of the lift, so the sample time has to be small enough to get a proper resolution of that ripple. As it has been already explained, the frequency of the main torque ripple component is six times the fundamental frequency which is equal to 19 Hertz. So the torque ripple has a period of 8.77ms. Thus, a sample time of 500μs is chosen so as to use 17 samples for the definition of a period of the torque ripple.

Another critical aspect that affects final results is the mesh resolution of the machine model in FLUX®. A too accurate resolution may slow down the simulation. As the sample time, the mesh resolution has to be carefully set in order to get enough accuracy in the results in a reasonable simulation time.

6.3. Results

In this subsection the co-simulation results are presented. The simulation has been carried out under 50% of rated conditions, with a load of 3 passengers. Two machine models have been taken into account: an ideal one which consist in a constant gain equal to the torque constant K_T, and the FEM model (see Fig 19). In Fig 21-A it could be seen the track of the lift speed in which a little overshoot can be noticed. That is because the dynamic of the regulator has been limited in order to avoid the excitation of the system resonance by the control. In Fig 21-B the torque produced by the FLUX® model is presented.

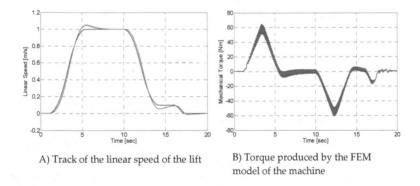

A) Track of the linear speed of the lift

B) Torque produced by the FEM model of the machine

Figure 21. Torque and speed obtained by co-simulation

In Fig 22 the resultant lift accelerations for an ideal machine model and for the FEM machine model are shown. Unlikely to the ideal case, the torque of the FLUX® model is not as smooth as application requires. Consequently, that torque ripple excites the mechanical resonances of the system, causing vibrations in the vertical acceleration. This phenomena lead to a notary worsening in the ride quality of the elevator.

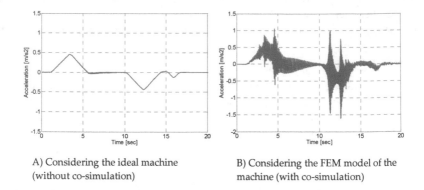

A) Considering the ideal machine   B) Considering the FEM model of the
(without co-simulation)   machine (with co-simulation)

Figure 22. Vertical acceleration of the cage obtained by simulation

7. Conclusions

In this chapter a co-simulation tool for analysis and design of electrical machines is proposed.

Two different case studies have been reported. In the first one co-simulation between the system simulator software and the FEM software are presented for the iron losses calculation under arbitrary voltages. A particular procedure is described to carry out current driven co-simulations in order to reduce as much as possible the computation load and the time consumption of the calculus.

The proposed method is validated by experimental tests. The estimated iron losses under sinusoidal and PWM voltages have a good agreement with the iron losses measured experimentally. So it can be stated that using this method it is possible to estimate the iron losses under arbitrary voltages without the need of prototyping, which could lead to less expensive and more flexible design processes.

In the second case study the performance of the electric machine in an elevator is evaluated. Thus, the vibrations caused by the motor in the elevator cage are studied applying the proposed co-simulation. It has been demonstrated that the torque ripple of the motor can affect negatively on the elevator comfort.

Probably the main drawback of these co-simulations is the required computation time. They ought to be carefully configured, on one hand to avoid too large computation times, and on the other hand to achieve an adequate accuracy.

As main conclusion it could be remarked that these co-simulations are very helpful tools which may allow accurate and relatively easy analysis of multi-domain systems in a relatively short development time.

Author details

Gaizka Almandoz, Gaizka Ugalde, Javier Poza
Faculty of Engineering,
University of Mondragon, Mondragon, Spain

Ana Julia Escalada
ORONA EIC. ELEVATOR INNOVATION CENTRE, Hernani, Spain

8. References

[1] CEDRAT. (2010). Flux 10 User Guide – Volume 3 – Physical Applications: Magnetic, Electric, Thermal,...

[2] Gieras, J.F. (2002) Permanent Magnet Motor Technology. Design and Applications. Marcel Dekker, Inc. 105p

[3] CEDRAT. (2005). Flux 9.1 User Guide - 2D and 3D Applications - New Features.

[4] Zhu, Z.Q., Ng, K., Schofield, N., Howe, D. (2004). Improved analytical modelling of rotor eddy current loss in brushless machines equipped with surface-mounted permanent magnets. *Electric Power Applications, IEE Proceedings*, vol. 151, no. 6, pp. 641-650,

[5] Zhu, Z.Q., Ng, K., Schofield, N., Howe, D. (2001). Analytical prediction of rotor eddy current loss in brushless machines equipped with surface-mounted permanent magnets. I. Magnetostatic field model. *Electrical Machines and Systems, 2001.ICEMS 2001.*Proceedings of the Fifth International Conference on 2 ed Beijing, China: Int. Acad. Publishers, pp. 806-809

[6] Bertotti, G. (1998). General properties of power losses in soft ferromagnetic materials. *Magnetics, IEEE Transaction on*, vol. 24, no. 1, pp. 621-630

[7] Fiorillo, F., Novikov,A. (1990). An improved approach to power losses in magnetic laminations under non-sinusoidal induction waveform. *Magnetics, IEEE Transactions on*, vol. 26, no. 5, pp. 2904-2910

[8] Boglietti, A., Cavagnino, A., Lazzari, M., Pastorelli,M. (2003) Predicting iron losses in soft magnetic materials with arbitrary voltage supply: an engineering approach. *Magnetics, IEEE Transactions on*, vol. 39, no. 2, pp. 981-989,

[9] Toda, H., Senda, K., Ishida, M. (2005). Effect of material properties on motor iron loss in PM brushless DC motor. *Magnetics, IEEE Transactions on*, vol. 41, no. 10, pp. 3937-3939

[10] Amar, M., Kaczmarek, R. (1995). A general formula for prediction of iron losses under nonsinusoidal voltage waveform. *Magnetics, IEEE Transactions on*, vol. 31, no. 5, pp. 2504-2509

[11] Boglietti, A., Lazzari, M., Pastorelli, M. (1997). Iron losses prediction with PWM inverter supply using steel producer data sheets. *Industry Applications Conference. Thirty-Second IAS Annual Meeting* vol 1, pp. 83-88

[12] Arakawa, A. and Miyata, K. (2002). A variable-structure control method for the suppression of elevator-cage vibration. *IECON 02, 28th annual Conference of the IEEE Industrial Electronics Society*, pp. 1830-1835.

Telecommunication-Communication Systems

MATLAB as a Design and Verification Tool for the Hardware Prototyping of Wireless Communication Systems

Oriol Font-Bach, Antonio Pascual-Iserte, Nikolaos Bartzoudis and David López Bueno

Additional information is available at the end of the chapter

1. Introduction

The ability to verify the capacity gains of novel signal processing techniques or the performance of new communication standards is one of the main research and development drivers of both academic and industrial entities. In this context, the signal processing community has adopted MATLAB as a flexible modelling, simulating and testing software development environment. MATLAB includes numerous toolboxes, open-source code and pre-compiled libraries, which facilitate the design of complex systems using high-level models and provides the means for rapid verification of signal processing algorithms and systems in a user-controlled environment. The growing number of its add-on features allows MATLAB to fill the gap between these high-level models and the physical implementation of systems; e.g., a real-time Field Programmable Array (FPGA)-based prototype. Moreover, the functionality of MATLAB is significantly extended with the use of Simulink [1], which serves as a schematic-entry design and programming environment. The integration of the System Generator blockset of Xilinx [2] to Simulink and the direct linking of the latter with the Xilinx FPGA-design toolchain enriches the target use-cases of the software. This approach allows the creation of FPGA binary executables from high-level models. MATLAB is also one of the most popular software-modelling environments, whose functionality is commonly interfaced nowadays with instruments to provide connectivity, control and programming solutions for rapid prototyping and testing. In fact, MATLAB scripts are increasingly used to program a wide variety of testing, signal generation and signal analysis hardware instruments. Thus, the programming versatility of MATLAB allows it to be used as a key software component in complex testbeds, which comprise a multitude of software programming interfaces and heterogeneous hardware instruments. The role of such testbeds is crucial because they enable the prototyping and validation of advanced research concepts under realistic conditions, providing at the same time a detailed account of hardware requirements and implementation feasibility.

The present chapter aims at describing how MATLAB can be used as a design and verification tool in the different phases of migrating a high-level model to a real-time hardware prototype, using as a case study the implementation of a real-life wireless communication system. The chapter proposes a generic design methodology and, finally, provides a practical case study related to the implementation of a real-time Multiple Input Multiple Output (MIMO) mobile WiMAX (i.e., IEEE 802.16e) system [3, 4].

1.1. Considered development scenarios

Real-time system-prototyping using FPGA devices is a painstaking and time-consuming process that goes beyond a controlled computer simulation. In this context, MATLAB is having a manifold contribution as a design and validation tool. In order to successfully leverage the advices, techniques and design methodology, it is required to define the specific development scenarios that have to be considered by digital design developers.

It is important to note that this chapter will not cover model-based, MATLAB-to-Register Transfer Level (RTL) design flows (e.g., by using the Simulink and System Generator tools). Adversely, a custom-code programming strategy will be followed, where the user carefully designs each component of the system and takes into account the constraints of real-world hardware and signals. Our focus is to unveil the key role that MATLAB plays when the design objective is the creation of custom Hardware Description Language (HDL) code (e.g., Very High Speed Integrated Circuit - VHSIC - HDL, VHDL) that targets high-performance wireless communication prototypes. In fact, converting a MATLAB model into a working VHDL code for such FPGA-based prototypes requires a considerable effort. Although the automatic MATLAB-to-HDL conversion is becoming increasingly popular, its efficiency is still under scrutiny by the FPGA designer community [5]. The main concern raised is that the MATLAB-to-HDL automatic conversion is not yet mature enough to cover the needs of processing demanding FPGA-based systems, where performance and constraints imposed by the size and the embedded resources of the target device, may occasionally render this option unsuitable. The direct MATLAB-to-HDL translation accepts only very limited constructs that can be automatically translated into hardware [6]. Other approaches, involving an intermediate stage of Matlab-to-C code generation, can be used as an alternative. The produced C code is consequently processed by C-to-HDL synthesis tools subject to certain modifications (i.e., the generated C code contains unsupported constructs that prevent a seamless translation to HDL code).

As already mentioned, the automatically-produced HDL code is usually not as efficient as the custom hand-written HDL one. This difference is becoming a significant factor to be considered when stringent FPGA area utilization conditions apply or when performance and achievable clock frequencies do matter [7]. The modern FPGA devices and the corresponding synthesis tools seem to address the issues mentioned before. This is due to the extraordinary capacities of the new devices in terms of embedded resources (logic, memories dedicated Digital Signal Processing - DSP - logic) and the significant improvement of the FPGA design and implementation tools. However, it is anticipated that the FPGA-based prototyping and the respective FPGA design tools are due to be challenged soon by the constantly aggregated performance requirements and algorithmic complexity of next generation wireless communication systems. Therefore, an incremental design approach based on custom-HDL coding is once again expected to be the most reliable solution to sort out well-established digital design problems (i.e., dense FPGA designs with compute intensive requirements and hard to achieve timing constraints [8]). The only difference is that the complexity of such problems is scaled because of the massive amount of FPGA logic, memories and embedded components that need to be addressed. Custom HDL coding provides the means to control every important aspect of the design, which requires an in-depth knowledge of the low-level RTL architecture.

The design and validation principles presented herein could be applied in many digital-design cases. Nonetheless, the application-domain will be narrowed down to well-characterized case studies, in order to help the reader to assimilate the described concepts, methodology and examples. Thus, this chapter explores the uses of MATLAB when the custom-HDL design flow is employed for the prototyping of systems with design and implementation requirements similar to the ones described next:

I Real-time system prototyping
- *Advanced wireless communication system*: Algorithms and hardware technologies able to offer data rates higher than current systems are needed to cope with the requirements of emerging wireless communication systems. The MIMO technology, using multiple antennas both at the transmitter and receiver sides, combined with Orthogonal Frequency Division Multiplexing (OFDM) constitute a suitable technique for the implementation of advanced wireless communication systems. Additionally, the Orthogonal Frequency Division Multiple Access (OFDMA) is used to target Multi-User (MU) scenarios in high mobility conditions. A prominent MIMO configuration scheme proposed in OFDMA systems is the closed-loop one, where the receiver is providing information to the transmitter related to the current channel conditions by means of a dedicated feedback link. This improves the performance and usage of resources in scenarios with multiple competing users and fast channel fading (e.g., it is applied adaptive carrier allocation, Adaptive Modulation and Coding - AMC). The scenario can be augmented by contemplating an adaptive power-aware PHY-layer that takes into account the interaction with higher layers of the communication stack and user requirements (e.g., in terms of quality of service, monetary cost or battery constraints). The compliance with a modern wireless communication standard (e.g., mobile WiMAX, Long Term Evolution - LTE) also adds strict design requirements.
- *Real-time operation*: The real-time operation implies transmission and reception of an uninterrupted data flow. To tackle the challenges of real-time operation, especially when accounting for wide bandwidth at baseband, a low-latency pipelined processing structure has to be designed. The latter requires a large amount of memory resources for the intermediate data storage and implies a complex control plane, which usually features multiple clock domains. Moreover, the operation of high performance wireless communication systems results in a growth of the design, implementation and validation complexity. Notwithstanding, the real-time operation gives the opportunity to realize closed-loop strategies requiring dynamic adaptation of the system in response to the actual channel conditions.

- *FPGA-based prototyping*: The inherent parallelism of FPGA devices is providing the means to prototype bit-intensive systems following an RTL-design approach. In this context, the designer has to evaluate the computational, storage and timing requirements of the target FPGA-based platform, in order to ensure that the implementation is feasible. Additionally, the FPGA-based prototyping of baseband DSP algorithms using a custom HDL design flow, typically implies the use of fixed-point logic. Therefore, an optimum trade-off between the implementation complexity and the precision of the internal calculations has to be defined (i.e., maximizing the dynamic range at baseband). The effort of interfacing the user design with the on-board buses, peripherals and components residing outside the FPGA device (e.g., Analog-to-Digital - ADC - and Digital-to-Analog - DAC - circuitry) is a critical part of the on-board validation, because it can be proved quite costly in terms of time. Finally, the losses introduced by the ADCs, DACs and baseband digital logic can be calculated to quantify the precision of the FPGA-based prototype.
- *Heterogeneous hardware setup*: The validation of high performance FPGA-based prototypes requires close to real-world testing conditions, which provide the means to properly tune the operating behaviour according to the defined deployment-scenarios. This in turn implies the use of a testbed which features a heterogeneous hardware setup. A real-time testbed typically comprises Radio-Frequency (RF) front-ends, signal generation and signal acquisition hardware boards, FPGA-DSP based baseband boards and other specialized equipment (e.g., radio channel emulator, digital oscilloscope). Moreover, testbeds have data-capturing interfaces that enable the performance characterization of the system (i.e., off-line data post-processing and metric calculation in MATLAB-space).

II Offline system prototyping

- *Advanced wireless communication system*: The goal in this case is the rapid prototyping of advanced techniques able to satisfy the requirements of future wireless communication systems. As it will be detailed in the following lines, the prototypes that principally operate offline make a series of assumptions to simplify the testing and deployment conditions and remove or ignore real-life implementation constraints. This inevitably results in a partial validation of the systems under test, especially for those cases where exhaustive offline data processing is practically impossible. Nonetheless, their contribution is also significant because they enable the design and preliminary experimental evaluation of algorithms beyond the state-of-the-art.
- *Off-line operation*: One of the main drivers of rapid prototyping is based on hybrid experimental testbeds that combine real-time processing and offline software-based post-processing. Such platforms, make use of commercial Vector Signal Generator (VSG) instruments equipped with arbitrary waveform generators. These are configured with user-generated MATLAB vectors, which represent the output of a baseband transmitter and eventually produce a real-time RF signal that is transmitted using either antennas or a direct cable connection. Offline testbeds may also use a RF channel emulator or other instruments that combine signal generation and channel fading. On the receiver side the data is stored in large buffers (e.g., FPGA) and retrieved in order to be post-processed offline. The captured signals are used as test vectors that facilitate the modelling of the baseband signal processing algorithms of the receiver (i.e., MATLAB high-level model of the system). This prototyping methodology allows the rapid verification of the functionality and performance of

algorithms. However, certain data capturing and post-processing limitations apply, especially when the testing requires reception of long data frames under high mobility conditions. In fact, although offline prototyping accelerates the design and testing of algorithms, it is important to understand its foundations and design particularities e.g., unconstrained computational and storage resources, unlimited precision using floating-point implementation, no need to account for real-life implementation constraints or the complexity of the control plane, perfectly synchronized signals or ideal channels are typically assumed. Thus it is clear that in order to achieve a thorough analysis of the implementation cost and feasibility of the target system (especially in scenarios requiring dynamic responsiveness or high mobility), real-time prototyping has to be employed.

- *Hardware/software partitioning*: the flexibility of non real-time prototyping in terms of resource requirements allows the designer to select an optimum hardware/software partitioning accounting for the implementation cost. It is a common practice to maintain the algorithms in MATLAB space, while only the RF section and the data capturing operates in real-time. Alternatively, a subset of the signal processing algorithms can be mapped to a DSP or a FPGA implementation, following a co-simulation or hardware-in-the-loop testing approach.

- *Hybrid prototyping*: the granularity of the prototyping strategy can be adjusted to fit the specific design and budget requirements. For instance a reduction in the prototyping complexity can be achieved by implementing/emulating more features in MATLAB-space or by making assumptions and system-wide simplifications. In hybrid prototypes a portion of the design resides in a computer simulation, while at the same time dedicated memory interfaces facilitate the communication with the bit-intensive portion of the design that runs on a FPGA device. This prototyping method downscales the real-time processing requirements in order to cope with the data-exchange constraints between the software and hardware processing domain.

1.2. The role of MATLAB in the design and validation process

As it has been described in the previous section, system-prototyping involving FPGAs and other specialized hardware equipment is subject to non idealities and certain signal impairments, which are not usually considered in a computer-based simulation (i.e., high-level models). Moreover, the heterogeneous hardware boards used for the prototyping of high performance real-time systems impose a series of hardware constraints in terms of processing capacity, available memory, maximum achievable clock frequency, I/O interfacing, DAC/ADC resolution and power consumption.

In the following sections, it will be shown how the previously described operating conditions and constraints can be either modelled or considered in MATLAB throughout the design and implementation process. The goal is to demonstrate the plural contribution of MATLAB in the FPGA-based rapid prototyping, beyond its well-established function as a high-level modelling tool:

I *Definition of system requirements*: Apart from its traditional operating perception, MATLAB can be used as a key companion throughout the analysis of system requirements in terms of computational resources and cost (e.g., implementation complexity, optimal hardware platform selection). Once the deployment scenario and specifications are strictly defined (e.g., operating frequencies, channel bandwidth, channel specifications, sampling frequencies, DAC-ADC resolution) the high-level MATLAB model of the system can be modified to satisfy real-life system characteristics, according to the following key points:

- Account for system-wide signal impairments introduced by the complete hardware processing chain (baseband, RF and channel).
- Identify the most critical signal-processing blocks that play a definitive role in system's performance and computational load.
- Select the optimum algorithms satisfying a trade-off between resulting precision, hardware specifications and implementation complexity (e.g., required FPGA-re-sources).
- Adjust the data quantization at the different baseband processing stages.
- Account for the specifications, operation and functionality of the memory and control planes.

II *Co-simulation*: A very useful practice during the early stages of prototype development is to implement and simulate different parts of the target system using different design approaches and tools; i.e., one part of the system remains modelled and simulated in MATLAB, while the rest is designed using lower-level HDL simulation tools. The co-simulation of the differently modelled parts requires the communication of MATLAB with third party simulation environments. This can be realised by utilizing the data importing and exporting capabilities of MATLAB, or as it will be discussed later, by exploiting the interfaces of MATLAB with certain third-party tools. For instance, the prototyping of systems or algorithms using offline testbeds typically implies that the complex signal processing algorithms, and other emulated functionalities that serve the testing scenario, remain modelled in MATLAB. Using standard I/O functions, binary data can be read, written and quantized in MATLAB-space, providing a direct way to communicate with the remaining portion of the system which resides in an HDL-based simulation (i.e., using equivalent I/O connectivity options). The same co-simulation methodology can be used to test an algorithm, an independent processing block or a complete system designed in MATLAB against its HDL-based counterpart (designed in third party RTL simulation tools). This type of co-simulations have a critical contribution in the prototyping of real-life FPGA-based systems, because they provide the means to assess the fixed-point precision of the independent processing blocks comprising a digital baseband system and also because they produce reliable test vectors, which enable the performance validation of the RTL-algorithms.

III *Verification of the hardware-produced results*: MATLAB supports data importing and exporting in various formats and includes a series of pre-compiled libraries and mathematical functions. The latter facilitate the post-processing of data captured by baseband processing boards and assist the verification of the results produced by a FPGA-based prototype. The only requirement as far as the baseband signal processing platform is concerned is its ability to capture large amount of data in files that could be imported in MATLAB.

IV *Rapid-prototyping*: the previously described features and design-capacities of MATLAB are making it a prime candidate for the off-line prototyping and validation of wireless communication systems. Indeed, MATLAB plays a key role in off-line testbeds that are used to prototype state-of-the-art MIMO-OFDM systems [9–13].

The process of mapping a high-level MATLAB model to HDL logic and consequently to FPGA-based hardware is a complex and costly process, where many crucial decisions need to be taken. These include among others the environment where the system will be deployed, the expected operating conditions and the target implementation technology. MATLAB can be easily interfaced with third-party EDA tools and hardware equipment [14], a fact that facilitates this decision-making process. Additionally, the use of MATLAB in all prototyping-stages makes easier the interaction between different design-teams by providing a common working framework.

2. Design methodology

The design, implementation and on-board testing of high performance wireless communication systems under realistic conditions implies an undertaking with high stakes. Thus, the adoption of a well-structured design, implementation and validation methodology is a paramount requirement. The aim of this section is to offer an insight to a robust, yet generic, methodology, which demonstrates the contribution of MATLAB during the FPGA prototyping stages using a custom HDL design entry. The effectiveness of the proposed methodology is analysed using a practical case study, which involves the prototyping of a real-time MIMO mobile WiMAX system.

A fundamental guideline that applies throughout the design, implementation and on-board validation phases is a multi-stage testing strategy (Fig. 1). This starts from a baseband-to-baseband system testing under ideal conditions. The latter is performed both in simulation-time (MATLAB and consequently HDL-based) and at real-time in the target hardware platform using a direct connection of the transmitter and receiver. The scenario can then be augmented by adding the conversion stages (i.e., ADC and DAC). This implies re-simulating the MATLAB and HDL code and finally validate the FPGA implementation in real-time (i.e., connecting via a cable the output of the DAC device with the input of the ADC device). The final testing stage can be divided in two sub-stages; the first includes a direct cable connection of the RF front-ends and the second the inclusion of channel either by using antennas or a real-time channel emulator (both sub-stages can be priorly simulated in MATLAB and in HDL). This incremental testing approach allows the step-by-step characterization of the system.

2.1. Starting point

The development of a processing demanding real-time wireless communication system requires a wide range of skills, resources and time. A commonly accepted commencing point is the design of a baseline version of the target system, which complies with the following design requirements:

- *Modularity:* This feature facilitates the substitution, modification, extension and/or reuse of specific parts of the design.

- *Downscaled specifications:* The initial design-efforts should focus on the core signal processing algorithms and on the most critical aspects of the overall system architecture (e.g., high-throughput pipeline structures combined with efficient memory and control planes).

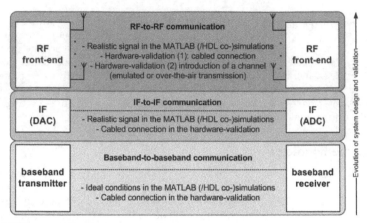

Figure 1. Multi-stage testing strategy

Once the baseline system-model is designed and validated, the proposed methodology can adjust the granularity of the system by accommodating more advanced features.

2.2. Proposed methodology

This section gives the details of the proposed design methodology, which is depicted in Fig. 2.

I *Basic transmitter modelling*: The first vital requirement for the design of any wireless communication system is the definition of the transmitted signal. The modelling of the transmitted signal is in most cases bound to the specifications of a wireless communication standard, which indicatively includes the OFDM parameters, the duplexing mode, the format and length of the frame, the number, value and location of the pilot tones, the guard-band size, the inter-carrier spacing, the available bandwidth sizes and the RF operating bands. At this initial stage the model of the transmitted signal is based on certain ideal conditions i.e., using floating-point logic, assuming unlimited processing resources during design-time and not accounting for signal-impairments (e.g., channel effects, noise).

II *Hardware-validation of the baseband transmitter model*: The output of the MATLAB model has two vectorial components, namely the in-phase and quadrature (I/Q). By writing the I and Q outputs in a MATLAB file (i.e., with file extension .mat), it is possible to make a direct hardware validation of the baseband transmitter model. As it was previously described, this is made feasible considering that numerous modern VSG instruments[1], provide the necessary API to download such files to an internal memory of the instruments. The latter with the help of an arbitrary waveform generator provides the real-time baseband digital I/Q signals, which then pass from the required DACs and RF conversion stages to produce the desired signal at the selected RF band. This is an indicative test and verification flow where MATLAB

---

[1] The described functionality is available, for instance, on the VSGs provided by Agilent (*http://www.agilent.com*) or Rode & Schwarz (*http://www.rohde-schwarz.com*). Further information on other hardware manufacturers supporting MATLAB communication may be found in *http://www.mathworks.com/products/instrument/hardware*.

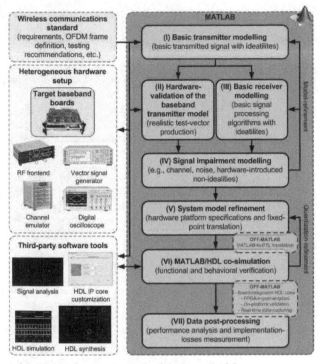

Figure 2. Proposed design, implementation and validation methodology

is directly interfaced with advanced instrumentation to produce a real-time signal. This signal can be then processed by specific testing hardware (e.g., signal analysers, digital oscilloscopes), which communicate with proprietary third-party software in order to perform standard-compliance tests. Additionally, the transmitted signal can be introduced via a cable connection to the receiver's RF down-converters (i.e., no channel should be used at this initial design stage) and after passing from the ADC stage at the receiver's acquisition boards, it can be retrieved using the FPGA devices and dedicated external memories of the baseband signal processing boards. The captured data constitute realistic test vectors that can be used for the development of the MATLAB model of the receiver, whereas the whole testing procedure permits a refinement of the initial transmitter model (see points IV and V). The testing setup described before could also include specialized equipment that add realistic signal impairments (e.g., real-time emulation of a selected channel, addition of noise or of Carrier Frequency Offset - CFO). However, such operating conditions make unreliable the capturing of test-vectors until the digital front-end of the receiver is developed and tested at the target FPGA board.

III *Basic receiver modelling*: The next step is the modelling of the signal processing algorithms at the receiver side. As in the case of the transmitter, the ideal MATLAB model of the receiver uses floating-point logic and does not have any design limitations in terms of processing and memory resources. The functional testing of the complete system is conducted by running a MATLAB simulation of the transmitter and receiver models (i.e., ideal baseband-to-baseband signal). This could be extended by using the test vectors captured in the previous step (i.e., hardware-validated MATLAB model of the transmitter). Although the design is still not constrained by the limitations of the entire hardware processing platform, the performance of different algorithms could be studied, including those whose computational complexity makes their real-time prototyping challenging. The designer has therefore the opportunity to estimate the ideal performance of the overall system.

IV *Signal impairment modelling*: After finishing the ideal MATLAB model of the entire system, it is time to start adding real-world impairments. The latter are inherent features of hardware components and effects applied to analogue signals when propagating in physical mediums. This implies modifications of the originally designed MATLAB model to meet new operating conditions. The most indicative impairments that need to be modelled in MATLAB is the transmission over a defined channel, the addition of noise and CFO, the coupling of the baseband signal with the Local Oscillator (LO) and the introduction of a Direct Current (DC) level by the hardware platform. As a result, it is obtained a model of the transmitted signal that is significantly closer to real-world conditions. The signal processing algorithms at the receiver have to be modified and upgraded to account for these signal impairments.

V *System model refinement*: Additional modifications are required to the MATLAB baseband model of the system, before starting the challenging stage of mapping it to RTL code. The MATLAB models of the transmitter and receiver have to account for the the hardware platform specifications (i.e., ADC/DAC features, internal buses, I/Os, available FPGA-resources - including embedded memory and specialized digital signal processing - DSP - blocks, etc.). Thus, the signal processing algorithms must be refined as follows:

- *RTL-implementation awareness*: it is widely known that not all MATLAB structures or functions are implementable in an FPGA. Even if equivalent HDL constructs exist, they are used during simulation time but do not serve for logic synthesis (e.g., a for-loop construct with undefined number of iterations). Moreover, MATLAB includes several pre-compiled DSP functions (e.g., Fast Fourier Transform - FFT) and provides abstract arithmetic operators (i.e., the user calls the same operator independently of the type of the operands). For instance, the '$*$' operator provides the multiplication for integer, real or complex numbers, arrays and matrices. Although these MATLAB features provide a powerful workbench for users, it is common quite a mistake to underestimate the computational complexity and the internal arithmetic calculations of such operations, especially when they are meant to be mapped on a real-time RTL-based implementation (see example 2.1). It is therefore a key design requirement to evaluate the implementability and arithmetic complexity of the algorithms comprising the target system, in relation to the maximum processing and memory capacity of the target FPGA device. This usually gives a first idea of which design partitioning strategy can be followed (e.g., using various FPGA devices or a combination of FPGA devices and DSP microprocessors). The importance of this evaluation stage for the mapping of the MATLAB model to RTL code is crucial and may result in selecting different algorithms and lightweight versions of pre-compiled arithmetic functions. Another important task is to estimate the storage and intercommunication needs. This is made feasible by including in the MATLAB model a high-level representation of the memory and control planes.

- *Translation to fixed-point arithmetic*: the FPGA-based prototyping of wireless communication systems implies the use of fixed-point logic at baseband. This is a significant design constraint that has to be evaluated considering that MATLAB modelling is based by default on floating point arithmetic. In general terms the floating-point operations dramatically increase the FPGA logic utilization and result in lower clock speeds and longer pipelined structures when compared to fixed-point logic[2]. The designers are responsible for mapping the MATLAB algorithms to an HDL-based fixed-point logic, which in fact is a demanding and non-trivial task. The latter implies that all internal processing stages of the transmitter and receiver (both in MATLAB-space and HDL-design space) have to be appropriately simulated to tune them at an optimum fixed-point dynamic range, applying numerous truncation and scaling steps to achieve the best arithmetic precision. Additionally, each of the implemented HDL blocks has to be co-tested with the equivalent portion of the floating point Matlab model to ensure that the system performance is not compromised (see point VI). A very handy modification of the MATLAB model that assists the comparison with the equivalent RTL code is to apply quantization at the outputs of selected processing blocks that represent functional partitions of the design. This quantization process emulates the fixed-point logic.
- *Hardware constraints and specifications awareness*: the functionality of the MATLAB model of the transmitter and receiver can be further adapted to account for hardware-introduced constraints, brining it more close to real-life testing conditions. For instance, the MATLAB model can be adjusted to the Dynamic Range (DR) of the DAC/ADC circuitry of the target boards. The system DR depends on the modulation scheme, the modelled signal-impairments and the DAC/ADC specifications (i.e., number of bits of the produced samples and applicable amplifier gains). Additionally, a number of pre-compiled HDL IP cores used in the prototyping stage of FPGA-based DSP algorithms (e.g., FFT, Digital Down Converter - DDC, pipelined divider) are offering a limited range of input/output data-width options. This results in further quantization analysis, assuming that the reception of samples is scaled within a certain dynamic range. The on-board FPGA implementation entails a series of other design limitation, which are hard to be emulated at MATLAB space. Indicative examples of such hardware implementation features include the interfacing of the FPGA design with high-speed buses and the latencies introduced by several FPGA IP cores; the latter increase the intermediate storage requirements and add more complexity to the control plane.
- *Satisfy a trade-off between numerical complexity and system performance*: The system designer has to discover the optimal achieved performance of the designed system (i.e., baseband, RF and channel propagation stages) through a recursive process, taking into account the processing and memory resources of the target FPGA device, the additional inherent constraints of the hardware platform and the minimum required yield of the system. The latter is subject to specific prerequisites related to numeric precision, throughput and compliance with certain performance metrics (e.g., Bit Error Rate - BER, average data rate). This means that the MATLAB model will be adjusted until the designer achieves the desired performance, which eventually will allow him to pass to the next design stage of RTL coding.

---

[2] It is useful to mention that specific floating-point arithmetic libraries, Intellectual Property (IP) cores, embedded microprocessors and other dedicated processing components can be used in FPGA devices to serve the needs of particular applications that require this type of arithmetic operations [15, 16]

Example 2.1: let's consider the simple multiplication of two complex numbers, $a = 2.5 + 3.2i$ and $b = 1.7 - 4.5i$. In MATLAB a user would simply type 'c = a * b' abstracting away the underlying calculation. However, when considering a RTL design many other aspects must be considered.

First, let us assume a dynamic range of input samples that satisfy the $(-8, 8)$ margin. Also let us consider a binary representation of samples with 16 bits, where 4 bits are used to represent the sign and the integer part and the remaining bits are used to represent the fractional part. The I and Q components of the complex numbers have to be represented separately. This can be modelled in MATLAB using the `quantizer`, `num2bin` and `bin2num` functions of the fixed-point toolbox:

```
q = quantizer([16 12]);
I_a = num2bin(q,real(a)); Q_a = num2bin(q,imag(a));
I_b = num2bin(q,real(b)); Q_b = num2bin(q,imag(b));
```

Furthermore, the complex multiplication has to be broken down to basic operations. In MATLAB this can be done as follows:

```
I_c = bin2num(q,I_a)*bin2num(q,I_b) - bin2num(q,Q_a)*
bin2num(q,Q_b);
Q_c = bin2num(q,Q_a)*bin2num(q,I_b) + bin2num(q,I_a)*
bin2num(q,Q_b);
```

A first approximation of the error introduced by quantization can be measured with a simple subtraction: `quant_loss_I = real(c) - I_c; quant_loss_Q = imag(c) - Q_c;`

Moreover, each arithmetic operation in RTL coding results in a bit-width grow: e.g., the multiplication of two N-bit operands results in $2N$ bits and the addition of two N-bit operands results in $N+1$ bits. Therefore, RTL coding implies that each of the previously described intermediate operations has to be considered separately:

```
intermediate_op1 = I_a * I_b, results in 32 bits
intermediate_op2 = Q_a * Q_b, results in 32 bits
intermediate_op3 = intermediate_op1 - intermediate_op2, results in 33
bits
```

To sum up, a quantization adjustment (i.e., bit-alignment in case the bit-width of the different operands grows differently) and/or a data-truncation will be required between the different intermediate calculations to limit the overall computational complexity. Additionally, in order to achieve a better timing performance of the FPGA design, the intermediate calculations of complex operations are placed in different clocked-processes: i.e., the calculation of 'intermediate_op3' 'intermediate_op1' and 'intermediate_op2' would be placed in a different clocked process. Therefore, a latency of one clock cycle would be introduced at each intermediate calculation. Although the bit-width growth and the introduced latencies are not modelled in MATLAB, it is highly recommended to analyse such aspects in order to assess the system's complexity. A complex calculation may result in a change of the quantization, which in turn will require further modifications of the MATLAB model.

VI *MATLAB/HDL co-simulation*: Each portion of the implemented HDL code that forms a functional component of the system has to be co-simulated with the equivalent partition of the MATLAB model. This allows to assess both the functional correctness and the achieved performance. As already mentioned before, there are several ways to use the co-simulation methodology. An indicative example is when part of the system simulation resides in MATLAB space, whereas another portion is hosted in a third party HDL design tool; the output of the MATLAB model can be quantized and saved to a file, which can be inserted to the HDL-based simulation. The results produced by the HDL simulation can also be quantized and written to a file, which is fed back to MATLAB. This is a very useful way to verify the functionality and inter-working of the system that is implemented in different simulation domains. In addition, it also enables the evaluation of the precision achieved by the HDL model by comparing its performance with the non-quantized results produced by the MATLAB model. It is important to highlight the vital role of co-simulations for selecting an optimum quantization that satisfies a trade-off between precision and computational complexity. Finally, the MATLAB/HDL co-simulations provide the best means to evaluate and test HDL IP cores and common signal processing operations (e.g., optimizing the trade-off between implementation complexity and result precision requires the calculation and truncation of the produced outputs).

VII *Data post-processing*: Data can be captured at different baseband processing stages once the system (or parts of it) is implemented in a target FPGA board. This data can be inserted in MATLAB after using the proper quantization to enable the off-line calculation of the required performance metrics (e.g., BER, Signal-to-Noise Ratio - SNR, Error Vector Magnitude - EVM). MATLAB can also be used to automate the post-processing of the captured data-frames, and provide a reliable calculation of the desired performance metrics (i.e., mean value over thousands of data samples).

The end of a major design cycle is reached when the performance of the RTL prototype is finally validated on real-time hardware and does not require any further modifications. This gives the opportunity to the system designer to introduce additional features by iterating over the previously described methodology. The proposed incremental design approach implies a relative low effort to augment the features of a working prototype. This is mainly due to the fact that a modular and reusable code is already available, while at the same time the critical parts of the design and the system bottlenecks are well defined. The same applies to the hardware platform which is already thoroughly studied and characterized.

3. A practical case study

This final section presents a practical case study of the manifold contribution of MATLAB throughout the entire design, development and prototyping stages of a real-time mobile WiMAX system [3, 4]. The use-cases focus on the Single Input Single Output (SISO) configuration of the system [17] that features one antenna at the transmitter and receiver sides respectively. Taking as an exemplar basis the development of the SISO system, the presented incremental design methodology can be reused to develop the MIMO system, which however is not covered in this chapter. The main specifications of the target system are summarized in table 1.

The GEDOMIS® testbed (see Fig. 3), was used to prototype and validate the system described in this chapter. GEDOMIS® features multiple APIs, dedicated signal analysis software tools

Parameter	Value
Wireless telecommunication standard	IEEE 802.16e-2005
Antenna schemes: SISO, SIMO, MIMO	1x1, 1x2, 2x2
RF band (GHz)	2.595
IF (MHz)	156.8
Channel bandwidth (MHz)	20
Baseband sampling frequency (MHz)	22.4
ADC sampling frequency (MHz)	89.6
Cyclic prefix (samples)	512 (1/4 of the symbol)
Modulation type	QPSK
Duplex mode	TDD
FFT size	2048
OFDM symbols per frame	48
Supported permutation schemes	PUSC and AMC (DL)
Diversity scheme (2x2 MIMO)	Matrix-A (Alamouti)

Table 1. Basic OFDM and PHY-layer specifications of the described system.

and a heterogeneous hardware setup. The latter comprises signal generation equipment, multi-channel signal conversion boards, a real-time radio channel emulator and FPGA-based baseband signal processing boards [18]. The examples detailed in the remaining of the chapter do follow the previously proposed multi-stage testing strategy (see Fig. 1) and do not always require the use of the full set-up of this testbed.

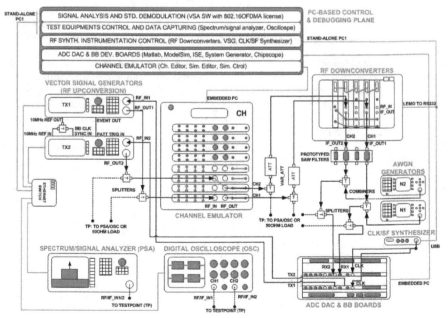

Figure 3. The GEDOMIS® testbed setup.

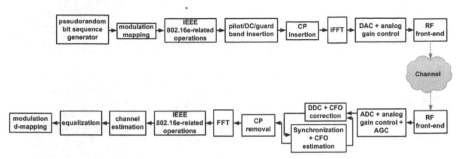

Figure 4. Basic architecture of the SISO transmitter and receiver systems.

3.1. PHY-layer prototype of a single antenna mobile WiMAX transceiver

Fig. 4 shows a simplified functional block diagram of the SISO mobile WiMAX system. Taking as a reference the design methodology presented before, this section gives an example of the MATLAB usage in each prototyping stage.

I *Basic transmitter modelling*: The first task is the accurate definition of the OFDM-based frame structure. Thus, it has to be identified the basic function of the different frequency subcarriers within each OFDM symbol. In our case, the frame is structured according to the Partial Used Subcarrier (PUSC) and the AMC subcarrier permutation schemes, which are defined in the mobile WiMAX standard [19]. The main characteristics of both OFDM symbol structures are summarized in table 2. Example 3.1 shows the MATLAB-modelling of the processing block responsible for inserting the pilot subcarriers, the DC and the guard bands, according to the mobile WiMAX specifications. The additional subcarrier organization and permutation operations required by the WiMAX standard can be easily designed in MATLAB-space. Finally, the use of a standard inverse FFT function provides the ideal I/Q baseband outputs of the transmitter (i.e., floating-point values).

Scheme	Parameter (per OFDM symbol)	Value
PUSC	Data subcarriers	1440
	Pilot subcarriers	240
	Null subcarriers	368
	Clusters	120
	Subcarriers per cluster	14
	Subchannels	60
	Data subcarriers per subchannel	24
AMC	Data subcarriers	1536
	Pilot subcarriers	192
	Null subcarriers	320
	Bands	48
	Bins per band	4
	Subcarriers per bin	9
	Subchannels	32
	Data subcarriers per subchannel	48

Table 2. Principal parameters of the PUSC and AMC permutation schemes.

Example 3.1: Fig. 5 shows the pilot distribution in the PUSC permutation scheme, described in the mobile WiMAX standard.

Figure 5. Location of the pilot symbols in the PUSC permutation scheme.

Taking into account this pilot distribution, the following MATLAB code represents the insertion of the pilot tones in a PUSC-structured OFDM frame:

```
%The PUSC-formatted OFDM symbols (i.e., outputs of the block in
charge of the IEEE 802.16e-related operations) are loaded in the
variable 'mWiMAX_PUSC_data'.
load('mWiMAX_PUSC_data')
PUSC_zone_length=30;

%There will be 240 pilots per OFDM symbol.
pilot=4/3+j*0; %Pilot value defined by the WiMAX standard.

%Each PUSC OFDM symbol contains 120 clusters of 12 contiguous
data subcarriers, where 2 pilots will be added.
evenSymb=1;
data_and_pilots=[];
for symb_index=0:PUSC_zone_length-1
symb_offset=symb_index*120*12;
ofdm_symbol=mWiMAX_PUSC_data(symb_offset+1:symb_offset+120*12);
cluster=[];
pilotCluster=[];

for cluster_index=0:119
subc_offset=cluster_index*12+1;
cluster=ofdm_symbol(subc_offset:subc_offset+11);
if evenSymb
pilotClus=[cluster(1:4) pilot cluster(5:7) pilot cluster(8:12)];
else
pilotClus=[pilot cluster(1:11) pilot cluster(12)];
end
ofdm_symbol=[ofdm_symbol pilotClus];
end

data_and_pilots=[data_and_pilots ofdm_symbol];
evenSymb=mod(evenSymb+1,2);
end

%A total of 368 null subcarriers are inserted.
ofdm_symbol=[zeros(1,184) ofdm_symbol(1:840) 0
ofdm_symbol(841:1680) zeros(1,183)];
```

II *Hardware-validation of the baseband transmitter model*: As already described before, the I/Q output vectors of the MATLAB model of the ideal transmitter can be stored (separately) in a MATLAB file. The latter can be downloaded to an internal memory of a VSG instrument (as described in Example 3.2). The VSG can be programmed to use these vectors in order to produce a real-time RF signal. This is made feasible by exploiting its embedded arbitrary waveform generator, DAC devices and RF upconversion circuitry. The validation of this signal using third party software tools and hardware instruments is very important, considering that several signal impairments and hardware constraints can be identified during early design stages.

Example 3.2: The first step for the prototyping and testing of the ideal transmitter MATLAB model using off-line testbed principles, requires the storage of the output I/Q components in two files.

```
%The frequency-domain data produced by the baseband transmitter
(i.e., before the IFFT) is loaded in the variable 'BB_data'.
load('BB_data')

%A short silence period precedes each frame.
silence_length=2560*5;
transmitted_signal=zeros(silence_period_length,1);

%The frame is composed by a preamble and 48 OFDM symbols.
for symb_index = 1:49
BB_ofdm_symbol=BB_data(2048*(symb_index-1)+1:(2048*symb_index));
%Conversion from frequency to time domain.
time_ofdm_symbol=zeros(512+2048,1);
time_ofdm_symbol(513:end)=ifft(BB_ofdm_symbol);

%Inclusion of the CP (i.e, the CP is a copy of the last 512
symbols of the OFDMA symbol).
preamble_length=512;
time_ofdm_symbol(1:preamble_length)=time_ofdm_symbol(1537:end);
transmitted_signal=[transmitted_signal; time_ofdm_symbol];
end

%I/Q component extraction.
custom_Tx_I=real(transmitted_signal);
custom_Tx_Q=imag(transmitted_signal);

%Creation of the 'custom_Tx_frame.mat' file to stimulate the VSG.
save('custom_Tx_frame.mat', 'custom_Tx_I', 'custom_Tx_Q');
```

Fig. 6, 7 and 8 show the configuration of the Agilent Signal Studio Toolkit. The latter is the software programming interface used to configure an Agilent E4438C VSG with the 'custom_Tx_frame.mat' file.

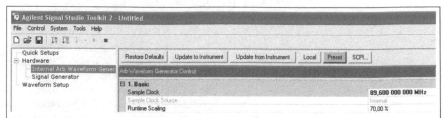

Figure 6. Agilent Signal Studio Toolkit configuration: ADC sampling frequency.

The principal parameters that need to be defined by the user to properly conduct the hardware-validation of the ideal transmitter, are the DAC sampling frequency, the desired RF band and the names of the variables of the MATLAB-generated file containing the I/Q components. The VSG is then able to apply the required IF-to-RF upconversion and provide a realistic RF signal.

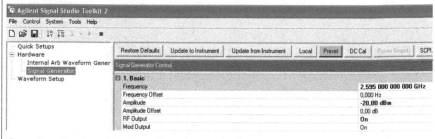

Figure 7. Agilent Signal Studio Toolkit configuration: RF band.

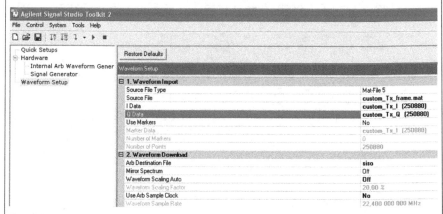

Figure 8. Agilent Signal Studio Toolkit configuration: loading of the I/Q components of the MATLAB model of the ideal transmitter.

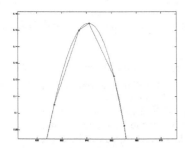
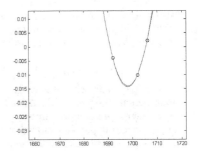

Figure 9. As it can be observed, the deviation between the ideal and the estimated channel is notable
when using a linear interpolation, which accounts only for the two closest pilots for each subcarrier. On
the contrary, the obtained results are better when applying a quadratic interpolation approach which
uses three neighbouring pilots in the calculations.

Using a RF-to-RF cable connection data can be captured at the receiver baseband boards.
This provides realistic test vectors that will be later used to design and debug the
MATLAB model of the receiver.

III *Basic receiver modelling*: The first step is to model the ideal received signal. In this sense, it
is assumed that the received signal is identical with the transmitted one, without making
use of quantizations or accounting for signal-impairments. In other words, an ideal
baseband-to-baseband communication is modelled as follows:

$$c(t) = \tilde{x}(t), \tag{1}$$

where $x(t)$ represents the equivalent transmitted baseband signal.

The modelling of the receiver is based on WiMAX-defined processing functions (e.g.,
permutation of the subcarriers) and common signal processing operations (e.g., FFT).
MATLAB provides the ideal modelling environment to compare the performance
tradeoffs of different signal processing algorithms. As an example, Fig. 9 shows the
comparison of a linear and a quadratic interpolation for a pilot-based channel estimation
algorithm. This type of algorithm design and benchmarking allows the designer to
make early decisions tailored for the specifications of the target hardware platform.
Nonetheless, the validation of the critical parts of the receiver, such as the synchronization
or the channel estimation requires a signal model that is closer to real-world conditions
(i.e., accounting for impairments and hardware constraints). Once this modified version
of the received signal is available, the designer is able to make a precise selection of
algorithms that are suitable for the anticipated channel conditions and the characteristics
of the target hardware platform.

IV *Signal impairment modelling*: Having already modelled the ideal system, the next step is
to modify the signal model to include the expected signal impairments. This requires
the analysis of the main specifications and performance of the target hardware. In
the test-case described herein, certain signal impairments such as the I/Q gain and
phase imbalances or LO drifts are ignored because of the performance indicators and
specifications of the equipment comprising the GEDOMIS® testbed. It is important
however that each designer exhaustively examines the complete set of potential signal
impairments and ignore only those that have negligible effects to the received signal.
This procedure is subject to generic signal processing and propagation principles, but

also requires a hardware-specific analysis of potential impairments (i.e., different for each testbed). In our case, the resulting refined received signal model at the output of the RF down-converters can be expressed as follows:

$$c(t) = \Re\{x(t) \cdot e^{j2\Pi(f_{IF} + \Delta f)t}\} + A \cdot cos(2\Pi(f_{IF} + \Delta f)t + \varphi) + w(t), \tag{2}$$

where $x(t)$ represents the useful part of the received baseband signal, f_{IF} is the Intermediate Frequency (IF), Δf is the Carrier Frequency Offset (CFO), $A \cdot cos(2\Pi(f_{IF} + \Delta f)t + \varphi)$ represents the unwanted residual carrier located at the center of the useful signal-spectrum (i.e., introduced by the LO coupling at the transmitter) and, finally, $w(t)$ is the Gaussian noise. The useful part of the received baseband signal can be expressed as:

$$x(t) = \tilde{x}(t) \star H(t), \tag{3}$$

where $\tilde{x}(t)$ is the equivalent transmitted baseband signal and $H(t)$ is the equivalent baseband of the time impulse response of the channel between the transmit and receive antennas. Example 3.3 shows the MATLAB model of the refined signal shown in equation (2). Additionally, other aspects related to the RF transmission, reception and downconversion of the signal are also contemplated (e.g., oversampling).

Example 3.3: MATLAB code for the signal impairment modelling.

```
%A custom IFFT function, providing an oversampled output is
required (i.e., the ADCs are oversampling by 4).
function samples = ifft_x4oversamp(BB_ofdm_symbol)
temp_symbols = zeros(8192,1);
temp_symbols(1:1024) = BB_ofdm_symbol(1:1024);
temp_symbols((8192-1024+1):8192) = BB_ofdm_symbol(1025:2048);
samples = ifft(temp_symbols,8192);
%----- function end -----

%To simulate the channel a coefficients file will be used.  The
channel will be loaded in the variable 'channel'.
load('channel_coefficients')
%The frequency-domain data produced by the baseband transmitter
(i.e., before the IFFT) is loaded in the variable 'BB_data'.
load('BB_data')

%A short silence period precedes each frame:  now we have to
account for the over-sampling of the ADCs.
silence_length=2560*5*4;
transmitted_signal=zeros(silence_period_length,1);

%The frame is composed by a preamble and 48 OFDM symbols.
for symb_index = 1:49
BB_ofdm_symbol=BB_data(2048*(symb_index-1)+1:(2048*symb_index));
%Introduction of the LO coupling (i.e., DC carrier is not 0).
BB_ofdm_symbol(1)=2;
```

```
%Conversion from frequency to time domain.
time_ofdm_symbol=zeros(2048+8192,1);
time_ofdm_symbol(2049:end)=ifft_x4oversamp(BB_ofdm_symbol);
%Inclusion of the CP (i.e, the CP is a copy of the last 512
symbols of the OFDMA symbol - oversampled by 4).
preamble_length=512*4;
time_ofdm_symbol(1:preamble_length)=time_ofdm_symbol(8193:end);
transmitted_signal=[transmitted_signal; time_ofdm_symbol];
end

%The modelled CFO will be equivalent to a third of the
intercarrier separation.
eps_freq=-1/3;

%Convolution of the frequency domain signal with the channel and
inclusion of the CFO and the noise.
SNR=25;
first_sample=silence_length+preamble_length+1;
mean_power = mean(abs(transmitted_signal(first_sample:end)).^2);
noise_power = mean_power/(10^(SNR/10));
received_signal = conv(transmitted_signal,channel);
rand_I=randn(size(received_signal));
rand_Q=randn(size(received_signal));
received_signal = received_signal+sqrt(noise_power/2)*(rand_I +
j*rand_Q);
received_signal = real(received_signal.*exp(j*2*pi*((156.8 +
(eps_freq*22.4/2048))*(1:length(received_signal))'/89.6)));
```

V *System model refinement*: In order to have a MATLAB model that provides a close match to the prerequisites of RTL coding, further modifications and refinements have to be conducted. This principally involves the emulation of fixed-point arithmetic in specific outputs of the MATLAB model. The trade-off between resulting precision and computational complexity has to be investigated. The more bits used to represent the fixed-point data, the more precision is achieved in the arithmetic operations. Considering that the prototyping target is a high performance real-time wireless communication system, it is required to use additional bits for the representation of signals, which consequently increases the FPGA processing and memory requirements. Different quantizations can be tested to analyse their effect both on independent processing stages, as well as on the overall system performance. An indicative example is when 16-bit words are used for the intermediate calculations of a custom MATLAB FFT function, featuring a radix-2 butterfly structure. This results in an aggregate quantization loss of $87 \cdot 10^{-2}$. The equivalent loss when using 32-bit words is reduced down to $13 \cdot 10^{-7}$. By inserting the quantized results to each of the remaining processing stages of the signal processing chain, it can be evaluated the performance-loss of the overall system. Hence, retaking the example mentioned before, the 16-bit quantized outputs of the FFT result in a performance degradation of the channel estimation (i.e., the precision-loss of the estimated coefficients for the pilot tones increases the error during the interpolation stage). Example 3.4 presents the modified version of the MATLAB signal, which accounts for hardware constraints and applies the desired quantization. It is assumed a 14-bit ADC, a QPSK modulation and a value of the pilot signals of $\pm 4/3$ (defined in the WiMAX standard). For this testing scenario the DR is set to $[-1.9, 1.9]$: i.e., 2 bits represent the sign and the integer part and the remaining bits represent the fractional part.

VI *MATLAB/HDL co-simulation*: this section gives representative examples of the MATLAB versus HDL co-simulations, which is a vital procedure that has to be applied in all FPGA prototyping cases. Continuing from the previous example, the digitized IF signal at the receiver (i.e., ADC outputs) will be processed by the DDC component, which comprises a programmable digital synthesizer and a complex Finite Impulse Response (FIR) lowpass filter that eliminates out-of-band components. The input signal at the DDC is multiplied with a sine and a cosine (produced by the digital synthesizer). This multiplication results in the I and Q vector components, which are finally filtered and decimated in order to produced the desired baseband signal. This procedure is considered a key functionality of the Software Defined Radio (SDR). The digital synthesizer can be tuned on-the-fly by accessing a digitally-controlled register. This fact allows designers to correct the CFO, an inherent impairment of real-life RF front-end systems.

Example 3.4: MATLAB code that models the constraints introduced by the utilization of a particular ADC.

```
ADC_quantization=quantizer([14 12]);
gain=1.9/max(abs(received_signal));
ADC_samples = (received_signal.*gain)';
ADC_samples_binary = num2bin(ADC_quantization, ADC_samples);
ADC_samples_quantized = bin2num(ADC_quantization,
ADC_samples_binary);
```

Example 3.5 describes how the Xilinx DDC IP core was configured using MATLAB. In more details, we have used the Filter Design and Analysis Tool (fdatool), to design the required low-pass filter and produce the filter coefficients required for configuring the DDC core. Considering the importance of the DDC for the correct operation of the receiver, the MATLAB versus HDL co-simulation provided a crucial contribution for the evaluation of the fixed-point precision and guided the tuning of the configurable parameters featured in the DDC IP core.

Example 3.5: the SISO mobile WiMAX receiver requires the design of a low-pass filter with a decimation stage (denoted as polyphase decimator filter in the DDC IP). The configuration parameters of the fdatool are shown in Fig. 10.

The resulting filter has 103 coefficients, which can be quantized and exported to a file (i.e., with file extension .coe). The latter can be used to configure the Xilinx DDC IP core, as depicted in Fig. 11.

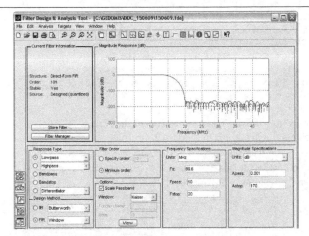

Figure 10. Utilization of the `fdatool` to design a FIR low-pass filter.

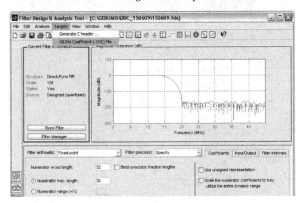

Figure 11. Exporting the FIR low-pass filter coefficients.

The code of the equivalent MATLAB model of the DDC, using the coefficients generated by `fdatool` is the following:

```
%The 'eps_freq' parameter represents the estimated CFO, as
returned by the synchronization block.
function baseband_signal = DDC(ADC_samples, eps_freq)

%The FIR-coefficients generated with 'fdatool' are loaded onto
the 'hfilter' variable.
load('hfilter')

%Modelling of the DDC functions (including CFO-correction).
cos_samples = ADC_samples.*cos(2*pi*(22.4-eps_freq*22.4/2048)*
(1:length(ADC_samples))/89.6);
```

```
sin_samples = -ADC_samples.*sin(2*pi*(22.4-eps_freq*22.4/2048)*
(1:length(ADC_samples))/89.6);
filter_cos = conv(cos_samples,hfilter);
filter_sin = conv(sin_samples,hfilter);
baseband_signal = filter_cos(1:4:end)+j*filter_sin(1:4:end);
%----- function end -----
```

Fig. 12 shows how the digital filtering stage of the Xilinx DDC IP can be configured using the coefficients file produced in MATLAB.

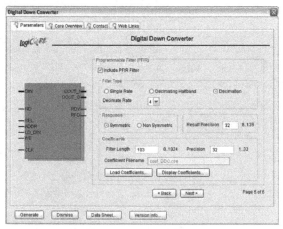

Figure 12. Configuration of the digital filtering stage of the DDC IP core using the MATLAB-generated coefficients.

Example 3.6 covers the main steps required to verify the behaviour and performance of an independent processing block (built using HDL code), by interfacing it with the MATLAB model of the remaining components of the system. The one-to-one comparison of the HDL model with its MATLAB counterpart provides a reliable analysis of the implementation losses (i.e., fixed-point versus floating point) and facilitates the selection of an optimum quantization (i.e., trade-off between precision and computational complexity, optimization of the bit-alignment and truncation operations).

Example 3.6: The MATLAB and VHDL code of the DDC processing stage that is required to run the co-simulation is quoted next. The output of the MATLAB model is written to a file, which is later used as a test vector of the RTL-simulation:

```
%The quantized outputs of the ADC are written to a file, which
will be used to stimulate the DDC IP core.
fileOut=fopen('DDC_core.in','w');
```

```
for k = 1:length(ADC_samples_quantized)
DIN = num2bin(ADC_quantization,(ADC_samples_quantized(k)));
fprintf(fileOut,'%s\n',DIN);
end
fclose(fileOut);
```

In the following simplified version of the VHDL code of the DDC block, the
MATLAB-generated signal will be used as input to the RTL code. Additionally, the
results produced by the HDL simulation are written to a file. This is used in recursive
manner for the MATLAB simulation of the remaining processing blocks of the receiver:

```
-The quantized outputs of the ADC are read from a file and used
as inputs to the DDC IP core.
FILE inputFile :  TEXT OPEN READ_MODE IS "DDC_core.in";

-The RTL-generated outputs are written to a file, which will be
used to stimulate the MATLAB model.
FILE outputFile :  TEXT OPEN WRITE_MODE IS "DDC_RTL.out";

-Instantiation of the Xilinx DDC IP core.
DDC_core_ins :  DDC_core PORT MAP (
 -Input ports
CLK => clock_adc,
SEL => reset,
DIN => data_in,
ND => data_valid_in,
LD_DIN => prog_DDS_value,
ADDR => prog_DDS_addr,
WE => prog_DDS_write_enable,
 -Output ports
RFD => ready_for_data,
RDY => output_ready,
DOUT_I => BB_I_comp,
DOUT_Q => BB_Q_comp);

-Read MATLAB-generated data from a file to stimulate the DDC.
PROCESS
VARIABLE L_IN : LINE;
VARIABLE DATA : STD_LOGIC_VECTOR(13 DOWNTO 0);
BEGIN
reset <= '1';
data_in <= (others => '0');
data_valid_in <= '0';
prog_DDS_addr <= cnt_DDCreg;
WAIT FOR 44.64 ns;
reset <= '0';
data_valid_in <= '1';
```

```
FOR k IN 0 TO cnt_lengthDDC LOOP
READLINE(inputFile,L_IN);
READ(L_IN, DATA); data_in <= <= DATA;
WAIT FOR 11.16 ns;
END LOOP;
WAIT;
END PROCESS;

- Write the RTL-results to a file to stimulate the MATLAB model.
PROCESS(clock_adc)
VARIABLE L_OUT : LINE;
BEGIN

IF RISING_EDGE(clock_adc) THEN
IF output_ready = '1' THEN
WRITE(L_OUT, BB_I_comp);
WRITELINE(outputFile, L_OUT);
WRITE(L_OUT, BB_Q_comp);
WRITELINE(outputFile, L_OUT);
END IF;
END IF;
END PROCESS;
```

When comparing the 32-bit words at the output of the HDL-based DDC processing block with the equivalent stage of the MATLAB model, we realize that we may truncate this word to 16 bits with negligible precision losses. The required quantization is also obtained during this stage. Finally, in order to use the HDL-generated outputs in the MATLAB-simulation of the remaining blocks of the receiver, the following MATLAB code is required:

```
-The RTL-outputs of the DDC are read from a file and used as
inputs to the MATLAB receiver.
fileIn=fopen('DDC_RTL.out','r');
VHDLResult=fscanf(fileIn,'fclose(fileIn);

DDC_quantization=quantizer([32 26]);
BB_I_comp=[];
BB_Q_comp=[];
k=1;
for l=1:(cnt_lengthDDC+1)/2
binTmp=VHDLResult(k:k+31);
BB_I_comp(l)=bin2num(DDC_quantization,binTmp);
k=k+32;
binTmp=VHDLResult(k:k+31);
BB_Q_comp(l)=bin2num(DDC_quantization,binTmp);
k=k+32;
end
```

```
-The simulations show that a truncation to 16 bits can be applied
(i.e., q([16 14]) -> (27 DOWNTO 12) in RTL).
BB_I_trunc=[];
BB_Q_trunc=[];
for l=1:(cnt_lengthDDC+1)/2
BB_I_trunc(l)=BB_I_comp(5:20);
BB_Q_trunc(l)=BB_Q_comp(5:20);
end
```

VII *Data post-processing*: Once the FPGA-based prototype presents a stable operation, data can be captured in different parts of the system to evaluate its performance. This data could then be processed in MATLAB to calculate the desired metrics. When the goal is to characterize the performance of a system under mobility conditions, hundreds of data captures (e.g., generated with different channel seeds) containing several complete frames have to be captured and processed under different operating conditions (e.g., modify the SNR). MATLAB can be used to automate the calculation of the performance metrics, as shown in example 3.7.

Example 3.7: A simplified version of a MATLAB function, which automates the calculation of the EVM. The function relies on a predefined name-structure for reading the files:

```
%Function to automate the calculation of the EVM from real-time
post-equalization data captures.
function automatic_EVM_calculation(channel_spec, initial_rep,
final_rep, SNR_steps)

EVM_experiment=[];

for repetition = initial_rep:final_rep
for scenario = 1:SNR_steps
%Generation of a predefined 'file_name'
file_name=['postequal_' channel_spec '_' SNR_step '_'
num2str(repetition)];
%Call to the function calculating the EVM
EVM_array=EVM_calculation_HW_capture(file_name);
%Calculation of the mean value, conversion to dB and storage
EVM_experiment(index,scenario)=10*log10(mean(EVM_array));
end
index=index+1;
end

save(['postequal_' channel_spec '_' SNR_step '_'
num2str(initial_rep) '_to_' num2str(final_rep)
'.mat'],'EVM_experiment');
%----- function end -----
```

The EVM calculation of the FPGA-based prototype is made possible by comparing the files captured in the equalization block with the equivalent ones of the ideal MATLAB receiver. To achieve this we have to feed the MATLAB model with all the different test vectors captured in the post AGC stage of the FPGA prototype and produce the same amount of files at the output of the equalization stage. For each OFDM symbol in each captured frame, we would apply the following MATLAB operations (a mean value for each captured-file has to be calculated in the end):

```
deviation=[];
for index=1:cnt_data_carriers_per_symbol
deviation(index)=equal_out_RTL(index)-ideal_equal(index);
end
EVM_symbol=mean(abs(deviation).^2)/1;
```

4. Conclusion

The message that this chapter intended to convey is that MATLAB is having nowadays a diverse usage that goes beyond its initial conception as a generic mathematic modeling environment. Its functionality is valuable because it can be directly interfaced with various third party software/hardware design tools and instruments. Moreover, MATLAB has a multi-level contribution in the conceptual high-level modeling of a system, and it is an ideal candidate for rapid prototyping, since it can emulate the baseband signal processing when used in instrumentation-based offline testbeds. MATLAB is also used to emulate real-life hardware constraints and it can be adapted to serve HDL co-simulations. Its role is particularly important for the prototyping of bit-intensive systems such as the PHY-layer of modern wireless communication systems. This chapter proposed a comprehensive design methodology and quoted indicative examples, in order to highlight the previously mentioned benefits of MATLAB. In concrete, this chapter provided a guideline for the use of MATLAB during the prototyping of a FPGA-based real-time transceiver based on the mobile WiMAX standard. Finally, its critical contribution was contemplated by quoting extracts of the source code of the previously mentioned system prototyping phases.

Acknowledgements

The research leading to the published work was partially supported by the European Commission under projects BuNGee (248267) and BeFEMTO (248523); by the Catalan Government under grant 2009 SGR 891; and by the Spanish Ministry of Economy and Competitiveness under projects TEC2011-29006-C03-01 (GRE3N-PHY) and TEC2011-29006-C03-02 (GRE3N-LINK-MAC).

Author details

Oriol Font-Bach, Nikolaos Bartzoudis and David López Bueno
Centre Tecnològic de Telecomunicacions de Catalunya (CTTC), Spain

Antonio Pascual-Iserte
Centre Tecnològic de Telecomunicacions de Catalunya (CTTC), Spain
Department of Signal Theory and Communications, Universitat Politècnica de Catalunya (UPC),
Spain

5. References

[1] *The MathWorks, Simulink.* http://www.mathworks.com, 2012.

[2] *Xilinx, System Generator for DSP.* http://www.xilinx.com, 2012.

[3] O. Font-Bach, N. Bartzoudis, A. Pascual-Iserte, and D. López Bueno. A Real-Time MIMO-OFDM Mobile WiMAX Receiver: Architecture, Design and FPGA Implementation. *Elsevier Journal of Computer Networks*, 55(16):3634–3647, November 2011.

[4] O. Font-Bach, N. Bartzoudis, A. Pascual-Iserte, and D. López Bueno. A Real-Time FPGA-based Implementation of a High-Performance MIMO-OFDM Mobile WiMAX Transmitter. In *Proc. International ICST Conference on Mobile Lightweight Wireless Systems (MobiLight)*, May 2011.

[5] M. Rupp, S. Caban, and C. Mehlführer. Challenges in Building MIMO Testbeds. In *Proc. European Signal Processing Conference (EUSIPCO)*, September 2007.

[6] A. Engel, B. Liebig, and A. Koch. Feasibility Analysis of Reconfigurable Computing in Low-Power Wireless Sensor Applications. In *Proc. International Symposium on Applied Reconfigurable Computing (ARC)*, March 2011.

[7] A. Sghaier, S. Areibi, and R. Dony. Implementation Approaches Trade-Offs for WiMax OFDM Functions on Reconfigurable Platforms. *ACM Transactions on Reconfigurable Technology and Systems*, 3(3):12:1–12:28, September 2010.

[8] M. Fernandez and P. Abusaidi. Virtex-6 FPGA Routing Optimization Design Techniques. White paper, Xilinx, October 2010.

[9] S. Caban, C. Mehlführer, R. Langwieser, A. L. Scholtz, and M. Rupp. Vienna MIMO Testbed. *EURASIP Journal on Applied Signal Processing*, 2006, 2006.

[10] S. Hu, G. Wu, Y. L. Guan, C. L. Law, Y. Yan, and S. Li. Development and Performance Evaluation of Mobile WiMAX Testbed. In *Proc. IEEE Mobile WiMAX Symposium*, March 2007.

[11] D. Ramírez, I. Santamaría, J. Pérez, J. Vía, J. A. García-Naya, T. M. Fernández-Caramés, H. J. Pérez-Iglesias, M. González-López, L. Castedo, and J. M. Torres-Royo. A comparative study of STBC transmissions at 2.4 GHz over indoor channels using a 2 x 2 MIMO testbed. *Wireless Communications and Mobile Computing, John Wiley and Sons*, 8(9):1149–1164, November 2008.

[12] G. Wang, B. Yin, K. Amiri, Y. Sun, M. Wu, and Jo. R. Cavallaro. FPGA Prototyping of a High Data Rate LTE Uplink Baseband Receiver. In *Proc. Asilomar Conference on Signals, Systems and Computers (ASILOMAR)*, November 2009.

[13] M. S. Khairy, M. M. Abdallah, and S. E. D. Habib. Efficient FPGA Implementation of MIMO Decoder for Mobile WiMAX System. In *Proc. IEEE International Conference on Communications (ICC)*, June 2009.

[14] *The MathWorks, Instrument Control Toolbox.* http://www.mathworks.com, 2012.

[15] M. Parker. Taking Advantage of Advances in FPGA Floating-Point IP Cores. White paper, Altera, October 2009.

[16] T. Vanevenhoven. High-Level Implementation of Bit- and Cycle-Accurate Floating-Point DSP Algorithms with Xilinx FPGAs. White paper, Xilinx, October 2011.

[17] O. Font-Bach, N. Bartzoudis, A. Pascual-Iserte, and D. López Bueno.   Prototying
     Processing-Demanding Physical Layer Systems Featuring Single Or Multi-Antenna
     Schemes. In *Proc. European Signal Processing Conference (EUSIPCO)*, September 2011.
[18] *CTTC, GEDOMIS® testbed*. http://engineering.cttc.es/gedomis, 2012.
[19] IEEE 802.16e-2005. IEEE Standard for Local and Metropolitan Area Networks. Part 16:
     Air Interface for Fixed Broadband Wireless Access Systems. Amendment 2: Physical and
     Medium Access Control Layer for Combined Fixed and Mobile Operation in Licensed
     Bands, 2005.

Chapter 10

Wireless Channel Model with Markov Chains Using MATLAB

Diana Alejandra Sánchez-Salas,
José Luis Cuevas-Ruíz and Miguel González-Mendoza

Additional information is available at the end of the chapter

1. Introduction

Emerging technology developed in last years is the result of the necessity of human to communicate in an effective and fast way from any point of the world. Since some type of loss is always present in a wireless link, new transmission and reception techniques for wireless communication systems require the study and characterization of the wireless channel.

Channel modeling is the characterization of the wireless channel; it describes how the characteristics of the sent signal can be affected or what the conditions of the environment are, i.e. frequency, obstacles in the path, etc. The channel model helps to evaluate the performance of the system and to compare different techniques to mitigate the perturbations so the best fitted solution can be implemented according to the presented problem.

The simplest model is the free space loss which considers no obstacles between transmitter and receptor. (Parsons, 2000) However this is an ideal model that does not exist in real scenario because there are other losses in the wireless channel. Another option to describe a channel is by using statistical models which are based on probability density functions (pdf). Although they do not describe the behavior of the sent signal in a complete way, they give a good approximation of the conditions of the channel in a certain moment. (Nakagami, 1960; Abouraddy & Elnoubi, 2000) The main statistical channels and their corresponding pdf are:

- Additive White Gaussian Noise, AWGN. This channel only includes the sum of the white noise that follows a normal or Gaussian density.

$$p(x) = \frac{1}{\sigma\sqrt{2\pi}} \exp\left(-\frac{(x-\mu)^2}{2\sigma^2}\right) \tag{1}$$

Where:

p(x),   Probability density function.
μ,   Mean.
σ,   Standard deviation.
σ²,   Variance.
- Rice: represents a signal which is the result of the sum of the different multipath plus a dominant signal, known as the line of sight (LOS) between transmitter and receptor.

$$p(x)=\frac{x}{\sigma^2}\exp\left(-\frac{(x^2+A^2)}{2\sigma^2}\right)I_0\left(\frac{Ax}{\sigma^2}\right), \qquad A \geq 0 \qquad (2)$$

Where:

p(x),   Probability density function.
σ²,   Variance of the signal or mean power of the signal before the detection of the envelope.
A,   Amplitude of the dominant signal.
I₀(),   Zero order modified Bessel function of the first kind.

The relation between the power of the dominant signal and the power of the multipath is represented in (3).

$$K(dB) = 10\log\left(\frac{A^2}{2\sigma^2}\right) \qquad (3)$$

Where:

K,   Rice factor.
σ²,   Variance of the signal or mean power of the signal before the detection of the envelope.
A,   Amplitude of the dominant signal.

As A value decrease, the function is closer to characterize a Rayleigh fading environment. Otherwise, if the A value increase, the function is used to model an AWGN channel.

- Rayleigh: represents fast fading and describes the multipath phenomenon with no LOS between transmitter and receptor which can be caused by a non stationary user.

$$p(x)=\frac{x}{\sigma^2}\exp\left(-\frac{x^2}{2\sigma^2}\right), \qquad x \geq 0 \qquad (4)$$

Where:

p(x),   Probability density function.
σ²,   Variance of the signal or mean power of the signal before the detection of the envelope.

Due to a wireless channel is a time variant channel, a better option to characterize a channel is Markov chains, which are a stochastic process with a limited number of states and whose transition between them is based on the probability of an event. States of Markov chains could be defined in agreement to channel conditions of an scenario, like it was done by E. Lutz who defined a two state channel model, one classified as good and the other one classified as bad depending on the conditions and therefore the attenuation level. Another important work is the one of B. Vucetic which characterizes the wireless channel of a certain area in Australia with a four state Markov chain by combining four different types of statistical channels.

Next sections explain in detail how to create a wireless channel model using Markov chains and its application in a communication system with a coder and modulator. To achieve this, it is also explained how to create a markovian chain using Matlab. The effects of this model are analyzed through BER curves. An analysis with a semimarkovian channel is explained in the last section and a comparative analysis is done between this model and that from Markov chains. Finally, conclusions about both subjects are given. All the analysis is also done with Matlab.

2. Markov chains

One type of stochastic process is Markov chains, named after Andrei Markov who studied the transitions between consonants and vowels in a poem at the beginning of the 20th century. In this process, a set is defined as $\{X(t), t = 0,1,2,...\}$ whose number of elements is finite and denoted with real positive numbers. $X(t) = i$ represents that the process is in state i at an instant of time t and take discrete values. It is said that there is a fixed probability p_{ij} that chain goes from a state i to a state j in the next time t. This process is represented in (5) and it is known as the Markov property.

$$P\left[X\left(t_{k+1}\right)=x_{k+1}|X(t_k=x_k,...,X\left(t_1\right)=x_1\right]=P\left[X\left(t_{k+1}\right)=x_{k+1}|X\left(t_k\right)=x_k\right] \tag{5}$$

Where,

$X(t_k)$,	Current sample.
$X(t_{k+1})$,	Future sample.
$X(t_1),...,X(t_{k-1})$,	Past samples.
x_k,	State of the sample in the moment k.

Markov property indicates that given the present state, the next state is conditionally independent of the past. This statement is illustrated in Figure 1 which shows that the system can change from one condition to another or continues in the same state.

2.1. Elements of Markov chains

There are three important elements in Markov chains:

- Probability transition matrix **P**.
- Transition diagram.
- Steady-state vector π

The characteristics of each element will be given in next sections.

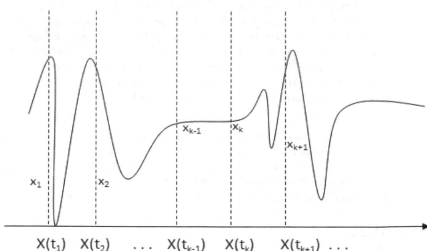

$$X(t_1) \quad X(t_2) \quad \ldots \quad X(t_{k-1}) \quad X(t_k) \quad X(t_{k+1}) \ldots$$

Figure 1. Markov Property

2.1.1. Probability transition matrix

The switch between states is established in the probability transition matrix **P**. Each element of it represents the probability that switches or remains in the state. These switches are called transitions. **P** is a square matrix whose order is the same to the number of states. Equation (6) shows the structure of a probability transition matrix.

$$\mathbf{P}=\begin{bmatrix} P_{00} & P_{01} & P_{02} & \cdots \\ P_{10} & P_{11} & P_{12} & \cdots \\ . & . & . & \\ P_{i0} & P_{i1} & \cdots & \\ . & . & \cdots & \end{bmatrix} \tag{6}$$

Each element of **P** must satisfy the next condition.

$$p_{ij} \geq 0, \qquad i,j=0,1,2,3\ldots \tag{7}$$

Where,

p_{ij},   Probability that current sample is in state i given the immediate precedent past time was in state j.

i,   Transition state i.

j,   Transition state j.

Condition of (7) is based on the argument that p_{ij} represents certain probability.

Another important characteristic of the probability transition matrix is that the sum of each row must be equal to one.

$$\sum_j p_{ij}=1, \qquad i=1,2,3,\dots \tag{8}$$

Where

p_{ij}, Probability that current sample is in state i given the immediate precedent past time was in state j.

i, Transition state i.

j, Transition state j.

An advantage of markovian models is that they describe in an efficient way the characteristics of the system and therefore they can be solved by mathematic methods. In communication systems, Markov chains characterize in a better way the channel because it represents the combination of some phenomena that affects the signal during its wireless transmission, having a better approach to a real channel.

2.1.2. Transition diagram

A probability transition matrix can be also represented as a diagram called transition diagram. Each node ○ represents a state of the Markov chain indicated with a number inside; an arrow → connects state i with state j if a transition exists and the transition probability p_{ij} is written on that connecting arrow, even if the transition is to the same state. (Nerlson, 2002) The transition diagram is also used to describe the model definitions; it is easy to see in this diagram the possible switches between states according to the probability. Next figures show the probability transition diagram for a two, three and four states Markov chain with its transition matrix.

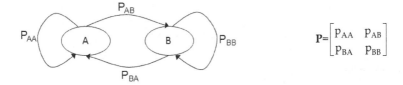

Figure 2. Probability transition diagram for 2-state Markov chain

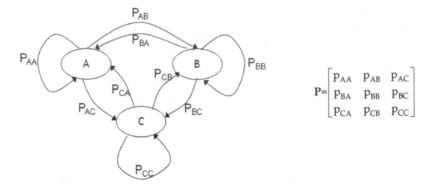

Figure 3. Probability transition diagram for 3-state Markov chain

$$P = \begin{bmatrix} P_{AA} & P_{AB} & P_{AC} \\ P_{BA} & P_{BB} & P_{BC} \\ P_{CA} & P_{CB} & P_{CC} \end{bmatrix}$$

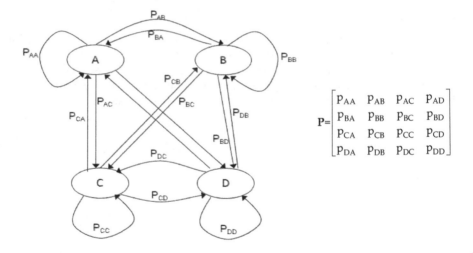

Figure 4. Probability transition diagram for 4-state Markov chain

$$P = \begin{bmatrix} P_{AA} & P_{AB} & P_{AC} & P_{AD} \\ P_{BA} & P_{BB} & P_{BC} & P_{BD} \\ P_{CA} & P_{CB} & P_{CC} & P_{CD} \\ P_{DA} & P_{DB} & P_{DC} & P_{DD} \end{bmatrix}$$

2.1.3. Steady-state vector

Another important element in Markov chains is the steady-state vector π, which represents the total appearing percentage of a state in a Markov chain. This vector can be computed by raising P to a large power. This is shown in (9).

$$P^n \rightarrow 1\pi \tag{9}$$

Where,

P,   Probability transition matrix.

π,   Steady state probability vector

1,   Column vector of ones: $\mathbf{1}^T = (1,1,\dots)$

One property of the π vector is that the sum of its elements must be equal to one as it is shown in (10).

$$\sum_i \pi_i = 1 \qquad (10)$$

Where,

π_i,   Steady state probability for state i.

3. Creation of a Markov chains in Matlab

In this section you will find the steps and the code to create a Markov chain using Matlab for two and three states. This code will be useful to create a wireless channel model that, within a wireless communications system, will be simulated using Matlab in next section.

3.1. Two-state Markov chains

The simpler case in Markov chains is the one with two states. The first step for the creation of a chain is to establish a transition matrix that indicates the switch between states. The transition matrix and the steady state vector for a two state model is shown in (11) and (12).

$$P_{2states} = \begin{bmatrix} P_{11} & P_{12} \\ P_{21} & P_{22} \end{bmatrix} \qquad (11)$$

$$\Pi_{2states} = \begin{bmatrix} \pi_1 & \pi_2 \end{bmatrix} \qquad (12)$$

The input data for the Matlab code will be the probability transition matrix and the size of the output vector. Since this is a stochastic event, the first sample and the switch between stated will be obtained in a random way but always following the characteristics of **P**. It is also possible to have an initial distribution for the first sample. The precise steps to create the Matlab code are listed below.

a) Generate a random integer number between 1 and 2 (because of the two state markovian chain).

b) Generate a random natural number between 0 and 1.

c) If previous sample was 1 and the generated number in step b) is equal or less to p_{12}, next sample of the chain is going to be 2; otherwise will be 1.

d) If previous sample was 2 and the generated number in step b) is equal or less to p_{21}, next sample will switch to 1, otherwise will be 2.

e) Repeat steps b) to d) until complete the number of samples required. The generated series is the resultant Markov chain.

The Matlab code for these steps is shown next.

```
function [channel] = markovChain2States(P,lengthChain)
channel   = zeros(1,lengthChain);              % 2-state Markov chain (output vector)
channel(1) = randint(1,1,[1 2]);               % Step a)

for i = 2:lengthChain
    event = randint(1,1,[1 100])/100;          % Step b)
    if channel(1,i-1) == 1                      % Step c)
       if event <= P(1,2)                       % Switch to state 2
          channel(1,i) = 2;
       else                                     % No switch
          channel(1,i) = 1;
       end
    elseif channel(1,i-1) == 2                  % Step d)
       if event <= P(2,1)                       % Switch to state 1
          channel(1,i) = 1;
       else                                     % No switch
          channel(1,i) = 2;
       end; end; end
```

The output vector will determine the moment when the sent signal will be affected by certain probabilistic channel established previously.

3.2. Three-state Markov chains

Another common case in Markov chains is the three-state case. The proceeding to create this type of chain in Matlab is similar to the two-state model. The input is the 3×3 size probability transition matrix, like the one shown in (13) and the output vector will be also the vector containing the Markov chain with the characteristics set by **P**.

$$\mathbf{P}_{3chan} = \begin{bmatrix} P_{11} & P_{12} & P_{13} \\ P_{21} & P_{22} & P_{23} \\ P_{31} & P_{32} & P_{33} \end{bmatrix} \tag{13}$$

The π vector for a three-state Markov chain is shown in (14).

$$\pi_{2chan} = \begin{bmatrix} \pi_1 & \pi_2 & \pi_3 \end{bmatrix} \tag{14}$$

The first step now will be to modify the probability transition matrix by computing the cumulative sum for each row because this will determine the transition between states. This step is show in (15).

$$\mathbf{P'}_{3chan} = \begin{bmatrix} P_{11} & P_{12}+P_{11} & P_{13}+P_{12}+P_{11} \\ P_{21} & P_{22}+P_{21} & P_{23}+P_{22}+P_{21} \\ P_{31} & P_{32}+P_{31} & P_{33}+P_{32}+P_{31} \end{bmatrix} = \begin{bmatrix} P_{11} & P_{12}' & 1 \\ P_{21} & P_{22}' & 1 \\ P_{31} & P_{32}' & 1 \end{bmatrix} \tag{15}$$

Once $\mathbf{P'}_{3chan}$ was computed, the proceeding to create the resulting Markov chain is the same as the two-state one. The steps are listed next.

a) Generate a random integer number between 1 and 3 (because now it is a three-state model). This will be the first sample of the chain, although an initial distribution can be established for this case.

b) Generate a random natural number between 0 and 1.

c) If previous sample was 1 and the generated number in step b) is less than p_{11}, the next sample will be 1; if it is greater than p_{12}', next sample will be 3, otherwise will be 2.

d) If preceding sample was 2 and the generated number in step b) is less than p_{21}, the next sample will be 1; if it is greater than p_{22}', next sample will be 3; if not, it will be 2.

e) If previous sample was 3 and the generated number in step b) is less than p_{31}, next sample will be 1; if it is greater than p_{32}', next sample will be 3, otherwise will be 2.

f) Repeat steps b) – e) until complete the required size of the Markov chain.

The Matlab code for the previous steps is presented next.

```
function [channel] = markovChain3States(P,lengthChain)
channel = zeros(1,lengthChain);         % 3-state Markov chain (output vector).
channel(1) = randint(1,1,[1 3]);        % Step a)

P1 = cumsum(P,2);                       % P'3chan

for i = 2:lengthChain
    event = randint(1,1,[1 100])/100;   % Step b)
    if channel(1,i-1) == 1              % Step c)
        if event < P1(1,1)             % No switch
            channel(1,i) = 1;
        elseif event > P1(1,2)          % Switch to state 3
            channel(1,i) = 3;
        else
            channel(1,i) = 2;           % Switch to state 2
        end
    elseif channel(1,i-1) == 2          % Step d)
        if event < P1(2,1)              % Switch to state 1
            channel(1,i) = 1;
        elseif event > P1(2,2)          % Switch to state 3
            channel(1,i) = 3;
        else                            % No switch
            channel(1,i) = 2;
        end
```

```
elseif channel(1,i-1) == 3          % Step e)
    if event < P1(3,1)              % Switch to state 1
        channel(1,i) = 1;
    elseif event > P1(3,2)          % No switch
        channel(1,i) = 3;
    else                            % Switch to state 2
        channel(1,i) = 2;
    end; end; end
```

The methodology explained above can be used as a base to create an n-state Markov chain.

To proof the created Markov chain follows a specific probability transition matrix is by counting the number of each one of possible transitions and dividing them by the sum of the total transitions for the corresponding state. To verify that the chain follows also the steady-state vector it is necessary to count the number of times each state appeared in the chain and divide each count by the total number of samples (size of the output vector).

Two and three-state Markov chains Matlab program described above represents the wireless transmission channel that will be implemented in a communication system. This will be done by simulating a message is being sent through it, all with Matlab.

4. Implementation of a Markov chains in Matlab

Another alternative to characterize a wireless channel is using Markov chains as it was said before. This model is a better option than statistic channels (AWGN, Rice, Rayleigh) because the former represent a statistical channel combination of the latter. To show the application of Markov chains in this area the next scenario is proposed.

"A wireless channel model must be created in such manner it characterizes the principal causes of attenuation, for instance: the obstacles between the transmitter and receiver, a mobile user or the influence of the line of sight (LOS)."

The statistic channels for the scenario area are defined as Rayleigh and Rice. The former characterize a mobile user and the latter the LOS between transmitter and receiver.

To simulate this scenario in Matlab, a communication system with a QPSK and rate 2/3 convolutional code is proposed. The block diagram of this system and the channel model are illustrated in Figure 3 and 4. Markov chains will be used as a base to create a wireless channel model and will represent the multiplicative fading, which is right after the transmitter, and will be switching between the possible channels according to the probability transition matrix, as it is shown in Figure 4. From now, this model will be called as a "markovian channel".

To have a better understanding of this markovian model, several examples with different probability transition with its steady-state vector, calculated using (9), are proposed. The codes for the creation of a two and three state Markov chains are used to produce results. Interpretations are based on BER curves obtained by implementing the communication system and the markovian channel of figures below. Next sections explain with details the examples and its results.

4.1. Two-state Markov channel model

As it was said before, this is the simplest model in Markov chains. According to the proposed scenario, the two statistical channels used for this case are:

- Channel 1: Rice K = 14 dB. This channel represents the better conditions because of its strong LOS.
- Channel 2: Rayleigh. This channel corresponds to a mobile user and multipath generated from the movement.

Now, three examples about two-state markovian channel model are proposed next.

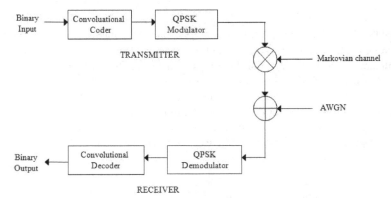

Figure 5. Block diagram for a communication system with markovian channel

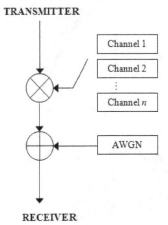

Figure 6. Block diagram of the markovian channel

Example 1. The next two Markov channels are proposed.

$$\mathbf{P}_{2chan1} = \begin{bmatrix} 1 & 0 \\ 1 & 0 \end{bmatrix} \tag{16}$$

$$\mathbf{P}_{2chan2} = \begin{bmatrix} 0 & 1 \\ 0 & 1 \end{bmatrix} \tag{17}$$

And their steady-state vectors are shown in (18) and (19).

$$\mathbf{\Pi}_{2chan1} = \begin{bmatrix} 1 & 0 \end{bmatrix} \tag{18}$$

$$\mathbf{\Pi}_{2chan2} = \begin{bmatrix} 0 & 1 \end{bmatrix} \tag{19}$$

Channel P_{2chan1} sets that channel 1 (Rice K = 14 dB) appears all the time, in other words, there is a strong LOS between transmitter and receiver, which can be referred as a rural environment where there is no tall buildings that blocks that line of sight. Conversely, channel P_{2chan2} establish that channel 2 (Rayleigh) will appear all the time, this channels can be seen as an urban environment where there is a lot of obstacles between transmitter and receiver that will cause the multipath or also it can represents an user who is moving from one point to another one. These two channels were simulated with the communication system of Figure 3 in Matlab and the BER curves obtained are shown in Figure 5.

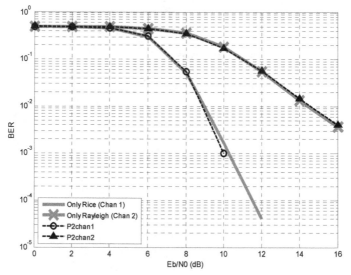

Figure 7. Two state Markov cannel for Example 1

To verify the results of the markovian channel, BER curves of systems using exclusively each statistical channel were obtained too. It can be appreciated in Figure 5 that the resulting BER curve for P_{2chan1} is exactly the same as the one resulting from the simulation of the Rice $K = 14$ dB statistical channel. Likewise, BER curve generated from P_{2chan2} is exactly the same to the simulation where only Rayleigh statistical channel is implemented.

To proof the Markov channel follows the characteristics of (16) and (17), a counting of the transitions and the number of times both channels appeared is realized from the created Markov chain. The size of the simulated sent message was 100,000 bits, so the results of the count are given as percentages, which is equivalent to the probabilities of the transition matrixes. Those results are given in Table 1 and 2.

Channel 1 to 1: 100 %	Channel 1 to 2: 0 %	Channel 1: 99.9 %
Channel 2 to 1: 100 %	Channel 2 to 2: 0 %	Channel 2: 0.01 %

Table 1. Counting of events for P_{2chan1}

Channel 1 to 1: 0 %	Channel 1 to 2: 0 %	Channel 1: 0 %
Channel 2 to 1: 0 %	Channel 2 to 2: 100 %	Channel 2: 100 %

Table 2. Counting of events for P_{2chan2}

As it can be observed, obtained results from counting are equal to the probability transition matrix of (16). This means that 100% of chances there was a transition from channel 1 to 1 and from channel 2 to 1. Channel 1 appeared 99.99% which says that at the first sample of the chain was channel 2 but immediately after switched to channel 1, that is why the third column of Table 1 is not the same to the steady-state vector of (18) but it is very close to it.

For the case of P_{2chan2}, it is appreciated that channel 1 never appeared in the Markov chain, thus 100% of chances remained in channel 1, so data from the third column of Table 2 has the same characteristics of the steady state vector of (19).

Example 2. In contrast to Example 1, these two probability transition matrixes and its steady-state vectors are proposed.

$$P_{2chan3} = \begin{bmatrix} 0.2 & 0.8 \\ 0.2 & 0.8 \end{bmatrix} \tag{20}$$

$$\Pi_{2chan3} = \begin{bmatrix} 0.2 & 0.8 \end{bmatrix} \tag{21}$$

$$P_{2chan4} = \begin{bmatrix} 0.8 & 0.2 \\ 0.8 & 0.2 \end{bmatrix} \tag{22}$$

$$\Pi_{2chan4} = \begin{bmatrix} 0.8 & 0.2 \end{bmatrix} \tag{23}$$

The interpretation for the channel of P2chan3 is that 80% of chances, Rayleigh channel will be present in the Markov chain meaning that the user is moving (walking, running) and LOS conditions are poor. For channel P2chan4 probabilities are opposite than the other channel, in other words, there is a greater probability of having LOS than multipath, like in a rural area. Resulting BER curves for both channels are shown in Figure 8, where it shows that BER curves from markovian channels of (20) and (22) are very close to that curves resulting from simulating only the correspondent statistical channel but they are not the same, proving the combination of the channels according to the probability transition matrixes.

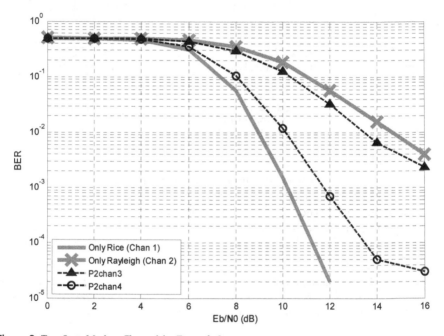

Figure 8. Two State Markov Channel for Example 2

Example 3. A probability transition matrix shown in (24) with its steady-state vector in (25) is presented as a new wireless channel model. In this channel model the user has LOS the most part of the time but in some instants experiments multipath. This seems a semi urban environment because it can exists some building that cause multipath but they are not that tall to block the line of sight. BER curve for this model is shown in Figure 9.

$$P_{2chan5} = \begin{bmatrix} 0.7 & 0.3 \\ 0.9 & 0.1 \end{bmatrix} \tag{24}$$

$$\Pi_{2chan5} = \begin{bmatrix} 0.75 & 0.25 \end{bmatrix} \tag{25}$$

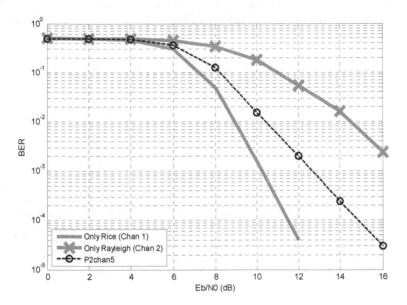

Figure 9. Two State Markov Channel for Example 3

To verify the channel model was well implemented the counting of switches and how many times a state appeared is presented next.

Channel 1 to 1: 70.15 %	Channel 1 to 2: 29.85 %	Channel 1: 75.29 %
Channel 2 to 1: 90.93 %	Channel 2 to 2: 9.07 %	Channel 2: 24.71 %

Table 3. Counting of events for P2chan5

The count of transitions between states and the times each state (or probabilistic channel) appeared in the Markov chains indicate probability transition matrix shown in (25) was followed. This can be observed also in Figure 9 where the BER curve for the channel model presents an inclination to the curve obtained when only Rice channel is simulated but it is not identically to it.

4.2. Three-state Markov channel model

A two-state channel model is not enough to characterize a wireless channel. To create a better model it is necessary to add more statistical channel. According to the proposed scenario at the beginning of the section, the three statistical channels proposed are:

- Channel 1: Rice K = 14 dB, very strong LOS.
- Channel 2: Rayleigh, multipath and moving user.
- Channel 3: Rice K = 7 dB, not a strong LOS like channel 1.

As it was done for the two-state channel model, different probability transition matrixes with are analyzed through BER curves to proof the correct implementation of the channel in a communication system of Fig. 5.

Example 4. Three markovian channels are proposed.

$$P_{3chan1} = \begin{bmatrix} 1 & 0 & 0 \\ 1 & 0 & 0 \\ 1 & 0 & 0 \end{bmatrix} \tag{26}$$

$$P_{3chan2} = \begin{bmatrix} 0 & 1 & 0 \\ 0 & 1 & 0 \\ 0 & 1 & 0 \end{bmatrix} \tag{27}$$

$$P_{3chan3} = \begin{bmatrix} 0 & 0 & 1 \\ 0 & 0 & 1 \\ 0 & 0 & 1 \end{bmatrix} \tag{28}$$

Its steady-state vectors are shown next.

$$\Pi_{3chan1} = \begin{bmatrix} 1 & 0 & 0 \end{bmatrix} \tag{29}$$

$$\Pi_{3chan2} = \begin{bmatrix} 0 & 1 & 0 \end{bmatrix} \tag{30}$$

$$\Pi_{3chan3} = \begin{bmatrix} 0 & 0 & 1 \end{bmatrix} \tag{31}$$

The goal of these models is to verify the correct implementation of the markovian channels into a communication system. Each one of them establishes that they must stay always in the same channel. Results are compared with BER curves when only statistical channels are simulated. Figure 10 shows each BER curve obtained from the Markov chains models of (26) – (28) are almost the same to the ones obtained when only the corresponding statistical channel is simulated.

Markovian channel of (26) can be compared to a rural area where LOS is very probable because there are no tall buildings. Channel model of (27) can be interpreted as an urban zone because the multipath and users are constantly moving. Markov channel of (28) indicates LOS but not as strong as channel 1, so it can be seen as a semi-urban area because there are not a lot of tall buildings to block the transmission.

Example 5. Another three markovian channel models are proposed where it is indicated that each channel must be present in the Markov chain 80% of times. Probability transition matrixes and steady-state vectors are shown in (32)-(37).

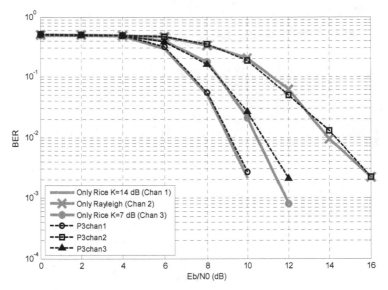

Figure 10. Three State Markov Channel for Example 4

$$\mathbf{P}_{3chan4} = \begin{bmatrix} 0.8 & 0.1 & 0.1 \\ 0.8 & 0.1 & 0.1 \\ 0.8 & 0.1 & 0.1 \end{bmatrix} \tag{32}$$

$$\mathbf{\Pi}_{3chan1} = \begin{bmatrix} 0.8 & 0.1 & 0.1 \end{bmatrix} \tag{33}$$

$$\mathbf{P}_{3chan5} = \begin{bmatrix} 0.1 & 0.8 & 0.1 \\ 0.1 & 0.8 & 0.1 \\ 0.1 & 0.8 & 0.1 \end{bmatrix} \tag{34}$$

$$\mathbf{\Pi}_{3chan1} = \begin{bmatrix} 0.1 & 0.8 & 0.1 \end{bmatrix} \tag{35}$$

$$\mathbf{P}_{3chan6} = \begin{bmatrix} 0.1 & 0.1 & 0.8 \\ 0.1 & 0.1 & 0.8 \\ 0.1 & 0.1 & 0.8 \end{bmatrix} \tag{36}$$

$$\mathbf{\Pi}_{3chan1} = \begin{bmatrix} 0.1 & 0.1 & 0.8 \end{bmatrix} \tag{37}$$

Results are shown in Figure 11 where each BER curve are very close to the curve resulted from the simulation of only statistical channels (according to each case), confirming what is indicated in each steady-state vector.

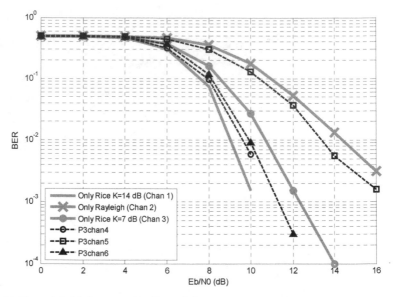

Figure 11. Three state Markov cannel for Example 5

Example 6. Once the behavior of the markovian channel model created with Matlab, probability transition matrix of (38) is proposed for the scenario explained above. This model indicates that the probability of a type of LOS (Rician channel K = 14 dB or K = 7 dB) is less than the probability when the user is moving (Rayleigh channel). This model focus on a mobile user and when there is a LOS but it is not the best conditions. The resulting curve presented in Figure 12 seems to follow a combination of the most probable statistical channel indicated in steady-state vector (but never equal to a particular channel), concluding that these model really represents a better characterization of the channel.

$$
P_{3chan7} = \begin{bmatrix} 0.1166 & 0.5072 & 0.3762 \\ 0.0675 & 0.4682 & 0.4643 \\ 0.1507 & 0.5208 & 0.3285 \end{bmatrix} \tag{38}
$$

$$
\Pi_{3chan7} = \begin{bmatrix} 0.1062 & 0.4940 & 0.4010 \end{bmatrix} \tag{39}
$$

The effect of the combination of statistical channels is proved with the counting of events (Table 4). These data is very similar to the probability transition matrix of (38).

Ch 1 to 1: 11.3 %	Ch 1 to 2: 50.4 %	Cha 1 to 3: 38.1 %	Channel 1: 10.1 %
Ch 2 to 1: 5.9 %	Ch 2 to 2: 46.9 %	Ch 2 to 3: 47.0 %	Channel 2: 49.3 %
Ch 3 to 1: 14.9 %	Ch 3 to 2: 52.0 %	Ch 3 to 3: 33.0 %	Channel 3: 40.4 %

Table 4. Counting of events for P_{3chan7}

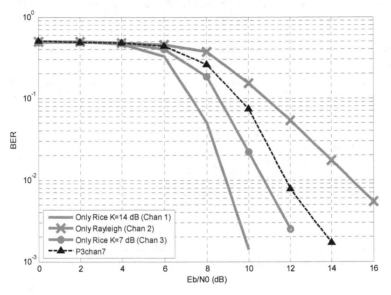

Figure 12. Three state Markov cannel for example 6

4.3. Four-state Markov channel model

The methodology applied to implement a markovian channel in a wireless communication system can be also used to create an n-state channel. Some authors have characterized channels up to four states. Let's take the probability transition matrix proposed by B. Vucetic shown in (40) with these probabilistic channels:

- Channel A: Rice K = 14 dB, strong LOS.
- Channel B: Rayleigh, mobile user and multipath.
- Channel C: Rice K = 7 dB, regular LOS.
- Channel D: Rice K = 5 dB, a channel with more noise but not as bad conditions as Rayleigh, user without movement.

$$P_{4chan} = \begin{bmatrix} 0.679 & 0.179 & 0.129 & 0.013 \\ 0.052 & 0.925 & 0.023 & 0 \\ 0.104 & 0.007 & 0.75 & 0.139 \\ 0 & 0 & 0.778 & 0.222 \end{bmatrix} \tag{40}$$

Computed steady-state vector of (41) was obtained by using property of (9).

$$\pi_{4chan} = \begin{bmatrix} 0.1753 & 0.4480 & 0.3171 & 0.0596 \end{bmatrix} \tag{41}$$

Through steady-state vector, this model establishes that the biggest probability is found between channel B (mobile user) and channel C (Rice K = 7 dB, regular LOS). This can be interpreted as an urban zone scenario where users are constantly moving and there is less possibility of line of sight. BER curve of Figure 13 shows this trend and the behavior of the markovian chain is proved by counting the transitions and states. These last results are confirmed in Table 5.

Channel 1 to 1: 67.22 % Channel 2 to 1: 5.36 % Channel 3 to 1: 11 % Channel 4 to 1: 0 %	Channel 1 to 2: 18.32 % Channel 2 to 2: 91.58 % Channel 3 to 2: 0.94 % Channel 4 to 2: 0 %
Channel 1 to 3: 12.53 % Channel 2 to 3: 3.06 % Channel 3 to 3: 74.98 % Channel 4 to 3: 81.50 %	Channel 1 to 4: 1.93 % Channel 2 to 4: 0 % Channel 3 to 4: 13.09 % Channel 4 to 4: 18.50 %
Channel 1: 18.12 % Channel 2: 43.14 % Channel 3: 33.01 % Channel 4: 5.73 %	

Table 5. Counting of events for P_{3chan7}

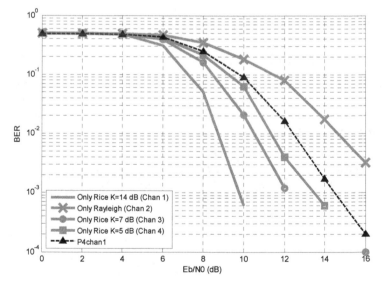

Figure 13. Four-state Markov channel

4.4. N-state Markov channel model

It has been proved until this point that the more statistical channels in a Markov chain wireless channel model, the better the channel will be characterized, however this must have a limit because maybe a large number of states in the chain could be exaggerated. Another analysis is suggested to demonstrate this hypothesis by proposing another markovian channels shown in Table 6. The common characteristic between all models is that Rayleigh channel (multipath, mobile user) has the biggest probability than a channel with some type of line of sight. The possible states are:

- Channel 1: Rice = 14 dB, strong LOS.
- Channel 2: Rayleigh, mobile user and multipath.
- Channel 3: Rice K = 7 dB, regular LOS.
- Channel 4: Rice K = 5 dB, the channel with more noise but "better" conditions than Rayleigh, user without movement.
- Channel 5: AWGN, without any type of multiplicative fading. This is the channel with best conditions because it represents practically no losses.

Using the same methodology of all examples above, BER curve was computed and it is presented in Figure 14. It can be appreciated from graphic that the curve for two, three and four states are different between them; nevertheless five-state channel is very similar to four-state model although they are not exactly the same. This is very peculiar because there is nothing similar to the other cases. So the conclusion is that until four-state markovian channel model is enough to characterize a wireless channel because results are going to be very similar with more states. (Sánchez-Salas & Cuevas-Ruíz, 2007)

Number of states	Transition Matrix	Steady-State Vector
2	$P_A = \begin{bmatrix} 0.32 & 0.68 \\ 0.25 & 0.75 \end{bmatrix}$	$\pi_A = \begin{bmatrix} 0.3 & 0.7 \end{bmatrix}$
3	$P_B = \begin{bmatrix} 0.1531 & 0.715 & 0.1319 \\ 0.1487 & 0.8221 & 0.0292 \\ 0.0714 & 0.816 & 0.1126 \end{bmatrix}$	$\pi_B = \begin{bmatrix} 0.14 & 0.8 & 0.06 \end{bmatrix}$
4	$P_C = \begin{bmatrix} 0.679 & 0.179 & 0.129 & 0.013 \\ 0.052 & 0.925 & 0.023 & 0 \\ 0.104 & 0.007 & 0.75 & 0.139 \\ 0 & 0 & 0.778 & 0.222 \end{bmatrix}$	$\pi_C = \begin{bmatrix} 0.1753 & 0.4480 & 0.3171 & 0.0596 \end{bmatrix}$
5	$P_D = \begin{bmatrix} 0.25 & 0.25 & 0.2 & 0.25 & 0.05 \\ 0.08 & 0.25 & 0.3 & 0.25 & 0.12 \\ 0.1 & 0.2 & 0.4 & 0.2 & 0.1 \\ 0.1 & 0.15 & 0.4 & 0.25 & 0.1 \\ 0.05 & 0.2 & 0.32 & 0.18 & 0.25 \end{bmatrix}$	$\pi_D = \begin{bmatrix} 0.11 & 0.201 & 0.349 & 0.2224 & 0.126 \end{bmatrix}$

Table 6. Markovian channels and steady-state vector for 1, 2, 3, 4 and 5 states

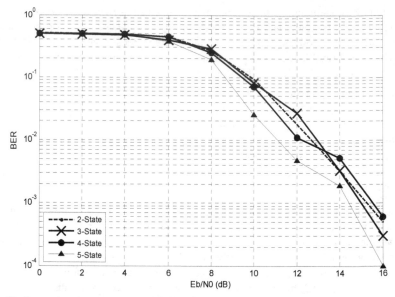

Figure 14. Comparison between n-states Markov channel model

5. Semi-markovian channel model

Now let's make the supposition that a process can be in any possible states $(1,2,...,N)$ and each time goes to state i remains there for a certain random amount of time with media μ_i and then makes a transition to state j with probability p_{ij}. This practice is called semi-markovian process and it is very similar to Markov chains because switches between states follow the Markov property. However, the remaining time in a state is a random variable with some probability distribution. (Ross, 2007)

The probability transition matrix for a semi-markovian process is shown in (42).

$$\mathbf{P}=\begin{bmatrix} 0 & P_{01} & P_{02} & \cdots \\ P_{10} & 0 & P_{12} & \cdots \\ . & . & & \\ P_{i0} & P_{i1} & 0 & \\ . & . & \cdots & 0 \end{bmatrix} \tag{42}$$

The most relevant characteristic of the matrix above is that it has a zero diagonal matrix because it only considers transitions between states. The second important element in this kind of processes is the mean sojourn time w_i in each state and it is represented as in (43).

$$\mathbf{w}=\begin{bmatrix} w_1 & w_2 & \cdots & w_i \end{bmatrix} \tag{43}$$

The evolution of a semi-markovian process is explained through probability transition matrix **P** and sojourn time vector **w** in this way: the process begins in state i and remains there for a mean amount of time w_i and then switches to state j with probability p_{ij}; after that remains in state j for another mean amount of time w_j and can switch to state k with probability p_{jk} or return to state i with probability p_{ji} and so on. The transition diagram for a two and three semi-markovian chain is shown in Figure 15 and 16.

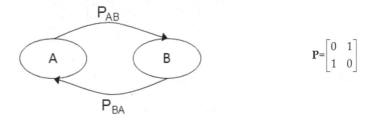

$$P = \begin{bmatrix} 0 & 1 \\ 1 & 0 \end{bmatrix}$$

Figure 15. Transition diagram for a 3-state semimarkovian process

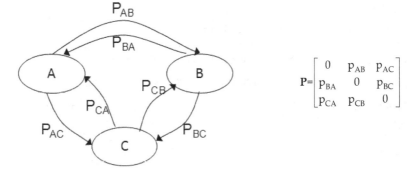

$$P = \begin{bmatrix} 0 & P_{AB} & P_{AC} \\ P_{BA} & 0 & P_{BC} \\ P_{CA} & P_{CB} & 0 \end{bmatrix}$$

Figure 16. Transition diagram for a 2-state semimarkovian process

If time follows an exponential probability density function, the process is called "continous-time Markov process". When time in each state and transition is the same (time does not vary and generally is 1), then the process is called "discrete Markov chain", consequently the analyzed models above are a particular case of semi-markovian process.

Semimarkovian process can be also applied to wireless channel model. The main difference between Markov chains and semimarkovian processes is that this last one includes the analysis of sojourn time in each state. In this way, the applications of the semi-markovian processes in a communication system centers in the analysis of the sojourn time in a particular condition. This can be useful to determine the performance of the designed communication system, the effectiveness of a fading mitigation technique in order to preserve optimal transmission conditions as long as possible, or to study some kind of fading that is only present in a certain hour or season, etc. An example is proposed to understand better the application.

Example 7. A three-state semimarkovian wireless channel model with probability transition matrix of (44) and mean sojourn time of (45) must be created. The remaining time follows an exponential probability density function. Analyze the model and give an interpretation of results for a wireless communication system like the one of Fig. 5.

$$
\mathbf{P}_{3semiM} = \begin{bmatrix} 0 & 0.5072 & 0.4928 \\ 0.5357 & 0 & 0.4643 \\ 0.1507 & 0.8493 & 0 \end{bmatrix} \tag{44}
$$

$$
\mathbf{w}_{3semiM} = \begin{bmatrix} 2 & 0.4 & 5 \end{bmatrix} \tag{45}
$$

The statistical channels that form this model are:

- Channel 1: Rice K = 14 dB, strong LOS.
- Channel 2: Rayleigh, multipath and moving user.
- Channel 3: Rice K = 7 dB, regular LOS.

Solution:

Markov chains Matlab code created in previous sections can be modified to create a semi-markovian process. The main change is that another random number is needed to determine the time in which the state will remain. The code is shown next.

```
function [channel,timeState] = semiMarkov3States(lengthChain,P,w,channel1)

channel = zeros(1,lengthChain);          % 3-state Markov chain (output vector).
timeState = zeros(1,lengthChain);        % Vector of time in each state
timeState1= zeros(1,lengthChain);        % Auxiliary vector of time
channel(1,1) = channel1;                 % First sample of the process

P1 = cumsum(P,2);                        % P'3chan

for i = 2:lengthChain
    eventP = randint(1,1,[1 100])/100;   %Event to decide the switch
    if channel(1,i-1) == 1               %If former sample was channel 1
        if eventP < P1(1,2)              %Switch to channel 2
            channel(1,i) = 2;
        else                             %Switch to channel 3
            channel(1,i) = 3;
        end
    elseif channel(1,i-1) == 2           %If former sample was channel 2
        if eventP < P1(2,1)              %Switch to channel 1
            channel(1,i) = 1;
        else                             %Switch to channel 3
            channel(1,i) = 3;
        end
```

```
    elseif channel(1,i-1) == 3              %If former sample was channel 3
        if eventP < P1(3,1)                 %Switch to channel 1
            channel(1,i) = 1;
        else                                %Switch to channel 2
            channel(1,i) = 2;
        end; end; end
% Sojourn time
for i = 1:lengthChain
    eventW = randint(1,1,[1 100])/100;      %Event to decide the sojourn time
    if channel(i) == 1
        timeState1(1,i)  = -w(1)*log(eventW);   %Sojourn time when Channel 1 appears
    elseif channel(i) == 2
        timeState1(1,i)  = -w(2)*log(eventW);   %Sojourn time when Channel 2 appears
    else
        timeState1(1,i)  = -w(3)*log(eventW);   %Sojourn time when Channel 3 appears
    end; end
timeState = cumsum(timeState1);         %Sojourn time for each element of the created chain
```

Next figure shows obtained results of how many time remains the process in each statistical channel by using the Matlab code above. It can be observed the time and exact moment when each channel is presented. The graphic can be useful in case a record of some phenomenon or fading exists, for example, the rain.

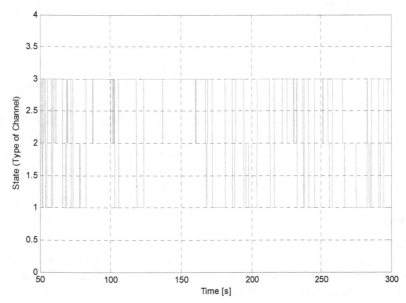

Figure 17. Three state semimarkovian channel

However this image may not be very clear at first sight. Probability transition matrix and sojourn time vector gives a good description of the channel. Also the steady-state vector can be computed using equation (9), which is shown in (46).

$$\Pi_{3semiM} = \begin{bmatrix} 0.2680 & 0.4097 & 0.3223 \end{bmatrix} \qquad (46)$$

From (45) and (46) it is observed that although channel 3 has not the largest probability, it does have the largest sojourn time of all of them. In other words, it is probable that channel with regular LOS is not experimented by the user so often but when it does it, remains there for much more time than any other channel. On the other hand, although the channel with multipath has the largest probability, it is not to be for a large amount of time and it will switch to better conditions (strong or regular LOS). The behavior of these channels seems to characterize an environment in an urban zone where there are mobile users or there are many obstacles. In this type of situations it is necessary to compensate multipath by designing a link between transmitter and receiver with effective fading mitigation techniques, this is why this type of channel remains shorts periods of time.

To prove all what was said above, the counting of transitions and states for the simulated semi-Markov process was done.

Channel 1 to 1: 0 %	Channel 1 to 2: 48.24 %	Channel 1 to 3: 51.76 %
Channel 2 to 1: 50.61 %	Channel 2 to 2: 0 %	Channel 2 to 3: 49.39 %
Channel 3 to 1: 14.33 %	Channel 3 to 2: 85.67 %	Channel 3 to 3: 0 %
Channel 1: 25.50 %		Mean time in Channel 1: 1.87
Channel 2: 41 %		Mean time in Channel 2: 0.38
Channel 3: 33.50 %		Mean time in Channel 3: 5.12

Table 7. Counting of events for P3semiM

The percentage of each transition is practically the same as the original transition matrix of (44), especially because there were no transitions to the same state in the semi-markovian process created. The percentages observed in the second row of Table 7 are the data of the steady state vector of (46). Finally, the same mean sojourn times was obtained than the one indicated in (45) proving the simulated process is correct.

6. Conclusion

The characterization of a wireless channel has become fundamental in the design of a communication system because of the rapid growing of telecommunications. The basic models are based on probability density functions although they represent real perturbations when a signal is sent through air, their characteristics are not enough because a real channel is composed by the combination of many statistical models.

A better choice to wireless channel modeling is Markov chains which are a type of stochastic processes and are based on the probability of an event given another past event. This type of model offers the combination of statistical channels. For this reason it is necessary to establish certain number of states for the probability transition matrix, which characterizes the channel. The larger the number of states (statistical channels) in the markovian chain, the better the channel is modeled but there is also a limit. The elements that model a Markov chains channel model are the probability transition matrix and steady-state vector.

Markov chains are a special case of semi-markovian processes. The main difference between them is that in the latter there are no transitions to the same state and have another element: the sojourn vector. This vector represents the mean time of sojourn of a state. This type of model gives information about how many time and in what exact moment stays in a particular state, therefore its application could be the analysis of time of a particular condition (LOS, multipath, shadows) or a cause of fading (rain, scintillation, snow). This model can be also useful to know the performance of the communication system or some fading mitigation technique.

Since the methodology exposed in this chapter is very flexible, explained models can be applied with other characteristics. Given the bases for a markovian and semi-markovian channel, the lector is invited to develop another application for wireless telecommunication channels.

Author details

Diana Alejandra Sánchez-Salas, José Luis Cuevas-Ruíz and Miguel González-Mendoza
Tecnológico de Monterrey, Campus Estado de México, México

7. References

Abouraddy, A.F.; Elnoubi, S.M.; (Sep 2000), Statistical modeling of the indoor radio channel at 10 GHz through propagation measurements .I. Narrow-band measurements and modeling, Vehicular Technology, IEEE Transactions on, vol.49, no.5, pp.1491-1507, ISSN : 0018-9545.

Feller, W. (1957). An Introduction to Probability Theory and Its Applications, Vol. 1, Second edition, Wiley, ISBN 0-471-25709-5.

Kijima, Masaaki. (1997). Markov Processes for Stochastic Modeling. Cambridge, England. The University Press. ISBN 0-412-60660-7.

Lutz, E.; Cygan, D.; Dippold, M.; Dolainsky, F.; Papke, W.; , (May 1991), The land mobile satellite communication channel-recording, statistics, and channel model, Vehicular Technology, IEEE Transactions on , vol.40, no.2, pp.375-386, ISSN : 0018-9545.

Nakagami, M.; (1960), The M-Distribution – A General Formula of Intensity Distribution of Rapid Fading, In W.C. Hoffman, Statistical Methods in Radio Wave Propagation, Pergamon Press, New York.

Nelson, Barry. (2002). Stochastic Modeling: Analysis & Simulation. USA. Dover Publications Inc. ISBN 0-07-046213-5.

Parsons, J.D. (1996). The Mobile Radio Propagation Channel, USA, Wiley, ISBN 0471964158

Rezaeian, M. (July 2006), Symmetric Characterization of Finite State Markov Channels, Information Theory, 2006 IEEE International Symposium on, pp.2734-2738, 9-14, E-ISBN 1-4244-0504-1.

Ross, S. (2007) Introduction to Probability Models, 9th edition, USA, Academic Press, ISBN 0-12-598062-0.

Sanchez-Salas, D.A.; Cuevas-Ruiz, J.L.; (2007), N-states Channel Model using Markov Chains, Electronics, Robotics and Automotive Mechanics Conference, 2007. CERMA 2007, vol., no., pp.342-347, 25-28 Sept. 2007. ISBN: 978-0-7695-2974-5

Trivedi, K. S. (2002). *Probability, Statistics with Reliability, Queueing and Computer Science* Applications, Second Edition, Wiley, ISBN 0-471-33341-7.

Vucetic, B.; Du, J.; (Oct 1992), Channel modeling and simulation in satellite mobile communication systems, Selected Areas in Communications, IEEE Journal on, vol.10, no.8, pp.1209-1218, ISSN : 0733-8716.

Yin, George. Zhang, Qing. (2005). Discrete-Time Markov Chains. Two Time-Scale Methods and Applications. Springer. USA. ISBN 978-0-387-21948-6.

Chapter 11

DVB-S2 Model in Matlab: Issues and Impairments

Bahman Azarbad and Aduwati Binti Sali

Additional information is available at the end of the chapter

1. Introduction

For the past two decades, the wide coverage and the reliable bandwidth offered by the broadband satellite systems has made them a promising media for IP streaming. Meanwhile, the demand for exploring new solutions concerning this industry has kept increasing to maintain the growth rate required by the various market sectors.

In order to minimize the design time as well as implementation costs, the initial steps in researches concerning satellite systems are often taken in simulation environments. In contrast with the actual satellite system test-beds which are expensive or sometimes not available to the academic research community, the simulation software packages like Mathworks MATLAB are widely used at the early stages of modeling and design process.However, such packages are mostly designed as general purpose tools and therefore, the built-in models provided by these tools are often incomplete or too simplistic.

The main objective of this research is to use MATLAB simulator for study of issues and impairments of Digital Video Broadcasting-Second generation (DVB-S2) standard in Geostationary (GEO) satellite as a broadcasting media.

In this study we model DVB-S2 standard using Matlab communication toolbox and built in DVB-S2 model in Simulink. However, it is noted that the model in Matlab does not include higher order modulations: 16APSK and 32APSK and also the main novelty of DVB-S2 which is the ACM algorithm. Therefore we need to rebuild the model using toolboxes to add the above mentioned capabilities.

In the following sections, we first provide background of DVB-S2 Standard and in the next section a brief overview on DVB-S2 Model in Matlab will be presented , and then we will go through the model improvement on the following section and afterwards we will analyze presented solution by means of BER performance of the system and the provided ACM engine. Finally, in the last section ,we will discuss the results and future work.

2. Background

The evolution of digital multimedia broadcasting over broadband communication systems in early 90's ,initiated the first stages of standardizing the digital TV broadcasting.In 1993, European Telecommunication Standards Institute (ETSI) started a project named Digital Video Broadcasting(DVB).The main objective of this standard was to introduce standards for digital multimedia services. DVB-S,the first standard for satellite video broadcasting over GEO satellite systems hired an outer shortened Reed Solomon(RS) and inner variable length convolutional code as its Forward Error Correction(FEC) technique[1].

For interactive applications and adaptive transmissions presence of a return link is compulsory.One return link can be established using terrestrial networks which has its own disadvantages like higher cost and unavailability of the link. The more interesting option would be using the same antenna at the receiver for the return link via satellite.This was the motivation for defining a new standard called Digital Video Broadcasting Return channel satellite (DVB-RCS).At the same time that ETSI was providing this standard , they had another project runing for second generation of satellite broadcasting,DVB-S2. In 2003, DVB-S2 specifications was provided by ETSI.

DVB-S2 standard exploits 30% channel efficiency improvement using same power and bandwidth as its ancestor DVB-S[2]. This improvement was resulted from the usage of new FEC techniques: Low Density Parity Check (LDPC) and Bose-Chaudhuri-Hochquenghem (BCH), higher order modulations: 16APSK, 32APSK and a dynamic selection of coding and modulations using instantaneous Channel State Information (CSI) so called Adaptive Coding and Modulation (ACM).

Fade mitigation techniques (FMT) are widely applied on satellite communication to tackle transmission errors and losses caused by atmospheric effects on these systems. Time variant nature of channel states in a Ka band channel affects severely performance of a satellite link,hence it necessitates a dynamic adjustment of Modulation and Coding (ModCods)used by physical layer for transmission. This dynamic adjustment is performed by an adaptive coding and modulation algorithm augmented in DVB-S2 systems deploying a feedback link via DVB-RCS terminals. ACM algorithm uses CSI sent by DVB-RCS return link from individual Earth Stations (ES) to Gate-way ,so called Network Control Center (NCC). NCC is responsible for making the proper selection of ModCods aiming best spectrum efficiency and the desired Bit Error Rate (BER) at the same time[3].

To overcome influences of fading events on transmission quality one of the Well-Known techniques among FMT's is ACM.ACM algorithm will make the proper switching in physical layer transmission mode to maintain channel quality.Different combinations of coding rates and modulation orders are given by ETSI standard.A low coding rate and modulation order will increase robustness of transmission in poor channel quality conditions with a lower spectral efficiency indeed. In case of clear sky by choosing higher coding rate and higher modulation orders spectral efficiency will be increased and system provides a higher throughput.The trade-off between spectral efficiency and BER is crucial in system performance and also transmission cost.In one hand, keeping in to account that although a spectral efficiency higher than appropriate according to channel state will increase system throughput ,it will introduce excessive BER to the system as well. On the other hand, if a ModCod with too low spectral efficiency is selected when the channel quality is in a good condition then capacity of the system will be wasted[4].

The satellite communication channel mostly suffers from signal fading mainly resulted from atmospheric rain attenuation and ionospheric scintillation.Rain attenuation affects these signals severely by absorbing properties of the water,while amplitude and phase of the received signal will be distorted frequently by scintillation in ionosphere caused by electron density irregularities[5].

Since scintillation effects rapidly occurs cannot be compensated by mode adaptation because of the long propagation delay in GEO satellite systems. But rain attenuation time scale is larger comparing to scintillation, hence deploying mode adaptation techniques is convincing to tackle these effects.ACM threshold offsets define thresholds for every ModCod a certain level of safe SNR to guarantee a quasi-zero BER transmission.Making the decision of switching among ModCods is the Gateways's responsibility. In one hand,this adaptation is crucial to tolerate fade attenuations by choosing an adequate ModCod according to the safe threshold defined in the ACM table,on the other hand very frequent changes in channel states due to scintillation may cause in recurrent crossing of thresholds subsequently frequent switchings which is not desirable[6].

Provided that with 11 coding rate and 4 modulation order available in the standard , there will be 44 possible combinations. Only 28 of them are covered by DVB-S2 standard.Considering complexity of terminal design and limited usage of some of these ModCods,there is some proposals suggesting a reduced subset of ModCods.A subset of less than one forth(5 or 7 out of 28)has been investigated in[7].They showed a close to optimum performance can be achieved using these reduced subset and consequently complexity of the terminal will be decreased.This reduced set of ModCods avoid system oscillations and will increase systems stability[8]

The tradeoff between terminal design complexity and achievable spectral efficiency has also been investigated in[9].In this research they proposed subsets of 8 and 5 Modcods with equidistant separation of adjacent ModCods.A simulated time series of one month was their SNR pattern targeting a BER at :

$$BER =\leq 10^{-5} \tag{1}$$

they assumed that a frame is corrupted if the SNR of received signal is less than the threshold offset and it means that comparison between sent and received signal has not been carried out.They obviously ignored the PSNR of received signal and effects of error concealment provided by other layers .

The design of different ACM thresholds and safety margins also play a significant role in the performance of the system.Although the zero-quasi BER offered by DVB-S2 standard is excellent,recent advances in audio and video codecs reduced their need for such outstanding BER level.About 15% packet loss can be accommodated without severe degradation in speech and also modern video codecs like MPEG-4 are capable of concealing errors in input stream by hiring error correction techniques (eg.interframe interpolation)they can accept a higher BER providing acceptable video quality[10].Hence BER rates as high as given below can be acceptable:

$$BER =\leq 10^{-3} \tag{2}$$

Considering the variation in application requirements of different threshold offsets can be implemented in ACM tables.As mentioned above , some applications can tolerate higher BER, so it is reasonable to decrease quality of the transmission in terms of allowing higher BER resulting in higher spectrum efficiency in the system.

3. DVB-S2 model in Matlab

3.1. Introduction

Matlab includes some of important digital video transmission models such as Digital Video Broadcasting-Terrestrial (DVB-T), Digital Video Broadcasting-Cable (DVB-C) and Digital Video Broadcasting-Satellite Second Generation (DVB-S2). Representation of these models are all based on European Telecommunication Standardization Institute (ETSI), in our case of study EN 302 307 [11].

Simulink function blocks are hired for this implementation which will be discussed in detail in the following sections and lack of some parts will be mentioned indeed.

3.2. Matlab DVB-S2 model hierarchy

Figure 1 shows block diagram of DVB-S2 model in Matlab . Each block and its functionalities are given in subsequent sections.

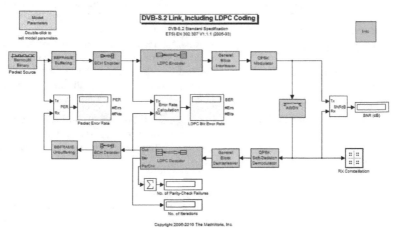

Figure 1. DVB-S2 Block Diagram in Matlab

3.2.1. Bernoulli sequence generator

The very first block is responsible for generating a balanced, in terms of probability of incidents, random binary sequence. Bernoulli sequence is a distribution of zeroes and ones by probabilities of p and (p-1) respectively. In this model, p equals to 0.5 resulting in equal probability of happening for 0 and 1. Output of this block is frame based with the same size as a MPEG-TS packet which is 188 bytes of 8 bits making it 1504 bits.

3.2.2. BBFRAME buffering/unbuffering

Output of packet source generator is buffered to make a Base Band Frame (BBFRAME).The size of this frame is related to the coding rate being used ,equal to BCH encoder input size

.Information bits or called Data FieLd (DFL)can be calculated as given in below formula:

$$DataField = K_b ch - 80 \tag{3}$$

Where Kbch is the size of outer FEC Encoder BCH input,and 80 is the BBFrame header size.Structure of a BBFRAME is shown In Figure 2.

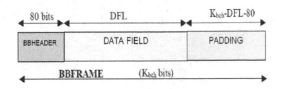

Figure 2. BBFRAME Structure[11]

Number of MPEG packets that can be fitted in one BBFRAME can be shown as:

$$Number of Packets = \left[\frac{K_b ch - 80}{1504}\right] \tag{4}$$

To fulfill BBFRAME size to match BCH encoder input ,post zero padding will be applied.At the receiver side Unbuffering block is responsible for excluding added zero pads and the BBHeader to generate MPEG packets from received frame.Number of zero pad added can be shown as:

$$ZeroPadNo = K_b ch - ((Number of Packets * 1504) + 80) \tag{5}$$

3.2.3. BCH encoder/decoder

One of DVB-S2 standard advances is the forward error correction which is deployed to reduce BER in transmissions is BCH error correction. Output of BBFrame buffering block at the sender side, as above mentioned ,are frames of kbch bits where a BCH(Nbch,Kbch) error correction with the correcting power of t will be applied to them . For each of 11 rate of coding presented in the standard Kbch and Nbch values are defined including the t-error correcting parameter. In tables 1 and 2 these values are shown for normal and short frames respectively.

The output of BCH encoder called BCHFEC frame will be created by adding parity check bits to make a frame with Nbch size.Nbch is the input of inner LDPC encoder which is also named Kldpc. The structure of whole FECFRAME is shown in the Figure 3.

3.2.4. LDPC encoder/decoder

Nbch,the BCH encoder out put as the input of inner FEC encoder will be processed at LDPC encoder to be protected from error with parity bits.The number of parity bits are given in tables 1 and 2, as :

$$number of LDPC parity bits = N_l dpc - N_b ch \tag{6}$$

LDPC encoder supports 11 coding rates.These coding rates are the ratio between information bits(Nbch bits) and LDPC coded block bits which is the FECFRAME. Fore example for rate

LDPC Code	BCH Uncoded Block Kbch	BCH coded block Nbch LDPC Uncoded Block kldpc	BCH t-error correction	LDPC Coded Block nldpc
1/4	16008	16200	12	64800
1/3	21408	21600	12	64800
2/5	25728	25920	12	64800
1/2	32208	32400	12	64800
3/5	38688	38880	12	64800
2/3	43040	43200	10	64800
3/4	48408	48600	12	64800
4/5	51648	51840	12	64800
5/6	53840	54000	10	64800
8/9	57472	57600	8	64800
9/10	58192	58320	8	64800

Table 1. Coding parameters for normal FECFRAMEnldpc=64800

LDPC Code identifier	BCH Uncoded Block Kbch	BCH coded block Nbch LDPC Uncoded Block kldpc	BCH t-error correction	Effective LDPC Rate kldpc/16 200	LDPC Coded Block nldpc
1/4	3072	3240	12	1/5	16200
1/3	5232	5400	12	1/3	16200
2/5	6312	6480	12	2/5	16200
1/2	7032	7200	12	4/9	16200
3/5	9552	9720	12	3/5	16200
2/3	10632	10800	12	2/3	16200
3/4	11712	11880	12	11/15	16200
4/5	12432	12600	12	7/9	16200
5/6	13152	13320	12	37/45	16200
8/9	14232	14400	12	8/9	16200
9/10	NA	NA	NA	NA	NA

Table 2. Coding parameters for short FECFRAMEnldpc=16200

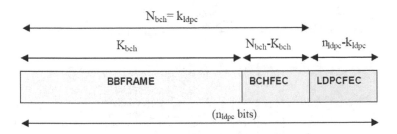

Figure 3. FECFRAME Structure[11]

Modulation	Rows(for nldpc=64800)	Rows(for nldpc=16200)	Columns
8PSK	21600	5400	3
16APSK	16200	4050	4
32APSK	12960	3240	5

Table 3. Bit Interleaver structure

1/4 in a normal frame it shows:

$$\frac{N_b ch}{n_l dpc} = \frac{16200}{64800} = \frac{1}{4} \tag{7}$$

This means that for every 1 bit of information sent from outer FEC coder(BCH),there will be 3 bits of parity checks added in LDPC encoder. The lower this ratio the more protection of data against error has been carried out in LDPC encoder. This will result in more robust data transmission,and it will reduce system throughput indeed. At the receiver side,LDPC decoder will check the received sequence till the parity checks are satisfied up to 50 iterations.This error correction uses the sparse parity-check matrices with a hard decision making algorithm.

3.2.5. Interleaver/deinterleaver

Interleaving process is the next step in DVB-S2 for modulations 8PSK,16APSK and 32APSK. Interleaving on QPSK is not going to be done and as for DVB-S2 model in Matlab ,16APSK and 32APSK modulations are not included so we will discuss them in our proposed model later.The interleaver structure is given in table 3.

Interleaver block in Matlab will make this on 8PSK by writing column wise serially the output of LDPC encoder in a 3 by nldpc(21600 for 8PSK) matric and then will read it out row wise.The MSB of BBHeader will be read-out first since for rate 3/5 it will be read-out as third.These processes are shown in figures 4 and 5.

Interleaving process creates rows in a matric from the LDPC encoder output according to the modulation order M, so each row will contain a symbol ready to be mapped in the next block ,modulation.At the receiver side Deinterleaver block will receive the output of demodulator block as input and will apply the reverse process to create a serial output for the LDPCdecoder input.

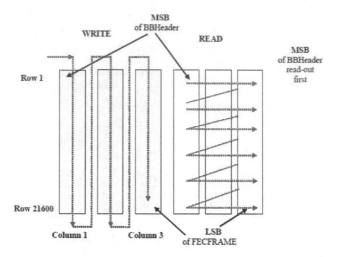

Figure 4. Bit Interleaving scheme for 8PSK and normal FECFRAME length (all rates except 3/5)[11]

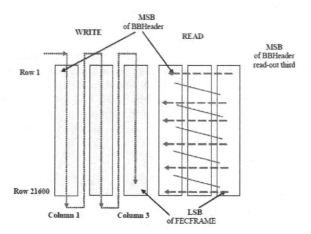

Figure 5. Bit Interleaving scheme for 8PSK and normal FECFRAME length (rate 3/5 only)[11]

3.2.6. Modulator/demadulator

Modulation block will process the interleaved vector by first mapping each row to a symbol which in our case is a gray mapping,then the mapped symbols will be assigned to constellations.Constellation and mapping for QPSK and 8PSK are given in figures 6 and 7 respectively.Modulator for QPSK and 8psk both orders have a phase offset given below and the average energy for normalized constellation per symbol should correspond to :

$$\rho^2 = 1 \tag{8}$$

$$Phase\,offset = \frac{\pi}{4} \tag{9}$$

At the receiver side,demodulator will analyze the received signal from the channel and will

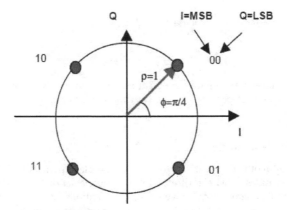

Figure 6. Bit mapping into QPSK constellation[11]

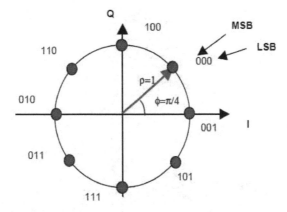

Figure 7. Bit mapping into 8PSK constellation[11]

approximately calculate LLR's using soft decision making LLR algorithm.Demodulator needs noise variance of the signal or at least an estimation of it. Noise variance calculation is given in below formula:

$$Noise\,variance = \frac{SignalPower * SymbolTime}{SampleTime * 10^{\frac{(\frac{E_s}{N_0})}{10}}} \tag{10}$$

3.2.7. AWGN channel

Additive Gaussian White Noise(AWGN) block in Matlab comply with Transmission channel in Ka band.This block adds a noise to the complex signal sent from modulator based on a manual parameter being set by the user.This parameter can be defined as Es/No,Eb/No or SNR,any how the block will calculate the noise variance and will add a noise with zero mean to the signal.The relation between Es/No,Eb/No and SNR is as follows:

$$\frac{E_s}{N_o} = (\frac{T_sym}{T_samp}) * SNR \tag{11}$$

$$\frac{E_s}{N_o} = (\frac{E_b}{N_o}) + 10\log(k) \tag{12}$$

Where Es is the signal energy in Joules ,Eb is bit energy in Joules, No is noise power spectral density,Tsym is the symbol period ,K is the information bits per symbol and Tsamp is the sample time.

4. Proposed DVB-S2 model

The most important motivation of this project was to implement a DVB-S2 link layer model in matlab which includes ACM algorithm with a complete set of ModCods and also video quality measurement system . To do so we added modulations for 16APSK and 32APSK and PSNR calculation to the system.Specificaly, we used communication toolbox in Matlab for this approach.The model is depicted in Figure 8.The model is defined in the following sections.

Figure 8. DVB-S2 proposed model

4.1. MPEG-TS input/output blocks

In Matlab DVB-S2 model as mentioned earlier they use a random Bernoulli sequence generator for input of the model.To analyze the effect of ACM algorithm on the quality of transmission of a real MPEG stream, we used MPEG-TS stored in a matrix with 188 columns (one MPEG packet) and 100000 rows(number of packets).This is used as the input of the system and at receiver side will be again stored for PSNR calculation.

4.2. PSNR calculation

Peak Signal to Noise Ratio(PSNR)which is a well-known metric for quality measurement of received video, is added to the proposed model.The computation of PSNR is in decibels and uses the Mean Square Error(MSE) which is also an error metric often used for video quality estimation[12].MSE computation is expressed as:

$$MSE = \frac{1}{N} \sum (P_i^s - P_i^r)^2 \tag{13}$$

where N represents the number of pixels in the image while P and P are the original image and received image respectively.The PSNR then is computed as follows:

$$PSNR = 10log \frac{(2^n - 1)^2}{MSE(I)} \tag{14}$$

where n is the number of luminance bits used in the image.

4.3. Interleaver/deinterleaver

Interleaving for 16 and 32 APSK are two blocks included to the model based on ETSI instructions.The number of rows and columns of this interleaver are given in table 3.In figure 9 the structure of Interleaver for 16 APSK is given , the only difference with 32 APSK is the number of columns which is 5 instead of 4, consequently number of rows also will be different.

4.4. Modulator/demodulator

Higher order modulations presented by DVB-S2,provides higher spectrum efficiency comparing to the earlier generation,DVB-S.To analyze the BER performance of DVB-S2 and also adding the ACM algorithm to our model, we include Modulations for 16 and 32 APSK. Modulation block is responsible for mapping and constellation generation to prepare the base band signal for transmission.

4.4.1. 16 APSK modulator

The modulation constellation for 16 APSK as described in ETSI uses two concentric rings R1 and R2.These rings are uniformly spaced with 4 and 12 points.The constellation is given in the Figure 10.The ratio between R1 and R2,gamma,is defined as:

$$\gamma = \frac{R_2}{R_1} \tag{15}$$

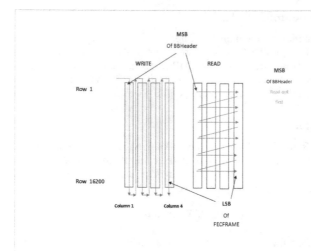

Figure 9. Bit Intereaving scheme for 16APSK and normal FECFRAME length

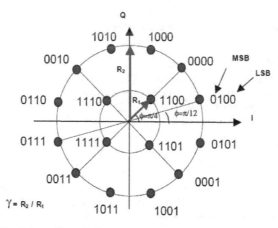

Figure 10. 16APSK Signal Constellation[11]

4.4.2. 32 APSK modulator

Three uniformly spaced rings are defined in the standard using 4 ,12 and 16 PSK points for 32 APSK modulator constellation :R1 ,R2 and R3.The outer ring R3 should be equal to one and gamma1 and gamma2 will define the ratio between rings as follows:

$$\gamma_1 = \frac{R_2}{R_1} \tag{16}$$

$$\gamma_2 = \frac{R_3}{R_1} \tag{17}$$

The symbol order and constellation defined by ETSI is given in Figure 11.

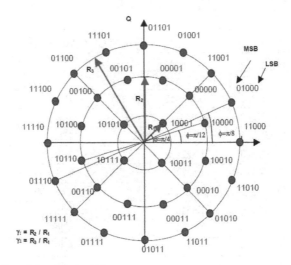

Figure 11. 32APSK Signal Constellation[11]

4.4.3. Demodulator

At the receiver side,demodulator will receive the signal from AWGN channel which is the noisy signal.To demodulate the signal ,demodulator needs noise variance of the channel for computation of the signal LLR's. For this computation we used approximate LLR algorithm.

4.5. ACM algorithm

In the current DVB-S2 model in Matlab,a Constant Coding and Modulation strategy has been developed .This strategy is based on the worst case adjustment for physical layer which will waste spectral efficiency at most of the time .This waste is costly and can be avoided by using state of the art ACM algorithm ,so any individual user can be treated according to its present channel state.

The last step of design in the proposed model is the implementation of the ACM engine.ACM algorithm included in this model is based on the standard required Es/No by ETSI to support a Quasi Error Free transmission.As depicted in table 4,for all 28 combinations of ModCods there is a required level of Es/No.To make decisions among ModCods threshold offsets are provided as equidistance thresholds between adjacent ModCods. The SNR of received signal at the receiver will be sent to ACM block to be used for next frame mode of transmission.

5. Simulation and results

We run simulations for different values of Es/No ranging from -3 to 17 dB and for each ModCod. The LDPC decoder was set to 50 iterations and normal frame size (64,800 bits)

Mode	Spectral efficiency	Ideal Es/No(dB) for FECFRAME Length 64800
QPSK1/4	0.490243	-2.35
QPSK1/3	0.656448	-1.24
QPSK2/5	0.789412	-0.30
QPSK1/2	0.988858	1.00
QPSK3/5	1.188304	2.23
QPSK2/3	1.322253	3.10
QPSK3/4	1.487473	4.03
QPSK4/5	1.587196	4.68
QPSK5/6	1.654663	5.18
QPSK8/9	1.766451	6.20
QPSK9/10	1.788612	6.42
8PSK3/5	1.779991	5.50
8PSK2/3	1.980636	6.62
8PSK3/4	2.228124	7.91
8PSK5/6	2.478562	9.35
8PSK8/9	2.646012	10.69
8PSK9/10	2.679207	10.98
16APSK2/3	2.637201	8.97
16APSK3/4	2.966728	10.21
16APSK4/5	3.165623	11.03
16APSK5/6	3.300184	11.61
16APSK8/9	3.523143	12.89
16APSK9/10	3.567342	13.13
32APSK3/4	3.703295	12.73
32APSK4/5	3.951571	13.64
32APSK5/6	4.119540	14.28
32APSK8/9	4.397854	15.69
32APSK9/10	4.453027	16.05

Table 4. Es/No performance at Quasi Error Free PER

Simulation Parameters	Settings
Frame size	64800(Normal)
LDPC Encoder Input Type	Bit
LDPC Decoder output Type	Information Part
LDPC Decoder Decision Input Type	Hard Decision
LDPC Decoder Number Of Iterations	50
Modulator Input Type	Bit
Modulator Symbol Order	Gray
Demodulator Output Type	Bit
Demodulator Decision Type	Soft Decision
LLR Algorithm	Approximate LLR
Channel Noise Factor	SNR

Table 5. Simulation Parameters and Settings

is used. Simulation parameters and settings are presented in Table 5. At the LDPC decoder output we calculate BER and number of violated parity checks.

To evaluate performance of the presented model in terms of BER we run simulation for all ModCods .The results are shown in Figure 12.It can be perceived,that the model performs transmissions with the expected BER levels for all ModCods.

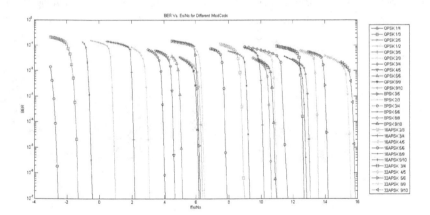

Figure 12. BER Vs. Es/No For Different ModCods

In order to analyze the video quality ,instead of sending a Bernoulli sequence , we send MPEG-TS and considering PSNR of received video and QEF requirements.In Figure 13, we showed that deploying the standardized ACM thresholds the model can perform the transmission with the desired quality with almost 0.3 dB less Es/No required.

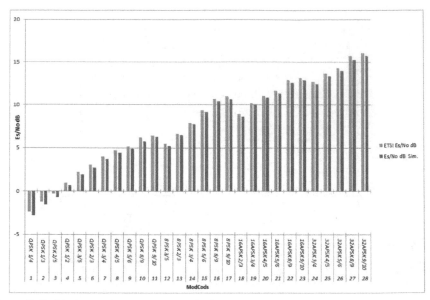

Figure 13. Es/No Comparison with ETSI Standard

In[8],the authors proposed SNR intervals for different ModCods based on ETSI standard.We also compared SNR performance of our proposed model with their intervals.We consider the PSNR of received video in conjunction with BER.The comparison result is given in Figure 14.

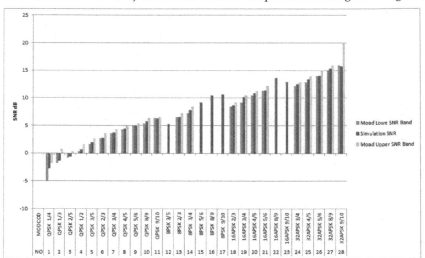

Figure 14. SNR Comparison with D.Moad et. al Offsets

6. Conclusion

In this study, we proposed a complete DVB-S2 model for GEO satellite communication system implemented in Matlab.Specifically, we added high order modulation schemes, 16APSK and 32APSK.On top of that, we include ACM algorithm with standard threshold offsets provided by ETSI.Instead of random inputs we used MPEG-TS and we analyzed the quality of the received video streams.By running extensive simulation runs, we showed that the model corresponds to the standard in terms of BER performance.Then we investigate the model performance according to the PSNR of received video and we compared the results with some results in the literature.The results show a 0.3 dB improvement in the required Es/No defined in ACM offsets by ETSI.For future work, we address the study of different ACM thresholds and their performance in terms of spectral efficiency versus PSNR of received video.

Acknowledgement

This project was funded by Malaysian Ministry of Science, Technology and Innovation (MOSTI) under its eScience fund program '3D Video Transmission over GEO Satellite Networks for Disaster Management Applications' (Project code: 01-01-04-SF1047). We would also take this opportunity to thank Mr Bernhard Shcmidt for his kind cooperation in some codes.

Author details

Bahman Azarbad and Aduwati Binti Sali
University Putra Malaysia, Malaysia

7. References

[1] ETSI. Ets 200 421 v1.2.2 digital broadcasting system for television, sound, and data services., 1994.

[2] Alberto Morello and Vittoria Mignone. Dvb-s2 ready for lift off. Technical report, RAI, Radiotelevisione Italiana, 2004.

[3] B. Azarbad, A. Sali, B.M. Ali, and H.A. Karim. Study of ber in dvb-s2 satellite implemented in matlab. In *Space Science and Communication (IconSpace), 2011 IEEE International Conference on DOI - 10.1109/IConSpace.2011.6015887*, pages 221–224, 2011.

[4] J.E. Barcelo, G. Giambene, and M. Castro. Cross-layer optimization of tcp throughput for dvb-s2 links. In *Satellite and Space Communications, 2008. IWSSC 2008. IEEE International Workshop on*, pages 13 –17, oct. 2008.

[5] S. Datta-Barua, P. H. Doherty, S. H. Delay, T. Dehel, and J. A. Klobuchar. Ionospheric scintillation effects on single and dual frequency gps positioning. In *16th international technical meeting of the satellite division of the institute of navigation(ION GPS/GNSS'03)*, pages 334–356, portland usa, september 2003.

[6] Matteo Berioli, Christian Kissling, and Rémi Lapeyre. Capacity versus bit error rate trade-off in the dvb-s2 forward link. *EURASIP Journal on Wireless Communications and Networking*, 2007:10, 2007.

[7] V. Boussemart, H. Brandt, and M. Berioli. Subset optimization of adaptive coding and modulation schemes for broadband satellite systems. In *Communications (ICC), 2010 IEEE International Conference on*, pages 1 –5, may 2010.

[8] D. Moad, Y. Hadjadj-Aoul, and F. Nait-Abdesselam. Predictive channel estimation for optimized resources allocation in dvb-s2 networks. In *Personal, Indoor and Mobile Radio Communications, 2009 IEEE 20th International Symposium on*, pages 2608–2612, sept. 2009.

[9] M. Smolnikar, T. Javornik, and M. Mohorcic. Target ber driven adaptive coding and modulation in hap based dvb-s2 system. In *Advanced Satellite Mobile Systems, 2008. ASMS 2008. 4th*, pages 262–267, aug. 2008.

[10] ETSI. Tr 126 975 v10.0.0 "digital cellular telecommunications system (phase 2+);universal mobile telecommunications system (umts);lte;performance characterization of the adaptive multi-rate (amr) speech codec" (3gpp tr 26.975 version 10.0.0 release 10), 04 2011.

[11] ETSI. En 302 307 v1.2.1 (2009-08)-digital video broadcasting (dvb);second generation framing structure, channel coding and modulation systems for broadcasting,interactive services, news gathering and other broadband satellite applications (dvb-s2), 2009.

[12] D. Pradas, Lei Jiang, M.A. Vazquez Castro, P. Barsocchi, and F. Potorti. Satellite phy-layer selector design for video applications in tropical areas. In *Satellite and Space Communications, 2009. IWSSC 2009. International Workshop on*, pages 407–411, sept. 2009.

Chapter 12

Simulation Framework of Wireless Sensor Network (WSN) Using MATLAB/SIMULINK Software

Qutaiba I. Ali

Additional information is available at the end of the chapter

1. Introduction

A wireless sensor network consists of spatially distributed autonomous sensors to cooperatively monitor physical or environmental conditions, such as temperature, sound, vibration, pressure, motion or pollutants. The development of wireless sensor networks was motivated by military applications such as battlefield surveillance. They are now used in many industrial and civilian application areas, including industrial process monitoring and control, machine health monitoring, environment and habitat monitoring, healthcare applications, home automation, and traffic control [1-2].

A smart sensor node is a combination of sensing, processing and communication technologies. Figure 1 shows the basic architectural components of a sensor node. The sensing unit senses the change of parameters, signal conditioning circuitry prepares the electrical signals to convert to the digital domain, the sensed analog signal is converted and is used as the input to the application algorithms or processing unit, the memory helps processing of tasks and the transceiver is used for communicating with other sensors or the base stations or sinks in WSN[3], see figure 1.

Sensors can monitor temperature, pressure, humidity, soil makeup, vehicular movement, noise levels, lighting conditions, the presence or absence of certain kinds of objects or substances, mechanical stress levels on attached objects, and other properties. Their mechanism may be seismic, magnetic, thermal, visual, infrared, acoustic, or radar. A smart sensor is also capable of self-identification and self-diagnosis. The mechanisms of smart sensors work in one of three ways: by a line of sight to the target (such as visual sensors), by proximity to target (such as seismic sensors), and by propagation like a wave with possible bending (such as acoustic sensors)[4,5].

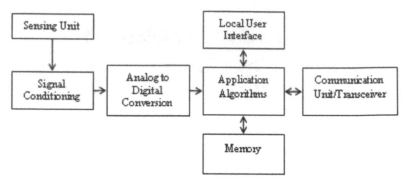

Figure 1. Basic architectural components of a smart sensor

2. Review of existing simulation environments for WSNs

In this section, a selection of existing simulation environments for WSNs is discussed. Basically, the investigated simulation environments can be divided into two major types: adaptive development and new development. The adaptive development covers simulation environments that already existed before the idea of WSNs emerged. These simulation environments were then extended to support wireless functionality and were then adapted for the use with WSNs. In contrast, new developments cover new simulators, which were created solely for simulating WSNs, considering sensor specific characteristics from the beginning. Both types have advantages and disadvantages, but basically it can be stated that while the evolutionary adaptation has some advantages in reusing well-tested ideas and source code as well as the bigger user and developer basis, the new developments have their advantages in focusing on the special characteristics and the functioning of sensor nodes.

a.   GloMoSim/QualNet

GloMoSim [6] is a scalable simulation environment for wireless and wired network systems, which uses the parallel discrete-event simulation capability provided by Parsec [7], a c-based simulation language for sequential and parallel execution of discrete-event simulation models. Both, GloMoSim as well as Parsec, were developed by the Parallel Computing Lab. at UCLA. GloMoSim offers basic functionality to simulate wireless networks, even for ad hoc networks (e.g. AODV, DSR). However, the current version of GloMoSim does not offer any sensor network specific features in the default package so that without any further efforts no WSNs can be simulated meaningfully. In 2000 QualNet [6], [7], a commercial derivate of GloMoSim, was created and with GloMoSim 2.0, the last version of GloMoSim, was released under an academic license. From this point in time, no further improvements to GloMoSim were made, whereas the development of QualNet expedited. In October 2009, version 5.0 of QualNet was released including enhancements such as a new sensor network library for ZigBee, new network security library, parallel updates, new models (e.g. battery and energy), updates to current models as well as performance improvements. Furthermore, a new QT based GUI was added providing a scenario designer, a visualizer to view network scenarios (2D and 3D), a packet tracer for debugging, an analyzer for statistics and a file editor to edit the scenarios directly.

b. OPNET Modeler Wireless Suite

OPNET Modeler Wireless Suite [8]–[10] is a commercial modeling and simulation tool for various types of wireless networks. It is developed by developed by OPNET Technologies, Inc. and based on the well-known product OPNET Modeler. The simulation environment uses a fast discrete event simulation engine operating with a 32-bit/ 64-bit fully parallel simulation kernel, which is available for Windows and Linux. The OPNET Modeler provides an object-oriented modeling approach and a hierarchical modeling environment. Although there are no special routing protocols for wireless sensor network available, at least different propagation and modulation techniques as well as a ZigBee (802.15.4) MAC layer are provided. Additional modules have to be customized or developed from the scratch. The simulations of wireless networks can be run as discrete event, hybrid or analytical, encompassing terrain, mobility and path-loss models. Due to the open interface external object files, libraries as well as other simulators can be integrated to the OPNET Modeler. Optional a System-in-the-Loop is available to interface simulations with live systems. Furthermore, the OPNET Modeler Wireless Suite provides grid computing support so that simulations can be executed in a distributed manner[11].

c. TOSSIM

TOSSIM (TinyOS mote simulator) [12]–[15] is a discrete event simulator for TinyOS sensor networks that is part of the official TinyOS package. TOSSIM takes advantage of the component based architecture of TinyOS by integrating it transparently by providing a new hardware resource abstraction layer that simulates the TinyOS network stack at the bit level for normal PCs. Due to this approach low-level protocols up to top-level applications can be simulated with TOSSIM. TOSSIM has an external communication system so that transmitted packets can be monitored and even new packets can be injected to network. Furthermore, the configuration of the debug options is fine grained providing the desired debug output at runtime. TOSSIM offers three network connectivity models: simple connectivity, static connectivity and space connectivity. The running simulations can be visualized and controlled by the Java-based GUI TinyViz[16].

d. OMNeT++

OMNeT++ [17]–[20] is an object-oriented discrete network simulation framework. The architecture is rather generic so that various problem domains can be simulated such as protocol modeling, validation of hardware architectures and modeling of wired and wireless communication networks. OMNeT++ is not a simulator, but it rather provides a framework and tools to write simulations. It is highly portable so that it can be run on the most common operating systems such as Windows, Linux and Mac OSX. There are a couple of simulation frameworks that enable OMNeT++ to be used for wireless sensor networks[21]. The most common of these frameworks are discussed in the following subsections.

Mobility Framework: The Mobility Framework [22]–[24], developed in the Telecommunication Networks Group (TKN) at the Technical University of Berlin, provides only basic support for mobile and wireless networks. It includes some basic layers such as MAC layers (Aloha, CSMA) and network layers (flooding) as well as some basic mobility functionality and some basic application layer.

MiXiM: MiXiM [25], [26] is a merger of several OMNeT++ frameworks to support mobile and wireless simulations. It uses the mobility support, the connection management, and the general structure from the Mobility Framework (MF); the radio propagation models from the CHannel SIMulator (ChSim); and the protocol library from the MAC simulator, the Positif frame- work [27], and the Mobility Framework.

Castalia: Castalia [28], [29] is a simulator for WSNs (WSN), body area networks (BAN) and generally networks of low-power embedded devices that is based on OMNeT++. It is developed at the National ICT Australia since 2006 and made public as open source under the Academic Public License in 2007.

INET Framework: The INET Framework [30], [31] is a framework for OMNeT++ that contains various implementations of common protocols, such as IPv4, IPv6, TCP, UDP etc., as well as several application models. The INET Framework is not specialized on mobile and wireless networks, but has some support for it.

NesCT: NesCT [32] is not a real framework, but rather a translator from the programming language NesC to C++ classes for OMNet++.

e. NS-2

NS (the Network Simulator) [33], [34] is an object-oriented discrete event simulator targeting at networking research. NS-2 is written in C++ and OTcl, an object-oriented version of Tcl. A huge amount of contributed protocol source codes can be found on the website http://nsnam.isi.edu/nsnam/index.php/Contributed Code. among them there are also some for WSNs interesting wireless protocols such as different variations of 802.11, 802.16, IR-UWB, BlueTooth and 802.15.4. Despite the great number of contributing researchers the support for wireless sensor network specific protocols is rather low. As special wireless sensor network framework the Mannasim Framework [36] should be highlighted that provides sensor network specific protocols such as LEACH and Directed Diffusion. Also the extension NS2-MIUN [37] provides some wireless sensor network specific contributions with the focus on intrusion detection. SensorSim: SensorSim [38]–[40] is a simulation framework for modeling sensor networks that built up on NS-2. It provides additional features for modeling sensor networks such as sensor channel models, power models (battery and radio), lightweight protocol stacks for wireless micro-sensors, scenario generation and hybrid simulation.

f. Avrora

Avrora [41]–[43] is a set of simulation and analysis tools for programs written for AVR micro-controllers. It has support for different sensor platforms, such as Mica2 and MicaZ, allowing wireless network simulation, dynamic instrumentation and static analysis. Since 2004, Avrora is developed in a research project of the UCLA compiler group. The special characteristic of Avrora is that it operates on the instruction-level, i.e. actual microcontroller programs can be run in the simulator, instead of just simulating software models.

g. J-Sim

J-Sim [44]–[46] is a component-based compositional simulation environment based on the autonomous component architecture (ACA). The basic entities of ACA are components, which communicated with each other by sending and receiving data using their ports. Application specific models can be defined by sub-classing the specified classes of the WSN simulation framework and adapting them to the desired behavior. At the moment, 802.11 is used as MAC Layer and AODV is provided as routing protocol.

h. ATEMU

ATEMU [47], [48] is one of the first instruction-level software emulators for AVR based systems. Additionally peripheral devices of the MICA2 sensor node platform such as radio is supported. Although at the moment only the MICA2 hardware is supported, ATEMU can be easily extended to support other sensor node platforms. Although ATEMU is the most accurate instruction-level emulator for wireless sensor network research, it lacks from simulation speed, being 30 times slower than TOSSIM, for example.

i. EmStar

EmStar [49]–[51] is an environment for WSNs built from Linux-class devices, so called micro servers. In comparison to motes, micro servers are much less constrained in computational power and data storage size so that they can handle more complex tasks such as image and audio processing. EmStar consists of simulation and emulation tools, which utilize a modular, but not strictly layered, architecture. EmStar provides different simulation modes: a pure simulation mode, an emulation mode, a real mode and a hybrid mode. EmStar provides various services that are used and combined to provide network functionality for wireless embedded systems. This includes link drivers for the lowest-layer interfaces to network resources, pass-through modules that implement various types of filter and passive processing, and routing modules such as Flooding, DSR, Sink, StateSync and Centroute.

j. SENS

SENS [52], [53] is an application-oriented simulator for WSNs. It has a modular, layered architecture so that components for applications, network communication and the physical environment can be easily interchanged and extended. Due to different component implementations, which varies in the degree of realism, application-specific environments can be created and simulated. Due to the chosen approach, SENS enables application portability because the same source code can be run with in a simulation or deployed on actual sensor nodes.

k. SENSE

SENSE (Sensor Network Simulator and Emulator) [54], [55] is a simulator for WSNs that is based on a novel component-oriented simulation methodology, which promotes extensibility and reusability. At the same time, the simulation efficiency and the scalability was considered. In the component repository of SENSE there are already different components available from the application to the physical layer including IEEE 802.11, AODV, DSR, SSR, SHR as well as Battery Models and a Power Model. At the moment, there does not seem to be any further tools included in SENSE so that, for example, a visualization tool to analyze the network behavior graphically is missing.

l. Shawn

Shawn [56]–[58] is customizable sensor network simulator based on an algorithmic approach. The primary design goals of Shawn are: simulate the effect caused by a phenomenon, scalability and support for extremely large networks and free choice of the implementation model. Models are the interfaces that are used by Shawn to control the simulation without knowing the exact implementation. Each implementation of a model specifies the actual behavior. Currently there are several implementations for the transmission model provided such as Pure CSMA & CSMA/CA, (Slotted) Aloha, Random Drop etc. Additionally to the three core models, there are several other models provided by Shawn for random variables, distance estimation and mobility. The simulation environment provides a sort of virtual world in which the different parts of the simulation are located. The simulated nodes are located in a single world instance and the nodes themselves are containers for processors. The application logic is implemented as instances of processors.

In this chapter, Simulink MATLAB was adopted to be the simulation tool of wireless sensor network (WSN). The main advantage of the suggested method is to determine the effect of the different channel parameters (i.e., Signal to Noise ratio, Attenuation and Interference) on the system behavior.

3. The proposed WSN simulation methodology

The environment in which we build our simulation model was MATLAB. The name MATLAB stands for matrix laboratory. *MATLAB*, developed by MathWorks Inc., is a software package for high performance numerical computation and visualization. The combination of analysis capabilities, flexibility, reliability, and powerful graphics makes *MATLAB* the premier software package for scientific researchers. *MATLAB* provides an interactive environment with hundreds of reliable and accurate built-in mathematical functions. These functions provide solutions to a broad range of mathematical problems including matrix algebra, complex arithmetic, linear systems, differential equations, signal processing, optimization, nonlinear systems, and many other types of scientific computations. The most important feature of *MATLAB* is its programming capability, which is very easy to learn and to use, and which allows user-developed functions. It also allows access to Fortran algorithms and C codes by means of external interfaces. There are several optional toolboxes written for special applications such as signal processing, control systems design, system identification, statistics, neural networks, fuzzy logic, symbolic computations, and others. *MATLAB* has been enhanced by the very powerful Simulink program[59].

Simulink is a software package for modeling, simulating, and analyzing dynamical systems. It supports linear and nonlinear systems, modeled in continuous time, sampled time, or a hybrid of the two. Systems can also be multi-rate, i.e., have different parts that are sampled or updated at different rates. For modeling, Simulink provides a graphical user interface (GUI) for building models as block diagrams, using click-and-drag mouse operations. With this interface, you can draw the models just as you would with pencil and paper (or as most textbooks depict them). Simulink includes a comprehensive block library of sinks, sources, linear and nonlinear components, and connectors. You can also customize and create your own blocks Models are hierarchical. This approach provides insight into how a model is organized and how its parts interact. After you define a model, you can simulate it, using a choice of integration methods, either from the Simulink menus or by entering commands in MATLAB's command window. The menus are particularly convenient for interactive work, while the command-line approach is very useful for running a batch of simulations (for example, if you are doing Monte Carlo simulations or want to sweep a parameter across a range of values). Using scopes and other display blocks, you can see the simulation results while the simulation is running. In addition, you can change parameters and immediately see what happens, for "what if" exploration. The simulation results can be put in the MATLAB workspace for post processing and visualization. And because MATLAB and Simulink are integrated, you can simulate, analyze, and revise your models in either environment at any point. [59].

3.1. Simulating a simple WSN in Simulink MATLAB

In order to demonstrate the concepts of the suggested simulation methodology, a simple WSN model was built as shown in figure 2[60]. This network consisted of three sensors (slaves) sending their measured data samples to a master node. In this chapter, MATLAB Simulink communication block set was used to build a complete WSN system. Simulation procedure includes building the hardware architecture of the transmitting nodes, modeling both the communication channel and the receiving master node architecture. Bluetooth was chosen to undertake the physical layer communication with respect to different channel parameters (i.e., Signal to Noise ratio, Attenuation and Interference). The simulation model was examined using different topologies under various conditions and numerous results were collected.

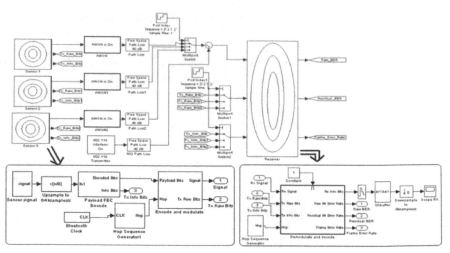

Figure 2. Simple WSN model

The architecture of the system could be explained as follows:

1. The transmitter

This system was based on Bluetooth technology that is considered as the backbone of transmission operation. Bluetooth is a short-range radio link technology that operates in the 2.4 GHz Industrial, Scientific, and Medical (ISM) band[60]. In this system we modulated the signal using Gaussian frequency shift keying (GFSK) over a radio channel with maximum capacity of 1 Mbps. The transmitter consists of the following blocks:

- Sensor signal stage: It is represented by a sensor to sense the physical signals such as temperature, pressure…etc, then transducing them into an electrical signal. In addition, this stage includes the A/D convertor which converts the signal from Analog to Digital using 256 quantization level.
- Up-sampling to 64ksamples/s: Up-samples the input to a higher rate by inserting zeros between samples.
- Payload FEC encode: Encodes the data to enable error correction(an FEC encoder may include a binary convolutional encoder followed by a puncturing device).
- Bluetooth Clock: Each Bluetooth device has a free-running 28-bit Bluetooth clock. The clock ticks 3,200 times per second or once every 312.5 μsec, representing a clock rate of 3.2 KHz.
- Hop Sequence Generator: For devices to communicate with each other, they must transmit and receive on the same frequency at the same time. The hop sequence generator generates a sequence of hop frequencies in the range 0 to 78. It can generate either the connection state hop sequence, a random white sequence, or be fixed.
- Encoder and modulator: The 366 data bits are transmitted at 1 Mbps and modulated using Gaussian frequency shift keying (GFSK). GFSK effectively transmits +150 kHz signal relative to the carrier for a 1bit, and a 150 kHz signal for a 0 bit. The carrier signal is

generated in the Simulink model by a baseband MFSK block set to 79 symbols and a separation of 1MHz. If a hop frequency value 0 is input, a -39MHz complex sinusoid is generated. If a 1 is entered, a -38 MHz complex sinusoid is generated and so on. In the model, the hop sequences are generated by a simple random number generator, not using the actual method specified in the standard. The transmitter is turned off after 366 bits using a Gain block to multiply the frame with a mask of 36600 ones and 26500 zeros.

2. **The medium which consists of the following blocks**

- AWGN Channel: The AWGN Channel block adds white Gaussian noise to a real or complex input signal. When the input signal is real, this block adds real Gaussian noise and produces a real output signal. When the input signal is complex, this block adds complex Gaussian noise and produces a complex output signal.

- Path Loss: This block reduces the amplitude of the input signal by an amount specified. The loss can be specified directly using the "Decibels" mode, or indirectly using the "Distance and Frequency" mode. The reciprocal of the loss is applied as a gain, e.g., a loss of +20 dB, which reduces the signal by a factor of 10 corresponds to a gain value of 0.1.

- 802.11b interferer: This block adds signals that have the same frequency of the data signal to make interference between the data signal and other signals(i.e. a Wireless Local Area Network (WLAN) transmission).

- Multiport Switch: In order to simulate the multiple access and multiplexing functions of the channel, this block was used. It chooses between a number of inputs. The first input is called the control input, while the rest of the inputs are called data inputs. The value of the control input determines which data input is passed through to the output port.

3. **The receiver consists of the following blocks:**

- Hop Sequence Generator: same as mentioned earlier.
- Demodulation and decoding: This block is used to extract the original information-bearing signal from a modulated carrier wave, and to recover the information contends in it.
- Zero-Order Hold: This block samples and holds its input for the specified sample period. The block accepts one input and generates one output, both of which can be scalar or vector. If the input is a vector, all elements of the vector are held for the same sample period.
- Un-buffer: This block un-buffers an Mi-by-N frame-based input into a 1-by-N sample-based output. That is, inputs are un-buffered row-wise so that each matrix row becomes an independent time-sample in the output. The rate at which the block receives inputs is generally less than the rate at which the block produces outputs.
- Down-sampling to 8ksamples/s: This block down-samples the input to a lower rate by deleting the repeating samples.
- Scope RX: It was used to display the received signal and compare it with the original signal to discover the system behavior.

As known, a piconet can includes up to seven slaves and one master. In this example three signals were sent from three sensors ' (slaves) to the receiving component (master) representing one piconet , the information obtained by the sensors are used to estimate the

Bluetooth performance as well as to study the media effect. Noise and interference are added to the signals in order to simulate the channel effect and measure Bit Error Rate (BER) and Frame Error Rate (FER). The following figures shows the system performance under different working conditions.

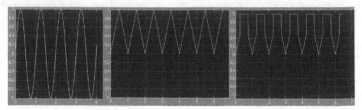

Figure 3. Signals sent from the three sensors

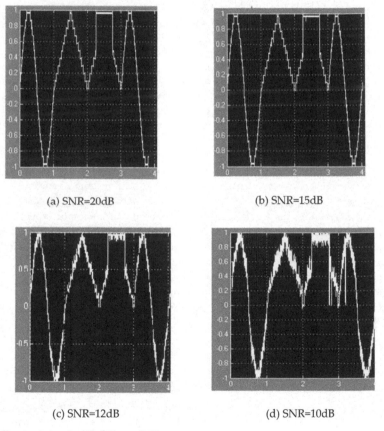

(a) SNR=20dB   (b) SNR=15dB

(c) SNR=12dB   (d) SNR=10dB

Figure 4. Received signals with different SNR

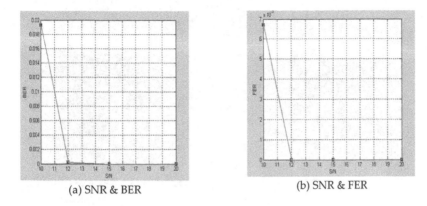

(a) SNR & BER   (b) SNR & FER

Figure 5. Relationship between SNR & (BER, FER)

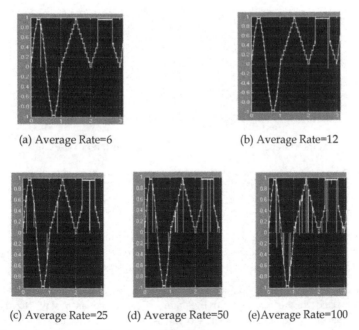

(a) Average Rate=6   (b) Average Rate=12

(c) Average Rate=25   (d) Average Rate=50   (e) Average Rate=100

Figure 6. Received signals with different rate of interference

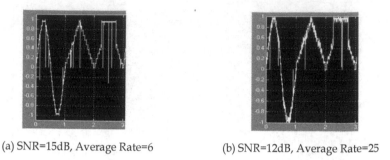

(a) SNR=15dB, Average Rate=6   (b) SNR=12dB, Average Rate=25

Figure 7. Received signals with different rate of interference & different SNR

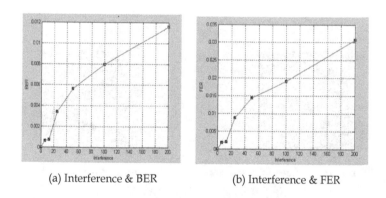

(a) Interference & BER   (b) Interference & FER

Figure 8. Relationship between interference & (BER, FER)

3.2. More complex example

As known from Blutooth operation, each piconet consists of one master and seven slaves and each master of a specific piconet may acts as a slave for another piconet which means the ability to expand the network to respond to more than seven sensors.

In this example two piconets are connected, so that the first piconet consists of three sensors connected to the master, and the later is connected as a slave to the second piconet. The second piconet consists of two slaves and one master as shown in Figure 9 below:

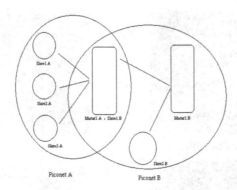

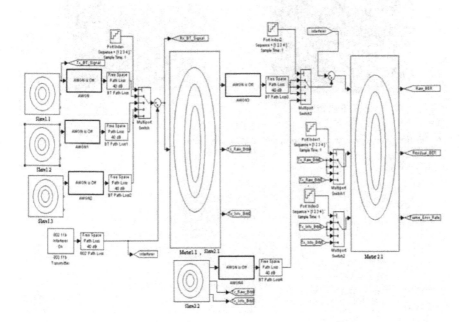

Figure 9. WSN model with masters & slaves

The following figures shows the system performance under different working conditions.

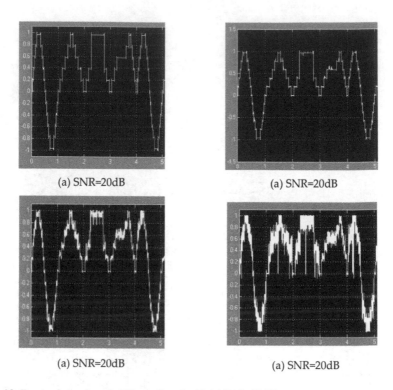

(a) SNR=20dB

(a) SNR=20dB

(a) SNR=20dB

(a) SNR=20dB

Figure 10. Received signals with different Signal to Noise Ratio (SNR)

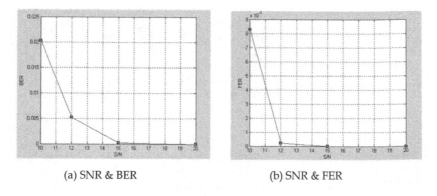

(a) SNR & BER

(b) SNR & FER

Figure 11. Relationship between SNR & (BER, FER)

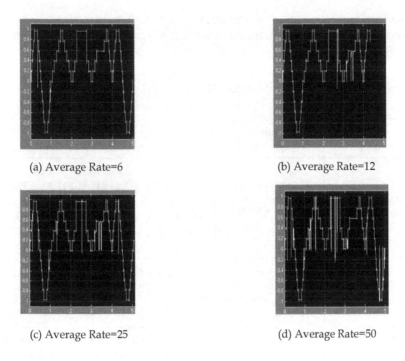

(a) Average Rate=6   (b) Average Rate=12

(c) Average Rate=25   (d) Average Rate=50

Figure 12. Received signals with different rate of interference

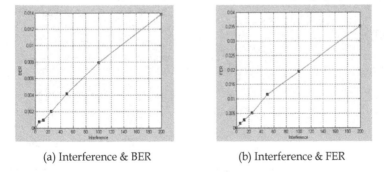

(a) Interference & BER   (b) Interference & FER

Figure 13. Relationship between interference & (BER, FER)

From the above results, it is obvious that the behavior of the system was successfully described using the suggested simulation methodology. It is also important to mention that this simulation method provides the ability to change the different system parameters to create new environment and hence, new simulation scenarios. This new simulation methodology proves the ability of the Simulink MATLAB to be a useful and flexible approach to study the effect of different physical layer parameters on the performance of wireless sensor networks.

Table (1) below, summarize the features of the different simulation methods of WSN including the suggested one in this chapter, MATLAB SIMULINK.

Simulation Environment	Programming Language	WSN support
GloMoSim/ QualNet	C and Parsec	GloMoSim: basic mobility and radio propagation models; 802.11; QualNet: additionally battery and energy model; ZigBee → GloMoSim seems to be outdated; QualNet seems to be more up-to-date, but commercial
OPNET Mod-eler Wireless Suite	configuration by GUI; internals C++	Different propagation models; 802.11, ZigBee; some MANET protocols, but no special WSN support → powerful tool with a nice GUI, but expensive
TOSSIM (part of TinyOS)	nesC	All TinyOS-based WSN protocols can be simulated with TOSSIM without modifications → good ap-proach especially if implementation should also be used with TinyOS-based nodes
OMNeT++	basic modules C++; larger structures NED	Several frameworks that add WSN functionality to OMNet++ such as MiXiM, Castalia, etc. → active project with a huge user base; Eclipse-based IDE for development
NS-2	C++; configu-ration OTcl	Huge amount of protocols available contributed by NS-2 users → complex configuration; unclear situa-tion due to large number of different user contributed implementations
Avrora	AVR micro-controller binaries	Particularly for programs written for AVR micro-controller with support for support for Mica2 and Mi-caZ → very special application area; project seems to be still active -still changes in CVS

J-Sim	Java; configuration Tcl/Java	Includes sensor network package containing models such as propagation, battery, radio model and sen-sor protocol stack including AODV and 802.11 → project seems to be abandoned
ATEMU	AVR micro-controller binaries	Complete emulation of the AVR instruction set with partial Mica2 support; TinyOS based code can be run → very special application area; slow simulation speed; project seems to be abandoned
EmStar	C	Provides network functionality for wireless embedded systems; EmTOS can be used to run TinyOS applications as EmStar module → project seems be abandoned (download links broken)
SENS	C++	Provides very basic network and physical layer sup-port. Source can be compiled for TinyOS. → project does not seem to be developed any further
SENSE	C++	Includes battery and power models, MAC layers (802.11) as well as network protocols (AODV, DSR, SSR, SHR) → does not seem to be developed any further
Shawn	C++	Algorithmic approach that concentrates on lower layers, no special WSN protocols → very active project -lot of recent changes in SVN
MATLAB SIMULINK	C , Java	Detailed simulation of the end nodes and their architecture, Physical layer parameters, different modulation & encoding techniques, communication channel modeling(SNR, effect of different Noise schemes, Interference, distance, etc..), various methods to monitor and record results, making use of the rich library of Matlab/Simulink.

Table 1. The features of the different simulation methods of WSN

4. Conclusions

In this chapter, a new simulation methodology of wireless sensor networks (WSN) was presented. MATLAB/Simulink was used as the tool to build the simulation environment. The strength of this simulation method falls in the ability to study the effect of different physical layer parameters (channel noise and interference, Signal to noise ratio...etc.) on the system behavior. The other advantage of this method is its flexibility in building the end nodes and sensors. This simulation methodology could be used to build different WSN types and opens the doors to use the MATLAB in this new field.

Author details

Qutaiba I. Ali
Mosul University, Computer Engineering Department, Iraq

Acknowledgement

Many thanks to my students Akram & Hussien for their assistance.

5. References

[1] Lewis, F "Wireless Sensors Networks, Smart Environments: Technologies, Protocols, and Applications', ed. Cook DJ, Das SK, John Wiley, New York, 2004; 1-18.

[2] Akyildiz, IF, Sankarasubramaniam, F, Cayirci, E, "A Survey on Sensor Networks", IEEE Commun Mag 2002; 102-114.

[3] Rabaey, J, Ammer, M, da Silva, J.L., D. Patel, and S. Roundy, "Picoradio supports ad hoc ultra-low power wireless networking," *Computer*, vol. 33, no. 7, pp. 42–48, July 2000.

[4] Gupta, G, Mukhopadhyay, SC, Sutherland, M., Demidenko, S., "Wireless Sensor Network for Selective Activity Monitoring in a home for the Elderly", Proceedings of 2007 IEEE IMTC conference. Poland, Warsaw 2007; 1(3): 1-6.

[5] Callaway, E., Gorday, P. , Hester, L., "Home Networking with IEEE 802.15.4: A Developing Standard for Low-Rate Wireless Personal Area Networks", IEEE Commun Mag 2002; 69-77.

[6] QualNet. [Online]. Available:
http://www.scalable-networks.com/products/qualnet/,2012.

[7] S. Technologies, "Qualnet v. 3.9. 5 user's guide," 2006.

[8] OPNET Technologies, Inc. [Online]. Available: http://www.opnet.com/,2012.

[9] Jiang, H., Wang, P. ,Liu, H., "Research on OPNET simulation model in wireless sensor networks," Jisuanji Gongcheng/ Computer Engineering, vol. 33, no. 4, 2007.

[10] Jurˇcˈik, P., Koubˆaa,A., "The IEEE 802.15. 4 OPNET Simulation Model: Reference Guide v2. 0," 2007.

[11] OPNET Technologies, Inc. [Online]. Available: http://www.opnet.com/support/des model library/images/MANET scrnsht.jpg, 2012.

[12] Computer Science Division at UC Berkeley. [Online]. Available: http://www.cs.berkeley.edu/_pal/research/tossim.html, 2012

[13] Levis, P., Lee, N.,Welsh, M., Culler, M., "TOSSIM: Accurate and scalable simulation of entire TinyOS applications," in Proceedings of the 1st international conference on Embedded networked sensor systems. ACM New York, NY, USA, 2003, pp. 126–137.

[14] Levis, P., Lee, N., "Tossim: A simulator for tinyos networks," UC Berkeley, September, 2003.

[15] Notani, S., "Performance Simulation of Multihop Routing Algorithms for Ad-Hoc Wireless Sensor Networks Using TOSSIM," in Advanced Communication Technology, 2008. ICACT 2008. 10th International Conference on, vol. 1, 2008.

[16] Computer Science Division at UC Berkeley. Visualisation of a TOSSIM simulation with TinyViz. [Online]. Available: http://www.tinyos.net/tinyos-1.x/doc/tutorial/imgs/tinyviz-screenshot1.gif, 2012.

[17] OMNeT++ Community. (2010, May) OMNeT++. [Online]. Available: http://www.omnetpp.org/

[18] Varga, A., et al., "The OMNeT++ discrete event simulation system," in Proceedings of the European Simulation Multiconference (ESM'2001), 2001, pp. 319–324.

[19] Varga, A., "OMNeT++ Discrete event simulation system. User Manual," Technical University of Budapest, Dept. of Telecommunications, 2006.

[20] Varga, A., Hornig, R., "An overview of the OMNeT++ simulation environment," in Proceedings of the 1st international conference on Simulation tools and techniques for communications, networks and systems & workshops table of contents. ICST (Institute for Computer Sciences, Social-Informatics and Telecommunications Engineering) ICST, Brussels, Belgium, Belgium, 2008.

[21] OMNeT++ Community. OMNeT++ 4.0 IDE.[Online]. Available: http://omnetpp.org/doc/omnetpp40/ide-overview/pictures/img1.png, 2012.

[22] Mobility Framework for OMNeT++ Community. [Online]. Available: http://mobility-fw.sourceforge.net, 2012.

[23] Drytkiewicz, W., Sroka, S., Handziski, V., Koepke, A., Karl, H., "A mobility framework for omnet++," in 3rd International OMNeT++ Workshop, 2003.

[24] L¨obbers, M., Willkomm, D., K¨opke, A., Karl, H., "Framework for Simulation of Mobility in OMNeT++(Mobility Framework)," 2004.

[25] MiXiM developers. MiXiM project. [Online]. Available: http://mixim.sourceforge.net/, 2012.

[26] K¨opke, A., Swigulski, M., Wessel, K., Willkomm, D., Haneveld, P., Parker, T., Visser, O., Lichte, H. Valentin, S., "Simulating wireless and mobile networks in OMNeT++ the MiXiM vision," in Proceedings of the 1st international conference on Simulation tools and techniques for communications, networks and systems & workshops table of contents. ICST (Institute for Computer Sciences, Social-

Informatics and Telecommunications Engineering) ICST, Brussels, Belgium, Belgium, 2008.

[27] University of Twente and TU Delft. Positif, MAC Simulator and T-MAC. [Online]. Available: http://www.consensus.tudelft.nl/software.html, 2012.

[28] National ICT Australia. Castalia. [Online]. Available: http://castalia.npc.nicta.com.au/, 2012.

[29] Boulis, A., "Castalia: revealing pitfalls in designing distributed algorithms in WSN," in Proceedings of the 5th international conference on Embedded networked sensor systems. ACM New York, NY, USA, 2007, pp. 407–408.

[30] OMNeT++ Community. INET framework for the OMNeT++. [Online]. Available: http://inet.omnetpp.org/, 2012.

[31] Ariza-Quintana, A., Casilari, E., Cabrera, A., "Implementation of MANET routing protocols on OMNeT++," in Proceedings of the 1st international conference on Simulation tools and techniques for communications, networks and systems & workshops table of contents. ICST (Institute for Computer Sciences, Social-Informatics and Telecommunications Engineering) ICST, Brussels, Belgium, Belgium, 2008.

[32] OMNeT++ Community. NesCT for the OMNeT++. [Online]. Available: http://nesct.sourceforge.net/, 2012.

[33] NS-2 developers. The Network Simulator – ns-2. [Online]. Available: http://www.isi.edu/nsnam/ns/, 2012.

[34] Downard I., DC, N., "Simulating sensor networks in ns-2,"2004.

[35] NS-2 developers. Visualisation of a ns-2 simulation with NAM. [Online]. Available: http://www.isi.edu/nsnam/nam/nambig.gif, 2012.

[36] Departamento de Ciência da Computac͎ ̃ao, Universidade Federal deMinas Gerais. Mannasim Framework for ns-2. [Online]. Available: http://www.mannasim.dcc.ufmg.br/, 2012.

[37] Computer Science, Mid Sweden University , Sweden. NS2-MIUN. [Online]. Available: http://apachepersonal.miun.se/_qinwan/resources.htm, 2012.

[38] Networked and Embedded Systems Laboratory (NESL) at the University of California at Los Angeles (UCLA). SensorSim framework. [Online]. Available: http://nesl.ee.ucla.edu/projects/sensorsim/, 2012.

[39] Park, S., Savvides, A., Srivastava, M., "SensorSim: a simulation framework for sensor networks," in Proceedings of the 3rd ACM international workshop on Modeling, analysis and simulation of wireless and mobile systems. ACM New York, NY, USA, 2000, pp. 104–111.

[40] "Sensor Sim: A Simulation Framework for Networks Sensors", Electrical Engineering Department, University of California, Los Angeles, Retrieved October, vol. 16, 2006.

[41] UCLA Compilers Group). Avrora. [Online]. Available:
http://compilers.cs.ucla.edu/avrora/, 2012.

[42] Titzer, B., "Avrora: The AVR simulation and analysis framework," Master's thesis, University of California, Los Angeles, 2004.

[43] Titzer, B., Lee, D. Palsberg, J., "Avrora: Scalable sensor network simulation with precise timing," in Proceedings of the 4th international symposium on Information processing in sensor networks. IEEE Press Piscataway, NJ, USA, 2005.

[44] Department of Computer Science at University of Illinois at Urbana-Champaign). J-Sim. [Online]. Available: http://sites.google.com/site/jsimofficial, 2012.

[45] Sobeih, A., Chen, W., Hou, J., Kung, L., "J-sim: A simulation environment for wireless sensor networks," in Proceedings of the 38th annual Symposium on Simulation. IEEE Computer Society Washington, DC, USA, 2005, pp. 175–187.

[46] Hou, J., Kung, L., "J-Sim: A Simulation and emulation environment for wireless sensor networks," IEEE Wireless Communications Magazine, vol. 13, no. 4, pp. 104–119, 2006.

[47] Center for Satellite and Hybrid Communication Networks (CSHCN) at University of Maryland. Atemu. [Online]. Available: http://www.cshcn.umd.edu/research/atemu/, 2012.

[48] Polley, J., Blazakis, D., "Atemu: A fine-grained sensor network simulator," in Sensor and Ad Hoc Communications and Networks, 2004. IEEE SECON 2004. 2004 First Annual IEEE Communications Society Conference on, 2004, pp. 145–152.

[49] Laboratory for Embedded Collaborative Systems (LECS) at UCLA. [Online]. Available: http://www.lecs.cs.ucla.edu/emstar/, 2012.

[50] Elson, J., Bien, S., "Emstar: An environment for developing wireless embedded systems software," Center for Embedded Networked Sensing (CENS) Technical Report, vol. 9, 2003.

[51] Girod, L., Ramanathan, N.," A Software Environment for Developing and Deploying Heterogeneous Sensor Actuator Networks," Center for Embedded Network Sensing, p. 101, 2007.

[52] Open Systems Laboratory at University of Illinois at Urbana-Champaign. [Online]. Available: http://osl.cs.uiuc.edu/sens/, 2012.

[53] Sundresh, S., Kim, W., Agha, G., "SENS: A sensor, environment and network simulator," in Proceedings of the 37th annual symposium on Simulation. IEEE Computer Society Washington, DC, USA, 2004.

[54] Computer Science Department at Rensselaer Polytechnic Institute (RPI). [Online]. Available: http://www.ita.cs.rpi.edu/sense/, 2012.

[55] Chen, G., Branch, J., "Sense: A sensor network simulator," Advances in Pervasive Computing and Networking, pp. 249–267, 2004.

[56] SwarmNet project. [Online]. Available: http: //shawn.sourceforge.net/, 2012.

[57] Kroeller, A., Pfisterer, D., "Shawn: A new approach to simulating wireless sensor networks," Arxiv preprint cs/0502003, 2005.

[58] Fekete, S., Kroller, A., Fischer, S., Pfisterer, D., "Shawn: The fast, highly customizable sensor network simulator," in Networked Sensing Systems, 2007. INSS'07. Fourth International Conference on, 2007, pp.299–299.

[59] MATLAB Web Site: http://www.mathworks.com/

[60] Ali, Q., Abdulmaojod, A., Ahmed, H.," Simulation & Performance Study of Wireless Sensor Network (WSN) Using MATLAB, IJEEE Journal,2010.

Chapter 13

Semi-Analytic Techniques for Fast MATLAB Simulations

Daniele Borio and Eduardo Cano

Additional information is available at the end of the chapter

1. Introduction

Advances in electronics and telecommunications are leading to complex systems able to efficiently use the available resources. Fast electronics, complex modulation schemes and correction codes enable transmissions on channels with unfavorable characteristics, coexistence between different services in the same frequency bands and high transmission rates. However, the complexity of such communications systems often prevents analytical characterizations. For example, figures of merit such as the Bit Error Rate (BER) are difficult to determine analytically for transmission schemes involving correction codes and communication channels with Inter-Symbol Interference (ISI) and fading. In such cases, the system is characterized through Monte Carlo simulations [1, 2]. The Monte Carlo framework involves simulations of the whole system under analysis. For example, when considering a communications system, the whole transmission-reception chain is simulated. A large number of sequences are sent through the simulated system and the message recovered by the simulated receiver is compared to the original transmitted sequence. This comparison allows one to determine the average number of transmission errors and compute the BER.

Monte Carlo simulations can be applied to almost any system although their implementation and computation requirements can be significantly high. In addition to this, precision problems can arise when the quantity to be estimated is significantly low. For example, BERs of the order of $10^{-8} - 10^{-9}$ require at least $10^9 - 10^{10}$ simulation runs. Conversely, analytical models have a limited applicability and usually adopt approximations (i.e., model linearization) that can yield a poor description of the system under analysis.

In order to overcome the limitation of Monte Carlo and analytical techniques, semi-analytic approaches have been previously implemented [1, 2]. In a semi-analytic framework, the knowledge of the system under analysis is exploited to reduce the computational load and complexity that full Monte Carlo simulations would require. In this way, the strengths of both analytical and Monte Carlo methods are effectively combined. Semi-analytic techniques are a powerful tool for the analysis of complex systems.

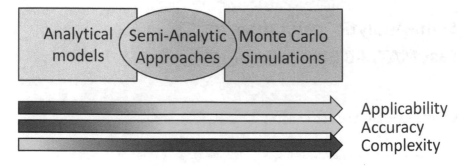

Figure 1. Different approaches available for the analysis of complex systems. Semi-analytic approaches represent a compromise in terms of applicability and complexity (computational and implementation) between analytical models and Monte Carlo simulations.

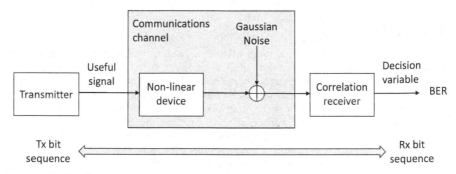

Figure 2. Model adopted for the evaluation of the BER using a semi-analytic approach. The communications channel is modeled as a non-linear device, which affects only the signal component, and the addition of a noise term supposed to be Gaussian.

The characteristics and relationships among the three aforementioned methods are shown in Figure 1: semi-analytic approaches represent a good compromise in terms of applicability and complexity, combining the strengths of Monte Carlo and analytical approaches.

The main goal of this chapter is to provide a general overview of semi-analytic techniques for the simulation of communications systems. Specific emphasis is given to their implementation in MATLAB and two examples from the communications context are analyzed in detail.

Despite their potential, semi-analytic techniques have received limited attention from the communications community. Reference books on simulation of communications systems such as [1], [2] and [3] dedicate only a few pages to this kind of techniques. The focus is usually on the computation of the BER, which represents one of the first applications of semi-analytic techniques in communication system analysis [4, 5]. In this case, the model depicted in Figure 2 is adopted. The communications channel is modeled as a non-linear device, which distorts the signal component alone, with the addition of a noise term that is assumed to be Gaussian. This model is quite general and can be used to represent several communications channels.

A classical example is the model of a transmission chain where a Traveling Wave Tube Amplifier (TWTA) is used to amplify the useful signal before transmission. The TWTA is highly non-linear and can lead to signal distortions. Since the signal is injected into the TWTA before transmission, the noise component entering the amplifier is negligible. In this case, the model depicted in Figure 2 is appropriate for describing the transmission chain including a non-linear amplifier.

The TWTA is a memory-less device and can be characterized using *AM-AM conversion* and *AM-PM conversion* (AM = Amplitude Modulation, PM = Phase Modulation) curves [3]. When a base-band signal model is used, the amplifier input and output are complex quantities; moreover, the response of the device usually depends only on the amplitude (instantaneous power) of the input signal. AM-AM and AM-PM conversion curves define the relationship between the input/output signal amplitudes and phases as a function of the input amplitude. Using these conversion curves, it is possible to simulate the behavior of the TWTA and other non-linear devices.

In the semi-analytic framework, the additivity of the noise component is exploited to compute the BER. More specifically, only the signal transmission chain is simulated and for each possible signal symbol, the Energy per bit (E_b) is computed. Since the noise properties are known, the BER for the ith symbol, s_i, is given by

$$BER_i = \frac{1}{2}\text{erfc}\left(\sqrt{\frac{E_{b,i}}{N_0}}\right), \tag{1}$$

where $E_{b,i}$ has been obtained by simulating the transmission chain (including the non-linear device) in the absence of noise and transmitting the symbol s_i. The parameter N_0 is the noise power spectral density and it is a known value of the system. Finally, the BER of the system is obtained from

$$BER = \text{E}\left[BER_i\right] = \frac{1}{2}\sum_{i=0}^{N_s-1} p_i \text{erfc}\left(\sqrt{\frac{E_{b,i}}{N_0}}\right), \tag{2}$$

where p_i is the probability that the symbol s_i will be transmitted and N_s is the number of symbols of the signal constellation.

This simple example clearly illustrates the principles of semi-analytic techniques: the analytical knowledge of the system is exploited to reduce the computation load and complexity that full Monte Carlo simulations would require. In this case, only the transmission of the signal component is simulated.

In the literature, several generalizations of the aforementioned BER computation technique have been proposed. For example, [5] considered the case where the noise term at the input of the non-linear amplifier is not negligible. An equivalent model is proposed where the noise at the input is propagated after the non-linearity. [5] also considered the presence of a bandpass channel. More recently, [6] proposed a methodology for estimating the BER in the presence of ISI. All these examples show the potential and flexibility of the semi-analytic approach.

1.1. Building blocks

When considering the previous example it is possible to identify three building blocks that play different roles in the semi-analytic framework:

- **simulation block**
- **estimation block**
- **analytical model**.

The simulation block corresponds to that part of the system that is actually simulated. In the previous example, this block corresponds to the signal generation, the non-linear amplifier and the correlation receiver simulation. These blocks were used to determine the decision variable employed for recovering the transmitted symbol. The analytical model exploits the properties of the system to determine the quantities of interest. In the previous example, the fact that the noise introduced by the communication channel is Gaussian was exploited to determine the BER as a function of the E_b of each transmitted symbol. The estimation block is used as the interface between the simulated and analytical parts of the system. In BER computation case, the simulation part allows one to generate the different decision variables, whereas the analytical model is expressed as a function of energy per bit. The estimation block is used to determine E_b from the simulated decision variables.

The three functional blocks can be connected according to different configurations leading to different types of semi-analytic approaches. In the next section, two of these configurations are briefly discussed. Examples for each type of semi-analytic system are given in Section 2 and Section 3.

1.2. Main configurations

When considering the BER example, it is possible to note that the simulation, estimation and analytical blocks are connected in series. The simulation block is used at first to compute the different decision variables. The estimation block determines the E_b associated with each variable and finally the analytical model is used to compute the BER from the Energy per bit to Noise power spectral density ratio (E_b / N_0).

This type of configuration is defined here as *sequential* since there is no feedback between the different blocks and each element of the chain is run sequentially. The principle of this configuration is shown in the upper part of Figure 3.

A second type of configuration has been recently considered for the analysis of tracking loops in Direct Sequence Spread Spectrum (DSSS) and Global Navigation Satellite System (GNSS) receivers. The most computationally demanding operation in a DSSS/GNSS receiver is despreading, i.e, the correlation of the incoming samples with local replicas of the code and carrier. This operation is performed by the Integrate and Dump (I&D) blocks that rely on simple operations that can be analytically modeled. For this reason, semi-analytic models exploiting the knowledge of the I&D blocks and simulating only the non-linear parts of the system have been developed [7–10]. This resulted in efficient analysis tools, which require reduced processing time with the applicability of Monte Carlo simulations.

Different techniques for modeling the output of the I&D have been suggested. [7] modeled the correlator outputs evaluated by the I&D blocks as linear combinations of independent Gaussian random variables. Correlation among the different correlators was obtained by using, for the generation of different I&D outputs, a subset of the same random variables. This technique becomes complex as the number of correlators increases. Another attempt made in [8] assumed that the correlator outputs were independent which, in general, is not a

Sequential approach

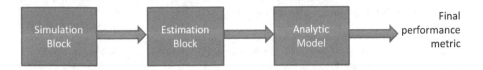

Closed-loop approach

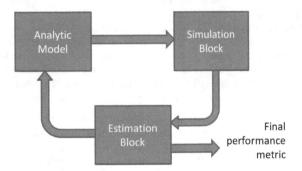

Figure 3. Basic blocks and main configurations adopted in semi-analytic approaches. An estimation block is used for determining key signal and system parameters and interfacing the simulation and analytic components of the system.

realistic condition. Finally, [9, 10] suggested the use of a technique based on the Cholesky decomposition detailed in [11]. This approach allows one to easily generate an arbitrary number of correlated Gaussian random variables. In this way, [9, 10] were able to simulate advanced tracking loops for new GNSS signals.

Regardless of the type of approach used for modeling the correlator outputs, the aforementioned semi-analytic configuration can be represented as in the bottom part of Figure 3. In this case, an analytical model is used to generate quantities that will be propagated by simulation. In the tracking loop case, an analytical model is used to generate the correlator outputs that are then processed through simulations. The non-linear parts of the system are fully simulated and quantities such as the loop discriminator and filter outputs are computed. Finally, an estimation block is used to interface the simulation and analytical components of the semi-analytic scheme. A new estimate of the signal parameters is obtained and used to generate new correlator outputs. The estimation block is also used to compute performance metrics such as tracking jitter or Mean Time to Lose Lock (MTLL) [12].

The three functional blocks described in Section 1.1 are connected in a loop and thus this type of configuration is named *closed-loop approach*. The technique developed by [9, 10] and the closed-loop approach will be detailed in Section 3.

2. Sequential approach: The inter-system interference case

As shown in Figure 3, the sequential approach, at first, requires an initial simulation block to generate the random processes and system functions that cannot be analytically described. Subsequently, the simulated processes are employed by the estimation unit to obtain key parameters required by the analytical model to compute metrics of interest. In the analytical model, the estimated parameters are plugged into mathematical expressions to obtain the desired final metrics. In the sequential architecture, the gain in computational load mainly depends on the simplifications allowed by the analytical model. The use of such a model allows one to simulate only a part of the system and eventually avoid computationally demanding error counting processes.

The computational complexity of Monte Carlo simulations increases significantly when two or more communication systems coexist within the same environment. In this case, it is necessary to account for the interaction of the different systems and determine potential inter-system interference. In addition, computational requirements of Monte Carlo simulations increase dramatically with the number of random elements included in each block of the communication chain. These requirements can be considerably reduced by adopting semi-analytic techniques in which the evaluated metrics are analytically expressed as a function of parameters estimated through simulations. This principle is the core idea behind the sequential semi-analytic approach.

In order to better illustrate the principles of the semi-analytic sequential approach, an inter-system interference scenario is considered in this section. The case of a satellite navigation receiver affected by interference generated by a communications system is considered. The primary system (i.e., the victim system) considered here is a Global Positioning System (GPS) L1 receiver affected by an interference signal caused by third order harmonics of a Digital Video Broadcasting - Terrestrial (DVB-T) signal. A comprehensive description of the sequential approach applied to an inter-system interference case is provided in the following.

The reception of GNSS signals is challenging due to low signal power, possible severe channel conditions and the presence of Radio-Frequency (RF) interference. The presence of RF interference can be particularly troublesome and the performance of a GNSS receiver can vary significantly depending on the type of interference. For this reason, significant research efforts have been devoted to the characterization of the receiver performance in the presence of different types of interference [13, 14]. Furthermore, the impact of interference originated by specific communication technologies, such as Ultra Wideband (UWB) transmissions [15], Distance Measuring Equipment (DME) signals [16] and DVB-T harmonics [17, 18], has been thoroughly investigated. It is noted that the interference impact strongly depends on the strategy adopted by a GNSS receiver for processing the useful signals. Moreover, different impacts are expected depending on the receiver operating mode. The first task of a GNSS receiver is to determine the presence of a specific GNSS signal. This task is accomplished by the acquisition block that implements a statistical test for the detection of useful signals. After acquisition, the useful GNSS signals are passed to the tracking stage that refines the estimates of different signal parameters. Since acquisition and tracking implement different processing strategies, RF interference will affect these two receiver blocks differently. In the following, the acquisition stage is considered. A semi-analytic approach for the analysis of GNSS tracking loops is discussed in Section 3.

The acquisition of a GNSS signal can be formulated as a classical detection problem [19], where the signal of interest is buried in noise. The outcome of the acquisition process is twofold. First, a decision relative to the signal presence is provided. If the signal is present, a rough estimate of signal parameters (defined in the following) is also obtained. The received useful GNSS signal, which is impaired by Additive White Gaussian Noise (AWGN) and interference, is processed by the acquisition block yielding a decision variable. If the decision variable is greater than a decision threshold the signal presence is declared. This decision variable is calculated by using the digital samples provided by the receiver front-end. The signal model and the acquisition process are briefly summarized in the following sections.

2.1. The GNSS signal

The signal at the input of a GNSS receiver, in a one-path AWGN channel and in the presence of RF interference, can be modeled as

$$r(t) = \sum_{l=0}^{L-1} y_l(t) + i(t) + \eta(t), \tag{3}$$

where $y_l(t)$ is the signal transmitted by the lth GNSS L1 satellite, L is the total number of satellites in view, $i(t)$ is the received interference signal and $\eta(t)$ is the noise term.

Each useful signal, $y_l(t)$, can be expressed as

$$y_l(t) = \sqrt{2C_l}d_l\left(t - \tau_{0,l}\right) c_l\left(t - \tau_{0,l}\right) \cos\left(2\pi(f_{RF} + f_{d0,l})t + \varphi_{0,l}\right), \tag{4}$$

where

- C_l is the power of the lth useful signal;
- $d_l(\cdot)$ is the navigation message;
- $c_l(\cdot)$ is the lth pseudo-random sequence extracted from a family of quasi-orthogonal codes and used for spreading the signal spectrum;
- $\tau_{0,l}$, $f_{d0,l}$ and $\varphi_{0,l}$ are the delay, Doppler frequency and phase introduced by the communication channel, and
- f_{RF} is the centre frequency of the GNSS signal.

It is noted that GNSS signals adopt a DSSS modulation. The pseudo-random sequences, $c_l(t)$, allow the simultaneous transmission of several signals at the same time and in the same band. Moreover, $c_l(t)$ sequences are characterized by sharp correlation functions that allow the precise measurement of the signal travel time. The travel time is then converted into distances that allows a GNSS receiver to determine its position.

The pseudo-random sequence, $c_l(t)$, is composed of several terms including a primary spreading sequence and a subcarrier:

$$c_l(t) = \sum_{i=-\infty}^{+\infty} c_{l,(i \bmod N_c)}s_b(t - iT_h). \tag{5}$$

The signal $s_b(t - iT_h)$ in (5) represents the subcarrier of duration T_h, which determines the spectral characteristics of the transmitted GNSS signal. The GPS L1 Coarse/Acquisition (C/A) component is Bi-Phase Shift Keying (BPSK) modulated, whereas the Galileo E1 signal adopts a Composite Binary-Offset Carrier (CBOC) scheme. The sequence $c_{l,i}$, of length N_c, defines the primary spreading code of the lth GNSS signal. In the following, only the BPSK case is considered. The results can be easily extended to different subcarriers.

A GNSS receiver is able to process the L useful signals independently since the spreading codes are quasi-orthogonal. Therefore, expression (3) can be simplified to

$$r(t) = y(t) + i(t) + \eta(t), \tag{6}$$

where the index l has been dropped for ease of notation.

The received signal in (6) is filtered and down-converted by the receiver front-end. Filtering is of particular importance since it determines which portion of the interfering signal, $i(t)$, will effectively enter the receiver. After down-conversion and filtering, the input signal is sampled and quantized. In this analysis, the impact of quantization and sampling is neglected. After these operations, (6) becomes:

$$r_{BB}[n] = y_{BB}(nT_s) + i_{BB}(nT_s) + \eta_{BB}(nT_s) = y_{BB}[n] + i_{BB}[n] + \eta_{BB}[n], \tag{7}$$

where the notation $x[n]$ is used to denote discrete time sequences sampled at the frequency $f_s = \frac{1}{T_s}$. In addition, the index "BB" is used to denote a filtered signal down-converted to baseband. Furthermore, the signal $y_{BB}[n]$ in (7) can be written as

$$y_{BB}[n] = \sqrt{C}d(nT_s - \tau_0)c(nT_s - \tau_0)\exp\{j2\pi f_0 nT_s + \varphi_0\}. \tag{8}$$

The noise term, $\eta_{BB}[n]$, is AWGN with variance σ_{BB}^2. This variance depends on the filtering, down-conversion and sampling strategy applied by the receiver front-end and can be expressed as $\sigma_{BB}^2 = N_0 B_{RX}$, where B_{RX} is the front-end bandwidth and N_0 is the Power Spectral Density (PSD) of the input noise $\eta(t)$. The ratio between the carrier power, C, and the noise PSD, N_0, defines the Carrier-to-Noise density power ratio (C/N_0), one of the main signal quality indicators used in GNSS.

2.2. The DVB-T interfering signal

The interference term in (6), $i(t)$, originates from DVB-T emissions. The DVB-T system is the European standard for the broadcasting of digital terrestrial television signals and has been adopted in many countries, mainly in Europe, Asia and Australia. The standard employs an Orthogonal Frequency Division Multiplexing (OFDM)-based modulation scheme operating in the VHF III ($174 - 230$ MHz), UHF IV ($470 - 582$ MHz) and UHF V ($582 - 862$ MHz) bands [20]. It is noticeable that none of these bands fall within the bands allocated for GNSS signals. However, the second harmonics of UHF IV and third order harmonics of UHF V could coincide with the GPS L1 band, and, thus cause harmful interference. The case of the third order harmonics of a DVB-T signal is considered here. The DVB-T transmitted signal can be represented as

$$i_{DVB-T}(t) = \frac{1}{\sqrt{M}} \sum_{p=0}^{N_d-1} \sum_{h=0}^{M-1} I_{p,h} \exp\left(\frac{j2\pi ht}{M}\right), \tag{9}$$

where M is the modulation order, h is the subcarrier index, p is the symbol index, N_d represents the total number of transmitted symbols and $I_{p,h}$ models the hth constellation point of the pth symbol. Here, the term "subcarrier" should not be confused with the subcarrier used to modulate the GNSS signals in (5). In the OFDM context, several components are transmitted in parallel on different overlapping frequency bands. The term subcarrier denotes each individual transmitted component. In GNSS, the subcarrier is an additional component that modulates the transmitted signal and plays a role analogous to the carrier used for the signal up-conversion.

Third order harmonics are the consequence of the malfunctioning of the transmitter electronics. In particular, the presence of these harmonics are due to the non-linearities of an amplifier. The output of an amplifier can be modeled using a polynomial expansion of the amplifier input/output function:

$$p(t) = \sum_{n=1}^{\infty} a_n i_{DVB-T}^n(t), \tag{10}$$

where a_n are the polynomial coefficients of the Taylor series expansion of the amplifier input/output function. This type of model is an alternative to the AM-AM and AM-PM conversion functions discussed in Section 1 for the TWTA case.

The terms of order $n > 1$ in (10) model the amplifier non-linearities and the ratios a_n/a_1 are expected to be small for $n > 1$. Since only the third harmonics will fall into the GPS L1 band, the interference signal at the antenna of a GNSS receiver is given by

$$i(t) = a_3 i_{DVB-T}^3(t). \tag{11}$$

The signal $i(t)$ is filtered and down-converted by the receiver front-end and signal $i_F(t)$, the filtered version of $i(t)$, will affect receiver operations.

Finally, the interference term in (7) can be modeled as $i_{BB}[n] = i_F(nT_s)$.

2.3. The acquisition process

After signal conditioning, the sequence $r_{BB}[n]$ is correlated with local replicas of the useful signal code and carrier as shown in Figure 4. Since the code delay, τ_0, and the Doppler frequency, f_0, of the useful signal in (8) are unknown to the receiver, several delays and frequencies are tested by the acquisition block. In addition to this, several correlators, computed using subsequent portions of the input signal $r_{BB}[n]$, can be computed in order to produce a decision variable less affected by noise and interference. In this way, the output of the kth complex correlator can be expressed as

$$S_k = \frac{1}{N} \sum_{n=kN}^{(k+1)N-1} r_{BB}[n] c(nT_s - \tau) \exp\{-j2\pi f_d nT_s - j\varphi\}, \tag{12}$$

where τ, f_d and φ are the code delay, Doppler frequency and carrier phase tested by the receiver. The parameter N is the number of samples used for computing a single correlation output and $T_c = NT_s$ defines the coherent integration time. It is noted that the computation of correlation outputs is essential for the proper functioning of a GNSS receiver and they are both used in acquisition and tracking modes [21]. To further improve the acquisition performance,

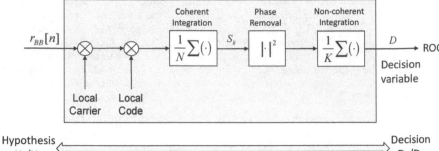

Figure 4. Schematic representation of the operations performed by the acquisition block of a GNSS receiver.

non-coherent integration can be implemented as illustrated in Figure 4. More specifically, the impact of the navigation message, $d(\cdot)$, is removed through squaring, $|S_k|^2$, and the final decision variable is computed as

$$D = \frac{1}{K} \sum_{k=0}^{K-1} |S_k|^2, \tag{13}$$

where K is the total number of correlation samples that are non-coherently integrated. It should be noted that for $K = 1$ only coherent integration is used. In order to determine the signal presence, the receiver compares D with a decision threshold, β. If D is greater than β then the useful signal is declared present.

It is noted that, as in any binary test, two hypotheses are possible:

- H_0: the signal is not present or it is not correctly aligned with the local code and carrier replica .
- H_1: the signal is present and the local code and carrier replica are aligned.

The null hypothesis, H_0 assumes that the correlator outputs, S_k, are made of noise alone. Since the pseudo-random sequences, $c(\cdot)$, are selected to have good autocorrelation properties, if the code delay and Doppler frequencies tested by the receiver do not match the parameters of the input signal, $y_{BB}[n]$, then the useful signal component is almost completely filtered out at the correlator output. Thus, also in this case, the H_0 hypothesis is verified.

Furthermore, H_1 is the alternative hypothesis and assumes that the signal is present and the local code and carrier replica are perfectly aligned. If H_1 is declared, then rough estimates of τ_0 and f_0 are also obtained.

Depending on the result of the test, $D > \beta$, two decisions can be taken by the receiver

- D_0: the signal is declared not present
- D_1: the signal is declared present

	D_0	D_1
H_0	Signal absence correctly declared	False alarm
H_1	Missed detection	Signal detection

Table 1. Confusion matrix describing the four events that can happen in the binary test performed by the acquisition process.

and the four events described in Table 1 can occur.

The off-diagonal events in Table 1 correspond to the different errors that the acquisition block can commit. The following probabilities are usually associated with the events in Table 1:

$$P_d(\beta) = \text{Prob}(D > \beta | H_1) \quad \text{Probability of detection} \tag{14}$$

and

$$P_{fa}(\beta) = \text{Prob}(D > \beta | H_0) \quad \text{Probability of false alarm.} \tag{15}$$

The probabilities of missed detection and correct signal absence decision are obtained as $1 - P_d(\beta)$ and $1 - P_{fa}(\beta)$, respectively. The performance of the acquisition process is characterized in terms of Receiver Operation Curves (ROC) [22], which plots the detection probability as a function of the false alarm rate. ROC curves capture the behavior of a detector as a function of the different decision thresholds.

2.4. The semi-analytic approach

The goal of the sequential semi-analytic approach considered in this section is the evaluation of the ROC in the presence of DVB-T interference. The full Monte Carlo approach would consist of simulating the full transmission/reception scheme shown in Figure 5 and generating several realizations of D both under H_0 and H_1. Probabilities of detection and false alarm would then be determined through error counting techniques. This approach is computationally demanding and does not exploit the analytical knowledge of the system. More specifically, under the hypothesis that the correlator outputs S_k are independent and identically distributed (i.i.d.) complex Gaussian random variables with independent real and imaginary parts, it is possible to show [23] that

$$P_{fa}(\beta) = \exp\left\{-\frac{\beta}{2\sigma_n^2}\right\} \sum_{i=0}^{K-1} \frac{1}{i!} \left(\frac{\beta}{2\sigma_n^2}\right)^i \tag{16}$$

and

$$P_{det}(\beta) = Q_K\left(\sqrt{K\lambda}; \sqrt{\beta\sigma_n^2}\right), \tag{17}$$

where $Q_K(a;b) = \int_b^{+\infty} x \left(\frac{x}{a}\right)^{K-1} \exp\left\{-\frac{x^2+a^2}{2}\right\} I_{K-1}(ax)dx$ is the generalized Marcum Q-function of order K. The function $I_K(\cdot)$ is the modified Bessel function of first kind and order K. In (16) and (17), σ_n^2 is the variance of the real and imaginary part of S_k. The parameter λ is given by

$$\lambda = \frac{|E[S_k]|^2}{\sigma_n^2} \tag{18}$$

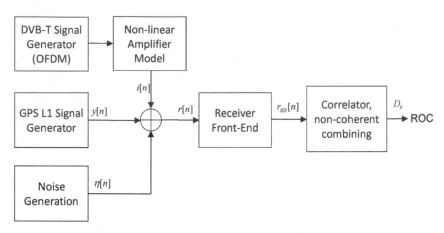

Figure 5. Schematic representation of the full Monte Carlo simulation system for the ROC evaluation of the acquisition of a GPS L1 signal in the presence of DVB-T third order harmonics.

and defines the Signal-to-Noise Ratio (SNR) at the correlator outputs.

The correlator output can be considered i.i.d. complex Gaussian random variables even in the presence of DVB-T interference. More specifically, the large number of terms in the sum performed in (12) allows one to invoke the central limit theorem and assume S_k is Gaussian. Independence derives from the down-sampling performed by the correlators. Since only one correlator is produced every N samples, the statistical correlation between subsequent correlators is significantly reduced. The lack of correlation translates into independence for Gaussian random variables. Thus, models (16) and (17) can be used and the only parameters that need to be estimated are σ_n^2 and λ.

The analytical knowledge of the system can be further exploited to simplify the evaluation of σ_n^2 and λ. In particular, since $i_{BB}[n]$ and $\eta_{BB}[n]$ are modeled as zero mean random processes, they only contribute to the variance of the correlator outputs. Thus, neglecting residual errors due to delay and frequency partial misalignments, yields

$$|E[S_k]|^2 = C, \tag{19}$$

where C is the useful signal power and is one of the known parameters of the system. Thus, λ can be derived from C and σ_n^2.

Finally, exploiting the linearity of the correlation process, it is possible to express S_k as

$$S_k = S_{r,k} + S_{\eta,k} + S_{i,k}, \tag{20}$$

which is a linear combination of a useful signal term, derived from $y_{BB}[n]$, a noise term, derived from $\eta_{BB}[n]$, and an interference term derived from $i_{BB}[n]$. The variance σ_n^2 can be obtained as

$$\sigma_n^2 = \frac{1}{2}\mathrm{Var}\{S_k\} = \frac{1}{2}\mathrm{Var}\{S_{\eta,k}\} + \frac{1}{2}\mathrm{Var}\{S_{i,k}\}. \tag{21}$$

Using the results derived in [24], [13] and [23], it is possible to show

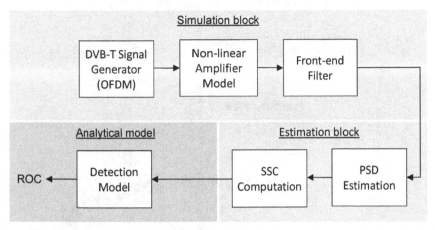

Figure 6. Schematic representation of the semi-analytic approach adopted for the evaluation of the ROC in the presence of DVB-T interference. The three functional elements of the semi-analytic approach are highlighted in different colors.

$$\frac{1}{2}\text{Var}\left\{S_{\eta,k}\right\} = \frac{N_0}{2T_c} \tag{22}$$

and

$$\frac{1}{2}\text{Var}\left\{S_{i,k}\right\} = \frac{C_i}{2T_c}k_a, \tag{23}$$

where C_i is the interference power and k_a is the Spectral Separation Coefficient (SSC) defined as [13, 24]

$$k_a = \int_{-B_{RX}/2}^{B_{RX}/2} G_i(f)G_c(f)df. \tag{24}$$

The function $G_i(f)$ in (24) is the normalized PSD of the DVB-T interference signal after front-end filtering. In addition, $G_i(f)$ is normalized such that

$$\int_{-B_{RX}/2}^{B_{RX}/2} G_i(f)df = 1. \tag{25}$$

The function $G_c(f)$ models the effect of the correlation on the interfering signal. Correlation can be modeled as an additional filtering stage and $G_c(f)$ can be shown to be well approximated by the PSD of the subcarrier used in the despreading process. Also, $G_c(f)$ is normalized to have a unit integral. It is noted that different subcarriers lead to different $G_c(f)$ and thus, $i_{BB}[n]$ will have different effects depending on the type of modulation considered.

The only unknown parameter in the previous equation is the SSC, which needs to be estimated using Monte Carlo simulations. Also, the interfering DVB-T signal is fully simulated. The resulting signal is filtered by the receiver front-end and the sequence $i_{BB}[n]$ is obtained. The samples of $i_{BB}[n]$ are used to estimate the normalized PSD, $G_i(f)$. This can be easily obtained using the MATLAB functions developed for spectral analysis. In this case, the `pwelch` function is used. The function $G_i(f)$ is used to compute the SSC, which is then used to determine the system ROC.

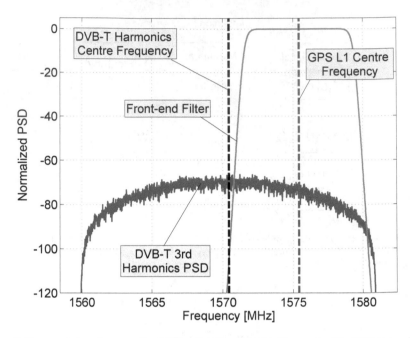

Figure 7. Representation of a normalized PSD realization of the third harmonic of the DVB-T signal and the frequency response of the GPS L1 front-end filter.

The developed semi-analytic approach is shown in Figure 6 where the simulation, estimation and analytic components are clearly highlighted.

2.5. Performance comparison

A comparison between a full Monte Carlo simulation and a semi-analytic technique, implemented for the evaluation of the acquisition performance of a GPS L1 receiver impaired by third order harmonics of a DVB-T signal, is presented in this section. Initially, the DVB-T interfering signal in time domain is programmed in MATLAB by following the DVB-T standard and the non-linear amplifier model, as illustrated in Figure 5. Note that the simulation of the interfering signal is required for both Monte Carlo and semi-analytic techniques. Subsequently, the estimated PSD of the interfering signal, needed for the estimation of the SSC in the semi-analytic method, is obtained by applying the `pwelch` function of MATLAB. A realization of the normalized PSD of the interfering signal is depicted in Figure 7. The centre frequency of the interfering signal is set to $f_I = f_{RF} + \Delta f$, where Δf is the frequency shift of the interference signal with respect to the centre frequency of the GPS L1 signal. The impact of selecting different values of Δf on the acquisition performance of a GPS L1 receiver is analyzed in [25]. Furthermore, the frequency response of the GPS L1 front-end filter is also plotted in Figure 7. In this case, the selected filter bandwidth is 8 MHz.

Sample results comparing ROC curves obtained using semi-analytic and Monte Carlo simulations are shown in Figure 8. The parameters used for the analysis are reported in

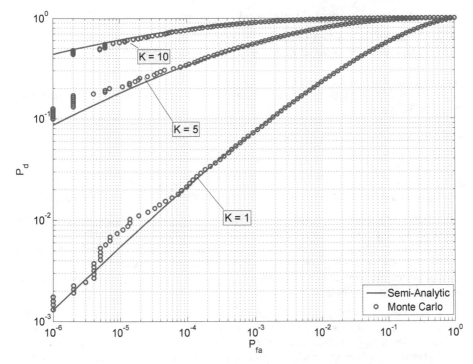

Figure 8. Comparison between ROC curves obtained using semi-analytic and Monte Carlo simulations. The semi-analytic framework considered provides increased precision and requires a lower computational complexity.

Parameter	Value
C/N_0	35 dB-Hz
Coherent integration time, T_c	1 ms
Interference to signal power ratio, $\frac{C_i}{C}$	30 dB
Centre frequency difference, Δf	0 Hz
Receiver bandwidth, B_{RX}	8 MHz
Number of Monte Carlo Simulation runs	10^6

Table 2. Parameters used for the evaluation of the ROC curves shown in Figure 8.

Table 2. From Figure 8, it can be observed that the Monte Carlo and semi-analytic approaches provide similar results and the curves obtained using the two methods overlap. However, the semi-analytic approach provides increased precision, particularly when small values need to be estimated, and a significant reduction in terms of computational complexity. Full Monte Carlo simulations require the implementation of the full transmission/reception chain and the evaluation of the ROC with a computational complexity significantly higher than that of the semi-analytic approach described above.

Additional results relative to the impact of DVB-T interference on GNSS can be found in [25].

3. Closed-loop approach: Digital tracking loops

As anticipated in Section 1, a second configuration, called *closed-loop approach*, has been recently proposed for the simulation of digital tracking loops in DSSS/GNSS receivers. The Semi-Analytic Tracking Loop Simulations (SATLSim) toolbox is a set of MATLAB functions implementing the semi-analytic closed-loop approach for the analysis of digital tracking loops. The SATLSim toolbox has been developed by [9, 10] and can be downloaded from the following websites:

- `http://www.ngs.noaa.gov/gps-toolbox/SATLSim.htm`
- `http://plan.geomatics.ucalgary.ca/publications.php.`

In the following, the closed-loop approach for the simulation of digital tracking loops is considered and the MATLAB code developed in the SATLSim toolbox is briefly analyzed.

A description of the correlator model used for reducing the computational complexity of the system is at first provided. The samples given by (7) at the input of a GNSS receiver are processed by the different functional blocks with different objectives. The acquisition process described in Section 2 is the first stage of a GNSS receiver and has the goal of determining the signal presence and provide a rough estimate of its parameters. These parameters include the code delay τ_0 and Doppler frequency f_0.

If the signal is successfully acquired then different tracking loops are used to refine the estimate of the signal parameters. A Delay Lock Loop (DLL) is usually used to provide accurate estimates of the code delay, τ_0, and track delay variations due to the relative motion between receiver and satellite. The Doppler frequency, f_0, is recovered using either a Frequency Lock Loop (FLL) or a Phase Lock Loop (PLL). If a PLL is used then the carrier phase, φ_0, is also estimated. The code delay and carrier phase allow the receiver to determine its position whereas the Doppler frequency can be used for computing the user velocity.

As indicated in Section 2, a subcarrier can be used for shaping the spectrum of the transmitted GNSS signal and improving its robustness against multipath. The presence of a subcarrier makes code tracking more complex since the correlation function of the transmitted signal may have multiple peaks. More specifically, fine delay estimation is obtained by maximizing the correlation between input signal and local code: the correlation function is maximized only when the delay of the locally generated code matches the delay of the input signal. The presence of several peaks in the correlation function may cause the DLL to converge to a local maximum causing biases in the delay estimation. For this reason, several solutions have been proposed to avoid lock on secondary correlation peaks [26, 27]. An effective solution is represented by the Subcarrier Lock Loop (SLL) proposed by [27]. In this case, the subcarrier is seen as a periodic waveform that further modulates the transmitted signal. The delays of code and subcarrier are decoupled and estimated separately. In this way, the ambiguous one-dimensional signal correlation is projected in an unambiguous bi-dimensional function. In the following, the joint simulation of DLL and SLL is considered.

In a GNSS tracking loop, the incoming signal is correlated with several locally generated code and carrier replicas and different correlator outputs are produced. This process is analogous to the correlation operations described in Section 2 and is performed by the I&D blocks.

Each correlator output is a function of the input signal and the parameters previously estimated by the tracking loop. The correlator outputs are passed to the non-linear discriminator that produces a first estimate of the tracking error that the loop is trying to minimize. The tracking error is filtered and passed to the Numerically Controlled Oscillator (NCO) that is used for generating new local signal replicas.

Efficient tracking loop simulations can be obtained by substituting the I&D blocks with their analytical model. More specifically, a correlator output can be modeled as:

$$\sqrt{C}\frac{\sin\left(\pi\Delta f_d T_c\right)}{\pi\Delta f_d T_c}R_l\left(\Delta\tau_d,\Delta\tau_s\right)\exp\left\{j\Delta\varphi\right\}+\eta_c,\tag{26}$$

where

- Δf_d and $\Delta\varphi$ are the residual frequency and phase errors;

- $\Delta\tau_d$ and $\Delta\tau_s$ are the code and subcarrier delay errors. The delay $\Delta\tau_s$ is present only when a SLL is used to correctly align the signal subcarrier [27];

- $T_c = NT_s$ is the coherent integration time where N is the number of samples used to compute a single correlator;

- $R_l\left(\Delta\tau_d,\Delta\tau_s\right)$ is the correlation function between incoming and locally generated code and is a function of both code and subcarrier delay errors. When the SLL is not used, $R_l\left(\Delta\tau_d,\Delta\tau_s\right)$ is replaced by the standard code correlation function;

- η_c is a zero-mean noise term whose variance depends on the input noise power, front-end filtering and the correlation process operated by the I&D blocks. More details on the properties of η_c can be found in [9].

From (26), it is possible to reconstruct the correlator outputs given the estimation errors generated by the tracking loops. Thus, the correlation process does not need to be simulated and only the estimation errors are determined using a Monte Carlo approach. Based on this principle, the simulation scheme shown in Figure 9 can be adopted for the fast simulation of digital tracking loops.

The functional elements in Figure 9 have been grouped to form the simulation block, the analytical model and the estimation part. The analytical model is used to convert the signal parameter errors, Δf_d, $\Delta\varphi$, $\Delta\tau_d$ and $\Delta\tau_s$, into the signal components of the correlator outputs. At the same time, the analytical model is used to determine the variance and correlation of the different noise terms used to simulate η_c. Since the noise components are simulated using parameters determined by the analytical model, the "noise generation" block is shared between the analytical and simulation parts. The remaining parts of the loop, including the non-linear discriminator, loop filter and NCO, are fully simulated. Finally, the estimation block determines the residual signal parameter errors by comparing true values (determined by the simulation scenario) and estimates produced by the NCO.

By modifying these functional blocks, it is possible to simulate different tracking loops. In the simulation scheme implemented in the SATLSim toolbox, a new estimate of the tracking parameters (Doppler frequency, carrier phase and code and subcarrier delays) is generated by

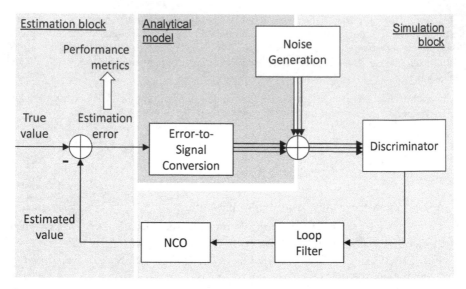

Figure 9. Semi-analytic scheme adopted for the simulation of GNSS tracking loops. Each element of the scheme proposed for the analysis of tracking loops has been implemented in a different function of the SATLSim toolbox.

an NCO model. This model accounts for the integration process performed by a real NCO and different update equations can be used [28]. A commonly used model is the rate-only feedback NCO [28], characterized by the following update equation:

$$\hat{\varphi}_k = \hat{\varphi}_{k-1} + \frac{T_c}{2} \left(\delta\hat{\varphi}_{k-1} + \delta\hat{\varphi}_{k-2} \right), \tag{27}$$

where $\hat{\varphi}_k$ denotes the k-th estimate of the tracking parameter under consideration and $\delta\hat{\varphi}_k$ is its estimated rate of change. The rate $\delta\hat{\varphi}_k$ is generally provided by the loop filter. It is noted that when several parameters are considered, equation (27) is used to update each term independently. The new parameter estimate is compared to the true value and a new estimation error is computed. This error is then used for the generation of the signal component at the output of the I&D block using equation (26). The noise term, generated separately, is then added to the signal component. When several correlators are required, the correlation among the different noise components has to be accounted for. This is simulated using the approach described in [9].

The operations required to convert the correlator outputs into a new estimate of the parameter rate, $\delta\varphi_k$, are fully simulated and correspond to the functional blocks that can be found in a real tracking loop. For instance, the correlator outputs are used to update the nonlinear discriminator and the loop filter. It is noted that a similar simulation scheme can be used for analyzing Kalman filter based tracking. In this case, the correlator outputs are fed to a Kalman filter that is used to produce new estimates of the tracking parameters.

Initialization:

- Initial parameters: sampling frequency, integration time...
- Loop filter design (`FilterDesign.m`)
- Input (true) parameters generation

<u>**Main Simulation Loop**</u>

Loop on the Early-minus-Late spacing:

    Loop on the C/N$_0$ values:

        - Noise generation (`GenerateNoiseVector.m`)

        Loop on the simulation runs:

          1. NCO update (`UpdateNCO.m`)
          2. Evaluation of the estimation error
          3. Error-to-Signal conversion (`GenerateSignalCorrelation.m`)
          4. Signal and Noise combining
          5. Discriminator update (`UpdateDiscriminator.m`)
          6. Loop Filter update (`UpdateFilter.m`)

        End Loop on the simulation runs

        - Evaluate tracking jitter

    End Loop on the C/N$_0$ values

    - Plot tracking results

End Loop on the Early-minus-Late spacing

Figure 10. Structure of the SATLSim toolbox and list of the different MATLAB functions.

3.1. Code structure

The structure of the code developed in the SATLSim toolbox is provided in Figure 10. In this case, the code is used to estimate the tracking jitter of the loop as a function of different parameters, such as the Early-minus-Late spacing and the input C/N_0. In particular, the non-linear discriminator may use several correlators to compute the cost function that the loop is trying to minimize. A DLL usually requires at least two correlators, named Early and Late correlators, computed for the delays

$$\hat{\tau} \pm \frac{1}{2}d_s \tag{28}$$

where $\hat{\tau}$ is the best code delay estimate and d_s is the Early-minus-Late spacing. Early and Late correlators are computed symmetrically with respect to the best delay estimate and the non-linear discriminator computes a cost function proportional to the misalignment between these two correlators. Since the code correlation function is symmetric, the output of the discriminator is minimized when $\hat{\tau}$ corresponds to the delay of the input signal. The SLL works using similar principles. The performance of DLL and SLL depends on the Early-minus-Late spacing that is a simulation parameter. The C/N_0 is used to determine the correlator amplitude and the variance of the noise component, η_c.

The parameters required for initializing the simulation procedure are accessible through the function `InitSettings`. These parameters include the sampling frequency, the loop bandwidth and the coherent integration time that are used to design the loop filters through the function `FilterDesign`. In the code provided, standard formulae from [21] are used. However, `FilterDesign` can be modified in order to adopt a different approach, such as the controlled-root formulation proposed by [28]. During the initialization phase, the true input parameters are also generated. The simulation core consists of three nested loops, on the Early-minus-Late spacing, for different C/N_0 values and for the number of simulation runs. The loop on Early-minus-Late spacing can be absent if, for example, only a PLL is considered. For each Early-minus-Late spacing and for a fixed C/N_0, a noise vector containing the noise components of the correlator outputs is generated. The vector length is equal to the number of simulation runs and all the noise components are generated at once for efficiency reasons.

All intermediate results, such as the discriminator and loop filter outputs, are stored in auxiliary vectors and are used at the end of the loop on the simulation runs to evaluate quantities of interest such as the tracking jitter.

In the code provided, theoretical formulae for the computation of the tracking jitter are also implemented and used as a comparison term for the simulation results.

3.2. Standard PLL (PLL.m)

The simulation of a standard PLL requires the generation of the Prompt correlator alone (`GenerateSignalCorrelation`). The Prompt correlator is the output of the I&D block computed with respect to the best delay estimate provided by the loop [21]. For this reason, the noise generation (`GenerateNoiseVector`) simply consists of simulating a one dimensional complex Gaussian white sequence with independent and identically distributed real and imaginary parts with variance [9]

$$\sigma_n^2 = \frac{1}{C/N_0 T_c}. \tag{29}$$

When simulating a standard PLL alone, perfect code synchronization is assumed and (26) simplifies to

$$\sqrt{C} \frac{\sin(\pi \Delta f_d T_c)}{\pi \Delta f_d T_c} \exp\{j \Delta \varphi\} + \eta_c, \tag{30}$$

where Δf_d is obtained by comparing the true Doppler frequency against the loop filter output. $\Delta \varphi$ is the phase error obtained as the difference between the true phase and the phase estimate produced by the NCO.

In SATLSim, the function `UpdateDiscriminator` implements a standard Costas discriminator. Different phase discriminators, as indicated in [21], can be easily implemented by changing this function.

3.3. Double estimator (DoubleEstimator.m)

In the Double Estimator (DE) case, i.e. when DLL and SLL are jointly used, the function `GenerateNoiseVector`, responsible for the generation of the correlator noise, produces a $5 \times N_{sim}$ matrix, where N_{sim} is the number of simulation runs. The five rows of this matrix correspond to the five correlators required by the DE that are characterized by the following correlation matrix

$$
C_n = \begin{bmatrix}
1 & R_l\left(\frac{d_s}{2},\frac{d_{sc}}{2}\right) & R_l\left(\frac{d_s}{2},0\right) & R_l\left(\frac{d_s}{2},\frac{d_{sc}}{2}\right) & R_l\left(d_s,0\right) \\
R_l\left(\frac{d_s}{2},\frac{d_{sc}}{2}\right) & 1 & R_l\left(0,\frac{d_{sc}}{2}\right) & R_l\left(0,d_{sc}\right) & R_l\left(\frac{d_s}{2},\frac{d_{sc}}{2}\right) \\
R_l\left(\frac{d_s}{2},0\right) & R_l\left(0,\frac{d_{sc}}{2}\right) & 1 & R_l\left(0,\frac{d_{sc}}{2}\right) & R_l\left(\frac{d_s}{2},0\right) \\
R_l\left(\frac{d_s}{2},\frac{d_{sc}}{2}\right) & R_l\left(0,d_{sc}\right) & R_l\left(0,\frac{d_{sc}}{2}\right) & 1 & R_l\left(\frac{d_s}{2},\frac{d_{sc}}{2}\right) \\
R_l\left(d_s,0\right) & R_l\left(\frac{d_s}{2},\frac{d_{sc}}{2}\right) & R_l\left(\frac{d_s}{2},0\right) & R_l\left(\frac{d_s}{2},\frac{d_{sc}}{2}\right) & 1
\end{bmatrix}, \tag{31}
$$

where d_{sc} is the subcarrier Early-minus-Late spacing.

The NCO update (UpdateNCO) is performed on both code and subcarrier loops and the estimated errors, $\Delta\tau_d$ and $\Delta\tau_s$, are used to compute new correlator signal components (GenerateSignalCorrelation). Two nonlinear discriminators (UpdateDiscriminator) and loop filters (UpdateFilter) are run in parallel to determine the rate of change of both code and subcarrier delay.

The DE provides an example of how several tracking loops, operating in parallel, can be easily coupled in order to provide more realistic simulations accounting for the interaction of different tracking algorithms [9].

3.4. Sample results

In this section, sample results obtained using the SATLSim toolbox are shown for the DE case. Results for the analysis of the PLL can be found in [10]. Specific focus is devoted to the analysis of the tracking jitter, which is one of the main metrics used for the analysis of digital tracking loops. The tracking jitter quantifies the amount of noise transferred by the tracking loop to the final parameter estimate [29]. The tracking jitter is the standard deviation of the final parameter estimate normalized by the discriminator gain. The non-linear discriminator is usually a memoryless device characterized by an input/output function relating the parameter estimation error to the discriminator output. The discriminator gain is the slope of this function in the neighborhood of zero (hypothesis of small estimation error).

Tracking jitter results obtained using non-coherent discriminators [21] for both DLL and SLL are shown in Figure 11. The figure is divided into three parts:

a) Tracking jitter of the DLL alone
b) Tracking jitter of the SLL alone
c) Jitter of the combined delay estimate.

This is due to the fact that the DE jointly uses a DLL, for estimating the code delay, and a SLL, for determining the subcarrier delay. Subcarrier and code delay are then combined to obtain the final estimate of the travel time of the transmitted signal [27]. Thus, three different jitters are evaluated for the different estimates produced by the system. Tracking jitter has been expressed in meters by multiplying the standard deviation of the delay estimates by the speed of light.

In addition to this, the curves are shown in Figure 11a) and Figure 11b). More specifically, three different methodologies have been employed for determining the tracking jitter.

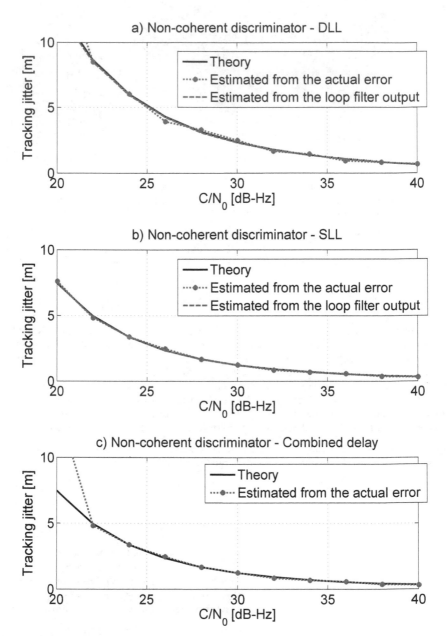

Figure 11. Tracking jitter obtained using the SATLSim toolbox. a) Tracking jitter of the DLL alone. b) Tracking jitter of the SLL alone. c) Jitter of the combined delay estimate.

Parameter	Value
Sampling Frequency	$f_s = 8\,\text{MHz}$
Integration Time	$T_c = 4\,\text{ms}$
DLL Early-minus-Late spacing	$0.1955\,\mu\text{s}$ (0.2 chips)
SLL Early-minus-Late spacing	$0.1955\,\mu\text{s}$ (0.2 chips)
DLL Loop Order	1
SLL Loop Order	1
DLL Loop Bandwidth	$0.5\,\text{Hz}$
SLL Loop Bandwidth	$0.5\,\text{Hz}$
Modulation type	$BOC(1,1)$

Table 3. Parameters used for the evaluation of the tracking jitter shown in Figure 11.

The theoretical curve corresponds to approximate formulas obtained by linearizing the input/output function of the non-linear discriminator. These formulas are valid only for small tracking errors or equivalently for high C/N_0. The jitter obtained from the actual error has been obtained by evaluating the variance of the code phase error. It is noted that in a real tracking loop the code phase error is not directly accessible since the true code phase is unknown. Thus, the tracking error can be evaluated by measuring the error at the loop filter output, which is an observable point, and propagating its variance through the loop. The tracking jitter obtained by propagating the variance at this measurable point corresponds to the curve denoted by "Estimated from the loop filter output". The relationship between the variances of the discriminator output and the true tracking error can easily be evaluated when the loop is working in its linear region. The measured curve was introduced to further validate the theoretical model and test the correctness of the simulation methodology. This latest curve is not available for the combined delay estimate.

The parameters used for the evaluation of the tracking jitter, shown in Figure 11, are provided in Table 3.

From the results shown in Figure 11, it is observed that the developed semi-analytic technique is able to effectively capture the behavior of the system. For high C/N_0 values, a good agreement between theoretical and simulation results is found. However, for C/N_0 lower than 22 dB-Hz theoretical and simulation results start diverging. This is more clear in parts a) and c) of the figures. For such low C/N_0 values, the loop is no longer working in the linear region of the discriminator input/output function. Thus, the theoretical model is unable to capture the behavior of the loop that is losing lock. The semi-analytic technique implemented in the SATLSim MATLAB toolbox is able to effectively describe the non-linear behavior of the loop requiring only limited computation resources.

4. Conclusions

In this chapter, the development of fast semi-analytic techniques using MATLAB has been analyzed. In the semi-analytic framework, the knowledge of the system under analysis is exploited to reduce the computational load and complexity that full Monte Carlo simulations would require. In this way, the strengths of both analytical and Monte Carlo methods are effectively combined.

Two examples of semi-analytic techniques have been thoroughly analyzed and used to illustrate the two main configurations developed within the semi-analytic framework. The first example illustrates the sequential configuration where simulations and the analytical model are used sequentially. This type of configuration provides increased precision with respect to full Monte Carlo simulations, particularly when the quantities to be estimated assume small values. In addition to this, a significant reduction in terms of computational complexity is achieved. In the example considered, full Monte Carlo simulations require the implementation of a full transmission/reception chain including the interaction between two different systems, DVB-T and GNSS. This requirement led to a significant computational and development complexity. The considered semi-analytic approach is an effective solution for alleviating those requirements.

The second example considered the closed-loop approach and specific focus was devoted to the SATLSim MATLAB toolbox. This toolbox has been developed for the analysis of digital tracking loops and fully exploits the flexibility of the MATLAB programming language. The code has been organized in functions that can be easily replaced by different MATLAB modules. In this way, different loop components such as discriminators, loop filters and NCO models can be integrated in the SATLSim toolbox. The efficiency of semi-analytic techniques and the reduced development time enabled by the MATLAB language are an effective tool for the analysis of complex communications systems.

Author details

Daniele Borio and Eduardo Cano
EC Joint Research Centre, Institute for the Protection and Security of the Citizen, Italy

5. References

[1] W. H. Tranter, K. S. Shanmugan, T. S. Rappaport, and K. L. Kosbar. *Principles of Communication Systems Simulation with Wireless Applications*. Prentice Hall, January 2004.

[2] M. C. Jeruchim, P. Balaban, and K. S. Shanmugan. *Simulation of communication systems*. Kluwer Academic/Plenum Publishers, new york edition, 2000.

[3] F.M. Gardner and J. D. Baker. *Simulation Techniques: Models of Communication Signals and Processes*. John Wiley & Sons, 2003.

[4] M. Jeruchim. Techniques for estimating the bit error rate in the simulation of digital communication systems. *IEEE Journal on Selected Areas in Communications*, 2(1):153 – 170, January 1984.

[5] M. Pent, L. Lo Presti, G. D'Aria, and G. De Luca. Semianalytic BER evaluation by simulation for noisy nonlinear bandpass channels. *IEEE Journal on Selected Areas in Communications*, 6(1):34 –41, January 1988.

[6] M.T. Core, R. Campbell, P. Quan, and J. Wada. Semianalytic BER for PSK. *IEEE Transactions on Wireless Communications*, 8(4):1644 –1648, April 2009.

[7] A. R. Golshan. Post-correlator modeling for fast simulation and joint performance analysis of GNSS code and carrier tracking loops. In *Proc. of the ION/NTM (National Technical Meeting)*, pages 312 – 318, Monterey, CA, January 2006.

[8] J. S. Silva, P. F. Silva, A. Fernandez, J. Diez, and J. F. M. Lorga. Factored correlator model: A solution for fast, flexible, and realistic GNSS receiver simulations. In *Proc. of ION/GNSS*, pages 2676 – 2686, Forth Worth, TX, September 2007.

[9] D. Borio, P. B. Anantharamu, and G. Lachapelle. Semi-analytic simulations: An extension to unambiguous BOC tracking. In *Proc. of the ION/ITM (International Technical Meeting)*, pages 1023–1036, San Diego, CA, January 2010.

[10] Daniele Borio, Pratibha Anantharamu, and Gérard Lachapelle. SATLSim: a semi-analytic framework for fast GNSS tracking loop simulations. *GPS Solutions*, 15:427–431, 2011.

[11] J.M. Geist. Computer generation of correlated gaussian random variables. *Proceedings of the IEEE*, 67(5):862 – 863, may 1979.

[12] A. R. Golshan. Loss of lock analysis of a firstorder digital code tracking loop and comparison of results to analog loop theory for BOC and NRZ signals. In *Proc. of the ION/NTM (National Technical Meeting)*, pages 299 – 305, San Diego, CA, January 2005.

[13] J. W. Betz. Effect of narrowband interference on GPS code tracking accuracy. In *Proc. of ION/NTM*, pages 16–27, Anaheim, CA, January 2000.

[14] D. Borio. GNSS acquisition in the presence of continuous wave interference. *IEEE Transactions on Aerospace and Electronic Systems*, 46(1):47 – 60, January 2010.

[15] T. Van Slyke, W. Kuhn, and B. Natarajan. Measuring interference from a UWB transmitter in the GPS l1 band. In *Proc. of the IEEE Radio and Wireless Symposium*, pages 887 – 890, Orlando, FL, March 2008.

[16] A. Simsky, T. De Wilde, D. Mertens, E. Koitsaly, and J.-M. Sleewaegen. First field experience with L5 signals: DME interference reality check. In *Proc. of ION/GNSS*, pages 29 – 37, Savannah, GA, September 2009.

[17] D. Borio, S. Savasta, and L. Lo Presti. On the DVB-t coexistence with galileo and GPS system. In *Proc. of the 3rd ESA Workshop on Satellite Navigation User Equipment Technologies (NAVITEC)*, Noordwijk, The Netherlands, December 2006.

[18] M. Wildemeersch, A. Rabbachin, E. Cano, and J. Fortuny. Interference assessment of DVB-t within the GPS l1 and galileo e1 band. In *Proc. of the 5th ESA European Workshop on GNSS Signals and Signal Processing (NAVITEC)*, pages 1 – 8, Noordwijk, The Netherlands, December 2010.

[19] Steven M. Kay. *Fundamentals of Statistical Signal Processing, Volume 2: Detection Theory*, volume 2. Prentice Hall, 1rt edition, February 1998.

[20] ETSI. Digital video broadcasting (DVB); framing structure, channel coding and modulation for digital terrestrial television, 2006. EN 300 744.

[21] E. D. Kaplan and C. Hegarty, editors. *Understanding GPS: Principles and Applications*. Artech House, 2nd edition, November 2005.

[22] H. L. Van Trees. *Detection, Estimation, and Modulation Theory - Part 1*. Wiley-Interscience, 1st edition, September 2001.

[23] Daniele Borio. *A statistical theory for GNSS signal acquisition*. Phd thesis, Politecnico di Torino, April 2008.

[24] John W. Betz. Effect of partial-band interference on receiver estimation of C/N_0. In *Proc. of the ION/NTM*, pages 817 – 828, Long Beach, CA, January 2001.

[25] J. Fortuny-Guasch, M. Wildemeersch, and D. Borio. Assessment of DVB-T impact on GNSS acquisition and tracking performance. In *Proc. of the ION/GNSS*, pages 347–356, San Diego, CA, January 2011.

[26] P. Anantharamu, D. Borio, and G. Lachapelle. Sub-carrier shaping for BOC modulated GNSS signals. *EURASIP Journal on Advances in Signal Processing*, 2011(1):133, 2011.

[27] M. S. Hodgart and P. D. Blunt. A dual estimate receiver of binary offset carrier (BOC) modulated signals global navigation satellite systems. *Electronics Letters*, 43(16):877–878, August 2007.

[28] S. A. Stephens and J. B. Thomas. Controlled-root formulation for digital phase-locked loops. *IEEE Transactions on Aerospace and Electronic Systems*, 31(1):78 –95, january 1995.

[29] A. J. V. Dierendonck, P. Fenton, and T. Ford. Theory and performance of narrow correlator spacing in a GPS receiver. *NAVIGATION: the Journal of The Institut of Navigation*, 39(3):265 – 283, Fall 1992.

Permissions

The contributors of this book come from diverse backgrounds, making this book a truly international effort. This book will bring forth new frontiers with its revolutionizing research information and detailed analysis of the nascent developments around the world.

We would like to thank Vasilios N. Katsikis, for lending his expertise to make the book truly unique. He has played a crucial role in the development of this book. Without his invaluable contribution this book wouldn't have been possible. He has made vital efforts to compile up to date information on the varied aspects of this subject to make this book a valuable addition to the collection of many professionals and students.

This book was conceptualized with the vision of imparting up-to-date information and advanced data in this field. To ensure the same, a matchless editorial board was set up. Every individual on the board went through rigorous rounds of assessment to prove their worth. After which they invested a large part of their time researching and compiling the most relevant data for our readers. Conferences and sessions were held from time to time between the editorial board and the contributing authors to present the data in the most comprehensible form. The editorial team has worked tirelessly to provide valuable and valid information to help people across the globe.

Every chapter published in this book has been scrutinized by our experts. Their significance has been extensively debated. The topics covered herein carry significant findings which will fuel the growth of the discipline. They may even be implemented as practical applications or may be referred to as a beginning point for another development. Chapters in this book were first published by InTech; hereby published with permission under the Creative Commons Attribution License or equivalent.

The editorial board has been involved in producing this book since its inception. They have spent rigorous hours researching and exploring the diverse topics which have resulted in the successful publishing of this book. They have passed on their knowledge of decades through this book. To expedite this challenging task, the publisher supported the team at every step. A small team of assistant editors was also appointed to further simplify the editing procedure and attain best results for the readers.

Our editorial team has been hand-picked from every corner of the world. Their multi-ethnicity adds dynamic inputs to the discussions which result in innovative outcomes. These outcomes are then further discussed with the researchers and contributors who give their valuable feedback and opinion regarding the same. The feedback is then collaborated with the researches and they are edited in a comprehensive manner to aid the understanding of the subject.

Apart from the editorial board, the designing team has also invested a significant amount of their time in understanding the subject and creating the most relevant covers. They scrutinized every image to scout for the most suitable representation of the subject and create an appropriate cover for the book.

The publishing team has been involved in this book since its early stages. They were actively engaged in every process, be it collecting the data, connecting with the contributors or procuring relevant information. The team has been an ardent support to the editorial, designing and production team. Their endless efforts to recruit the best for this project, has resulted in the accomplishment of this book. They are a veteran in the field of academics and their pool of knowledge is as vast as their experience in printing. Their expertise and guidance has proved useful at every step. Their uncompromising quality standards have made this book an exceptional effort. Their encouragement from time to time has been an inspiration for everyone.

The publisher and the editorial board hope that this book will prove to be a valuable piece of knowledge for researchers, students, practitioners and scholars across the globe.

List of Contributors

Muhammad Ahsan and Tapio Saramäki
Tampere University of Technology, Tampere, Finland

Mariano Raboso and Myriam Codes
Universidad Pontificia de Salamanca (Facultad de Informática), Spain

María I. Jiménez, Lara del Val, Alberto Izquierdo and Juan J. Villacorta
Universidad de Valladolid, Spain

Farhad E. Mahmood
Electrical Department, College of Engineering, University of Mosul, Iraq

Prashant M. Menghal
Radar & Control System Dept., Faculty of Electronics, Military College of Electronics
and Mechanical Engineering, Secunderabad, Andhra Pradesh, India

A. Jaya Laxmi
Electrical & Electronics Engineering Dept., Jawaharlal Nehru Technological University,
Hyderabad College of Engineering, Kukatpally, Hyderabad, Andhra Pradesh, India

Walid Hassairi, Moncef Bousselmi, Mohamed Abid and Carlos Valderrama
UMons University of Mons, Electronics & Microelectronics Dpt., Mons, Belgium
Laboratory CES, National School of Engineers of Sfax, Tunisia

Moulay Tahar Lamchich and Nora Lachguer
Cadi Ayyad University, Faculty of Sciences Semlalia, Department of Physics, Work group
EERI, Marrakech, Morocco

Libor Pekař, Eva Kurečková and Roman Prokop
Tomas Bata University in Zlín, Czech Republic

Gaizka Almandoz, Gaizka Ugalde and Javier Poza
Faculty of Engineering, University of Mondragon, Mondragon, Spain

Ana Julia Escalada
ORONA EIC. ELEVATOR INNOVATION CENTRE, Hernani, Spain

Oriol Font-Bach, Nikolaos Bartzoudis and David López Bueno
Centre Tecnològic de Telecomunicacions de Catalunya (CTTC), Spain

Antonio Pascual-Iserte
Centre Tecnològic de Telecomunicacions de Catalunya (CTTC), Spain
Department of Signal Theory and Communications, Universitat Politècnica de Catalunya (UPC), Spain

Diana Alejandra Sánchez-Salas, José Luis Cuevas-Ruíz and Miguel González-Mendoza
Tecnológico de Monterrey, Campus Estado de México, México

Bahman Azarbad and Aduwati Binti Sali
University Putra Malaysia, Malaysia

Qutaiba I. Ali
Mosul University, Computer Engineering Department, Iraq

Daniele Borio and Eduardo Cano
EC Joint Research Centre, Institute for the Protection and Security of the Citizen, Italy

Printed in the USA
CPSIA information can be obtained
at www.ICGtesting.com
JSHW011504221024
72173JS00005B/1195